BIRDING TRAILS™
MONTANA

INCLUDING
GPS

240 Birding Trails for the Avid Birder
With GPS Coordinates for All Locations

FROM THE COVER - THE SANDHILL CRANE

Sandhill Cranes are common throughout Montana. Their inimitable calls are unmistakable and can be heard long distances; especially prior to fall migration when huge flocks, sometimes thousands, stage in traditional spots known to generations. Normally pale gray, the rusty pair on the cover have been dusting in iron-rich soils.

Unless otherwise noted, all photos are copyright Chuck and Gale Robbins.

Other titles from Sandhill Crane Press™

Birding Trails™

Birding Trails™ Texas Panhandle, Prairies and Pineywoods

Birding Trails™ Texas Gulf Coast

Upcoming titles from Sandhill Crane Press™

Birding Trails™

Birding Trails™ Wisconsin

Birding Trails™ Eastern Oregon

BIRDING TRAILS™
MONTANA

INCLUDING GPS

240 Birding Trails for the Avid Birder
With GPS Coordinates for All Locations

By Chuck Robbins

Birding Trails Series™

Sandhill
Crane
Press™

Birding Trails™ Series

Published by Sandhill Crane Press ™,
An imprint of Wilderness Adventures Press, Inc.™
45 Buckskin Road
Belgrade, MT 59714
866-400-2012
Website: www.wildadvpress.com
email: books@wildadvpress.com

First Edition 2014

Printed in South Korea

ISBN 978 -1-932098-99-0 (8-09206-98990-0)

Table of Contents

ACKNOWLEDGEMENTS 1
DEDICATION 1
INTRODUCTION 3
Symbols Legend 8
Web Sites for Birding Trails Montana 9
Montana Important Birding Areas (IBAs) 9
State Land Recreation Use Permit 10
GLACIER COUNTRY 11
  Eureka/Tobacco Plains/ Dancing Prairie Preserve 15
  Kootenai Falls WMA 16
  Ross Cedar Grove 19
  Lost Trail National Wildlife Refuge 20
  Smith Lake Waterfowl Production Area 23
  Lake Mary Ronan State Park 24
  Safe Harbor Marsh (IBA) 26
  Pablo National Wildlife Refuge (IBA) 28
  Ronan Hawk Roost (IBA) 30
  Ninepipe National Wildlife Refuge (IBA) 31
  National Bison Range (IBA) 32
  Erskine Fishing Access Site 35
  Clark Fork River Float 37
  Kelly Island Fishing Access Site 39
  Tower Street Park 41
  Maclay Flat Nature Trail 42
  Council Grove State Park 43
  Clark Fork River/Grass Valley IBA 45
  Blue Mountain Nature Trail 47
  Traveler's Rest State Park 49
  Fort Fizzle/Lolo Creek Campground/East Fork Lolo Creek 51
  Lolo Pass 52
  Bass Creek Fishing Access Site 54
  St. Mary's Peak 57
  Bitterroot River (IBA) 58
  Bear Creek Trail 61
  Blodgett Canyon/Cow Creek Burn (IBA) 62
  Coyote Coulee Trail 63
  Lake Como National Recreation Trail 64
  Hannon Memorial Fishing Access Site 66
  Sam Billings Mem. Campground/Boulder Creek Trail 69
  Crazy Creek Campground 71
  Indian Trees Campground 73
  Chief Joseph Pass Ski Trails 74
  Broad Ax Lodge 76
  River and Hieronymus Parks 78

Centennial Grove Nature Trail 80
Teller Wildlife Refuge. 81
Lee Metcalf National Wildlife Refuge 83
Pattee Canyon National Recreation Area 86
Mount Sentinel 87
Greenough Park 88
Waterworks Hill 89
Rattlesnake National Recreation Area. 91
Mount Jumbo 93
Blackfoot-Clearwater Wildlife Management Area 95
Boy Scout Road. 97
Clearwater River Canoe Trail. 98
Chain of Lakes. 100
Swan River State Forest. 102
Swan River Oxbow Preserve. 103
Swan River National Wildlife Refuge 104
Owen Sowerwine Natural Area (IBA) 106
Lower Valley Road 108
Lawrence Park. 109
West Valley Ponds. 110
Tally Lake 111
Danny On Trail 113
Glacier National Park (IBA) 114
CENTRAL MONTANA **119**
Jarina Waterfowl Production Area 122
Blackleaf Wildlife Management Area. 123
Choteau Loop 126
Ear Mountain Wildlife Management Area 128
Freezout Lake Wildlife Management Area (IBA) 130
Arod Lakes Waterfowl Production Area (IBA). 133
Marias River State Park/ Wildlife Management Area. 135
Kevin Rim (IBA) 136
Toole County Waterfowl Production Areas 138
Furnell Waterfowl Production Area 140
Sanford Park 141
Fresno Reservoir Wildlife Management Area 143
Wild Horse Lake 146
Holm Waterfowl Production Area 147
Rookery Wildlife Management Area 149
Sands Waterfowl Production Area 151
Nez Perce National Historic Park/Bears Paw Battlefield. 152
Beaver Creek Park. 153
Pah-Nah-To Recreation Park 155
Wood Bottom Recreation Area 156
Kingsbury Lake Waterfowl Production Area 158
Beckman Wildlife Management Area 159
Woodhawk Recreation Site 161

Kipp Recreation Area. 163
War Horse National Wildlife Refuge 164
Brewery Flats Fishing Access Site 166
Crystal Lake 168
Ackley Lake State Park. 170
Stanford Bluebird Trail 171
Judith River Wildlife Management Area 173
Haymaker Wildlife Management Area 175
Smith River Wildlife Management Area 177
Newlan Creek Reservoir Fishing Access Site 179
Jumping Creek. 182
Kings Hill Pass/Porphyry Peak Lookout 183
Memorial Falls. 185
Dry Fork Road (Hughesville Road). 186
Sluice Boxes State Park 187
Giant Springs State Park 189
Benton Lake National Wildlife Refuge. 191
Hartelius Waterfowl Production Area 194
First Peoples Buffalo Jump State Park 195
Schrammeck Lake Waterfowl Production Area. 196
Pelican Point Fishing Access Site 197
SOUTHWEST MONTANA. 199
Sun River Wildlife Management Area 202
Sun River Backcountry Loop 205
Blackfoot Valley (IBA) 207
Beartooth Wildlife Management Area. 210
Little Prickly Pear Creek 212
Causeway (Lake Helena to Hauser Lake) 213
Lake Helena Wildlife Management Area (IBA) 214
Lake Helena Drive/Merritt Lane. 216
Helena Valley Regulating Reservoir 218
Floweree Drive/Sierra Road /McHugh Drive 219
Lower Skelly Gulch. 221
Fairgrounds/Spring Meadow State Park/Scratchgravel Hills. 222
Mount Helena City Park 224
Grizzly Gulch/Orofino Gulch 226
James P. Sunderland Park. 227
Canyon Ferry Wildlife Management Area (IBA) 228
Grant Kohrs Ranch/Arrow Stone Park. 231
Warm Springs Wildlife Management Area/ Anaconda Settling Ponds 233
Lost Creek State Park. 236
Mount Haggin Wildlife Management Area. 238
Big Hole River 241
Big Hole Battlefield/Surrounding Area 245
Burma Road 247
Birch Creek/Thief Creek/ French Creek Loop 249
Poindexter Slough Fishing Access Site 251

Beaverhead River 254
Bannack State Park 256
Clark Canyon Reservoir 258
Lemhi Pass. 261
Beaverhead Sage-Steppe (IBA) 262
Blacktail Road 265
Robb-Ledford/Blacktail Wildlife Management Areas 267
Red Rock Lakes National Wildlife Refuge. 271
Raynold's Pass Bridge 274
Earthquake Lake Boat Launch 276
Madison Valley IBA 277
Harrison Reservoir (IBA)(Willow Creek Reservoir FAS) 280
YELLOWSTONE COUNTRY. 283
Old Town Road 286
Bench Road 287
Missouri Headwaters State Park (IBA)/Three Forks Area 288
Central Park Pond 291
Fir Ridge Cemetery 292
Whit's Lake Road (FR 971) 293
Ghost Village Road (FR 989) 294
Beaver Creek Viewing Site 295
Baker's Hole Campground. 296
South Fork Madison River 298
Hebgen Lake Road(Denny Creek Road). 299
Springhill-Dry Creek Loop. 301
Cherry River Fishing Access Site. 302
East Gallatin Recreation Area 304
Hyalite Canyon 305
Kirk Hill. 306
Sourdough Nature Trail 307
Triple Tree Trail 308
Lindley Park. 309
Bozeman Trail System. 310
Mount Ellis. 311
Trail Creek Road 312
Fish Hatchery/"M" Trail 313
Bridger Raptor Festival 314
Battle Ridge Campground 315
Cottonwood Reservoir 316
Livingston County Parks and Surrounding Area. 317
Boulder River. 319
Big Timber City Parks 323
Otter Creek Road 324
Pelican Fishing Access Site. 325
Sweet Grass Creek Loop 328
Hailstone National Wildlife Refuge 329
Halfbreed National Wildlife Refuge (IBA). 331

Molt/Big Lake Complex 333
Itch-Kep-Pe Park and the Stillwater River 335
Cooney Reservoir State Park 338
Bear Canyon Important Bird Area (IBA) 340

SOUTHEAST MONTANA **343**
Chief Plenty Coups (Alek- Chea-Ahoosh) State Park 346
Audubon Center 348
Mystic Island Park 350
Pictograph Cave State Park 351
Four Dances Natural Area 353
Earl Guss Park 355
Norm Shoenthal Island 356
Two Moon Park 357
Lake Elmo State Park 358
Pompey's Pillar National Monument 360
Howrey Island Recreation Area 362
Isaac Homestead Wildlife Management Area 363
Grant Marsh Wildlife Management Area 366
Afterbay Dam 368
Bighorn Canyon National Recreation Area 370
Little Bighorn National Monument 372
Tongue River Birding Route 373
Tongue River Reservoir State Park 374
Black's Pond 376
Tongue River (IBA) 378
Powder Carter Sage-Steppe (IBA) 380
McNab Pond 382
Medicine Rocks State Park 383
Makoshika State Park 385
Terry Badlands Wilderness Study Area 387
Matthews Recreation Area 390
Pirogue Island State Park 391
Miles City Parks 393
Roundup River-Walk Heritage Trail 395
Musselshell Sage-Steppe (IBA) 397
Lake Mason National Wildlife Refuge 400

MISSOURI RIVER COUNTRY **403**
Charles M. Russell National Wildlife Refuge (IBA) .406
American Prairie Reserve 410
Camp Creek Campground /Little Rockies 413
Korsbeck Waterfowl Production Area 415
Milk River Wildlife Management Areas 416
Dyrdahl/Webb Waterfowl Production Areas 418
Grasslands National Park (Canada) 419
Bowdoin National Wildlife Refuge (IBA) 421
Beaver Creek Waterfowl Production Area 425
Nelson Reservoir 426

McNeil Slough Waterfowl Production Area 428
Cole Ponds 429
Bjornberg Bridge Fishing Access Site 430
Hinsdale Wildlife Management Area. 432
Bitter Creek Wilderness Study Area 434
Vandalia Wildlife Management Area 436
Faraasen Park Recreation Site 438
Paulo Reservoir 439
Little Beaver Creek (IBA) 440
Fort Peck Dredge Cut Ponds 443
Fort Peck Campground (Downstream Rec. Area) 445
Manning Lake Wetland Complex (IBA) 447
Medicine Lake National Wildlife Refuge (IBA) 448
Brush Lake State Park 451
Westby City Park 453
Westby Prairie-Wetland Complex (IBA) 455
Fox Lake Wildlife Management Area 458
Elk Island Fishing Access Site 461
Seven Sisters Fishing Access Site 463
Diamond Willow Fishing Access Site. 465
Fort Union Trading Post/Fort Buford National Historic Site 467

Audubon Christmas Bird Count **469**

Great Backyard Bird Count. **470**

Montana Bird Festivals And Such. **471**

Hire a Guide **472**

Important Bird Areas (IBAs) **473**

Montana Bird Species of Conservation Concern **476**

Recent Rare (Vagrant) Bird Records **477**

Chambers of Commerce **478**

Audubon Societies. **481**

FWP Regional Offices **481**

Montana Bird List **482**

Index **491**

ACKNOWLEDGEMENTS

To all the many expert birders, biologists, refuge managers and staff, and others who willingly shared their knowledge; and to the Montana Audubon Societies and the Nature Conservancy without whose guidance this book might never have happened. And to my friend, Livingston photographer Keith Szafranski, Gary Swant, and the U.S. Fish and Wildlife Service Digital Library for their help in filling out the photo list. And to Chuck and Blanche Johnson and the hard working staff at Sandhill Crane Press...my sincere thanks.

DEDICATION

For Gale, who has somehow managed to put up with me all these years and somehow manages to keep all our many projects moving forward on a somewhat even keel. And to wild lands, good soil, clean air and water.

Killdeer

INTRODUCTION

For as far back as I can remember birds have fascinated me, although it took awhile to eventually turn fascination into yet another obsession — I have a lot of obsessions. At first I viewed birds mostly as a sidelight to whatever else I happened to be up to at the moment — fly fishing, bird hunting, photography, hiking, canoeing, whatever. The first time I recall actually traveling somewhere just to bird was to Freezout Lake for the annual early spring Snow Goose fest. I was awed by the experience – blown away actually – when I learned biologists estimated that more than 100,000 snow and Ross's Geese visited that day.

It pains me to confess how many other birds were out there that day of which I had no clue. As I leafed frantically through my tattered Sibley's, the guy next to me looked away from his spotting scope long enough to offer a piece of sage advise, "Why fret, just call 'em LBJs and move on." "Little Brown Jobs?" Now why hadn't I thought of that? By the way, LBJs still show up way too often but rather than obsess…well, like the man said… forget it, move on.

Since then I have studiously practiced observing and photographing every chance, in all seasons, and in a lot of different places — all across and up and down Montana and the Arizona deserts for example. Alas, I remain not much more than a reasonably informed, avid birder possessed of far less than master class skills. One thing I lack big time is the ability to hear and translate bird song — most I don't hear at all and some I hear clearly only under certain ideal conditions. Gale will say, "Oh listen, the goldfinches are back feeding on the sunflowers." Listen? What goldfinches? I don't hear a damn thing except the ringing in my ears, the neighborhood dogs barking, and the car speeding by the front gate.

The good news is mostly through the process of osmosis I've come to recognize good bird habitat. And because in our travels over the years there is scarcely a stone in the state we haven't at least wandered by at one time or another, we've been able to compile quite a list of pretty good birding spots. Thanks to the nine state chapters of the Audubon Society, we've discovered many more. And by talking with and asking questions of experts — birders, biologists, refuge managers and staff, and so forth — we have uncovered even more.

It should go without saying, but Montana is indeed a big place — 550 miles wide, 320 miles north to south. With a mean elevation of about 3,400 feet, elevations range from 1,820 feet in Lincoln County where the Kootenai River enters Idaho to towering Granite Peak at 12,799 feet in Park County. In January 1954, the temperature bottomed out at 70 degrees below zero, coldest ever recorded in the lower 48 states, while summer afternoons often soar well into the 90s and sometimes beyond to triple digits. Much of the state is semi-arid, actually high desert, with a statewide average of just 15 inches annual precipitation, the 5th driest in the U.S.

A vast and diverse landscape, featuring wide valleys surrounded by tall, forested mountains in the western one-third giving way to the High Plains — immense grass, sagebrush, and agricultural lands dotted with several island mountain ranges, badlands, and lush river bottoms — which roll on and on all the way to the Dakotas, from Canada to Wyoming. Largely empty, some of it pretty much unchanged since Lewis and Clark marched across some 200 years ago. Considering most of the birds and every mammal, including bison and grizzly bear, roamed here at the time of settlement still live here, no wonder so many of us label Montana "Last Best Place." A diverse landscape lends itself to an equally diverse wildlife base, one unmatched anywhere within the Lower 48 states. About 150 mammal species and 400 bird species live here; in short, a four-season bird (wildlife) viewing paradise.

Birding Trails Montana is divided into the Six Tourism Regions: Glacier Country, Central Montana, Southwest Montana, Yellowstone Country, Missouri River Country, and Southeast Montana. Each "Region" describes dozens of birding sites — name, location, GPS coordinates, key birds, best seasons, area description, directions, and contact information. While I would like to have included "all" the birding hotspots out there alas, as I'm sure once you delve into birding Montana, you will come to agree, such coverage is hugely impossible.

Truth is, just step out the back door, and in most cases you will find birds aplenty to pique your interest. For example, our little town (typical of most, by the way) sports two tree- and brush-lined streams running through it, a couple small public parks, tree and shrub filled backyards, tree-lined streets, and vacant lots overgrown in brush and grass — all bird habitat. Toss in our cattail-rimmed kids' fishing pond and hiking trail area which features trees, assorted grass and brush, and a tiny cattail, willow, and buffalo berry choked spring run and...Why leave town? Even our biggest "cities" afford similar, though in every case many more, birding opportunities. For example, Helena our state capital, boasts dozens of top-notch birding areas; ditto Billings our largest city, population 100,000-plus. In a state still boasting not quite one million residents, as you can imagine there is a lot of room as they say "for the birds."

In addition to the many sites listed here, you can add about 300 more by going to The Montana Fishing Access Sites Field Guide (http://fwp.mt.gov/fishing/ guide/fasGuide. html). State-owned Fishing Access Sites (FAS) are found on Montana's streams, rivers, and lakes and vary in size from less than one acre to several hundred acres. All hold at least the potential for sighting a variety of birds; some of the more outstanding I've included, though none I know of aren't worth at least a brief stop. In our travels, these sites rank high among our favorite pit stops — light the stove, brew a cup'a Joe, cook a burger, check off a few birds — what better way to cut a long road trip down to size.

But before you dig in, a few disclaimers. While I've visited more of these sites than not, I make no claim to having visited them all. Wherever possible I have leaned on local experts to provide the key birds and other details. In all cases, should you find errors (like, no way could he have seen such-and-such here,) you're right, I probably did not…though trust me nothing in this book is meant to deceive but rather to give you birders a clear place to start all wrapped up in one package.

So there you have it, turn the pages of the book, enjoy, and by all means get out there and go birding.

Chuck Robbins
Dillon, MT
2014

Cedar Waxwing

FOR YOUR INFORMATION

Nickname: Treasure State, aka, Big Sky Country; Land of the Shining Mountains; Mountain State; Bonanza State and Headwaters State (depending, our rivers flow to the Pacific, Atlantic, and Arctic Oceans)

State Animal: Grizzly bear

State Bird: Western Meadowlark

State Dance: Square dance

State Fish: Black-spotted cutthroat trout

State Flower: Bitterroot

State Fossil: Duck-billed dinosaur (*Maiasaura peeblesorum*)

State Gemstones: Sapphire & agate

State Grass: Bluebunch wheatgrass

State Tree: Ponderosa pine

State Butterfly: Mourning cloak

State Song: "Montana" – written one night by a Montana newspaper editor and famous songwriter in 1910.

State Ballad: "Montana Melody" – Montana is one of few states to have a state song and ballad.

Admitted to the Union: Nov. 8, 1889, the 41st state.

Population: 926,865, 6.2 persons per square mile, the 44th most populous state.

Capital City: Helena – population, 26,718

Largest City: Billings – population, 95,220

State Name: "Montana" is from the Latin word for "mountainous region"

Size:

147,046 square miles in total area

145,556 square miles in land area

1,490 square miles in water area

94,109,440 total acres

Fourth largest state in the union

Greatest distance from east to west boundary: approximately 550 miles

Greatest distance from north to south boundary: approximately 320 miles

Geographic Center: Fergus County, about 11 miles west of Lewistown

Number of Counties: 56

Highest Point: 12,799 feet (3,901 meters) above sea level at summit of Granite Peak in Park County near south-central boundary

Lowest Point: 1,820 feet in Lincoln County in the northwest corner where the Kootenai River enters Idaho

Mean Elevation: 3,400 feet

Time Zone: Mountain

Area Code: 406

Postal Abbreviation: MT

Resident: Montanan

Motto: Oro y Plata (Spanish for "gold and silver")

Birding Manners

A few suggestions guaranteed to improve your birding and insure a pleasant outing for all concerned—birds included.

- Exercise restraint observing, videoing, photographing, recording, digiscoping, whatever.
- Never approach a bird near enough to stress, flush, or in any way disturb it.
- Limit the use of voice recordings, predator calls and such, especially with birds of conservation concern and/or rare to your area.
- Maintain a distance from nesting and feeding sites that do not disturb the birds in any way.
- Whenever possible use a blind, natural cover, or other means to mask your presence; vehicles work well in most cases.
- Park in designated parking areas.
- Drive only on designated roads and trails.
- Strive to eliminate the spread of noxious weeds; maintain a clean vehicle.
- Walk/hike on designated roads and trails in high use areas.
- Private land trespass requires written landowner permission.
- Follow all rules and regulations on public lands; do not violate closed seasons/restrictions designed to protect breeding/nesting/brood rearing birds.
- Do not block gates, roads, trails, or other means of access.
- Do not litter. Litter is the best way I know to insure locked gates.
- Use common courtesy around fellow birders and photographers.
- Quiet rocks; the sneakier you are, the more birds you will find.

Symbols Legend

 Bicycling

 Hunting

 Blinds

 Picnicking

 Boat Access

 Fee

 Camping

 Restrooms

 Fishing

 Visitor's Center

 Handicapped Access

 Wildlife Viewing

 Hiking

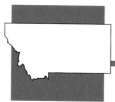

BIRDING TRAILS: MONTANA

Web Sites for Birding Trails Montana

Montana State Parks: www.stateparks.mt.gov
Montana Fish Wildlife and Parks: www.fwp.mt.gov
Montana Wildlife Management Areas: www.fwp.mt.gov/fishandwildlife/wma
Montana Audubon: www.mtaudubon.org

Montana Important Birding Areas (IBAs)

The Important Birding Area program is a global initiative of Birdlife International, implemented by Audubon and their state Audubon. The purpose of the program is to identify and conserve areas that are important to birds and other biodiversity. The Montana Audubon has currently identified 40 IBAs in Montana. These sites are identified in our book. The web address for Montana Audubon's site is www.mtaudubon.org/birds/areas.html

BIRDING TRAILS: MONTANA

State Land Recreation Use Permit

A State Land Recreation Use Permit is required for anyone conducting a non-commercial activity on State Trust Lands not related to hunting and fishing. State Trust Lands are properties managed by the Department of Natural Resources and Conservation (DNRC) for the sole purpose of generating income for public schools and other public institutions. Applicable non-commercial activities include, but are not limited to, bird and wildlife viewing, photography, hiking, biking, skiing, sightseeing, and day horseback use.

The State Land Recreation Use Permit is not required when using State Trust Lands for hunting or fishing, because a $2 fee is included in the Montana Conservation License for use of these lands.

BIRDING TRAILS: MONTANA

GLACIER COUNTRY

Glacier Country is comprised of Flathead, Glacier, Lake, Lincoln, Mineral, Missoula, Ravalli and Sanders Counties. Glacier National Park IBA lists over 260 species. The region's 10 other IBAs form an impressive core to the fabulous birding opportunities found here. Take the Bitterroot south of Missoula, explore the Flathead Lake region, the Seeley-Swan corridor to the east, or the sprawling Kootenai River country to the west; enough birding ops to last all but the most jaded amongst us several lifetimes.

Unlike much of Montana the northwest is wetter. Rivers, creeks, marsh and wetlands abound. There are more trees and the feel is more western Washington-Oregon rainforest than what most think of as Montana.

Commercial airports in Missoula and Kalispell, I-90 and US 2 and 93 are the major highways. Kootenai, Flathead, and Lolo National Forests provide plenty of camping ops and public access. The Flathead and Bitterroot Valleys are among the state's fastest growing population centers offering travelers any and everything in amenities.

Lake McDonald, Glacier National Park

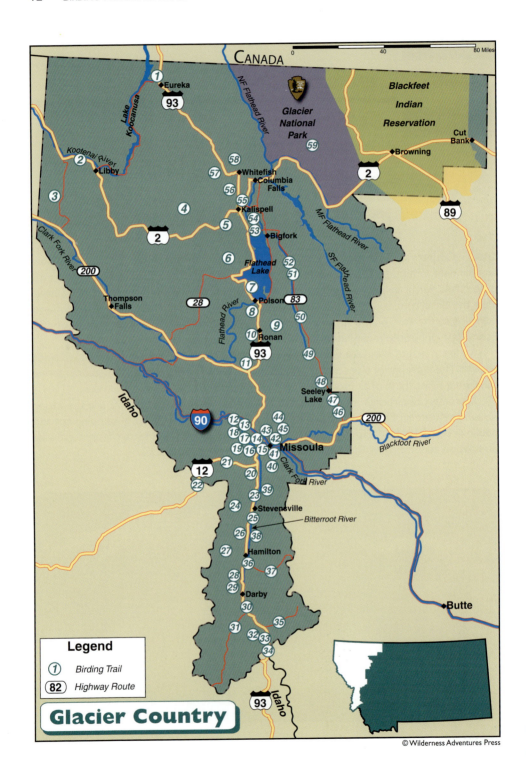

Glacier Country

Glacier Country Locations

1. Eureka/Tobacco Plains/Dancing Prairie Preserve
2. Kootenai Falls Wildlife Management Area
3. Ross Creek Cedar Grove
4. Lost Trail National Wildlife Refuge
5. Smith Lake Waterfowl Production Area
6. Lake Mary Ronan State Park
7. Safe Harbor Marsh IBA
8. Pablo National Wildlife Refuge
9. Ronan Hawk Roost IBA
10. Ninepipe National Wildlife Refuge
11. National Bison Range
12. Erskine Fishing Access Site
13. Clark Fork River Float
14. Kelly Island Fishing Access Site
15. Tower Street Open Space Park
16. Maclay Flat Trail
17. Council Grove State Park
18. Clark Fork River/Grass Valley IBA
19. Blue Mountain Nature Trail
20. Traveler's Rest State Park
21. Fort Fizzle
22. Lolo Pass
23. Bass Creek Fishing Access Site
24. St. Mary's Peak
25. Bitterroot River IBA
26. Bear Creek Trail
27. Blodgett Canyon
28. Coyote Coulee
29. Lake Como National Recreation Trail
30. Hannon Memorial Fishing Access Site
31. Sam Billings Memorial Campground
32. Crazy Creek Campground
33. Indian Trees Campground
34. Chief Joseph Pass Ski Trails
35. Broad Ax Lodge
36. River And Hieronymus Parks
37. Centennial Grove Nature Trail
38. Teller Wildlife Refuge
39. Lee Metcalf National Wildlife Refuge
40. Pattee Canyon National Recreation Area

41. Mount Sentinel
42. Greenough Park
43. Waterworks Hill Trail
44. Rattlesnake National Recreation Area
45. Mount Jumbo
46. Blackfoot Clearwater Wildlife Management Area
47. Boy Scout Road
48. Clearwater River Canoe Trail
49. Chain Of Lakes
50. Swan River State Forest
51. Swan River Oxbow Preserve
52. Swan River National Wildlife Refuge
53. Owen Sowerwine Nature Area
54. Lower Valley Road
55. Lawrence Park
56. West Valley Ponds
57. Tally Lake
58. Danny On Trail
59. Glacier National Park

GLACIER COUNTRY
Eureka/Tobacco Plains/ Dancing Prairie Preserve

GPS 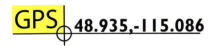 **48.935,-115.086**

EUREKA

KEY BIRDS
Typical grassland species such as Mountain and Western Bluebird, Bobolink, Baird's, Savannah and Grasshopper Sparrows, Long-billed Curlew, Sprague's Pipit, McCown's and Chestnut-collared Longspur, Lark Bunting, Swainson's and Ferruginous Hawks, Mountain Plover, Horned Lark, Lazuli Bunting and Turkey Vulture

BEST SEASONS
Spring through early fall

AREA DESCRIPTION
Mix of remnant Palouse prairie, intermountain grasslands, agricultural fields, cottonwood, aspen, willow stream bottoms, interspersed with pothole lakes

More or less surrounded by national forest – predominantly ponderosa pine-Douglas fir forest – the preserve itself offers the best remaining example of the Palouse prairie in Montana.

The preserve harbors the world's largest known population of the rare flowering plant, Spalding's catchfly. Once the site of the last known Columbian Sharp-tailed Grouse dancing ground (lek) in Montana, alas no grouse have been seen here recently.

Hike in from the interpretive kiosk. Please do not pick or otherwise disturb wildflowers, and keep your distance from singing, nesting birds. Remember that, in Montana, private land access requires landowner permission.

DIRECTIONS
From Eureka, take MT 37 west 1 mile; turn on Airport Road 2 miles to the preserve.

CONTACT
Nature Conservancy phone: 406-443-0303

GLACIER COUNTRY
Kootenai Falls WMA

GPS 48.456, -115.761

DOWNSTREAM OF LIBBY

KEY BIRDS
Bald Eagle (over 150 have been sighted in a single day), Harlequin Duck, Osprey, and American Dipper, Long-billed Curlew

BEST SEASONS
Year around, spring through fall offers best variety; winter and spring for Bald Eagles

AREA DESCRIPTION
River habitat with 30-foot high waterfall surrounded by mountains

Over 150 bald eagles have been sighted here in a single day. Our best day here, in addition to the four key birds listed above, we also checked off Great Blue Heron, Bullock's Oriole, Red-Winged Blackbird, Black-Capped and Boreal Chickadees, Steller's Jay, Common Raven, American Crow, American Wigeon, Blue-Winged Teal, Canada Goose, Common Goldeneye, Mallard, Wood Duck, Belted Kingfisher, Golden-Crowned Kinglet, Great Horned Owl, Song and Chipping Sparrows, Western Tanager, Veery, Dusky Flycatcher, Yellow Warbler, Pileated Woodpecker, Red-naped Sapsucker, and Pacific Wren. Admittedly pale by comparison to local experts, but for us a pretty good day.

Here the Kootenai River drops 90 feet in less than a mile; the main falls is 30 feet high. It is the last major falls in the northwest not harnessed for electricity. The Kootenai Tribe considers the falls a sacred site; commercial use requires tribal permission. In 1808, David Thompson became the first white man to view the falls. *"The River had steep banks of rocks and only 30 yards in width; this space was full of violent eddies, which threatened us with destruction; at wherever the river contracted, the case was always the same, the current was swift; yet to look at the surface, the eddies make it appear to move as much backward as forward."*

The Falls Trail (from the County Park on US 2) provides benches and interpretive signs. Trail-wise, within the WMA you are on your own.

The WMA is managed for bighorn sheep, white-tailed deer, mule deer, and black bear as well as beaver, mink, muskrat, otter, and the occasional moose and elk. Though rarely seen, bobcat, fisher, and mountain lion also frequent the area.

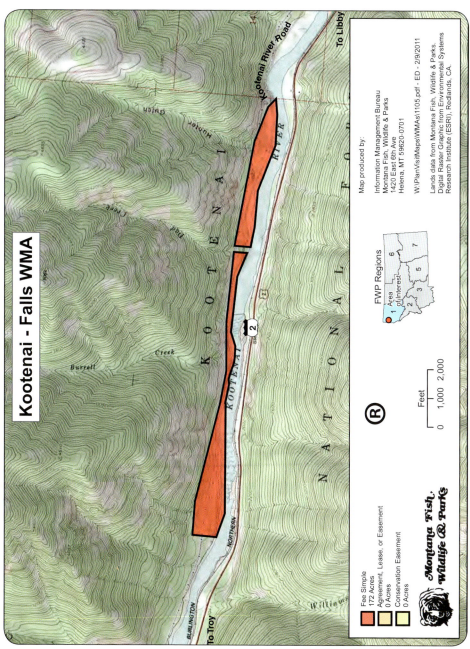

Kootenai - Falls WMA

Fee Simple
172 Acres

Agreement, Lease, or Easement
0 Acres

Conservation Easement
0 Acres

Montana Fish,
Wildlife & Parks

FWP Regions

1 Area
of Interest

Feet
0   1,000   2,000

Map produced by:

Information Management Bureau
Montana Fish, Wildlife & Parks.
1420 East 6th Ave
Helena, MT 59620-0701

W:\Plan\VisitMaps\WMAs\1105.pdf - ED - 2/9/2011

Lands data from Montana Fish, Wildlife & Parks.
Digital Raster Graphic from Environmental Systems
Research Institute (ESRI), Redlands, CA.

Used with permission

Other activities include fishing, mountain biking, hiking, picnicking, photography, boating (non-motorized) and hunting for big game, upland birds, and waterfowl.

DIRECTIONS
From Libby, take MT-37 north 7 miles to Kootenai River Road to the WMA. To reach the county park and access the trail to the falls, follow U.S. 2 approximately 10 miles west. A swinging bridge allows access and viewing across the river.

CONTACT
Montana Fish, Wildlife & Parks phone: 406-444-2535
Tonya Chilton-Radandt phone: 406-293-4161
Email: tchilton@mt.gov

Long-billed Curlew

GLACIER COUNTRY
Ross Cedar Grove

#3

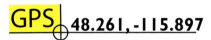 

GPS 48.261, -115.897

SOUTH OF TROY NEAR BULL LAKE

KEY BIRDS
Pileated, Hairy, and Downy Woodpeckers, Great Gray Owl, Red-naped Sapsucker, Townsend's and MacGillivray's Warblers, Red-eyed Vireo, Brown Creeper

BEST SEASONS
Spring through early fall

AREA DESCRIPTION
Mainly old-growth western cedars

For us this one is more about just spending some quality time amid old growth western red cedars, though naturally we keep one eye peeled for birds. As trees go, the cedars are huge — 175 feet tall and 8 feet in diameter — and old — 200 or more years old. Initially spared by area loggers, in 1960 the Forest Service set the grove aside as a scenic area affording permanent protection for future generations to explore and enjoy.

The best birding is weekdays, early morning and evening. Belted Kingfisher, Bohemian and Cedar Waxwings, Pygmy and Great Horned Owls, Common Loon, Ruffed Grouse, American Dipper, Steller's Jay, Rufous and Calliope Hummingbirds, Mountain and Western Bluebirds, Black-capped and Boreal Chickadees, Bald Eagle, Osprey, Harlequin and Wood Duck, Common and Barrow's Goldeneye, Ruby- and Yellow-crowned Kinglets, White- and Brown-breasted Nuthatches frequent the area.

Activities include hiking, biking, picnicking. At nearby Bull Lake visitors enjoy fishing, camping, boating, and canoeing. The surrounding national forest offers more good birding and is also a popular hunting destination.

Camping is available at Bad Medicine Campground on Bull Lake: 18 sites, tables, fire rings, RV limit 32 feet, potable water, vault toilets, and boat ramp/dock. Season: Memorial Day-Labor Day, though camping is allowed year around.

Also, be sure to check out nearby Ross Creek Falls.

DIRECTIONS
From Troy, take US 2 east, turn south on MT 56 for 18 miles to a well-signed turnoff to Bull Lake and the Ross Creek Cedars. From Thompson Falls, follow MT 200 north to MT 56, turn north 16 miles to the turnoff at the south end of Bull Lake. Follow signs 4 miles west to the Ross Creek trailhead.

CONTACT
Kootenai National Forest phone: 406-293-6211

GLACIER COUNTRY
Lost Trail
National Wildlife Refuge

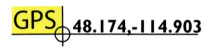

GPS 48.174,-114.903

WEST OF KALISPELL
AND NORTH OF MARION

KEY BIRDS

Willow Flycatcher, Wild Turkey, Western Tanager, Warbling Vireo, Yellow Warbler, Red-naped Sapsucker, Sandhill Crane, Gadwall, Cinnamon and Green-winged Teal, Lesser Scaup (Bluebill), Wood and Redhead Ducks, Spruce, Dusky, and Ruffed Grouse, Killdeer, Dowitcher, Sandpipers, Common Snipe, Bitterns, Black Terns

BEST SEASONS

Year around, with certain areas restricted during nesting seasons. Spring and fall migrations offer the best viewing ops.

AREA DESCRIPTION

Partially-drained lake surrounded by irrigated wet meadows

Consisting of 7,800 acres, the heart of the refuge is partially-drained, 160-acre Dahl Lake which is surrounded by irrigated wet meadows and primarily non-native reed canary grass. Despite being fed by several drainages, water levels tend to fluctuate widely according to the season. Upland areas are typically dry, a mosaic of prairie grasslands dominated by a variety of native and non-native grasses and woods — both coniferous and deciduous species.

The main parking area overlooks the lake, surrounded by grass. A spotting scope works best. There are no developed trails but roads, game trails, and cross-country hiking offer unlimited birding ops. Vehicle access is permitted on designated roads only (no off-road) and parking is in designated parking areas only.

The refuge is bordered by Plum Creek Timberlands, two private ranches, and four state tracts totaling 1,440 acres. These tracts are managed by the MT Department of Natural Resources Conservation (DNRC) and are open to recreational uses according to state law.

Refuge literature lists mule and white-tailed deer, elk, moose, black bear, muskrat, badger, fisher, pine marten, lynx, wolverine, and bobcat. Columbian ground squirrels inhabit the drier uplands. Grizzly bears and gray wolves are seen occasionally.

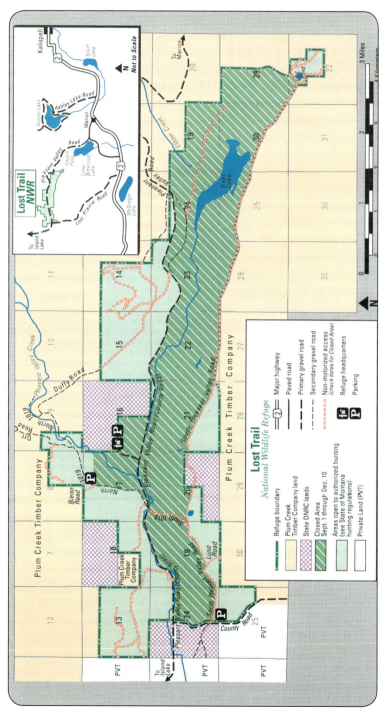

Credit: U.S. Fish and Wildlife Service

Activities include hiking, mountain biking, photography, fishing, picnicking, and hunting (with restrictions).

There are also excellent birding ops at Little Bitterroot Lake (waterfowl) and all along the road from Marion to the refuge (forest birds).

DIRECTIONS

Follow US 2 west of Kalispell, and turn north at Marion on Pleasant Valley Road. The refuge is approximately 20 miles.

CONTACT

Lost Trail National Wildlife Refuge
Phone: 406-644-221
Website: bisonrange@fws.gov

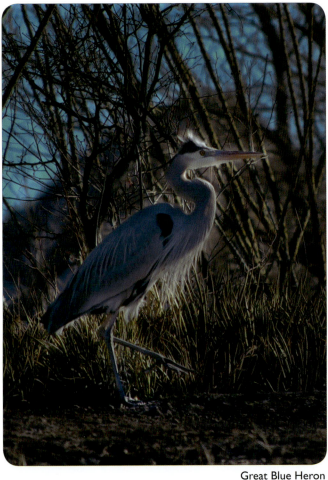

Great Blue Heron

GLACIER COUNTRY

#5 Smith Lake Waterfowl Production Area

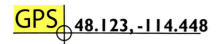 **GPS** 48.123, -114.448

WEST OF KALISPELL

KEY BIRDS
Avocet, Killdeer, Phalarope, Yellowlegs, American Wigeon, Mallard, Pintail, American Bittern, Gadwall, Tundra Swan, Sandhill Crane, Wild Turkey

BEST SEASONS
August best for shorebirds, spring & fall migrations for waterfowl

AREA DESCRIPTION
Wetlands surrounding open water

Get out early to scan the extensive wetlands that surround the open water. There are no trails and much of the area is wet, so be sure to bring along appropriate foot gear. The best way to view the lake and associated creek mouth and shoreline is from a boat.

Smith Lake and Ashley Creek are open year around, but the wetlands are closed to public access from March 1 to July 15 to reduce the disturbance of nesting birds. Smith is a popular fishing spot and is especially busy weekends.

White-tailed deer, muskrat, skunk and red fox frequent the area.

DIRECTIONS
From Kalispell, take US 2 west 7 miles to Kila.

CONTACT
Smith Lake WPA
Phone: 406-644-221
E-mail: bisonrange@fws.gov

GLACIER COUNTRY

#6 Lake Mary Ronan State Park

GPS 47.56, 114.23

WEST OF FLATHEAD LAKE

KEY BIRDS

Ruby-crowned Kinglet, Pileated Woodpecker, Common Loon, Bald Eagle, Osprey, Pied-billed, Eared, Red-necked, and Western Grebes, Calliope Hummingbird, Cassin's Vireo, Northern Saw-whet Owl, Green-winged Teal

BEST SEASONS

Open year around; best viewing is spring and fall

AREA DESCRIPTION

Lakeside habitat surrounded by forest

First check out the lake and then head for the hills. Several trails lead through the forest into the surrounding Flathead National Forest offering birders plenty of chances. Easy hiking, a variety of birds, wildflowers galore, the chance to gorge on

Green-winged Teal

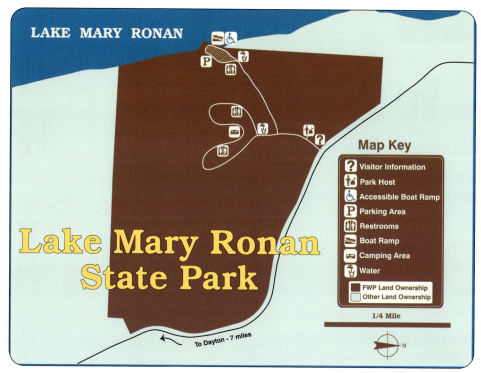

huckleberries (late summer) and gaze at wildflowers and plentiful wildlife. Little wonder that the park ranks high with local birders. Summer weekends tend to draw a crowd.

Dippers frequent Ronan Creek, and hearing a Pileated Woodpecker or two pounding away is almost a given. Many of the 14 owls known to nest in Montana have been observed in the area. As you might expect, late winter owling excursions are popular among locals.

Other activities include photography, fishing, boating, camping, mountain biking, and picnicking.

DIRECTIONS
Follow US 93 to Dayton, turn west on Mary Ronan Road (MT 352).

CONTACT
Park Manager phone: 406-849-5082

GLACIER COUNTRY

#7 Safe Harbor Marsh (IBA)

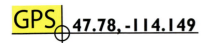 GPS 47.78, -114.149

NORTH OF POLSON ON WEST SIDE FLATHEAD LAKE

KEY BIRDS
Bald Eagle, Red-Winged, Yellow-Headed and Brewer's Blackbirds, Ruffed Grouse, Calliope and Rufous Hummingbirds, Willow and Hammond's Flycatchers, Cassin's Finch, Song Sparrow, Common Yellowthroat, Pacific Wren, Osprey, Prairie Falcon, Wood Duck, Western Screech Owl, Song Sparrow, Red-breasted Nuthatch, Western Wood-pewee, Pileated Woodpecker

BEST SEASONS
Year round

AREA DESCRIPTION
Freshwater marsh surrounded by coniferous forest

From the kiosk, a trail winds through the preserve. Please stay on the trail and avoid disturbing singing males and, especially, nesting sites.

Douglas fir is predominant in the cool, damp areas and ponderosa pine on the drier uplands. The marsh is actually a small bay connected by a narrow channel to Flathead Lake, a remnant of glaciers 12,000 years ago. In spring and summer, the marsh comes alive with nesting songbirds, waterfowl, and wading birds. The wildflower show is spectacular. Walk the trail which winds through the marsh, and watch birds flit about in every direction. During migrations, 81 neotropical migrant species have been observed.

At times, especially early morning, the birdsong is deafening. On a recent spring morning we thrilled to the sound of a Wild Turkey gobbling, several Ruffed Grouse drumming, watched and listened as a Pileated Woodpecker hunted breakfast, while a Wood Duck hen made multiple trips to a cavity nest in a nearby tree…what a nifty way to start the day, eh?

The marsh was acquired by the Nature Conservancy in 1989. Flathead Lake is the largest natural freshwater lake west of the Mississippi.

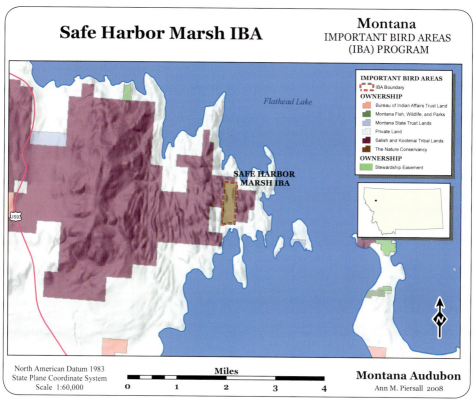

Used with permission.

DIRECTIONS

From Polson, at the south end of Flathead Lake, take US 93 northwest for a half mile. Turn right on Rocky Point Road and go 4.5 miles to King's Point Road. Turn right (east) 1.5 miles and look for a gravel turn-out on the north side of the road next to a fence marked with yellow Nature Conservancy signs.

CONTACT

Nature Conservancy phone: 406-837-0066

GLACIER COUNTRY
#8 Pablo National Wildlife Refuge (IBA)

GPS 47.628,-114.153

SOUTH OF POLSON ON TRIBAL TRUST LANDS OF THE CONFEDERATED SALISH AND KOOTENAI TRIBES

KEY BIRDS
Trumpeter Swan, Gadwall, Northern Pintail, Ruddy Duck, Common Loon, Blue- and Green-winged Teal, Coot, Wester and Red-necked Grebes, Bald Eagle, Warbling Vireo, Yellow and Yellow-rumped Warblers, Snowy Owl, Rough-legged Hawk (winter), Mallard

BEST SEASONS
Year around, spring and fall for waterfowl and songbirds, August for shorebirds

AREA DESCRIPTION
Reservoir surrounded by upland habitat

Many consider the Mission Valley to be perhaps the best winter raptor viewing site in the state.

The refuge is comprised of the 1,850-acre Pablo Reservoir and surrounding 692 acre uplands. The IBA includes the 400-acre state wildlife management area. Cottonwoods at the north end of the refuge and the willows on the south and west end of the reservoir, as well as the surrounding uplands, offer excellent viewing ops for songbirds and raptors. The wetlands, lake, and associated potholes attract large numbers of waterfowl and shorebirds during migration. Many ducks and Canada Geese nest within the IBA as well.

Dale Becker, manager of the Flathead Tribal Wildlife Program, says 159 captive-raised Trumpeter Swans have been released on the reservation since 2001. The swans have produced 69 cygnets since 2004.

Low water years expose extensive mudflats. As many as 18 shorebird species — including Baird's, Least, Semipalmated and Stilt Sandpipers, and Semipalmated Plover — and 1,000 individuals have been observed in a single August day. Thousands of Redhead ducks congregate annually during the fall migration.

Largemouth bass and yellow perch fishing, picnicking, hunting on the WMA, and nature photography are popular activities.

DIRECTIONS
South of Polson off US 93, west of highway, watch for signs.

CONTACT
Pablo NWR phone: 406-644-2211
Website: bisonrange@fws.gov
WMA, John Grant – phone: 406-644-2510

Mallard hen

GLACIER COUNTRY

Ronan Hawk Roost (IBA)

#9

GPS 47.53,-114.038

SOUTHEAST OF RONAN

KEY BIRDS
Rough-legged Hawk, Short-eared Owl, Red-tailed Hawk, Bald Eagle, Ferruginous Hawk and other raptors including Snowy Owl

BEST SEASONS
Winter

AREA DESCRIPTION
Stand of conifers in the foothills of the Mission Valley, now dominated by irrigated farmland and pastures

This area has the largest communal roost of wintering rough-legged hawks in the world. In peak vole years, more than 300 Rough-legged Hawks use the roost nightly. Some years, as many as 1,000 raptors — hawks, eagles, and Short-eared Owls — winter in the valley. Snowy Owls also show up in the valley when there are lean lemming years up north.

Look for the short-eared owl at the roost. The best viewing is to drive the roads and scan the fields. Nearly all private and, assuming you remembered to pack the 60X spotting scope, there is really no reason to leave your vehicle or to approach the roost site itself on foot.

DIRECTIONS
In Ronan (US 93) turn east on Terrace Lake Road, and in approximately 2.5 miles turn right (south) on Glacier Lilly Lane; hawk roost is on left. Please remain in your vehicle, hawks are easily disturbed.

CONTACT
Montana Audubon Society - Amy Cilimburg, Director of Conservation and Climate Policy
phone: 406-465-1141
Email: amy@mtaudubon.org

Rough-legged Hawk

GLACIER COUNTRY

#10 Ninepipe National Wildlife Refuge (IBA)

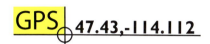

GPS 47.43,-114.112

SOUTH OF RONAN

KEY BIRDS
Northern Shoveler, American Wigeon, Redhead and Ruddy Ducks, Canada Goose, Red-necked and Western Grebes, Song Sparrow, Yellow-headed and Red-winged Blackbirds, Ring-necked Pheasant, Osprey, American Bittern, Sora

BEST SEASONS
Year around: summer for nesting songbirds; shorebirds in August, and winter is primetime for raptor sightings

AREA DESCRIPTION
Reservoir surrounded by grasslands, potholes, marshes, and wetlands

Ninepipes is comprised of the 1,652-acre Ninepipe Reservoir and 348 acres of surrounding grasslands interspersed with numerous potholes, marshes and wetlands, many of which remain wet year round. The IBA includes the refuge, the 3,800-acre state-managed Ninepipes WMA, 3,000 acres of Flathead Tribal Lands, and 2,000 acres of USFWS conservation easements.

"The IBA hosts the only known western grebe nesting colony in the Mission Valley and is an important nesting and staging area for a large portion of the Flathead Valley's Canada goose population. Active great-blue heron and double-crested cormorant rookeries can be seen from the roads—some of which are closed during nesting season—March through mid-July. The gravel road at the dam is a good place to view the cormorant rookery. Cattails offer the best chances for viewing marsh loving birds such as yellow-headed blackbirds, marsh wrens, bitterns and sora." Quote per Ninepipes literature

We've found a spotting scope works best for identifying waterfowl which often raft up way out on the main lake. Binoculars seem to work best on the smaller potholes. Gunlock and Olson Roads pass by potholes that offer numerous birding ops.

The Mission Valley is perhaps the premier winter hawk and owl viewing area in the state. Bald Eagles frequent the area, especially over winter and early spring. Snowy Owls often show up during lean lemming years up north.

CONTACT
Ninepipes NWR phone: 406-644-2211
Website:bisonrange@fws.gov
WMA – John Grant – phone: 406-644-2510

GLACIER COUNTRY
#11 National Bison Range (IBA)

GPS 47.319,-114.21

SOUTH OF POLSON, JUST OUTSIDE MOIESE

KEY BIRDS
Species of conservation concern known to nest here include Bald Eagle, Lewis's Woodpecker, Red-naped Sapsucker, Willow Flycatcher, Lazuli Bunting, Grasshopper Sparrow; also Long-eared Owl

BEST SEASONS
Open year around (with restrictions) but best viewing is spring through early fall

AREA DESCRIPTION
Native grasslands, brushy draws, Douglas fir/ponderosa pine and aspen forest dominate the uplands; cottonwoods, willows, choke cherry and other shrubs dominate the riparian areas

Over 200 species have been observed here. Rough-legged (winter) and Red-tailed Hawks, Northern Harrier, Mountain Bluebird, Western Meadowlark, Mourning Dove, Vesper Sparrow, Tree, Cliff, Barn and Northern Rough-winged Swallows are easy to find in the open grass.

In the brushy draws, riparian zones, and forested areas look for Northern Oriole, Clark's Nutcracker, Dusky Grouse, Great Horned and Northern Saw-whet Owls, Belted Kingfisher, Steller's And Gray Jays, Lewis's, Hairy, and Downy Woodpeckers, Mountain and Black-capped Chickadees, and Red-breasted and Pygmy Nuthatches. Of this group, all but the Northern Oriole are year-round residents.

There are four trails. **Nature Trail** (1 mile) starts at the picnic area and **Grassland Trail** (1/4 mile) starts at the visitor center. Both **Bitterroot Trail** (1/2 mile) and **High Point Trail** (1 mile) are located off Red Sleep Mountain Drive and allow for easy hiking and good birding ops. Otherwise, walking away from your vehicle is prohibited.

Prairie Drive/West Loop is a 5-mile gravel road open year round to vehicles, including trailers and large RVs.

Red Sleep Mountain Drive is a 19-mile, one-way, gravel road. Elevation gain is 2,000 feet with switchbacks and 10% grades; maximum vehicle length is 32 feet. Allow one and a half to two hours. Open mid-May to late October.

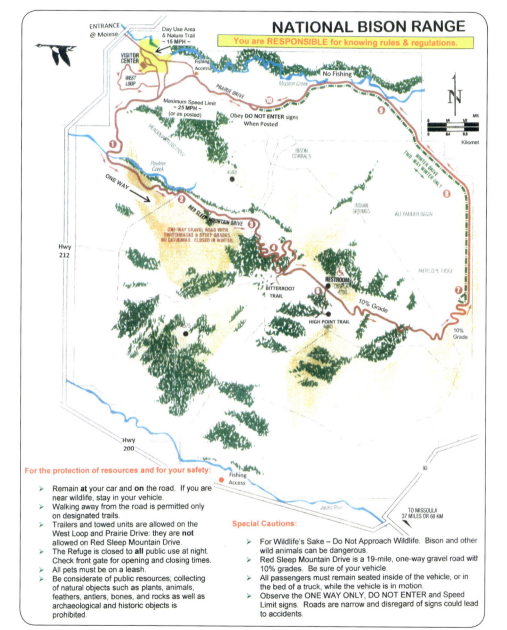

NATIONAL BISON RANGE

You are RESPONSIBLE for knowing rules & regulations.

ENTRANCE @ Moiese

Day Use Area & Nature Trail ~ 15 MPH ~

VISITOR CENTER

WEST LOOP

Fishing Access

No Fishing

PRAIRIE DRIVE

Mission Creek

Maximum Speed Limit ~ 25 MPH ~ (or as posted)

Obey DO NOT ENTER signs When Posted

HEADQUARTERS 2160

Pauline Creek

ONE WAY

4088

BISON CORRALS

WINTER DRIVE TWO-WAY WINTER ONLY

RED SLEEP MOUNTAIN DRIVE

ONE-WAY GRAVEL ROAD WITH SWITCHBACKS & STEEP GRADES. NO GUARDRAIL. CLOSED IN WINTER.

INDIAN SPRINGS

ALEXANDER BASIN

Hwy 212

BITTERROOT TRAIL

RESTROOM DISPLAY

ANTELOPE RIDGE

10% Grade

HIGH POINT TRAIL

10% Grade

Hwy 200

Fishing Access

Jocko River

93

TO MISSOULA 37 MILES OR 60 KM

For the protection of resources and for your safety:

- Remain **at** your car and **on** the road. If you are near wildlife, stay in your vehicle.
- Walking away from the road is permitted only on designated trails.
- Trailers and towed units are allowed on the West Loop and Prairie Drive: they are **not** allowed on Red Sleep Mountain Drive.
- The Refuge is closed to **all** public use at night. Check front gate for opening and closing times.
- All pets must be on a leash.
- Be considerate of public resources; collecting of natural objects such as plants, animals, feathers, antlers, bones, and rocks as well as archaeological and historic objects is prohibited.

Special Cautions:

- For Wildlife's Sake – Do Not Approach Wildlife. Bison and other wild animals can be dangerous.
- Red Sleep Mountain Drive is a 19-mile, one-way gravel road with 10% grades. Be sure of your vehicle.
- All passengers must remain seated inside of the vehicle, or in the bed of a truck, while the vehicle is in motion.
- Observe the ONE WAY ONLY, DO NOT ENTER and Speed Limit signs. Roads are narrow and disregard of signs could lead to accidents.

Credit: U.S. Fish and Wildlife Service

No bicycles or motorcycles allowed off paved roads.

Bison (300-400) are of course the main attraction, but the refuge supports a healthy critter base including elk, deer, pronghorn, bighorn sheep, mountain goat, black bear, coyote, ground squirrel and, while seldom observed, prairie rattlesnake.

"Visitors should be aware bison are unpredictable and can be dangerous. Appearing slow and docile bison are quite agile; run as fast as a horse. Bear in mind, tail down and flagging usually indicates indifference; straight out with a droop at the end indicates mild agitation; straight up, you need to be someplace else....DO NOT RUN.

Bulls top out about 2,000 lbs; cows about half that. Bulls sport heavy horns and are especially ill-tempered during rut, mid-July through August. Calves are born from mid-April through May; wear a rust red color for the first month or so. Cows are extremely protective; with calf in tow often more dangerous than bulls." Quote from National Bison Range literature

The annual fall roundup is a highlight; check headquarters for specific dates. Be sure to stop at the visitor center for the latest info on unusual bird sightings.

Fee area in summer (mid-May to late October); Golden Age Passes and Federal Waterfowl Stamps are accepted. Day use only, hours vary seasonally and the visitor center is closed weekends from late October to mid-May. No camping.

Picnicking, wildflower and wildlife photography, and trout fishing are popular activities. The nearest amenities are in Ronan and Polson.

DIRECTIONS

From Missoula: Follow US 93 north to Ravalli, turn left (west) on MT 200 approximately 5 miles to the junction of MT 200 and 212; turn right (north) approximately 5 miles to Moiese.

From Kalispell: Follow US 93 or MT 35 south to Polson, through Pablo and Ronan to the junction of US 93 and MT 212; follow MT 212 (through Charlo) to Moiese.

From the west: Take MT 200 through Dixon to the junction of MT 200 and MT 212, turn left (north) on MT 212 to Moiese.

CONTACT

National Bison Range
phone: 406-644-2211
Website: bisonrange@ fws.gov

Long-eared Owl

GLACIER COUNTRY
#12 Erskine Fishing Access Site

GPS 47.015,-114.28

WEST OF FRENCHTOWN

KEY BIRDS
Wood Duck, Least and Willow Flycatchers, Lewis's Woodpecker, Common Yellowthroat, MacGillivray's Warbler

BEST SEASONS
Spring through early fall offers the best variety

AREA DESCRIPTION
River habitat with a mix of cottonwoods, ponderosa pines, aspens, willows, cattails and shrub thickets

The oxbow and island, the result of centuries of floods, add an interesting footnote to an already diverse mix in this 425-acre area which birds of all sorts find attractive. Erskine is part of the IBA that includes Kelly Island, Council Grove State Park, and Grass Valley.

Local birders rate it the "best spot in the valley" to see willow flycatchers and least flycatchers. Three hummingbirds — Black-chinned, Calliope and Rufous — also nest here. Northern Waterthrush, Cedar Waxwing, Western Tanager, Gray Catbird, and American Redstart are common. In February, listen for the distinctive hooting of Great Gray Owls. Oxbow beaver ponds provide attractive nesting sites for teal, Gadwall, Wood Duck, and Mallard.

White-tailed deer, beaver, and painted turtles also frequent the area.

Expect wet conditions and difficult access to much of the area during runoff — typically May and June. Fishing, hiking, and wildlife viewing are popular activities. Camping is allowed, but there are no facilities, and trailers and RVs are not recommended. Pack-in, pack-out rules apply. Hunting is not allowed.

DIRECTIONS
From I-90, Frenchtown Exit, turn south onto Ducharme Street, then west on Mullan Road for 2 miles; turn south at the FAS sign for 1 mile to parking area; two trails, east and west, lead into the area.

CONTACT
Montana Fish, Wildlife and Parks phone: 406-542-5500

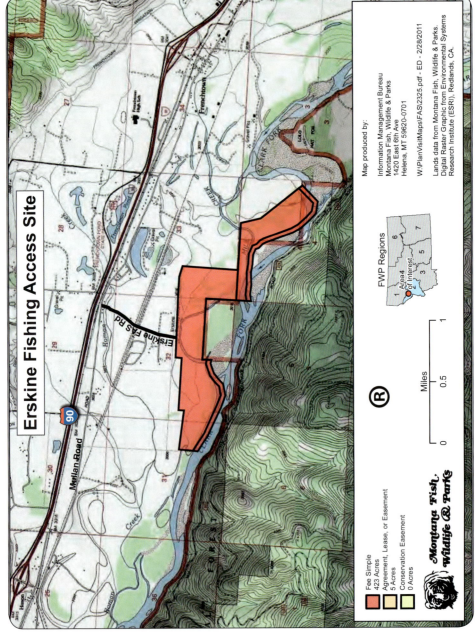

Erskine Fishing Access Site

Fee Simple
423 Acres

Agreement, Lease, or Easement
5 Acres

Conservation Easement
0 Acres

Montana Fish,
Wildlife & Parks

FWP Regions

Miles
0   0.5   1

Map produced by:

Information Management Bureau
Montana Fish, Wildlife & Parks
1420 East 6th Ave
Helena, MT 59620-0701

W:\Plan\VisitMaps\FAS\2325.pdf - ED - 2/28/2011

Lands data from Montana Fish, Wildlife & Parks.
Digital Raster Graphic from Environmental Systems
Research Institute (ESRI), Redlands, CA.

Used with permission.

GLACIER COUNTRY

#13 | Clark Fork River Float

GPS 46.837,-114.105

SOUTHWEST OF MISSOULA

KEY BIRDS

Belted Kingfisher, Willow Flycatcher, American Redstart, Western Tanager, Spotted Sandpiper, Bald Eagle, Osprey, Ring-necked Duck

BEST SEASONS

Year around; spring and fall migrations best for waterfowl

AREA DESCRIPTION

River habitat with willows and alders

Except during high water, the river is easy to float in a canoe; otherwise, better use a more seaworthy craft. Keep an eye peeled for shorebirds. Bank and Rough-winged Swallows colonize sandy banks; Great Blue Heron rookery (Kelly Island); Belted Kingfishers also build nest holes in sandy banks. Yellow Warblers and American Redstarts nest in the bank-side willows and alders. Common and Hooded Mergansers frequent the river, and hens with broods in tow provide endless entertainment. As with most sites, best viewing is either early in the morning, or late in the day.

There are a number of active beaver lodges on the banks throughout the stretch of river; painted turtles, white-tailed deer, and muskrat are common sights. Endangered bull trout live here (illegal to target) but the river is excellent fishing for other trout.

Ring-necked Ducks

Old Harper Bridge Site
GPS

Kona Bridge
GPS

Council Grove
State Park
GPS

Flow

Mullan Road

Missoula◆

90

93

Kelly Island
GPS

GPS

Kelly Island: 46.861912, -114.101296
Kona Bridge: 46.899434, -114.150495
Council Grove State Park: 46.913020, -114.154836
Old Harper Bridge Site: 46.931909, -114.208269

CLARK FORK RIVER FLOAT

© 2014 Wilderness Adventures Press, Inc.

Montana Audubon Society notes: *"About 15,000 years ago a glacial ice dam blocked the Clark Fork River, created the 3,000-square-mile Lake Missoula. Several times the ice dam broke and drained the lake, sent catastrophic floods downriver which shaped the landscape as we see today."*

DIRECTIONS

To reach the put-in from the stoplight on US 93 just south of Missoula, head north 2 miles on Blue Mountain Road to the Maclay Flat parking area. Take out at Kona Bridge (6 miles – two to three hours at high water; six hours low water) off Mullan Road; or site of Old Harper Bridge (10 miles).

GLACIER COUNTRY

#14 Kelly Island Fishing Access Site

 **GPS** 46.863,-114.108

WEST OF MISSOULA

KEY BIRDS
Osprey, Bald Eagle, Turkey Vulture, Pileated and Lewis's Woodpeckers, Black-chinned, Rufous and Calliope Hummingbirds

BEST SEASONS
Year around; spring and fall migrations best for waterfowl; August for shorebirds

AREA DESCRIPTION
River and island habitat with cottonwood and pine forests

Kelly Island features a Great Blue Heron rookery. The extensive cottonwood and ponderosa pine forest attracts a variety of tree nesters including Osprey and Bald Eagle, Bullock's Oriole, and Tree Swallow. Yellow and Yellow-rumped Warblers frequent the shrub and willow thickets. Look for Western Tanager, Northern Waterthrush, and Mountain Bluebird in the edges around shrub thickets and meadows. From spring through fall, a wide variety of ducks and the ubiquitous Canada Goose haunt the river while shorebirds such as sandpipers and Killdeer frequent the shoreline, seemingly at every bend.

The islands are accessible by boat, except during low water in late summer and early fall when the river can usually be forded on foot.

DIRECTIONS
From Reserve Street south of the river, turn west on Spurgin Road and go to the end of Spurgin. Continue one block north of Spurgin at the end of N. 7th Street West. Or, off Reserve Street north of the river, turn west on Mullan Road up the hill, past the cemetery to Cote Lane and follow the signs.

CONTACT
MT-FW&P phone: 406-542-5500

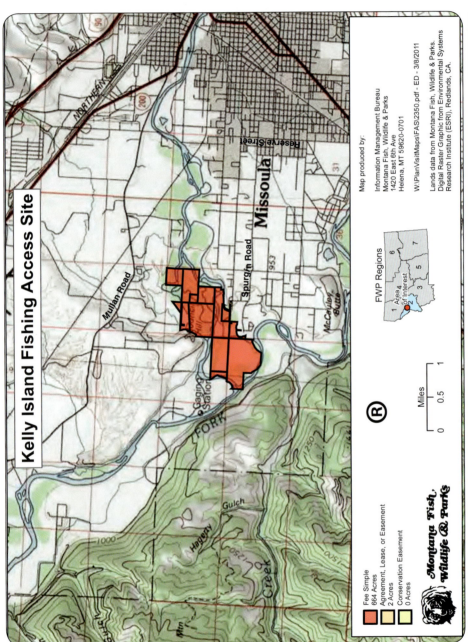

Kelly Island Fishing Access Site

Map produced by:

Information Management Bureau
Montana Fish, Wildlife & Parks
1420 East 6th Ave
Helena, MT 59620-0701

W:\PlanVisitMaps\FAS\2350.pdf - ED - 3/8/2011

Lands data from Montana Fish, Wildlife & Parks.
Digital Raster Graphic from Environmental Systems
Research Institute (ESRI), Redlands, CA.

Used with permission.

FWP Regions

Area
of Interest

Miles

0   0.5   1

Fee Simple
664 Acres

Agreement, Lease, or Easement
2 Acres

Conservation Easement
0 Acres

Montana Fish,
Wildlife & Parks

GLACIER COUNTRY
#15 Tower Street Park

GPS 46.871, -114.063

MISSOULA

KEY BIRDS
Bank Swallow, Gray Catbird, Red-Shafted Flicker, Bohemian (winter) and Cedar Waxwings, Hammond's Flycatcher, Orange-crowned Warbler

BEST SEASONS
Spring through early fall offers the best variety

AREA DESCRIPTION
River habitat with willows, cottonwood, and aspen

Early morning walks on the banks of the Clark Fork River offer the best birding ops. Trails wind through the park and connect with other Missoula parks and open spaces along the river. In early spring, be on the lookout for nesting Great Horned Owls and Red-tailed Hawks; later, Ospreys can be seen hunting the river to feed nestlings. Cedar Waxwings are common throughout the summer, while their Bohemian cousins can be found in great numbers during the winter months.

DIRECTIONS
From Reserve Street in Missoula, turn west on 3rd Street for 2 miles; turn north on Tower Street; the park is at the end of the street.

CONTACT
Missoula Parks & Recreation phone: 406-721-7275
MTFWP phone: 406-542-5500

GLACIER COUNTRY

#16 Maclay Flat Nature Trail

GPS 46.836,-114.105

SOUTHWEST OF MISSOULA

KEY BIRDS
Red-winged and Yellow-headed Blackbirds, Sora, Pileated Woodpecker, Pygmy Nuthatch, Wood Duck, Great Blue Heron, Wilson's Snipe, Vaux's Swift, Western Bluebirds

BEST SEASONS
Year around; spring and fall migrations best for waterfowl

AREA DESCRIPTION
Forested river habitat

An easy hike on the graveled 2-mile loop trail winds through the area. The first section is 1¼ miles and features 16 interpretive trail signs. The trail is also popular with joggers and dog walkers. Dogs must be leashed. Bicycles, horses, and all motorized vehicles are not allowed.

Lots of water, trees, and bushes attract a wide variety of avian wildlife. Black-headed Grosbeaks, Western Tanagers, Yellow, Yellow-rumped and Orange-crowned Warblers nest in the trees and bushes. Wood Ducks, Tree Swallows, and Wilson's Snipe frequent the ponds. Bald Eagles and Ospreys are common sights, soaring above the river. Look and listen for winter birds such as Pileated Woodpeckers, Pygmy Nuthatches, and Northern Pygmy Owls.

In summer the grasslands host a variety of butterflies, and wildflowers grow profusely in the wet areas.

Salish once camped here annually to dig roots of the Bitterroot, Montana's state flower.

DIRECTIONS
From the stoplight on US 93 just south of Missoula, head north on Blue Mountain Road for 2 miles to a signed parking area.

CONTACT
Missoula Ranger District phone: 406-329-3750

GLACIER COUNTRY

#17 Council Grove State Park

GPS 46.913,-114.155

NORTHWEST OF MISSOULA

KEY BIRDS
American Kestrel, White-breasted Nuthatch, Sandhill Crane, Osprey, Bald Eagle, Western Wood-pewee, Pygmy Nuthatch

BEST SEASONS
Spring through early fall offers the best variety

AREA DESCRIPTION
Old-growth ponderosa pine and cottonwood forest, open meadows and aspens

The trail leads from the parking area to the Clark Fork River, offering viewing opportunities for forest-, shrub-, and grassland-loving songbirds, such as mountain and Western Bluebirds, Savannah and Song Sparrows, Western Tanager, Gray Catbird, Spotted Towhee, Veery, and Bullock's Oriole. Look for shore and wading birds along the banks of the river. Raptors, Osprey, Bald Eagles, and Red-tailed Hawks are common.

Beyond nature study, the park offers visitors an interesting cultural learning experience. Council Grove is the site of the July, 1855

Western Wood-pewee

Hellgate Treaty signing between the Confederated Tribes of the Flathead, Kootenai, and Upper Pend d'Oreille and then Territorial Governor Isaac Stevens.

Day use only, handicap accessible, open all year, picnic tables, restrooms, pets allowed on leash. Other activities include fishing, wildlife viewing, photography, and history study. As with most parks, sunny summer weekends are best avoided.

DIRECTIONS
From I-90, Reserve Street Exit, go 2 miles; turn west on Mullan Road, and then 10 miles to the turn-off for Council Grove State Park.

CONTACT
Park Manager phone: 406-542-5500

Northern Shrike

GLACIER COUNTRY

#18 Clark Fork River/ Grass Valley IBA

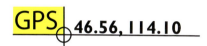

GPS 46.56, 114.10

BETWEEN MISSOULA AND HUSON

KEY BIRDS

Lewis's and Pileated Woodpeckers, Bald Eagle, Red-naped Sapsucker, Pacific Wren, Lazuli Bunting, Red-eyed Vireo, Swainson's Hawk, Peregrine Falcon, Hooded Merganser, and Willow, Hammond's, and Cordilleran Flycatchers

BEST SEASONS

Year round; spring and fall migrations best for waterfowl; August for shorebirds

AREA DESCRIPTION

Diverse mix of riparian cottonwoods, wetlands, and grasslands along the Clark Fork River

The IBA encompasses the Erskine FAS, Council Grove State Park, Kelly Island, and Grass Valley. In 2009, the IBA was awarded status as "continentally significant" because of the numbers of nesting Lewis's Woodpeckers — 55 nesting pairs, along with 12 other species of conservation concern that nest here — see above list of key birds.

Consisting of 25,000 acres, this is a diverse mix of riparian cottonwoods, wetlands, and grasslands along the Clark Fork River between Missoula and Huson, and is comprised of city, state, federal, and private lands including lands protected by conservation easements. About 230 bird species (over half of Montana's total) have been observed in the Missoula Valley, many of which have been observed within this IBA.

In late summer during the southbound migration, local birders have found as many as 27 shorebird species, and up to 1,000 individuals.

Obviously, viewing such a large area requires some planning and effort. A good place to start is the Montana Natural History Center (see below). Also visit Five Valleys Audubon Society website: www.fvamissoula.org. They will be able to put you in touch with local experts who keep tabs on the IBA.

DIRECTIONS

Grass Valley is located off MT 263 west of Missoula toward Huson. Access the IBA off the highway and associated side roads. Directions to the other sites included in the IBA can be found in the appropriate site descriptions elsewhere in this section.

CONTACT

Montana Natural History Center phone: 406-327-0405

Montana Audubon Society - Amy Cilimburg phone 406-465-114 — email: amy@ mtaudubon.com

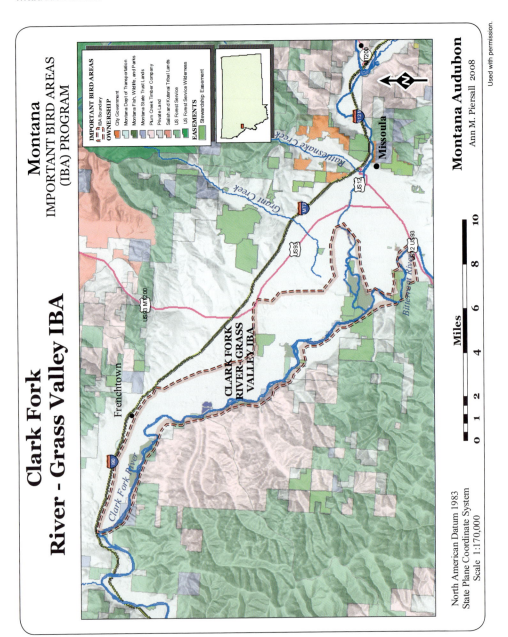

Clark Fork
River - Grass Valley IBA

Montana
IMPORTANT BIRD AREAS
(IBA) PROGRAM

Montana Audubon
Ann M. Piersall 2008

North American Datum 1983
State Plane Coordinate System
Scale 1:170,000

Miles

Used with permission.

GLACIER COUNTRY

#19 Blue Mountain Nature Trail

GPS 46.84,-114.117

SOUTHWEST OF MISSOULA

KEY BIRDS
Black-backed, Three-toed, and Pileated Woodpeckers, Western Tanager, bluebirds, Red-naped Sapsucker

BEST SEASONS
Year around; spring and summer best for variety and of course wildflower viewing

AREA DESCRIPTION
Mountain trail habitat

Hike or mountain bike in from the trailhead on the established trail which traverses a portion of the Black Mountain wildfire that scorched about 7,000 acres in 2003. An easy hike, interpretive posts scattered along the way point out interesting sites. The trail is wheelchair accessible about halfway to a scenic overlook with a view of the distant mountains, valley, and the confluence of the Bitterroot and Clark Fork Rivers.

Red-naped Sapsucker

Like most birding sites, this one offers much more. Now, several years after the fire, you can see in graphic detail how quickly nature begins the healing process. Typical of most wildfires, this one left a mosaic of live and dead trees in its wake. Green grass and wildflowers erupted almost before the ashes cooled. Soon after, shrub and tree seedlings popped and the once-blackened landscape came alive with forest birds — cavity nesters such as woodpeckers, creepers, nuthatches, sapsuckers, and bluebirds; nest builders such as jays, vireos, veery, orioles, and flycatchers. Local birders rate this *the* best place in the Missoula Valley to see fire dependent insects, plants, and birds such as the Black-backed Woodpecker.

The spring and summer wildflower display is spectacular — arrowleaf balsamroot, fireweed, pinegrass, fire moss, and Bicknell's geranium and a host of other unique flowering plant species. Summer butterfly viewing can be equally impressive.

Morel mushrooms (others too, assuming you know what to pick), while perhaps not as abundant as right after the fire, can still be found.

DIRECTIONS
From the stoplight on US 93 just south of Missoula, turn north onto Blue Mountain Road for 1½ miles, and then turn west onto FS #365 for 1½ miles to the trailhead.

CONTACT
Missoula Ranger District phone: 406-329-3750

GLACIER COUNTRY
#20 Traveler's Rest State Park

GPS 46.757,-114.089

WEST OF LOLO

KEY BIRDS
Black-headed Grosbeak, Warbling Vireo, Western Tanager, Lazuli Bunting, Yellow Warbler, Yellow-rumped Warbler, Common Snipe, Marsh and Pacific Wrens

BEST SEASONS
Open year around; best birding spring through early fall

AREA DESCRIPTION
Creekside habitat surrounded by tall cottonwoods, dense willows, and other bushes

The park is a good spot to stop for that quick bird fix, perhaps to kill time in between more important engagements or on the way to someplace else. No matter how brief our visits, it seems we almost always nab an interesting bird or two. The trail leads to Lolo Creek, which provides the best birding opportunities and some pretty fair fishing, should you have a hankering. If birding per se is your plan, best to get there early or late, especially during the tourist season.

DIRECTIONS
One half mile west of Lolo via US 12

CONTACT
Park Manager phone: 406-273-4253

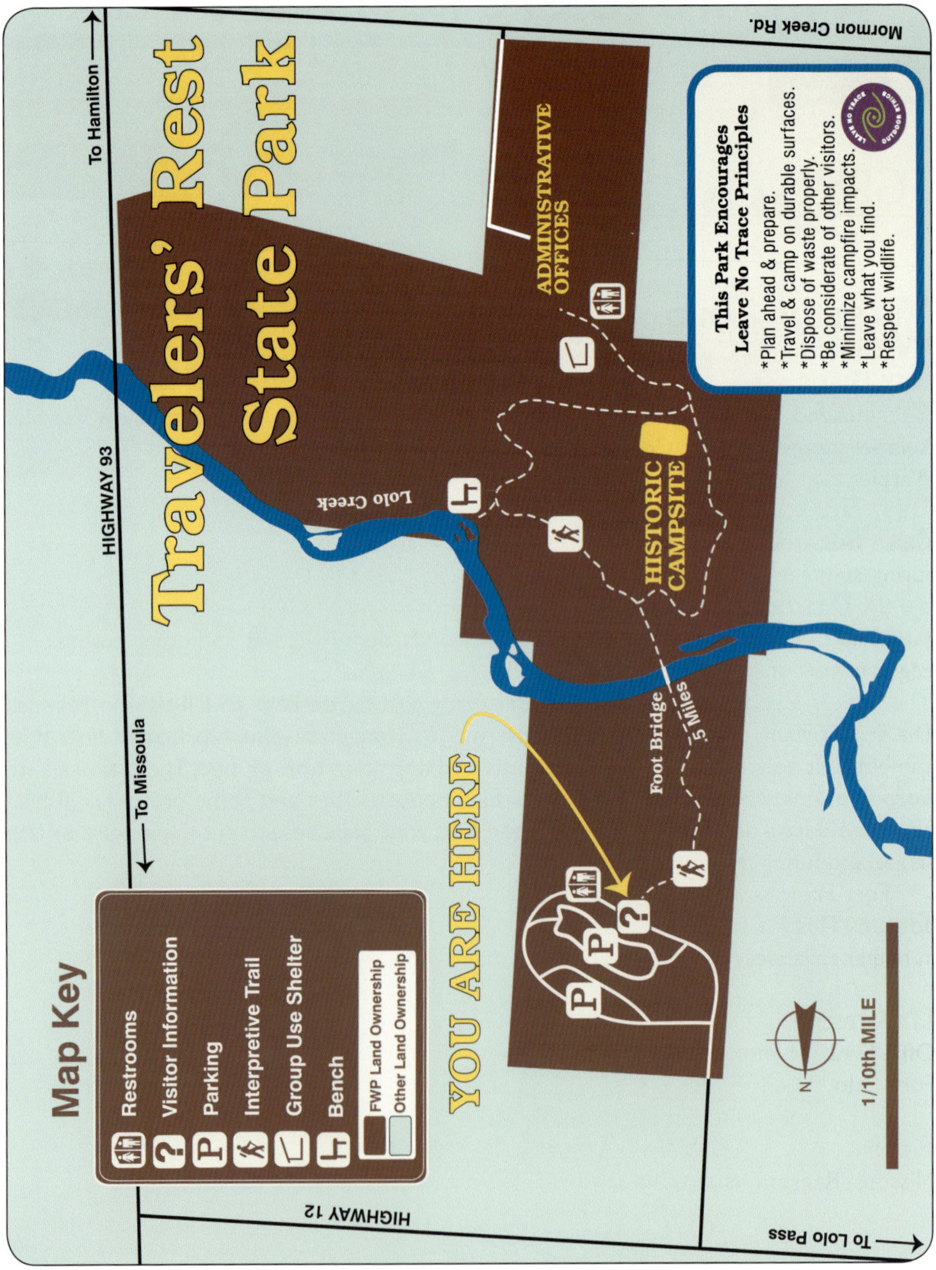
Travelers' Rest State Park
Map Key
Restrooms
Visitor Information
Parking
Interpretive Trail
Group Use Shelter
Bench
FWP Land Ownership
Other Land Ownership
YOU ARE HERE
To Hamilton
HIGHWAY 93
To Missoula
HIGHWAY 12
To Lolo Pass
Mormon Creek Rd.
Lolo Creek
ADMINISTRATIVE OFFICES
HISTORIC CAMPSITE
Foot Bridge
.5 Miles
N
1/10th MILE
This Park Encourages
Leave No Trace Principles
*Plan ahead & prepare.
*Travel & camp on durable surfaces.
*Dispose of waste properly.
*Be considerate of other visitors.
*Minimize campfire impacts.
*Leave what you find.
*Respect wildlife.

Used with permission.

GLACIER COUNTRY
#21 Fort Fizzle/Lolo Creek Camp-ground/East Fork Lolo Creek

FORT FIZZLE:
46.746, -114.171
GPS **LOLO CREEK CAMPGROUND:**
46.776, -114.384

WEST OF LOLO

KEY BIRDS
A variety warblers, flycatchers, and woodpeckers such as Willow Flycatcher, Townsend's Warbler, Pileated Woodpecker, American Redstart

BEST SEASONS
Spring, summer and fall; June for nesting and migrant songbirds

AREA DESCRIPTIONS
Edge between forest and meadow wetlands along creek

The East Fork Lolo Creek and the campground's dense alder, willow, and cottonwoods in combination with open water provides a diverse habitat. Some local birders consider the campground *the* top spot on the Bitterroot Birding Trail for viewing neotropical migrants.

We like to find a quiet spot with a good view, grab the binoculars, set up the spotting scope, and have at it; seldom do we come away without finding a surprise or two.

Fort Fizzle features a paved accessible trail that provides access to forested creek bottoms. This is a good stop if pressed for time, or just on the way to someplace else and in need of a bird fix.

DIRECTIONS
Off US 12 west of Lolo, Fort Fizzle is about 5 miles; Lolo Creek Campground and East Fork Lolo Creek about 15 miles.

CONTACT
Missoula Ranger District phone: 406-329-3750

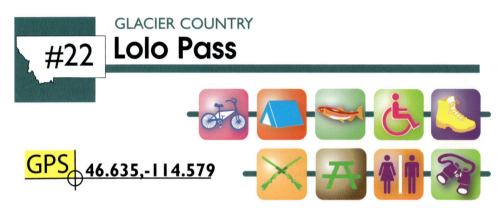

GLACIER COUNTRY
#22 | Lolo Pass

GPS 46.635,-114.579

ON US 12 AT THE IDAHO-MONTANA BORDER

KEY BIRDS
Varied thrush, Wilson's and Townsend's Warblers, Clark's Nutcracker, White-crowned and Fox Sparrows, Steller's Jay, Boreal Owl (winter), Cassin's Finch

BEST SEASONS
Year around (heavy snow in winter); best birding opportunities in June through September

AREA DESCRIPTION
High mountain meadows and forests

To get an idea of what to expect at any given time, stop at the visitor center (good birding, by the way). Packer Meadows (1½ miles east on FS 373) is perhaps the best site to check off multiple species. Driving and/or hiking any of the roads and trails in the area will reveal many spots not on every birder's radar. A variety of raptors frequent the area, such as northern goshawk and boreal owl (February dusks and dawns are the best times).

In June, the wildflower display is awesome — camas, glacier lily, trillium, shooting star, spring beauty, marsh marigold, you name it. Pine marten, fisher, bobcat, elk, and mule deer frequent the area; though uncommon moose and wolves occasionally show up.

September 13, 1805, William Clark declared, *"The country as usial except the Glades which is open boggey, water Clare and Sandey"*. After poking around a bit, we find "the country" eerily similar today.

Other activities include snowshoeing, cross-country skiing, hunting, fishing, hiking, mountain biking, as well as developed and dispersed camping in the national forest on both sides of the Continental Divide.

DIRECTIONS
Follow US 12 west of Lolo, MT approximately 32 miles to the top of the pass

CONTACT
Powell Ranger District phone: 208-942-3113

Cassin's Finch

GLACIER COUNTRY
#23 Bass Creek Fishing Access Site

GPS 46.567, -114.101

SOUTHWEST OF FLORENCE AND NORTHWEST OF STEVENSVILLE

KEY BIRDS
Kinglets, Lewis's Woodpecker, Red Crossbill, Western Wood-pewee, American Redstart, American Dipper

BEST SEASONS
Year around; June for nesting songbirds

AREA DESCRIPTION
Varied habitat from creekside to hay meadows to pine and aspen forests

In the spring be sure to stop, look, and listen for singing Bobolinks and Western Meadowlarks in the hay meadows beside the county road. Kestrels and Mountain Bluebirds often share the fence posts. Northern Harrier and Swainson's Hawk are also common.

Continue on to the trailhead where a trail follows Bass Creek to Bass Lake and beyond, into the Selway-Bitterroot Wilderness. American Dipper, Pacific Wren, Northern Goshawk, Pileated and Lewis's Woodpeckers, Red Crossbill, White-breasted Nuthatch, Ruby-crowned Kinglet, Warbling Vireo, and Western Wood-pewee are common.

Park in the day-use area to access the nature trail (1/2 mile) and fire-ecology trail (2½ mile); both are loop trails. Wildflowers attract a variety of butterflies, while the ponderosa pine, grand fir, aspen forest, and willows attract a variety of raptors, songbirds, and woodpeckers.

The campground features 22 sites, with water, garbage pick-up, and vault toilet. Maximum trailer/RV length allowed is 35 feet.

Elk and deer frequent the area as well as the occasional black bear. Look for pika in the rocks higher up.

Other activities include mountain biking, horseback riding, fishing, hunting, and cross-country skiing. Bass Creek contains brook trout, and westslope cutthroats are planted periodically in Bass Lake.

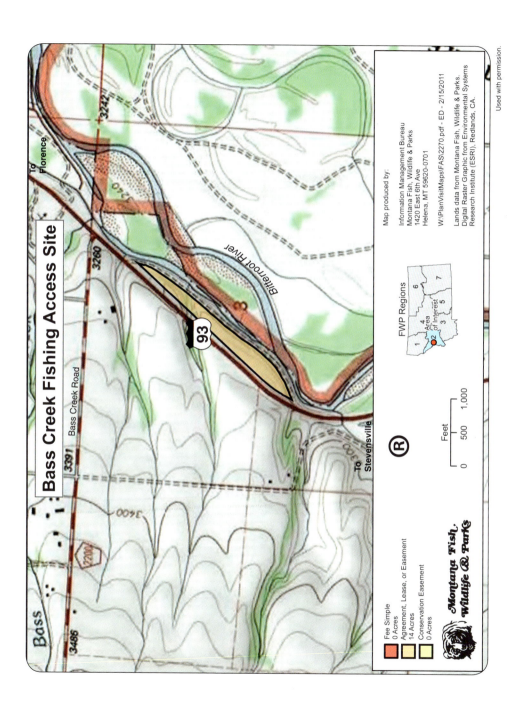

Bass Creek Fishing Access Site

Bass Creek Road

Bitterroot River

93

To Florence

To Stevensville

Map produced by:

Information Management Bureau
Montana Fish, Wildlife & Parks
1420 East 6th Ave
Helena, MT 59620-0701

W:\PlanVisitMaps\FAS\2270.pdf - ED - 2/15/2011

Lands data from Montana Fish, Wildlife & Parks.
Digital Raster Graphic from Environmental Systems
Research Institute (ESRI), Redlands, CA.

FWP Regions

Area of Interest

Feet

0   500   1,000

Fee Simple
0 Acres

Agreement, Lease, or Easement
14 Acres

Conservation Easement
0 Acres

Montana Fish,
Wildlife & Parks

Directons

From US 93, go 4 miles south of Florence or 5 miles north of Stevensville. Turn west on Bass Creek Road, and go 2 miles to trailhead.

Contact

Stevensville Ranger District phone: 406-777-5461

American Dipper

GLACIER COUNTRY
#24 St. Mary's Peak

GPS 46.512, -114.246

SOUTHWEST OF STEVENSVILLE

KEY BIRDS
Golden Eagle, Peregrine Falcon, Gray-crowned Rosy Finch, American Pipit, Rock Wren, Steller's Jay

BEST SEASONS
Late spring through early fall

AREA DESCRIPTION
Narrow mountain trail

This one is not for the faint of heart. The road to the trailhead is steep, narrow, and winding. The trail to the fire lookout is steep (elevation gain 2,500 feet) and long (9 miles round trip). The good news for birders is the rewards, though few, can be spectacular. Soaring Golden Eagles and swift-flying Peregrine Falcons top the list, but other birds you might not see every day such as Rock Wren and Gray-crowned Rosy Finch occasionally show up. Toss in scenic views, healthy pika and hoary marmot populations and, heck, why not just suck it up and go for it, eh?

DIRECTIONS
From US 93, about 4 miles south of Stevensville turn right (west) on Indian Prairie Road. Follow USFS signs to the trailhead, about 13 miles in. Road is narrow and winding, use caution. Parking is available for about 10 vehicles and can be full, especially on sunny weekends so plan accordingly.

CONTACT
Stevensville Ranger District phone: 406-777-5461

GLACIER COUNTRY
Bitterroot River (IBA)

#25

GPS 46.30, 114.08

NORTH OF HAMILTON TO SOUTH OF LOLO

KEY BIRDS
Lewis's Woodpecker, Bald Eagle, Red-naped Sapsucker, Northern Harrier, Wilson's Phalarope, Short-eared Owl, Willow Flycatcher, Red-eyed and Warbling Vireos, MacGillivray's and Orange-crowned Warblers

BEST SEASONS
Early spring through October

AREA DESCRIPTION
35-mile long floodplain of the Bitterroot River

This IBA is a mix of state, federal, and private lands — a number of which are private stewardship easements. It is a diverse mix of riparian cottonwood and pine forest, shrubs, grasslands, wetlands, ponds, the river itself, and parts of several tributaries.

Floating is the best way to view the area. Stop often to glass, especially in the side channels and sloughs. Expect to see a variety of songbirds, waterfowl, raptors, and shorebirds. If you have time, drop anchor and walk about the refuge.

Interesting to note, there are 240+ bird species; of which at least 115 species nest here, including nine species of conservation concern — Pileated and Lewis's Woodpeckers, Red-naped Sapsucker, Bald Eagle, Northern Harrier, Wilson's Phalarope, Short-eared Owl, Willow Flycatcher, and Red-eyed Vireo. Local birders have identified nine active Bald Eagle nest sites in the corridor, at least 100 nesting Red-naped Sapsuckers, 75 nesting Willow Flycatchers, and 40 nesting Lewis's Woodpeckers.

The river is a popular trout fishing destination and, especially week-ends, sees a lot of non-fishing recreational use. In other words, early birds get the most worms! If pressed for time, leave the boat at home and check out Lee Metcalf and/or the river trail below Stevensville.

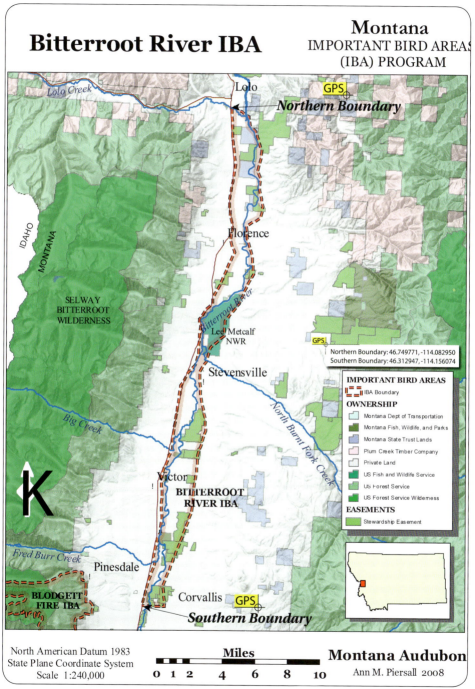

Bitterroot River IBA

Montana
IMPORTANT BIRD AREAS
(IBA) PROGRAM

Lolo Creek

Lolo

GPS

Northern Boundary

IDAHO

MONTANA

Florence

SELWAY
BITTERROOT
WILDERNESS

Bitterroot River

Lee Metcalf
NWR

GPS

Northern Boundary: 46.749771, -114.082950
Southern Boundary: 46.312947, -114.156074

Stevensville

North Burnt Fork Creek

Big Creek

IMPORTANT BIRD AREAS

- - - IBA Boundary

OWNERSHIP

Montana Dept of Transportation

Montana Fish, Wildlife, and Parks

Montana State Trust Lands

Plum Creek Timber Company

Private Land

US Fish and Wildlife Service

US Forest Service

US Forest Service Wilderness

EASEMENTS

Stewardship Easement

K

Victor

**BITTERROOT
RIVER IBA**

Fred Burr Creek

Pinesdale

**BLODGETT
FIRE IBA**

Corvallis   GPS

Southern Boundary

North American Datum 1983
State Plane Coordinate System
Scale 1:240,000

Miles

0 1 2   4   6   8   10

Montana Audubon

Ann M. Piersall 2008

Fishing Access Sites allow for arranging floats to suit most any schedule. Except during high water, the river is relatively easy to float though, as with floating any river, inquire locally before launching, exercise safe boating practices, and proceed with caution.

DIRECTIONS
The IBA starts upstream at Woodside Bridge FAS below Hamilton and ends at Chief Looking Glass FAS (6.5 miles south of Lolo). Off US 93, turn east (or west off MT 269) onto MT 373 to the Woodside Bridge FAS. Boat launch sites such as Bell Crossing (just below Victor, off either US 93 or MT 269); Florence Bridge FAS can be accessed off US 93 in Florence or MT 203. All are well-signed and easy to find. Before launching, check locally for conditions, approximate float times, and other pertinent information.

CONTACT
Montana Audubon Society - Amy Cilimburg, Director of Conservation and Climate Policy
Phone: 406-465-1141
Email: amy@mtaudubon.org

Lewis's Woodpecker
Credit: Dan Casey

GLACIER COUNTRY
#26 Bear Creek Trail

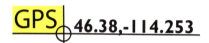

GPS 46.38,-114.253

SOUTHWEST OF VICTOR

KEY BIRDS
Peregrine Falcon, woodpeckers, American Dipper, Western Tanager, Mountain Chickadee

BEST SEASONS
Late spring (after runoff) through early fall

AREA DESCRIPTION
Mountain trail along creek

The trail follows the creek, which in spring looks spectacular, but the roar drowns out the bird song. The creek, trees — western larch, grand fir, ponderosa pine — and western yew understory attract numerous forest-dwelling birds: Ruby-crowned Kinglet, Red- and White-breasted and Pygmy Nuthatches, Black-capped Chickadee, Pacific Wren, American Dipper, Yellow-rumped Warbler, Warbling Vireo, Red Crossbill, Pine Grosbeak, Northern Goshawk, Western Tanager, and Northern Flicker to name just a few.

Peregrine Falcons are a main attraction, but you'll need your hiking boots (about an hour up the trail) and a spotting scope. The fierce birds have been known to nest here since 1996.

Elk and deer frequent the area along with an occasional black bear. Pika and hoary marmot frequent the rocky areas higher up. The creek harbors brook, brown, and rainbow trout.

Other activities include hiking, mountain biking, photography, hunting, and fishing.

DIRECTIONS
Follow US 93 approximately 3 miles south of Victor; turn west on Bear Creek Road (across from Tucker Crossing FAS) for 2½ miles. Turn right (north) on Red Crow Road for 1 mile; turn left (west) 3 miles to trailhead.

CONTACT
Stevensville Ranger District phone: 406-777-5461

GLACIER COUNTRY

#27 Blodgett Canyon/ Cow Creek Burn (IBA)

GPS 46.273,-114.29

NORTHWEST OF HAMILTON

KEY BIRDS
Williamson's Sapsucker, Olive-sided Flycatcher, Lewis's and Three-toed Woodpeckers, Townsend's Solitaire, Mountain Bluebird, Peregrine Falcon

BEST SEASONS
April-November

AREA DESCRIPTION
Canyon habitat including large burn areas

Public land, two good trails, and decent roads provide excellent access to this IBA, which comprises the nearly 12,000-acre burn in Mill and Blodgett Canyons. Terrain differences and variation in fire temperatures created a typical wildland fire mosaic, severe (total stand replacement) to minor (low-impact). Leaving in its wake the sort of diverse habitat attractive to a wide variety of birds, especially woodpeckers such as the black-backed, which is rarely found outside recent burns. The birds are attracted by wood-boring beetles — as beetle numbers dwindle, so too do woodpecker numbers.

Look for warblers, Veery, American Redstart, Western Tanager, Red Crossbill, Red-eyed and Warbling Vireos, White-breasted Nuthatch, and Brown Creeper in the post-fire shrubs and trees in the less-impacted areas.

Two pairs of Peregrine Falcons are known to nest within the IBA. Tote along a spotting scope and good binoculars if you want a good view of the Peregrine Falcons, as well as the White-throated Swifts which nest in the towering cliffs. Interesting to note, many locals refer to the area as Montana's Yosemite. Pika and hoary marmot can be found in the rocky areas.

DIRECTIONS
At the stoplight on US 93 at Woodside, 3 miles north of Hamilton, turn west onto Dutch Hill Road for 2 miles, then turn right (north) at the "T" on Bowman Road for approximately 2 more miles. Just before Pinesdale, turn (left) west onto FS #438 (Cow Creek Road). It is about half a mile to a gate and small parking area. The road beyond the gate is open from June to October; area is open to foot travel year round.

CONTACT
Stevensville Ranger District phone: 406-777-5461

GLACIER COUNTRY
#28 Coyote Coulee Trail

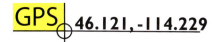

GPS 46.121, -114.229

SOUTHWEST OF HAMILTON

KEY BIRDS
Veery, Townsend's and Yellow-rumped Warblers, White-breasted Nuthatch, Ruby-crowned Kinglet, Pine Grosbeak, Hairy Woodpecker, Red-naped Sapsucker, Warbling Vireo, Western Tanager

BEST SEASONS
Accessible year around but best birding is spring, summer, and fall

AREA DESCRIPTION
Creekside habitat with trails through old orchards and pine forests and aspens

Two moderately difficult loop trails (about 8 miles long with elevation gain of nearly 1,500 feet) pass through old apple orchards and Douglas fir-ponderosa pine forest beside small creeks with scattered aspen stands. The upper loop passes through more open terrain with good views of the higher peaks of the Bitterroot Range. The edges between habitats and especially along Camas Creek, in and around the old apple trees provide the easiest viewing. Look for sapsuckers, warblers, and Western Tanagers frequenting the scattered apple trees. Lost Horse Road is a good hike, which usually provides ample viewing ops.

Remnant apple trees, stone foundations, and railroad bed date back to around 1880. The rail spur was used primarily to haul logs north to the mills around Missoula.

Deer, elk, and snowshoe hare are common, and black bears come to eat the apples in early fall.

Other activities include hiking, mountain biking, horseback riding (trails are maintained by Bitterroot Backcountry Horsemen), snow-shoeing, cross-country skiing, and hunting.

Amenities can be found in Hamilton and Darby.

DIRECTIONS
Eight miles south of Hamilton on US 93, turn west on Lost Horse Road for 2½ miles to FS 496 to Coyote Coulee Trailhead.

CONTACT
Darby Ranger District phone: 406-821-3913

GLACIER COUNTRY
#29 Lake Como National Recreation Trail

GPS 46.066, -114.247

NORTHWEST OF DARBY

KEY BIRDS
Common and Red-throated Loons, Double-crested Cormorant, Western Tanager, Osprey, Bald Eagle, Ruby- and Yellow-crowned Kinglets, Yellow-rumped Warbler, Red-naped sapsucker, Pileated and Lewis's Woodpeckers, Mountain Bluebird, Olive-sided Flycatcher, and American Dipper (in Rock Creek), Bufflehead

BEST SEASONS
Waterfowl numbers peak spring and fall; June for nesting songbirds

AREA DESCRIPTION
Lakeside habitat with surrounding trail and pine forests

Lake Como National Recreation Trail circles the lake (7 miles). The first quarter mile is paved and has natural history interpretive signs. It passes through old growth ponderosa pine and Douglas fir forest with stunning views of the high peaks of the Bitterroot Range.

In the trees, look for forest-dwelling songbirds such as Brown Creeper, Junco, and Brown-breasted Nuthatch. The upper end of the lake is the best place to view waterfowl. Rock Creek is a sure bet for American Dipper and Western Tanager, while sapsuckers and woodpeckers still find the old burn (1998) attractive. Good birding ops are found along any of the forest roads and trails, such as along Rock and Little Rock Creeks.

As you might expect, the lake is a popular recreation and boating spot, especially summer weekends when there is enough water. We avoid the chaos by birding on weekdays, early and late in the day.

The reservoir was built in the early 1900s to feed the "Big Ditch" — an irrigation canal which bisects much of the Bitterroot River Valley. In dry years, the reservoir experiences severe dewatering in late summer and fall.

A fee area is in effect Memorial Day through Labor Day; Golden Age Passes are accepted.

DIRECTIONS
Lake Como Road is approximately 10 miles south of Hamilton and 5 miles north of Darby off US 93.

CONTACT
Darby Ranger District phone: 406-821-3913

Bufflehead (drake)

GLACIER COUNTRY
#30 Hannon Memorial Fishing Access Site

GPS 45.973, -114.141

SOUTH OF DARBY ON THE BITTERROOT RIVER

KEY BIRDS
Red-shafted Flicker, Western Bluebird, Common Merganser, Mallard, Osprey, Bald Eagle, Great Blue Heron, Orange-crowned Warbler, American Redstart, Killdeer, Spotted Sandpiper, Gray Catbird, Bullock's Oriole, Willow Flycatcher

BEST SEASONS
Year round; best variety during spring and fall migration; June for nesting songbirds

AREA DESCRIPTION
Varied habitat from river to sagebrush

The river, cottonwoods, shrub understory, and sagebrush provide the sort of habitat mix attractive to a wide variety of avian wildlife. To avoid the rush during fishing season, stick to birding week days; quiet times are early and late in the day.

Eight other state-owned fishing access sites scattered up and down the river provide similar birding ops.

The campground offers six sites, vault toilet, and picnic tables on first come, first served basis. This is a fee area, and pack-in, pack-out rules apply. Nearby Darby offers lodging, food, and gas.

DIRECTIONS
Off US 93, 4 miles south of Darby (signed).

CONTACT
MT FW&P phone: 406-542-550

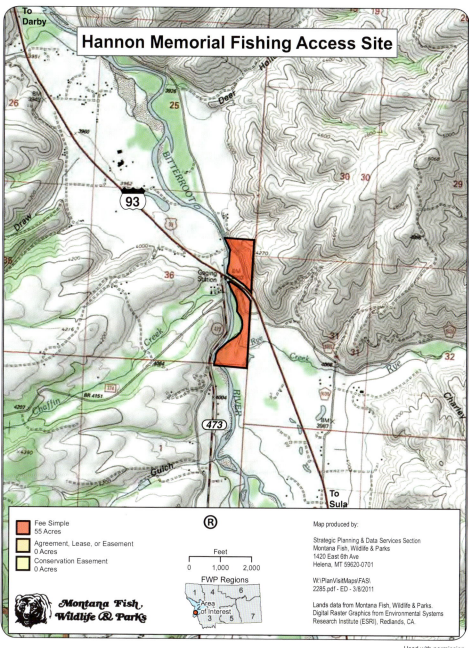

Hannon Memorial Fishing Access Site

To Darby

93

473

To Sula

Fee Simple
55 Acres

Agreement, Lease, or Easement
0 Acres

Conservation Easement
0 Acres

®

Feet

0   1,000   2,000

FWP Regions

Area of Interest

Map produced by:

Strategic Planning & Data Services Section
Montana Fish, Wildlife & Parks
1420 East 6th Ave
Helena, MT 59620-0701

W:\PlanVisitMaps\FAS\
2285.pdf - ED - 3/8/2011

Lands data from Montana Fish, Wildlife & Parks.
Digital Raster Graphics from Environmental Systems
Research Institute (ESRI), Redlands, CA.

Montana Fish,
Wildlife & Parks

Barn Owl

GLACIER COUNTRY

#31 Sam Billings Mem. Campground/Boulder Creek Trail

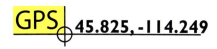

GPS 45.825, -114.249

SOUTH OF DARBY ON THE WEST FORK OF THE BITTERROOT RIVER

KEY BIRDS

Hairy, Lewis's and Pileated Woodpeckers, Red-shafted flicker, Brown Creeper, Western Screech Owl, Hammond's Flycatcher, Calliope and Rufous Hummingbirds, Pacific Wren, American Dipper, Dark-eyed Junco, White-breasted Nuthatch, Black-capped Chickadee

BEST SEASONS

Spring through early fall; late winter owling excursions are popular among local birders

AREA DESCRIPTION

Old growth forest with trail along creek

Huge ponderosa pines in the campground attract a variety of woodpeckers and songbirds typically associated with old growth forest. The trail ascends the creek through pine, fir, and spruce forest with western yew dominating the understory.

For us, as photographers and all around nature lovers, we come here mostly for the big trees and the chance to shoot scenic Trapper Peak (10,000 feet), kinnikinnick blossoms and berries (spring and summer) and Oregon grape (fall) but, truth be known, the brass ring often goes to the birds.

Interesting to note, Sam Billings, forester, first championed the idea of saving the big pines; alas, an increasingly rare item these days throughout the Bitterroot and elsewhere.

Deer, elk, and moose (common), the occasional black bear; also look for pika and hoary marmot upstream in the talus and rocks.

Other activities include fishing, hiking, hunting (outside campground), mountain biking, snowshoeing, cross-country skiing, owling (winter), picnicking, and photography.

DIRECTIONS

From the junction of US 93 and the paved West Fork Road, drive 13 miles; turn right (north) at the sign to the Sam Billings Memorial Campground. It's then 1 mile to the campground and trailhead beyond.

CONTACT

West Fork Ranger District Phone: 406-821-3269

Spruce Grouse

GLACIER COUNTRY
#32 Crazy Creek Campground

GPS 45.815,-114.071

NORTHWEST OF SULA

KEY BIRDS
American Dipper, Great Horned Owl, Lewis's and Pileated Woodpeckers, Red-naped and Williamson's Sapsuckers, Belted Kingfisher, Hammond's Flycatcher, Cassin's Vireo, Pacific Wren, Townsend's and Yellow-rumped Warblers

BEST SEASONS
Spring, summer and fall; especially spring and fall migration

AREA DESCRIPTION
Old growth ponderosa pine and Douglas fir forest, willows, wetlands, stream, beaver dams, and a recovering burn

The 2000 burn is the place to look for Lewis's and Pileated Woodpeckers and Red-naped and Williamson's Sapsuckers. Warblers and flycatchers flit about the aspens and shrubs beside the creek. Dipper and kingfisher ply the creek while teal and Wood Ducks are especially fond of the beaver dams. The trail above the campground is as good a place as any to start your search.

Moose, deer, elk, and beaver frequent the area; black bear wander through on occasion.

Hiking, mountain biking, horseback riding, camping, hunting, fishing, picnicking, wildflower viewing, and photography are popular.

The campground features seven sites and includes picnic tables, water, and vault toilets. Pack in-pack out rules apply. Maximum trailer length is 26 feet. The lower portion of the campground is for horse campers only.

Darby offers lodging, food, and gas.

DIRECTIONS
At Spring Gulch Campground along US 93 (about 3 miles north of Sula), turn west on Medicine Springs Road (FS 370) and go 4 miles to the campground.

CONTACT
Sula Ranger District phone: 406-821-3201

Dark-eyed Junco

GLACIER COUNTRY

#33 Indian Trees Campground

GPS 45.756,-113.954

SOUTH OF SULA

KEY BIRDS
MacGillivray's and Yellow-rumped Warblers, Warbling Vireo, Western Wood-pewee, Rufous, Calliope, and Black-chinned Hummingbirds, Pileated Woodpecker, Ruffed Grouse

BEST SEASONS
Late April through October

AREA DESCRIPTION
Centuries old ponderosa pines (many peeled, see below) and shrub understory

This site attracts a variety of forest-dwelling songbirds and woodpeckers, including numbers of neotropical migrants in spring and fall. Binoculars are needed to view birds in the tallest trees.

Interesting to note, Bitterroot Salish, Kootenai, Nez Perce, and Shoshone all came here to peel the ponderosas for the cambium layer beneath the bark. *Like rumor has it: oh so sweet and oh so delicious…Right!* Apparently the Corps of Discovery agreed to try it, stopping by here in early September, 1805 to lunch with the Bitterroot Salish encamped there.

Deer, elk, and black bear also frequent the area.

Other activities include camping, picnicking, hunting, fishing, mountain biking, hiking, and cultural history study. The campground features 16 sites and includes water, handicapped accessibility, garbage pickup, and vault toilets. The maximum trailer length is 50 feet.

DIRECTIONS
From US 93, go 6 miles south of Sula Ranger Station and turn west on FS 729 for 10 miles.

CONTACT
Sula Ranger District phone: 406-821-3201

GLACIER COUNTRY

#34 Chief Joseph Pass Ski Trails

GPS 45.695,-113.949

WEST OF WISDOM AND SOUTH OF SULA

KEY BIRDS
Northern Goshawk, Boreal and Great Gray Owls, Clark's Nutcracker, Mountain and Black-capped Chickadees, Red-breasted Nuthatch, Red Crossbill, Gray and Steller's Jays

BEST SEASONS
Typically June through October, but snow conditions vary

AREA DESCRIPTION
Eight cross-country ski trails loop through high elevation lodgepole forest and open meadows

The ski trails provide miles of birding opportunities during the off season. Loop trails of various lengths and difficulty allow birding jaunts to suit most anyone — none however are paved. Summertime deer flies can be thick, so come prepared.

Interesting to note: Lewis and Clark crossed the divide in early September, 1805 on their way west. Nez Perce Chief Joseph led his people across the pass in early August, 1877 to eventually engage the US Army at the Big Hole Battlefield several miles east of here.

Indian Trees Campground is approximately 10 miles north on US 93, and May Creek Campground is approximately 8 miles east on MT 43. Both are Forest Service fee areas; no hookups, vault toilets, picnic tables, or fire rings. Both are good birding spots, by the way.

Hiking, mountain biking, wildflower viewing, and photography are popular activities.

Keep an eye peeled for elk and mule deer and the occasional black bear and pine marten.

Sula and Wisdom provide limited lodging, food, and gas.

DIRECTIONS

Follow US 93 south of Missoula about 100 miles to Chief Joseph Pass; turn left on MT 43; parking area is on the left. From Wisdom, follow MT 43 west, approximately 23 miles; parking area is on right just before the intersection with US 93.

CONTACT

Wisdom Ranger District phone: 406-689-3243

Black-capped Chickadee

GLACIER COUNTRY
#35 Broad Ax Lodge

GPS 45.864, -113.886

EAST OF SULA

KEY BIRDS
Black-capped Chickadee, American Dipper, Great Horned and Western Screech Owls, Golden and Bald Eagles, Osprey, Prairie Falcon, Ruffed Grouse, Eastern and Western Kingbirds, Belted Kingfisher, Cliff Swallow, Western Tanager, White-throated Swift

BEST SEASONS
Open year round; best songbird viewing is during spring and fall migration

AREA DESCRIPTION
Conifer, aspen, and shrub riparian areas beside the East Fork Bitterroot River surrounded by drier uplands comprised of grass, rocky outcrops, and shrubs

Bighorn sheep frequent the area as well as other indigenous big game animals.

The lodge provides birders free parking and will direct visiting birders to key spots. Please stop in and let them know you are here. The restaurant tables feature binoculars and bird ID books. The lodge features guest accommodations and dining, and can arrange for just about any outdoor activity including fly fishing, floating, photography, hiking, biking, and cross-country skiing.

Nearby Darby offers lodging, meals, gas, and groceries.

DIRECTIONS
At Sula, on US 93, take the East Fork Bitterroot Road 5½ miles to the lodge.

CONTACT
Broad Ax Lodge
1237 E. Fork Road Rd., Sula, MT 59871
Phone: 406-821-3878
Website: www.broadaxlodge.com

Bald Eagle

GLACIER COUNTRY
#36 River and Hieronymous Parks

GPS HIERONYMUS PARK: 46.266,-114.159
RIVER PARK: 46.24,-114.167

HAMILTON

KEY BIRDS
Wood Duck, Osprey, Great Horned Owl, a variety of warblers and flycatchers, Black-headed Grosbeak, Bald Eagle, Spotted Sandpiper, Common Merganser, American Dipper, American Goldfinch, various sparrows and Bullock's Oriole, Costa's Hummingbird

BEST SEASONS
Year around, but the best chance for checking off multiple species is spring through early fall

AREA DESCRIPTION
Both parks feature a healthy mix of shrub, grass, and cottonwood river bottom

Look for ducks, shorebirds, and water birds in the braided river channels. Shrub thickets line the Corvallis Canal along the east side, and attract songbirds such as Green-tailed Towhee, Song Sparrow, Yellow Warbler and Common Yellowthroat. The fishing pond in Hieronymous Park attracts the usual mix of waterfowl, wading birds, and songbirds.

Trails provide easy access to both parks. Hieronymous Park features a 2-mile unpaved interpretive loop while River Park offers a choice of accessible paved trails as well as unpaved trails. Interpretive signs help to explain relations between the Salish and Corps of Discovery.

A popular spot for picnicking (many tables overlook the river), biking, and walking. Naturally, dawn and dusk provide the best birding ops.

White-tailed deer, muskrat, striped skunk, and mink are common; occasionally moose, river otter, and beaver show up.

DIRECTIONS
River Park: Turn west at the light on Main Street off US 93 in downtown Hamilton. Drive eight blocks and turn left (south) on 9th Street to the park.

Hieronymus Park: In Hamilton, driving south on US 93, turn right (west) into the Bitterroot River Inn (139 Bitterroot Plaza Drive). Park in the grassy field at the entrance to the park.

CONTACT
River and Hieronymus Parks phone: 406-363-1519

Costa's Hummingbird

GLACIER COUNTRY

#37 Centennial Grove Nature Trail

GPS 46.162,-113.945

SOUTHEAST OF HAMILTON

KEY BIRDS
Hairy and Pileated Woodpeckers, Western Screech and Great Gray Owls, Hammond's Flycatcher, American Dipper, Belted Kingfisher, Calliope and Rufous Hummingbirds

BEST SEASONS
Spring through early fall; owls in winter

AREA DESCRIPTION
Old growth forest, shrub understory, and creek

This site attracts a variety songbirds, raptors, hummingbirds, and water-loving birds. The half-mile trail loops through old-growth ponderosa pine. An easy hike, the first part is paved. Nearby Bear Gulch Trail provides similar viewing ops and a longer hike on a more primitive trail.

Black Bear Campground offers six sites, with a 50-foot trailer maximum and no fee.

The road over Skalkaho Pass is spectacular, narrow, and winding. Rock Creek on the other side provides world class trout fishing as well as bird and wildlife watching.

Hamilton has all the amenities.

DIRECTIONS
From US 93, go 3 miles south of Hamilton and turn east on MT 38, Skalkaho Highway; about 12 miles to the campground.

CONTACT
Darby Ranger District phone: 406-821-4244

GLACIER COUNTRY
#38 Teller Wildlife Refuge

GPS 46.327,-114.113

NEAR CORVALLIS

KEY BIRDS
Osprey, Bald Eagle, Canada Goose, White-breasted, Red-breasted, and Pygmy Nuthatches, Ring-necked Pheasant, Townsend's and Orange-crowned Warblers, Great Blue Heron, Red-naped Sapsucker, Western Bluebird, Savannah Sparrow, Western Meadowlark, Bullock's Oriole, Sora, Marsh Wren

BEST SEASONS
Year around; best birding spring through fall

AREA DESCRIPTION
Riverside habitat with cottonwood and pine forests

A private non-profit conservation organization, trails provide birders access to the cottonwood/ponderosa pine forest, riparian areas, ponds, sloughs, and upland habitats including 3 miles of Bitterroot River frontage. The 1,200-acre refuge is an idea brought to fruition by the Otto Teller family and the donations of over 3,000 conservationists and numerous volunteers.

A healthy and diverse habitat makes the refuge attractive to a variety of indigenous wildlife, such as white-tailed deer, moose, red fox, coyote, porcupine, beaver, otter, muskrat, and skunk.

Other activities include hunting (limited waterfowl, pheasant, and white-tailed deer) as well as fly fishing, conservation education, volunteering, guest accommodations (contact refuge for details), hiking, picnicking, photography, and biking.

DIRECTIONS
Go approximately 45 miles south of Missoula on US 93, past Victor to flashing stop at Woodside junction. Turn left (east) at the flashing yellow light in Corvallis, and then turn left (north) onto Eastside Highway. Go approximately 1 mile to Quast Lane. Turn left and the refuge office is immediately on your right.

CONTACT
Teller Wildlife Refuge
PO Box 548
Corvallis, MT 59828
Phone: 406-961-3507
Webite: www.tellerwildlife.org

American Goldfinch

GLACIER COUNTRY
#39 Lee Metcalf
National Wildlife Refuge

 **46.553,-114.077**

North of Stevensville

Key Birds
Osprey, Great Blue Heron, Double-crested Cormorant, Bald Eagle, Belted Kingfisher, Wood Duck, American Wigeon, Blue-winged, Green-winged, and Cinnamon Teal, Northern Pintail, Semipalmated Plover, Western Wood-pewee, Willow Flycatcher, Song Sparrow, Western Tanager, Ring-necked Pheasant

Best Seasons
Spring and fall migration; August for shorebirds; June for nesting songbirds; late spring/ early summer for viewing waterfowl broods

Area Description
Many connected ponds surrounded by cottonwood forests

If birding sites, like trout streams, were given blue ribbon ratings, LM NWR would be a shoo-in. No matter when we've visited — spring, summer, fall, winter — multiple bird species sightings were a given — how many of course, depends. But with many visits over many years, I can honestly say not once have we been disappointed. According to refuge literature, 238 species have been observed.

On the way in, check for dippers around the Stevensville Bridge. The ponds attract a variety of waterfowl — Trumpeter Swan to Hooded Merganser. At one time or another, it seems just about every species indigenous to the area show up. The nature trail winds through cottonwood forest with willow and shrub understory and a few small wet areas. In spring, look for tree-nesting Canada Geese and listen for the noisy ratcheting calls of a hunting kingfisher and the distinct, loud drumming of Pileated Woodpeckers. Scan the bushes for Yellow and Yellow-throated Warblers, Marsh Wrens, and Song Sparrows. Wildfowl Lane affords seat-of-the-pants viewing of everything from nesting Ospreys to crowing rooster pheasants to gangs of painted turtles basking on partially submerged logs. Red-winged and Yellow-headed Blackbirds are common. Clamp a spotting scope to the side door window and you might be surprised what turns up.

Cinnamon Teal (drake)

Lewis's Woodpecker, Red-naped Sapsucker, Bald Eagle, Northern Harrier, Wilson's Phalarope, Short-Eared Owl, Pileated Woodpecker, Willow Flycatcher, and Red-eyed Vireo, all species of conservation concern, nest here.

White-tailed deer, muskrats, and skunks are common as is the occasional elk, moose, and river otter.

While in the area, be sure to check out the Stevensville River Trail. A half-mile trail runs north from the Stevensville Bridge and passes through a cattail marsh before looping back through cottonwood forest to the main parking lot. Waterfowl, songbirds, sandpipers, and native plants highlight the short walk.

You can kill two birds (sorry) with one stone, so to speak, by combining bird viewing with fish catching by floating the Bitterroot River IBA (Glacier Country # 25)

DIRECTIONS
Via Stevensville Cutoff Road (MT 269) off US 93, turn left on the Eastside Highway 1/4 mile to Wildfowl Lane. Turn left (north), for 2 miles to the refuge.

CONTACT
Lee Metcalf National Wildlife Refuge
4567 Wildfowl Lane
Stevensville, MT 59870
Phone: 406-777-5552

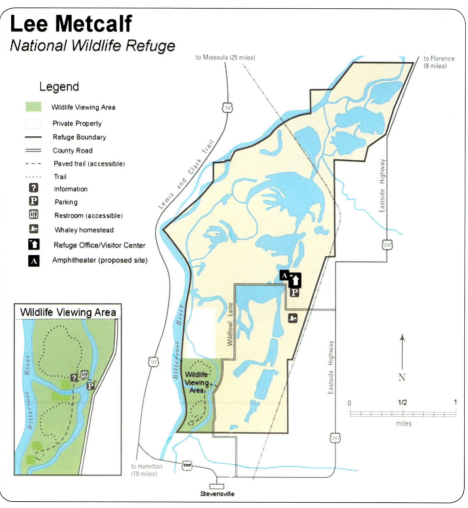

Credit: U.S. Fish and Wildlife Service

GLACIER COUNTRY

#40 Pattee Canyon National Recreation Area

GPS 46.828,-113.925

SOUTHEAST OF MISSOULA

KEY BIRDS
Brown Creeper, Lewis's and Pileated Woodpeckers, Red-naped Sapsucker, Pacific Wren, Western Tanager, Flammulated Owl, Northern Goshawk, and Hermit Thrush

BEST SEASONS
Year round; spring and summer offer the best viewing ops; winter offers fewer bird species.

AREA DESCRIPTION
Diverse area from open meadows to old growth pines

This 3,200-acre recreation area has 27 miles of connecting trails that wind through the old growth ponderosa pine and western larch forest, brushy understory, and open meadows. The trails are open year round. Wildfires in 1977 and 1985 burned a portion of the canyon, adding to the diversity of the landscape.

The canyon is named after David Pattee, an early Bitterroot Valley settler, who filed a homestead claim for some land near the mouth of the canyon. In 1926, the Forest Service acquired the property and in the 1930s, the CCC constructed the picnic area.

In early summer, be on the lookout for the beautiful calypso orchid as well as the many other colorful wildflowers that bloom here.

Other activities include hiking, hunting (with restrictions), disc golf (with restrictions), excellent cross-country skiing and mountain biking, picnicking, photography, as well as wildflower and butterfly viewing. No paintballing. There are picnic tables, but no drinking water. There are handicap-accessible vault toilets at the Pattee Canyon and Crazy Canyon Main Trailheads.

DIRECTIONS
Take Higgins Avenue S.W. to Pattee Canyon Drive. Turn east about 3½ miles to the picnic area or to where the pavement ends at the Sam Braxton Trails parking area. Area is closed from 9:00pm to 6:00am.

CONTACT
Missoula Ranger District phone: 406-329-3750

GLACIER COUNTRY
#41 Mount Sentinel

GPS 46.852,-113.963

MISSOULA

KEY BIRDS
Chipping and Vesper Sparrows, Lazuli Bunting, Ruby-crowned Kinglet, Nashville Warbler, Rock Wren, Cassin's Vireo, Prairie Falcon, Spotted Towhee, Dusky Grouse

BEST SEASONS
Year round; spring and summer offer the best viewing ops

AREA DESCRIPTION
From river habitat to mountain trails

The most popular hiking trails — the "M," Hellgate Canyon, and Kim Williams Trails — also offer the best birding opportunities. Local birders rate Sentinel "among the best spots in the area to find Cordilleran Flycatchers and Nashville Warblers nest here." The open rocky slopes attract hunting raptors such as Red-tailed and Cooper's Hawks and Prairie Falcon.

The "M" Trail passes through rocky grasslands attractive to Western Meadowlarks, Savannah and Vesper Sparrows, Lazuli Buntings, Bobolinks, and Horned Larks.

The Kim Williams Trail follows an old railroad bed beside the Clark Fork River before passing through the Hellgate Canyon natural area. Keep an eye peeled for Common Merganser hens with broods in tow and Great Blue Herons; Red-winged Blackbirds, Tree Swallows, and Cedar Waxwings are common as are Ospreys and Bald Eagles.

DIRECTIONS
Take Sixth Avenue to the University. By the field house turn right onto Campus Drive, that circles the east edge of campus and leads to the parking area. There are just four free spaces, but metered parking is available next to the University Center.

CONTACT
Missoula Parks & Recreation phone: 406-721-7275

GLACIER COUNTRY
#42 Greenough Park

GPS 46.877,-113.977

MISSOULA

KEY BIRDS
Pileated Woodpecker, American Dipper, Wood Duck

BEST SEASONS
Year round; best variety spring and fall

AREA DESCRIPTION
A diverse mix of cottonwood, ponderosa pine, Douglas fir, and non-native Norway maple overstory with willow, elderberry, mountain ash, and snowberry understory

The Greenough family donated the property in 1905 to the city with the codicil, "the park must be maintained in its natural state". They also asked "that the land forever be used as a park and for park purposes to which the people of Missoula may during the heated days of summer, the beautiful days of autumn, and the balmy days of spring find a comfortable, romantic and poetic retreat."

For such a small area, the park hosts a surprising number and variety of birds. The highlight has been the dipper nest beneath the lower footbridge; hopefully it will remain active in the foreseeable future and please, do not get too close.

Colorful male American Redstarts, Lazuli Buntings, Yellow-throated, Yellow and the occasional Wilson's Warblers add spice to an already tasty spot. Western Screech Owls and Red-shafted Flickers compete with Pileated and Lewis's Woodpeckers for the limited cavity nesting space.

Equally impressive as the bird list is the Arnold Bolle Interpretive Birding Trail that winds through the park. Bolle was "a famous conservationist and former UM professor said to have spent countless hours birding the trails within the park."

FYI...On occasion, black bears are known to frolic here also.

DIRECTIONS
From Van Buren St./Rattlesnake Drive side, turn west on Locust and go one block north on Monroe Street.

CONTACT
Missoula Parks & Recreation phone: 406-721-7275

GLACIER COUNTRY

#43 Waterworks Hill

GPS 46.876,-113.982

NORTH OF MISSOULA

KEY BIRDS
Calliope Hummingbird, Lazuli Bunting, Spotted Towhee, Bullock's Oriole, Chipping Sparrow, Killdeer, Western Tanager

BEST SEASONS
May through July

AREA DESCRIPTION
Hilly open area of grassland

Expect to see Mountain Bluebirds, Eastern Kingbirds, and Tree Swallows on the fence lines. By the way, the nesting boxes are courtesy of the folks at Five Valleys Audubon. One thing hard to miss is the loud chorusing of meadowlarks and Vesper Sparrows. Unlike their cousins, Western Bluebirds seem to prefer the more brushy areas. Look for Western Kingbirds who like to nest atop telephone poles; Red-tailed Hawks share the poles but, good news for the kingbirds, the hawks prefer the ground squirrels to nestlings. Cliff Swallows and raptors such as Kestrel, Merlin, and the occasional Cooper's Hawk can be seen hunting the open areas. Bullock's Orioles nest in the trees at the bottom of the hill.

Barren looking though far from lifeless, in addition to over 60 bird species, wildflowers abound — all beautiful, some rare — such as white Missoula phlox, pink Douglasia, royal blue lupine, and sunshine yellow dog's tooth groundsel. The bad news is the hills also support a healthy population of invasive weed species; control of which has long been a point of contention among Missoula county residents; e.g., to spray or not to spray is indeed a touchy subject.

Waterworks is a popular hiking, mountain biking, and dog-walking area.

DIRECTIONS
From Broadway, turn north on Madison Avenue and then turn right at Greenough Drive. Follow the dirt road to the parking area.

Western Tanager (fm)

CONTACT
Missoula Parks & Recreation phone: 406-721-7275

GLACIER COUNTRY
#44 Rattlesnake National Recreation Area

GPS 46.999,-113.876

MISSOULA

KEY BIRDS
American Dipper, Steller's Jay, Rufous and Calliope Hummingbirds, Mountain and Western Bluebirds, Blue and Spruce Grouse

BEST SEASONS
Spring through early fall offers the best variety

AREA DESCRIPTION
Very diverse mountain habitat with an elevation gain of 5,000 feet

This 61,000 acres is about as diverse as habitat gets — brushy creeks, springs, lakes, meadows, wetlands, cottonwood and conifer forests, rocky cliffs, and high, treeless peaks. Little wonder local birders have observed upwards of 40 species in a single day, including Vaux's and White-throated Swifts, Tree, Cliff, Violet-green, and Barn Swallows, Western Tanager, and Townsend's and MacGillivray's Warblers. American Dippers nest on the cliffs above Rattlesnake Creek.

Late summer huckleberry picking, butterfly and wildflower photography, and wildlife viewing can be spectacular — especially the stunning fall western larch display. Mountain goat and mountain lion frequent the area, though odds of spying the latter rank right up there with winning the lottery. Word on the street is, despite the name, rattlesnakes are indeed rare to non-existent but, then again, keeping one eye peeled can't hurt…you know, just in case. The remnant apple orchard near the bottom is a good spot to view Red-naped Sapsuckers, Bullock's Orioles, and Western Bluebirds and, in a good year, don't be surprised to find a black bear sampling the goods.

The view up top on a clear day is also well worth the effort although, anytime, come prepared for just about any sort of weather and, depending where, count on at least hiking 7-10 miles and a couple thousand feet up. Trails are mostly in the open and afford little shade on a hot, sunny day. There is plenty of water but be sure to pack along a filter. Overnight camping is allowed and is a popular spot for backpackers. Mountain biking and horseback riding are also popular, so be prepared to share the trails. There

Ruffed Grouse

are restrictions to using the area, especially the designated wilderness, as well as fishing restrictions on Rattlesnake Creek. The high peaks and a cluster of alpine lakes lie mostly within the wilderness area.

DIRECTIONS
Follow Broadway Avenue 4 miles north until you see the sign for the Rattlesnake NRA.

CONTACT
Missoula Ranger District phone: 406-329-3750

GLACIER COUNTRY
#45 Mount Jumbo

 46.879,-113.957

MISSOULA

KEY BIRDS
Vesper Sparrow, Red-tailed Hawk, Rock Wren, Cassin's Vireo, Prairie Falcon, Spotted Towhee, Dusky Grouse

BEST SEASONS
Spring through early fall

AREA DESCRIPTION
Grassland and brushy draws on south slope, and pine and fir forests on north side

Native grassland — blue-bunch wheatgrass, rough and Idaho fescue, and brushy draws — hawthorn, service berry, and ninebark — dominate the hotter, drier south slope. While the cooler, wetter north side supports a ponderosa pine and Douglas fir forest.

It should go without saying the view at the top is spectacular and well worth the effort. The southern portion of the mountain is closed December 1-March 15; the northern portion is closed December 1-May 1 to protect the resident elk herd.

"Mt Jumbo's name reflects its likeness to an elephant with its head and trunk facing north." Quote from montanabirdingtrail.org.

Wilson's Warbler

Hiking (dog on leash please) and mountain biking are popular. Trails can be crowded, especially on sunny weekends. The "L" trail is steep, while the Saddle Trail follows the ridgeline to the summit.

DIRECTIONS
"L" Trail and South Trail: From Van Buren Avenue turn right on Cherry Street to trailhead.
Mt. Jumbo Saddle Trail: About 2 miles up Van Buren/Rattlesnake Drive, turn right at Lincoln Hills and drive to the end of the paved road.

CONTACT
Missoula Parks & Recreation phone: 406-721-7275

Black-headed Grosbeak

GLACIER COUNTRY
#46 Blackfoot-Clearwater Wildlife Management Area

GPS ⊕ **47.024,-113.375**

NORTHEAST OF CLEARWATER JUNCTION

KEY BIRDS
Cordilleran Flycatcher, Solitary Vireo, Lincoln's Sparrow, Dark-eyed Junco, Mountain Chickadee

BEST SEASONS
Spring through fall

AREA DESCRIPTION
Grassland, wetland, cottonwood and willow bottoms, aspen, and coniferous forest

Songbirds and raptors can be found just about everywhere and at every season in this 67,000-acre WMA. Roads and game trails afford easy access, although travel can be difficult during wet periods and especially so, given deep snow and/or mud. Numerous potholes, several small lakes, and nearby Upsata Lake provide ample opportunities for viewing waterfowl and water birds. Woodworth Road more or less parallels Cottonwood Creek and offers perhaps the best chance for checking off multiple species. Cottonwood Lakes and Monture Creek Roads are always worth a shot.

Known locally as simply "the game range", it typically hosts around 1,000 elk, 1,000 mule deer, and 1,000 white-tailed deer during winter. Black bears frequent the area and, although rare, grizzly bears.

Dispersed camping is allowed; no facilities, and pack-in, pack-out rules apply. Motorized access is restricted to designated roads and trails. The WMA is closed to visitation December 1-May 15.

DIRECTIONS
Located about 40 miles east-northeast of Missoula on MT 200. Road access from MT 83 and 200 from May 15 to mid-November; otherwise closed to all visitation.

CONTACT
Jay Kolbe, WMA
Phone: 406-210-9830
Email: jkolbe@mt.gov

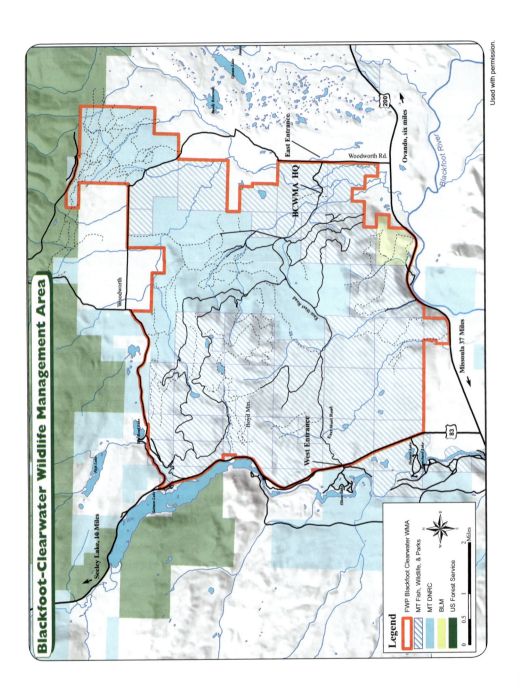

Blackfoot-Clearwater Wildlife Management Area

Legend

- FWP Blackfoot Clearwater WMA
- MT Fish, Wildlife, & Parks
- MT DNRC
- BLM
- US Forest Service

Miles
0   0.5   1   2

East Entrance

BCWMA HQ

Woodworth Rd.

Ovando, six miles

Blackfoot River

200

Missoula 37 Miles

83

Woodworth

East-West Road

East-West Road

Boyd Mtn.

West Entrance

Seeley Lake, 10 Miles

GLACIER COUNTRY
#47 Boy Scout Road

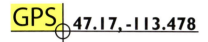

GPS 47.17, -113.478

OUTSKIRTS OF SEELEY LAKE

KEY BIRDS
Common Loon, Gray Catbird, Wilson's Snipe, Great Blue Heron, Belted Kingfisher, Great Gray Owl, Western and Red-necked Grebes

BEST SEASONS
Spring through fall

AREA DESCRIPTION
Forest, marsh, wetlands, and lakeside habitat

Just outside town, Boy Scout Road passes through old-growth grand fir, western larch, and ponderosa pine forest, several natural wetlands, a cattail marsh, and along a portion of Seeley Lake and the Clearwater River. Great places to get those quick bird fixes between other more pressing activities.

Seth Diamond Nature Trail is a leisurely hike (about 1 mile) through old growth forest and explains what makes a northern old growth forest tick and how it is best managed for all concerned…birds, of course, included.

Girard Grove is the home of the Grand National Western Larch Tree — 1,000 years old, 153 feet tall, 7 feet 3 inches diameter at breast height, 22 feet 9 inches around at breast height (4½ feet above ground) — and at least one Great Gray Owl (ask Gale).

DIRECTIONS
From MT 83 north, turn left at 1st Street past Redwood Lane (on your right). From MT 83 south, about 3 miles out of town, take the first road to the right after passing Sawyer Creek Road. The road skirts the west side of Seeley Lake.

CONTACT
Lolo National Forest phone: 406-677-2233

GLACIER COUNTRY
#48 Clearwater River Canoe Trail

GPS ⊕ **47.226, -113.536**

NORTH OF SEELEY LAKE

KEY BIRDS
Warblers, Common Loon (nesting), American Bittern, Gray Catbird, Wilson's Snipe, Great Blue Heron, Belted Kingfisher, Ruffed Grouse, Common Goldeneye, Wood Duck

BEST SEASONS
Spring and fall migrations offer the best variety

AREA DESCRIPTION
Riverside habitat with willow marsh and hiking trail

A 3½ mile (allow 1-2 hours) leisurely float through a dense willow marsh on an isolated portion of the Clearwater River offers excellent birding ops throughout.

The take-out is at the north end of Seeley Lake. A 1.5-mile return hiking trail winds by the river, through thick forest, open meadows, and wetlands, eliminating shuttle problems and providing bird viewing access for non-floaters. A viewing blind beside the hiking trail is a good place to view and photograph a variety of waterfowl, Yellow-headed Blackbirds, Sandhill Cranes, and marsh-loving songbirds.

A no-wake speed restriction for motorized craft applies while on the Clearwater River portion of the trail.

White-tailed deer, snowshoe hare, painted turtle, trout (bring your rod), beaver, and damsel- and dragonflies are common.

Wood Duck (drake)

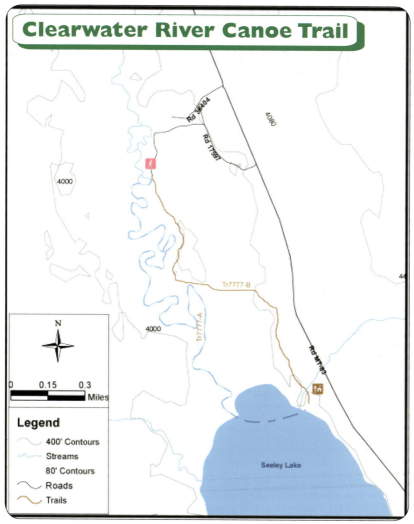

Credit: U. S. Department of Agriculture

There are a number of excellent Forest Service campgrounds in the area and Seeley Lake provides limited rooms, excellent food, gas, and groceries.

DIRECTIONS
From Seeley Lake, drive 4 miles north on MT 83. Turn left (west) at the Clearwater Canoe Trail sign (Elaines Way) and proceed half a mile to the put-in. There's an information board with maps at the put-in. The take-out and start of the return trail are at the Seeley Lake Ranger Station. Brochures are available at the Ranger Station.

CONTACT
Lolo National Forest phone: 406-677-2233

#49 Chain of Lakes

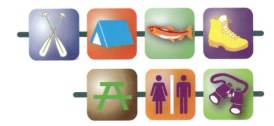

GPS | **SEELEY LAKE:**
47.173,-113.489

NORTH AND SOUTH OF SEELEY LAKE

KEY BIRDS

Common Loon, Gray Catbird, Wilson's Snipe, Great Blue Heron, Belted Kingfisher, Dusky and Ruffed Grouse, Cinnamon Teal, Northern Harrier, Swainson's Hawk, Red-tailed Hawk, Great Horned Owl

BEST SEASONS

Spring and fall offer the best variety; mosquitoes and deer flies can be troublesome

AREA DESCRIPTION

Pine forests with open grasslands and wetlands

Flanked by the Swan Range to the east and the Mission Mountains to the west, the valley is dominated by grand fir, western larch, and ponderosa pine forest with scattered open ranch and grass lands, wetlands, and cattail marshes. From the height of land near Summit Lake, the Clearwater River courses south through Rainy, Alva, Inez, Seeley, Salmon, and Blanchard Lakes to join the Blackfoot River at Clearwater Junction near the intersection of MT 200 and MT 83. The river, all the above lakes, and other lakes nearby — Lindbergh, Holland, Clearwater, Placid and Harper's — provide excellent birding opportunities from ice-out to freeze-up. The Clearwater Canoe Trail (Ranger Station north of town to Seeley Lake Campground) is another popular and productive option.

The vast majority of land in the area is public — state and federal — or private timber lands open, for the most part, for recreation.

With over 170 species observed to date, obviously the Seeley-Swan is something of a birder's paradise. Armed with a bird list, an ID book or two, and a good pair of binoculars, turn off any side road, hike any trail, peer into any thicket, and get ready!

The campgrounds and land immediately surrounding any of the lakes listed above are good for starters. Once we camped for a week or so in the fall at Lake Alva and, while it rained most of the time, not a day passed without sighting a few interesting birds right around our campsite. One morning at dawn, I opened the door to our camper to let our two bird dogs out and two ruffed grouse flushed from a nearby tree. On the lake, loons and grebes greeted us each morning. A Steller's Jay checked the picnic table for leftover crumbs each afternoon. And a Northern Goshawk, no doubt hunting the grouse, lurked about the campsite almost daily. During our stay, we sighted Sora and Virginia Rails, American Bittern, Marsh Wren, Song Sparrow, and Yellow-headed Blackbird in nearby wetlands.

Seeley Lake is a small, friendly town offering travelers all the amenities. In our experience, Arrow Head Resort offers excellent meals and lodging. Hungry Bear, Moose River, and Chicken Coup all serve good meals at reasonable rates. Lake Alva campground (USFS) is top notch.

CONTACT
Lolo National Forest phone: 406-677-2233

GLACIER COUNTRY

#50 Swan River State Forest

 GPS 47.605,-113.76

NORTH OF CONDON

KEY BIRDS
American Dipper, Ruffed Grouse, Wild Turkey, Lewis's Woodpecker, Red-naped Sapsucker

BEST SEASONS
Spring through fall; migration time offers the best variety

AREA DESCRIPTION
Varied forest habitat of diverse ages and logging evidence

As Montana forests go, this one is among the more intensely managed. Evidence of logging and timber stand improvement is everywhere you look. For birders, the forest offers numerous opportunities for viewing a wide variety of songbirds, raptors, and wetland and water-loving birds. Numerous regenerating logging operations provide the sort of diverse uneven age-class forest habitat — grass, brush, young and old trees — that birds find attractive.

The Swan River carves a watery path the entire length of the forest, and several nearby lakes attract a variety of waterfowl especially during spring and fall migrations.

Black bear and white-tailed deer frequent the area, as does the occasional grizzly bear.

Condon offers limited lodging, food, and gas.

DIRECTIONS
North of Condon on MT 83, both sides of the highway. The river is on the west side at varying distances from the road.

CONTACT
Swan River State Forest phone: 406-754-2301

GLACIER COUNTRY
#51 Swan River Oxbow Preserve

GPS 47.887,-113.837

SOUTH OF BIGFORK

KEY BIRDS
More than 170 species have been observed including Common Loon (important nesting site), Black Tern, Eared, Western, Pied-billed, Horned, and Red-necked Grebes, Willow Flycatcher, Northern Goshawk, Great Gray Owl, Wild Turkey, Ruffed Grouse

BEST SEASONS
Spring and fall migrations offer the best variety

AREA DESCRIPTION
Mix of forested and riparian area with brushy wetlands and grassy meadows

The preserve derives its name from a now mostly dry oxbow of the Swan River. The area attracts a similar mix of bird and wildlife species that are found at the nearby Swan River NWR.

Five rare plant populations are found here, including a state plant species of concern — water howelia.

The Sally Tollefson Memorial Trail winds through the preserve; kiosks and trailside plaques help guide the way. Mosquitoes are thick during spring and summer months. Hip boots, binoculars, and guide books are essential. Stay on trail, be bear aware, and watch out for sensitive plants and spring holes. Please report any bear activity (sightings, tracks, scat) to the Forest Service, Swan Lake District at 406- 837-5081. Fishing is allowed. No camping, hunting, or shooting.

DIRECTIONS
Located 2.5 miles south of Swan Lake NWR, from MT 83 turn west on Porcupine Creek Road for a quarter mile. Turn right on FS 10229A to a parking area and kiosk at the trail head.

CONTACT
Nature Conservancy phone: 406-837-0066

GLACIER COUNTRY

#52 Swan River National Wildlife Refuge

GPS 47.907,-113.859

SOUTH OF BIGFORK

KEY BIRDS
More than 170 species have been observed including Common Loon (important nesting site), Black Tern, Eared, Western, Pied-billed, Horned and Red-necked Grebes, Willow Flycatcher, Northern Goshawk, Great Gray Owl, Wild Turkey, Ruffed Grouse

BEST SEASONS
Spring and fall migrations offer the best variety

AREA DESCRIPTION
Floodplain area

The 1,600 acres are situated within the floodplain of the Swan River, upstream of Swan Lake in the shadow of the Swan Mountain Range to the east and the Mission Mountain Range to the west. The refuge is an important stopover for north/south migrating birds. In spring and fall large numbers of birds — waterfowl, wading birds, perching birds, and raptors — are attracted to the healthy mix of habitats, approximately 80% of which is non-native reed canary grass. Except for the river itself, the remaining 20% is forested — old growth grand fir, spruce, western cedar, and larch (tamarack) with cottonwood trees scattered beside the river.

Common Loon

Bog Road (approximately 2 miles south of the village of Swan Lake) is the only "official" access to the refuge. The gravel road leads to a kiosk and viewing platform but, in wet years such as 2011, the reed canary grass makes for difficult viewing. Beyond the kiosk, the road is not maintained, not recommended for vehicles, and impassable when wet. The "road" crosses several sloughs and eventually ends at the river, offering limited but sometimes productive viewing. Cross-country foot travel, game trails, and by boat are the only other means of getting around. The wooded area beside Bog Road is a good place to photograph colorful skunk cabbage and other early spring wildflowers.

Continue south on MT 83 to Porcupine Road and turn right; bearing right (north) at the fork in road will get you to the other side of the refuge and eventually to Swan Lake. Heavily forested but worth a shot, assuming you have the time.

White-tailed deer and black bear frequent the area, and keep an eye peeled for the occasional grizzly bear, which use the area as a migration route between the Bob Marshall and Mission Mountains Wildernesses.

There are no facilities on the refuge. Be sure to include adequate rubber boots and plenty of bug juice in your travel kit.

DIRECTIONS
From Swan Lake, take SR 83 south about 2 miles. Porcupine Road is farther south of SR 83.

CONTACT
Swan River NWR
Phone: 406-727-7400
Email: bentonlake@fws.gov

GLACIER COUNTRY

#53 Owen Sowerwine Natural Area (IBA)

GPS 48.19,-114.283

CONFLUENCE OF THE FLATHEAD AND STILLWATER RIVERS NEAR KALISPELL

KEY BIRDS
Red-naped Sapsucker, Pileated Woodpecker, Willow Flycatcher, Red-Eyed Vireo, Lazuli Bunting

BEST SEASONS
Year around; spring and fall migration best for waterfowl; August for shorebirds

AREA DESCRIPTION
River habitat with islands, cottonwoods, and brush

Open water, a mainland parcel, and several islands — little wonder this one attracts a variety of birds. Over 80 species have been observed to date, 65 of which are known to nest here. Wood Duck, Wild Turkey, Great Blue Heron, Osprey, Red-tailed Hawk, Great Horned Owl, Vaux's Swift, Belted Kingfisher, and Northern Rough-winged Swallow are common.

Several trailheads provide easy access to the mainland parcel. You can also access the mainland area and the several islands by boat via the Stillwater and Flathead Rivers.

Cottonwoods, green ash, river and paper birch, Douglas fir, ponderosa pine, and Englemann spruce dominate the overstory. Dense brush — willow, alder, buffalo berry, wild rose, chokecherry, and such — underneath provides the sort of diverse mix attractive to Red-eyed and Warbling Vireos, Black-headed Grosbeak, Calliope Hummingbird, Bullock's Oriole, Ruffed Grouse, Cooper's Hawk, swallows, Veery, Gray Catbird, Cedar Waxwing, Townsend's Warbler, and Ovenbird. Legions of waterfowl, water birds and shorebirds show up during spring and fall migrations.

Some of the islands are privately owned and landowner permission is required for trespass.

Owen Sowerwine was a well-known local avid outdoorsman and conservationist who led the fight to designate the natural area. It is the only IBA on state school trust land and Montana's only designated natural area.

DIRECTIONS

On the east side of Kalispell, follow Willowglen Drive and turn on Treasure Lane or Leisure Drive.

CONTACT

Montana Audubon Society, Amy Cilimburg
Phone: 406-465-1141
Email: amy@mtaudubon.org

Redhead

#54 Lower Valley Road

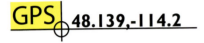

GPS 48.139,-114.2

SOUTH OF KALISPELL, EAST OF FOUR CORNERS

KEY BIRDS
Bald Eagle, Northern Pintail, Redhead, American Wigeon, Greater Scaup, Short-eared Owl, Clay-colored and Savannah Sparrows, Snow Bunting, Marsh Wren

BEST SEASONS
Year around but spring and fall migration provides the best viewing ops

AREA DESCRIPTION
Wetlands, uplands, croplands, potholes, ponds, and sloughs of the river

The route courses between Flathead River and Flathead Lake, a mix of residential and agricultural land that provides a diverse habitat attractive to a wide variety of birds. Extensive private lands (landowner permission required) make good map skills almost a prerequisite to stretching your legs. A busy road, so be sure to pull well off the road before reconnoitering and glassing the area.

From late March through April, thousands of Tundra Swans, Northern Pintails, and American Wigeon congregate on Church Slough and the surrounding wetlands.

The route passes by both the Blasdel WPA (North Somers Road) and Flathead Lake WPA (see North Shore Flathead Lake IBA). Both are closed to visitation from March 1 thru July 1 to protect nesting birds, but walk-in access is allowed otherwise.

A good spot to get out and hike is the recently purchased (FWP) Foy's Bend site off Lower Valley Road; over 2 miles of Flathead River shoreline provides numerous opportunities for observing waterfowl, water birds and shorebirds.

Interesting to note, the Porter Barn on Blasdel Waterfowl Production Area, built in 1909, is listed on the National Register of Historic Places.

DIRECTIONS
From US 2 in Kalispell, turn south on US 93 past the airport, turn left (east) on Lower Valley Road; side trips on North Somers and Farm Roads are also worthwhile.

GLACIER COUNTRY
#55 Lawrence Park

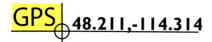 48.211,-114.314

KALISPELL

KEY BIRDS
Pileated Woodpecker, Wood Duck, Vaux's Swift, Red-naped Sapsucker, Lazuli Bunting, Black-chinned Hummingbird, Cooper's Hawk, Hooded Merganser, Great Blue Heron, Osprey

BEST SEASONS
Open year round, dawn to dusk

AREA DESCRIPTION
Developed parkland by river with trees and wetlands

Several trails allow for excellent viewing throughout. You can also park your canoe or raft and hike into the park from the river. Close to town, the park is a popular spot in summer, so avoid weekends for the best viewing ops.

Fox squirrel and white-tailed deer frequent the area; also watch for the occasional beaver, river otter, and mink.

Hiking, picnicking, cross-country skiing, canoeing, and rafting are popular activities.

DIRECTIONS
In Kalispell off US 2, turn north on US 93 and bear right onto Main Street to its end.

CONTACT
Kalispell Parks and Recreation phone: 406-758-7849

GLACIER COUNTRY
#56 West Valley Ponds

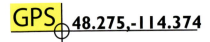

GPS 48.275,-114.374

NORTHWEST OF KALISPELL

KEY BIRDS
Pectoral and Stilt Sandpipers, Black-bellied and American Golden Plovers, Long-billed Dowitcher, Ring-billed Gull

BEST SEASONS
Year round; shorebirds (August); raptors (winter); neotropical migrants (spring and fall); waterfowl (spring-fall)

AREA DESCRIPTION
Pothole ponds in agricultural setting

Private lands make this one an auto tour all the way. Parking well off the road and setting up a spotting scope is the best way to view the ponds and the surrounding agricultural lands. Look for Cinnamon Teal and other ducks, Sandhill Crane, Long-billed Curlew, Snow and Ross's Geese (during migration), Lapland Longspur, Snow Bunting, and raptors including Snowy Owls which show up occasionally.

DIRECTIONS
From US 2 in Kalispell, turn north on US 93 and turn left (west) on Reserve Drive (about 3 miles north of US 2); drive 3 miles west to West Valley Drive; turn north 2 miles to Clark Road (dirt). Turn right (east), and then bear left on Spring Creek, to Church Road (paved). Turning right takes you back to Highway 93, or you can turn south on Stillwater Road back to Reserve Drive.

CONTACT
Kalispell Chamber of Commerce
15 Depot Park
Kalispell, MT 59901
Phone: 406-758-2800
Website: www.kalispellchamber.com

Ring-billed Gull

GLACIER COUNTRY
Tally Lake

#57

GPS 48.396, -114.559

WEST OF WHITEFISH

KEY BIRDS
Townsend's, Tennessee, MacGillivray's, and Orange-crowned Warblers, American Redstart, Northern Waterthrush, Dusky Grouse, Willow Flycatcher, Cassin's Vireo, Swainson's Thrush, Black-headed Grosbeak, Western Tanager, Rufous and Calliope Hummingbirds, Canvasback

BEST SEASONS
April through October

AREA DESCRIPTION
Conifer forest, open water, and riparian habitat along creek

Spring is a good time to view loons, Bald Eagles, and ospreys in and around the lake. Barred and Great Horned Owls are common, but look carefully for Great Gray and Northern Saw-whet Owls as they frequent the area as well. The most consistent birding occurs along FS 913, along the trail up Logan Creek and in the campground.

Tally Lake Warbler Weekend is held usually around June 10. Contact Flathead Audubon Society for more information.

Tally Lake is the deepest natural lake in the state at 492 feet.

The Forest Service campground offers 38 sites, no hookups and May through September it is a fee area. The lake is a popular summer weekend destination for hiking, mountain biking, picnicking, camping, boating, and swimming. In other words, plan your birding excursions accordingly.

White-tailed deer, black bear, and porcupine frequent the area.

DIRECTIONS
From Kalispell, take US 93 to Reserve Drive, turn left (west) 4 miles to Farm to Market Road. Turn right (north) 9 miles to the Tally Lake Road (FS 913).

From Whitefish, take US 93 north 4 miles to Twin Bridges Road; turn left (south) 3.4 miles on Twin Bridges Road. Turn left (south) onto Farm to Market Road for 2 miles to Tally Lake Road.

CONTACT
Flathead National Forest phone: 406-758-5204
Flathead Audubon Society – website: www.flatheadaudubon.org

Canvasback
Credit: Gary Swant

GLACIER COUNTRY
#58 Danny On Trail

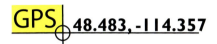

GPS 48.483, -114.357

BIG MOUNTAIN SKI RESORT OUTSIDE WHITEFISH

KEY BIRDS
Loggerhead Shrike, Steller's Jay, Townsend's Solitaire, Townsend's, Orange-crowned, and MacGillivray's Warblers, Warbling Vireo, Hermit and varied thrushes, Fox and White-crowned Sparrows

BEST SEASONS
Late spring, summer, and early fall

AREA DESCRIPTION
Ski trail on forested mountain

Danny On was a silviculturist with the Forest Service who died in a skiing accident on Big Mountain in 1979. Open 10am to 5pm late spring, summer, and early fall. Snow on the upper trail is common through mid-July or so. Be prepared for winter-like conditions anytime.

The trail begins in the upper parking lot and ends at the summit of Big Mountain. Elevation gain is about 2,000 feet. The good news is for four bucks you can take the ski lift and hike or bike back down. And, of course, there are no trail police forcing you to summit or else.

Typical forest birds are found throughout and the trail offers good exercise, scenic views, waterfalls, huckleberries, and wildflowers as added attractions. Mountain biking is popular, although not allowed on the DOMT.

Keep an eye peeled for deer which frequent the mountain, as do the occasional bobcat, mountain lion, coyote, wolf, and black bear.

Other activities include mountain biking (fee), hiking, picnicking, and photography.

DIRECTIONS
Follow the many signs in Whitefish.

CONTACT
Whitefish Mountain Resort
3889 Big Mountain Road
Whitefish, MT 59937
Phone: 406-862-2900 / Website: www.skiwhitefish.com / Email: info@skiwhitefish.com

GLACIER COUNTRY
#59 Glacier National Park (IBA)

GPS ⊕ 48.506,-113.988

ENTRANCES AT WEST GLACIER, EAST GLACIER, MANY GLACIER, TWO MEDICINE, POLEBRIDGE AND ST. MARY

KEY BIRDS
Harlequin Duck, American Dipper, Black and Vaux's Swifts, Clark's Nutcracker, Brewer's Sparrow (subspecies: Timberline), Gray-crowned Rosy Finch, White-tailed Ptarmigan, Golden Eagle

BEST SEASONS
Open all year; roads and facilities open as snow conditions permit

AREA DESCRIPTION
National park with lakes, creeks, forests, mountains and meadows

About one million acres, with more than 260 species observed (well over half the total found in Montana) Glacier ranks right up there with the best birding spots in the country. Better yet, you have a good chance of checking off all the key birds listed above by visiting just two sites: MacDonald Creek is as good a spot as any for "clown ducks", dippers and swifts; while Logan Pass is the place to check off nutcrackers, Timberline Sparrows, Rosy Finches, and ptarmigan. Just look up once in a while and you are almost guaranteed to see a soaring eagle or two. Thanks to the park, we've also added Band-tailed Pigeon (fall), Black-bellied Plover, and Black Turnstone (spring), and Three-toed Woodpeckers to our growing — though admittedly pale by comparison to many — life list.

Lake MacDonald is a good spot to view Yellow-billed Loons (spring) and Red-throated Loons (fall) and Long-tailed Ducks (fall) — like Harlequins, not your everyday waterfowl, at least not for us.

Harlequin Duck
(Credit: U.S. Fish and Wildlife Service)

Grizzly and black bears, mountain goat, wolverine, moose, elk, mule and white-tailed deer, gray wolf, beaver, river otter, lynx, bobcat, fisher, and pine marten are residents — in all, over 60 mammals have been observed.

There are 13 campgrounds in the park — amenities vary. Visitor center hours vary seasonally. Day-use fee and Golden Age Pass applies. Regulations and restrictions apply; check first for up-to-date information.

Other activities include hiking, biking, photography, fishing (no license required but restrictions apply), camping, cross-country skiing, ranger-guided hikes, and boating (restrictions apply). There are 151 maintained hiking trails totaling over 700 miles that crisscross the park; motorized travel is restricted to designated roads.

DIRECTIONS

From Kalispell, take US 2 east to the main gate at West Glacier. Inside the park at Apgar, connect onto Camas Road or Inside North Fork Road to Polebridge. At West Glacier, continue on US 2 to East Glacier, turn north on US 49 and turn west on Two Medicine Road or merge onto US 89 north to St. Mary. Farther north on US 89, you can enter the park at Babb; turn west on Many Glacier Road or continue north on US 89 and turn west on Chief Mountain Road. Going-to-the Sun Highway runs from Apgar over Logan Pass to St. Mary.

CONTACT

Glacier National Park Important Bird Area phone: 406-888-7800

Clark's Nutcraker
First discovered by Lewis and Clark in 1805 during
the Lewis and Clark Corps of Discovery Expedition.
(Credit: Gary Swant)

Lewis's Woodpecker
First discovered by Lewis and Clark in 1805 during
the Lewis and Clark Corps of Discovery Expedition.
(Credit: Dan Casey)

Sweet Grass Hills

CENTRAL MONTANA

With exceptions for Great Falls and to a lesser extent, Havre and Lewistown, small towns separated by large expansive ranches, prairie grasslands and badlands dominate the counties of Blaine, Cascade, Chouteau, Fergus, Hill, Judith Basin, Liberty, Meagher, Petroleum, Pondera, Teton, Toole, and Wheatland. Often, even on a clear night north of the Hi-Line, not a single light bulb as far as the eye can see, save of course the moon and, oh, about a zillion flickering stars.

Freezout Lake IBA (Fairfield), well known during fall and especially spring migration, is one the premier year-round birding sites anywhere. Other regional highlights include Arod Lakes IBA (Choteau), Benton Lake NWR (Great Falls), Beaver Creek Park (Havre), Choteau Loop, Kevin Rim IBA, (Shelby), Milk River corridor, Sanford Bluebird Trail, and Sweet Grass Hills.

Great Falls offers commercial air service. We've enjoyed the friendly hospitality and some really great meals in Chinook, Choteau, Denton, Fort Benton, Havre, Lewistown, and Shelby. Interstate 15, and US 2, 87, 89, and 191 are about it for major roads.

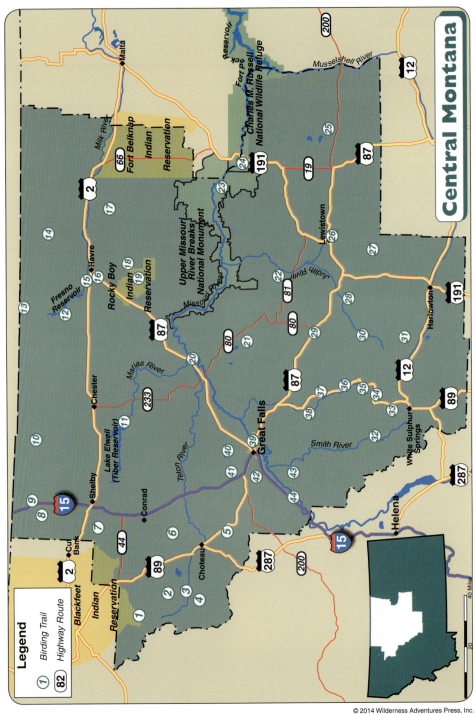

Central Montana

Legend
1 Birding Trail
82 Highway Route

© 2014 Wilderness Adventures Press, Inc.

Central Montana Locations

1. Jarina Waterfowl Production Area
2. Black Leaf Wildlife Management Area
3. Choteau Loop
4. Ear Mountain Wildlife Management Area
5. Freezout Lake Wildlife Management Area
6. Arod Lake Waterfowl Production Area
7. Marias River State Park/Wildlife Management Area
8. Kevin Rim IBA
9. Toole County Waterfowl Production Area
10. Furnell Waterfowl Production Area
11. Sanford Park /Tiber Dam
12. Fresno Reservoir Wildlife Management Area
13. Wild Horse Lake
14. Holm Waterfowl Production Area
15. Rookery Wildlife Management Area
16. Sands Waterfowl Production Area
17. Nez Perce National Historic Park/Bear Paw Battlefield
18. Beaver Creek Park
19. Pah-Nah-To Recreational Park
20. Wood Bottom Recreation Area
21. Kingsbury Lake Waterfowl Production Area
22. Beckman Wildlife Management Area
23. Woodhawk Recreation Site
24. Kipp Recreation Area
25. War Horse National Wildlife Refuge
26. Brewery Flats Fishing Access Site
27. Crystal Lake
28. Ackley Lake
29. Stanford Bluebird Trails
30. Judith River Wildlife Management Area
31. Haymaker Wildlife Management Area
32. Smith River Wildlife Management Area
33. Newlan Creek Reservoir
34. Jumping Creek
35. Kings Hill /Porphyry Peak Lookout
36. Memorial Falls
37. Dry Fork Road
38. Sluice Boxes State Park
39. Giant Springs State Park
40. Benton Lake National Wildlife Refuge
41. Hartelius Waterfowl Production Area
42. First Peoples Buffalo Jump
43. Schrammeck Lake Waterfowl Production Area
44. Pelican Point Fishing Access Site

CENTRAL MONTANA

#1 Jarina Waterfowl Production Area

GPS 48.176,-112.814

WEST OF DUPUYER

KEY BIRDS
Common Loon, American Avocet, Golden Eagle, gulls, grebes, Red-Breasted Merganser, Ruddy Duck, Canada Goose

BEST SEASONS
Spring and fall migrations

AREA DESCRIPTION
600 acres of small lakes, potholes, and wetlands

About 14 miles out on Swift Dam Road, Jarina is situated in the shadow of the awesome Rocky Mountain Front and just south of the sprawling Blackfeet Nation and is one of many wet places between Dupuyer and Swift Reservoir offering, if not *the* best birding for sure, some of the most stunning scenery on the planet.

Howes Lakes are actually dozens of small lakes and potholes, each of which holds the potential for a surprise bird encounter. Sheep Creek and nearby Dupuyer Creek both feature numerous birding ops, as do Swift Dam, Twin Lakes, and Tredson Reservoir. Armed with a good map and an adventurous soul, birding ops are nearly unlimited.

Camping is allowed at Swift Dam. Access to the WPA is on foot or horseback only.

DIRECTIONS
From Choteau, take US 89 north to Dupuyer. One half mile north of town, take Swift Lake Road west about 14 miles to the WPA.

CONTACT
Benton Lake NWR; 406-727-7400

CENTRAL MONTANA
Blackleaf Wildlife Management Area

GPS **47.993,-112.638**

NORTHWEST OF CHOTEAU

KEY BIRDS

Golden Eagle, Red-tailed and Rough-legged Hawks (winter), Alder and Dusky Flycatchers, Rufous and Calliope Hummingbirds, Sharp-tailed Grouse, White-throated Swift, Sora

BEST SEASONS

Spring through fall; be bear aware, grizzly and black bears frequent the area especially in spring. Closed December to May 15.

AREA DESCRIPTION

Water, grass, trees, and brush create the sort of mix that attracts a lot of birds

Scenic and wild, this 10,000-acre area is one you don't want to miss. There may be better (easier) birding spots, but there sure aren't many that can boast a more rugged, beautiful setting.

Local birders have observed about 70 species; Blue-winged Teal, Snipe, Long-billed Curlew, Sandhill Crane, White-crowned and Song Sparrows, and Swainson's Thrush are common.

Any of the several trails through the WMA are worthwhile. Knowlton Reservoir is a good spot to view waterfowl and shorebirds.

Bynum Reservoir (follow signs from Bynum) seems to always have a decent variety of ducks and, especially in dry years, often wall-to-wall shorebirds.

One more time: Trust me, this *is* major grizzly country. Avoid brushy creek bottoms, be alert, do not hike alone, and above all DO NOT be sneaky; mandatory bear-proof food storage is required.

Mule and white-tailed deer, elk, and a variety of lesser mammals are common.

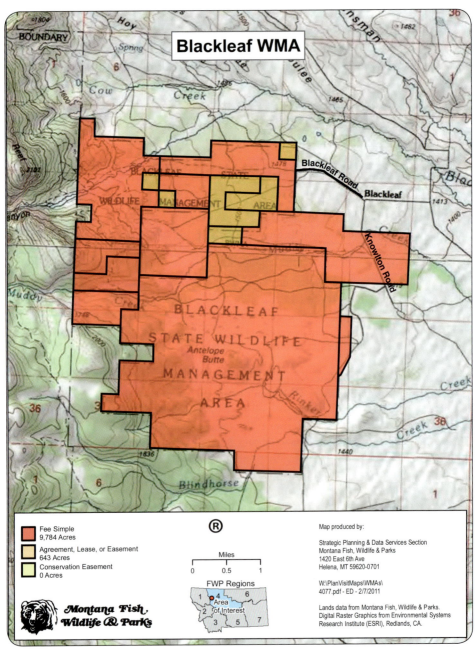

Blackleaf WMA

Fee Simple
9,784 Acres

Agreement, Lease, or Easement
643 Acres

Conservation Easement
0 Acres

Miles

0   0.5   1

FWP Regions

Area
of Interest

Map produced by:

Strategic Planning & Data Services Section
Montana Fish, Wildlife & Parks
1420 East 6th Ave
Helena, MT 59620-0701

W:\PlanVisitMaps\WMAs\
4077.pdf - ED - 2/7/2011

Lands data from Montana Fish, Wildlife & Parks.
Digital Raster Graphics from Environmental Systems
Research Institute (ESRI), Redlands, CA.

Montana Fish,
Wildlife & Parks

DIRECTIONS

From Choteau, travel about 14 miles north on US 89. Turn left (west) on Blackleaf Road and then it's about 15 miles to the WMA. The road ends at the trailhead leading into Blackleaf Canyon and the Bob Marshall Wilderness. To return, take the Cutacross Road to Teton Canyon Road, turn left (east) to US 89, just north of Choteau — good birding the entire loop.

CONTACT

Gary Olson, WMA, phone: 406-271-7033

Sora

CENTRAL MONTANA
Choteau Loop

GPS ⊕ **47.888,-112.61**

NORTHWEST OF CHOTEAU

KEY BIRDS
Red-necked Grebe and Caspian Tern at Eureka Reservoir; Mountain Bluebird, Prairie Falcon, Lazuli Bunting, Black-necked Stilt

BEST SEASONS
Spring through early fall

AREA DESCRIPTION
Route starts out along the Teton River where trees and brush and scattered grasslands and wetlands dominate the river bottom. Prairie, scattered conifer forest, and wetlands dominate the upland areas.

Depending on the season and the habitat, a large variety of bird species are possible. Calliope and Rufous Hummingbirds, Veery, Cordilleran Flycatcher, American Dipper and varied thrushes, Three-toed Woodpecker, Ferruginous Hawk, Merlin, Sandhill Crane, Long-billed Curlew, Marbled Godwit, Golden Eagle, Bobolink, Sharp-tailed Grouse, Alder Flycatcher, and Clay-colored Sparrow are just a few of many.

Interesting and worthwhile side trips include the Blackleaf and Ear Mountain Wildlife Management Areas, West and South Fork Teton Roads, and a hike to Our Lake.

Another excellent side trip is to Pine Butte Swamp Preserve (Nature Conservancy), the largest wetland complex (18,000 acres) on the Rocky Mountain Front. The preserve protects about 150 bird species, 45 mammals, and at least a third of the plant species in Montana. Rare wetland species such as yellow lady's slipper, Macoun's gentian, green-keeled cotton grass, and Craw's sedge flourish in proximity to common upland prairie plants such as shrubby cinquefoil, rough fescue, and Montana's state grass — bluebunch wheatgrass. Dozens of distinct plant communities have been identified on the preserve. Entry is restricted to protect bears and rare plants. Call 406-443-0303 for further information.

The wild and scenic Rocky Mountain Front in itself is reason enough to go. The Front boasts the largest herd of bighorn sheep in the country, as well as grizzly and black bear, elk, and mule deer.

DIRECTIONS

From Choteau, follow US 89 about 5 miles north to Teton Canyon Road. Turn left (west) about 17 miles to Bellview Cutacross (Teton) Road. Turn left (south) and stop at Pine Butte Swamp Preserve and then continue on Bellview to US 287 (about 19 miles), and then turn left (north) to Choteau.

CHOTEAU CHAMBER OF COMMERCE

Phone: 406-466-5316
Website: www.choteaumontana.us

Black-necked Stilt

CENTRAL MONTANA
Ear Mountain Wildlife Management Area

GPS ⊕ **47.843,-112.643**

WEST OF CHOTEAU

KEY BIRDS
Merlin, Prairie Falcon, Willow Flycatcher, Red-naped Sapsucker, Common Raven, Dusky Grouse, Cliff Swallow, Mountain Bluebird

BEST SEASONS
Spring through fall; be bear aware, grizzly and black bears frequent the area especially in spring. Closed December to May 15.

AREA DESCRIPTION
Grass, trees, and brush create the sort of mix that attracts a lot of birds

Like its Blackleaf neighbor, this 3,000-acre WMA is scenic and rugged, lots of birds, wildlife and, of course, keep one eye peeled for bears. Same precautions and rules apply. Less water here but nonetheless, the sort of varied habitat that birds love.

For a more adventurous outing, backtrack from road's end about 4 miles and turn right (south) onto Deep Creek Road for about 15 miles. Turn left (east) on Pishkun Road and, at the east end of Pishkun Reservoir, take the right fork and proceed southeast and then east to US 287. Turn north to Choteau. Pishkun is a great spot to view waterfowl, shorebirds, and wading birds. Raptors and songbirds are common throughout.

Just north of the WMA, the BLM trailhead is a good spot to picnic or just kick back and enjoy the view and the birds.

Bighorn sheep, mule and white-tailed deer, elk, and grizzly and black bears frequent the area; mandatory bear-proof food storage is required.

DIRECTIONS
Just south of Choteau turn right onto Bellview Road. The WMA is approximately 20 miles out. No motorized travel is allowed within the WMA.

CONTACT
Brent Lonner, WMA, phone: 406-467-2488

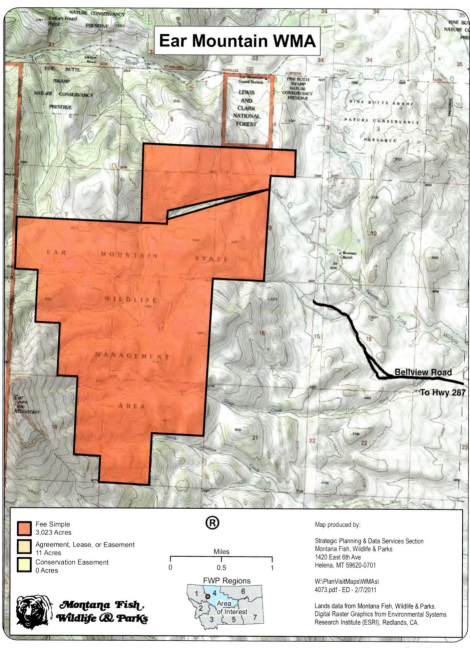

Ear Mountain WMA

Bellview Road
To Hwy 287

Fee Simple
3,023 Acres

Agreement, Lease, or Easement
11 Acres

Conservation Easement
0 Acres

Miles
0   0.5   1

FWP Regions
Area of Interest

Montana Fish, Wildlife & Parks

Map produced by:

Strategic Planning & Data Services Section
Montana Fish, Wildlife & Parks
1420 East 6th Ave
Helena, MT 59620-0701

W:\PlanVisitMaps\WMAs\
4073.pdf - ED - 2/7/2011

Lands data from Montana Fish, Wildlife & Parks.
Digital Raster Graphics from Environmental Systems
Research Institute (ESRI), Redlands, CA.

CENTRAL MONTANA

#5 Freezout Lake Wildlife Management Area (IBA)

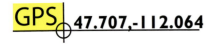 

GPS 47.707,-112.064

Between Fairfield and Choteau

Key Birds
Snow and Ross's Geese, Eared and Western Grebes, Wilson's Phalarope, Franklin's Gull, Marbled Godwit, Long-billed Curlew

Best Seasons
Mid-March to mid-April for snow geese; mid-May to mid-July for waterfowl and songbirds; mid-July to mid-August for shorebirds.

Area Description
Marsh, grasslands, shelterbelt, lake, and potholes

As many as 300,000 snow and Ross's Geese have been observed in a single day during spring migration. A large colony of Franklin's Gulls nest here, as do Eared and Western Grebes. Breeding shorebirds include Long-billed Curlews, Marbled Godwits, and Wilson's Phalaropes. Toss in countless shorebirds, ducks, and songbirds, and it's little wonder that Freezout shows up on most of our bucket lists.

Along with the area around Freezout, nearby Priest Lake and six potholes offer the sort of diversity avian wildlife just cannot ignore. A brochure, *Birding At Freezout Lake*, includes a check-off list for the 227 species observed to date, and is available at the main entrance kiosk. Among other interesting tidbits, it points out the various hotspots for viewing, say, grebes, shorebirds, nesting raptors, and so forth. It also tells what to expect in the various seasons and what to look out for, such as gumbo roads and rattlesnakes. Note to skeptics: Not to point the finger of fear at our fanged friends but our bird dog, Annie the Wirehair, suffered a recent run-in. And while she survived and eventually recovered fully, trust me it wasn't pretty.

According to the brochure, as many as 13,000 ruddy ducks have been observed in a single day. Other notable single day counts include 15,000 Tundra Swans, 15,000 Ross's Geese, 5,000 Canada Geese, 2,200 American Wigeon, 7,100 Northern Shovelers and 23,000 Northern Pintails.

In case you wondered, Freezout is <u>not</u> a typo; said to be a card game that winter travelers contrived way back when to while away the long, bitter-cold nights in an apparently less than cozy bivouac.

Camping and hunting are allowed. Tables and vault toilets are available, no hook-ups. Pack-in, pack-out rules apply. There is an auto tour route open seasonally.

DIRECTIONS
From Great Falls, take US 89 north to Fairfield. Just past town, turn left into the WMA.

CONTACT
Montana Fish, Wildlife and Parks phone: 406-467-2646

Snow Geese

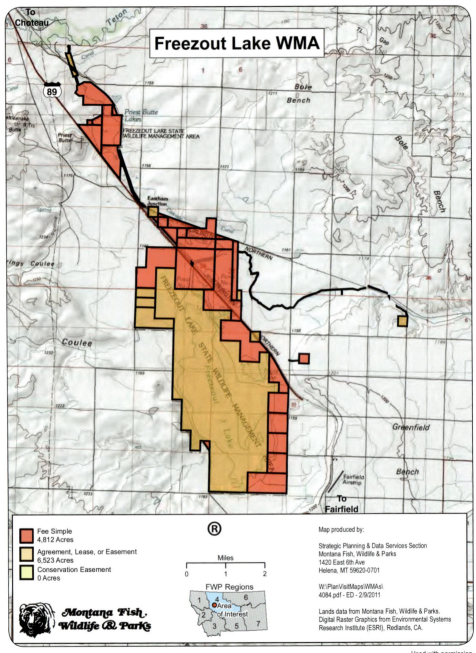

Freezout Lake WMA

Fee Simple
4,812 Acres

Agreement, Lease, or Easement
6,523 Acres

Conservation Easement
0 Acres

®

Miles

0   1   2

FWP Regions

Area of Interest

Montana Fish, Wildlife & Parks

Map produced by:

Strategic Planning & Data Services Section
Montana Fish, Wildlife & Parks
1420 East 6th Ave
Helena, MT 59620-0701

W:\PlanVisitMaps\WMAs\
4084.pdf - ED - 2/9/2011

Lands data from Montana Fish, Wildlife & Parks.
Digital Raster Graphics from Environmental Systems
Research Institute (ESRI), Redlands, CA.

CENTRAL MONTANA
#6 Arod Lakes Waterfowl Production Area (IBA)

GPS 47.989,-112.048

NORTHEAST OF CHOTEAU

KEY BIRDS
Ring-necked Pheasant, Gray Partridge, Snow, Ross's and Canada Geese, American White Pelican, Ring-billed and California Gulls, Double-crested Cormorant, Black-crowned Night-heron

BEST SEASONS
Spring through fall

AREA DESCRIPTION
Varied water habitat with upland habitat

This 800-acre WPA includes three main lakes — Arod, Middle, and Round — several smaller lakes and ponds, and an irrigation canal, all of which provide plenty of water for a variety of waterfowl and water birds. Arod is the largest, but all deserve equal billing as far as birding ops go; many migrants and year-round residents nest and rear young on the WPA.

Large concentrations of Snow Geese (40,000+), Ross's Geese (5,000+) and other waterfowl are common during spring migration. Large numbers of Ring-billed and California Gulls, Double-crested Cormorants, Canada Geese, and White Pelicans nest on the islands; one of only four known nesting colonies of American White Pelicans in the state. Ring-necked

Black-crowned Night-heron (im)

Pheasant and Gray Partridge are common throughout.

Water birds and numerous songbirds breed and nest in the marshy areas. Yellow-headed Blackbirds, Sora, Wilson's Snipe, Western Meadowlark, and Mountain Bluebird are common.

Mule and white-tailed deer frequent the area. Camping is allowed at the Arod Lake Fishing Access Site. There are tables, fire rings, and a vault toilet. Pack-in, pack-out rules apply.

Choteau is pronounced *show-toe*, just in case you wondered.

DIRECTIONS
Drive one mile east of Choteau on MT 221. Turn north on MT 220 for 6 miles. Turn east on gravel road for 5 miles. Turn north at intersection and go 6 miles to the WMA.

CONTACT
Montana Fish, Wildlife and Parks phone: 406-454-5840

Mourning Doves

CENTRAL MONTANA

#7 Marias River State Park/ Wildlife Management Area

 48.459,-112.099

SOUTHWEST OF SHELBY

KEY BIRDS
Bald Eagle, Burrowing Owl, Sprague's Pipit, Baird's and Grasshopper Sparrows, Spotted Sandpiper, Northern Harrier, Ferruginous Hawk, Short-eared Owl, Northern Rough-winged, Bank, Tree, and Cliff Swallows, Mourning Dove

BEST SEASONS
Open April 1 through January 1; best viewing spring through fall

AREA DESCRIPTION
River habitat with cliffs and coulees

The 5,845 acres of this state park and WMA contain a 14-mile river corridor; cottonwood, shrub, riparian areas, short grass prairie, sagebrush, cliffs, and brushy coulees that attract just about every bird indigenous to the area. Canada Goose, Wild Turkey, Sharp-tailed Grouse, Great Horned Owl, Osprey, Yellow, Yellow-rumped and Orange-crowned Warblers, Common Yellowthroat, American Redstart, Brewer's, Baird's, Vesper, Chipping and Song Sparrows, Hairy and Downy Woodpeckers, Bullock's and Baltimore Orioles, Western Wood-pewee, Least and Willow Flycatchers, Eastern and Western Kingfishers, Mountain Bluebird, and Loggerhead Shrike frequent the area. The best shorebird viewing is in late summer during migration.

Access is hike-in from designated parking areas; no vehicle access. Camping is allowed in designated spots and from the river. One of the best ways to view birds is from the river, though low water can make floating difficult for some types of watercraft.

Mule- and white-tailed deer and antelope are common.

DIRECTIONS
From I-15 Exit 358 (south of Shelby) drive east to Marias Valley Road, then turn north 3.5 miles. Turn west on Hjartarson Road for about 10 miles, then south 2.5 miles. Turns are signed.

CONTACT
Montana Fish, Wildlife and Parks phone: 406-454-5840

CENTRAL MONTANA
#8 Kevin Rim (IBA)

GPS 48.827,-111.96

NORTH OF SHELBY

KEY BIRDS
Raptors: Species of Global (Ferruginous Hawk); Continental (Swainson's Hawk and Prairie Falcon) and State (Golden Eagle) Conservation Concern nest here

BEST SEASONS
Spring through fall

AREA DESCRIPTION
Cliffs and eroded hillsides surrounded by sagebrush and grasslands

According to Montana Audubon, "Kevin Rim is a prominent series of sandstone cliffs and outcrops, associated with steep, eroded hillsides. The rims tower over surrounding grasslands and sagebrush-dominated habitat—making the area ideal for hawks to nest on cliff faces, as well as on the ground." American Kestrel, Red-tailed Hawk, Northern Harrier, Peregrine Falcon, and Great Horned and Burrowing Owls, have also nested here.

   PLEASE DO NOT DISTURB NESTING RAPTORS. Raptors, especially nesting ferruginous hawks, are intolerant of disturbance. Existing oil and gas wells and increasing oil and gas exploration along with a proposed wind farm (Spanish owned, by the way) pose looming threats, certain to affect raptor nesting — how it will play out in the long run remains to be seen.

DIRECTIONS
From Shelby, take I-15 north about 17 miles, and turn west (Exit 379) on MT 215 (Kevin Hwy.) to Kevin. The IBA is northwest.

CONTACT
Montana Audubon phone: 406-443-3949

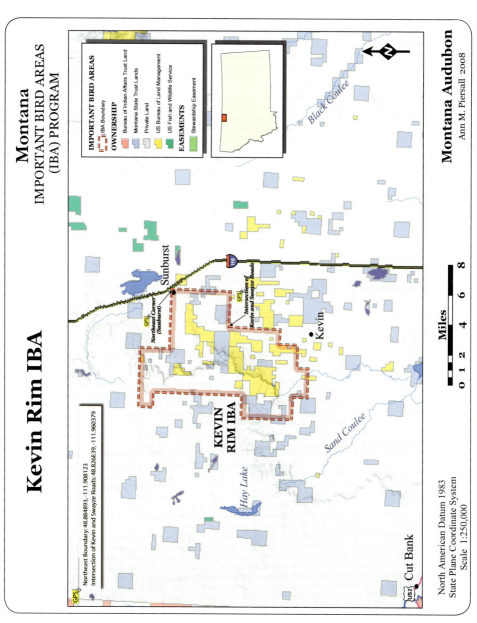

Montana
IMPORTANT BIRD AREAS
(IBA) PROGRAM

Kevin Rim IBA

Montana Audubon
Ann M. Piersall 2008

Used with permission

North American Datum 1983
State Plane Coordinate System
Scale 1:250,000

Miles
0 1 2 4 6 8

#9 Toole County Waterfowl Production Areas

GPS 48.885,-111.841

EAST OF SUNBURST

KEY BIRDS
Clay-colored, Brewer's, Vesper, and Lark Sparrows, Wilson's Phalarope, McCown's Longspur, Lark Bunting, Ferruginous Hawk, waterfowl, and shorebirds

BEST SEASONS
Spring and fall migrations

AREA DESCRIPTION
Grasslands with potholes and wetlands

Seven WPAs are strung out more or less on a north-south line just east of Sunburst. Potholes, wetlands, and grasslands attract a variety waterfowl, shorebirds, grassland-loving songbirds, and raptors. Northern Harrier, Prairie Falcon, Ferruginous and Swainson's Hawks, and American Kestrel as well as upland gamebirds — Sharp-tailed Grouse and Gray Partridge — live here.

This area and the Sweet Grass Hills to the east are largely wide-open, empty country — e.g. by any definition, good country. Antelope and mule deer are common throughout. Camping requires a bit of ingenuity, but is doable. Most of the landowners we've met are open to most any reasonable, courteous request.

Should you wish to extend your adventure, there are wetlands and potholes scattered all over the place; most any road is a good one. By the way, with exceptions for inclement weather, area gravel roads are usually pretty good.

DIRECTIONS
North of Shelby on I-15 Exit 389, follow Nine Mile Road (MT 552) east and turn north on Three Mile Road.

CONTACT
Benton Lake NWR phone: 406-727-7400

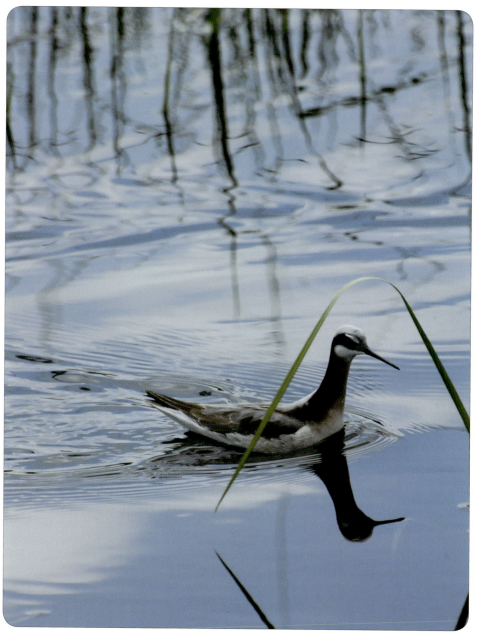

Wilson's Phalarope

CENTRAL MONTANA
#10 Furnell Waterfowl Production Area

GPS 48.861,-111.288

SWEET GRASS HILLS

KEY BIRDS
Mallard, Blue-winged, Green-winged, and Cinnamon Teal, Northern Harrier, Swainson's Hawk, Golden Eagle, Short-eared Owl, Sharp-tailed Grouse

BEST SEASONS
Spring and fall migrations offer best variety; summer and early fall offer best road conditions

AREA DESCRIPTION
Grasslands scattered with potholes

The first thing we noticed driving into the Sweet Grass Hills was, yes, there sure is a lot of grass but, man, is there a bunch of water; water as in potholes everywhere. Get out and take a hike and see for yourself how topping just about every grassy knob, at the bottom there is yet another pothole.

In such a landscape ducks, of course, are givens. But as we all know, water attracts all sorts of birds and of course birds attract raptors and, well, to our way of thinking the Hills rank high on our annual bucket list.

Gray Partridge, American Avocet, Long-billed Curlew, Common Snipe, Wilson's Phalarope, Common Nighthawk, Horned Lark, American and Sprague's Pipits, Vesper and Savannah Sparrows, Western Meadowlark, Red-winged and Yellow-headed Blackbirds, Snow Bunting, and Mountain Bluebird appear with fair regularity on our lists.

Mule deer and pronghorn abound, as well as a small but growing elk herd, and if you're lucky, you might see a moose.

Extensive roads — some good, some fair, some not so hot — wind throughout the Hills, offering enough birding ops to keep even the most jaded busy for some time. The WPA consists of 2,000 acres. There is plenty of public land — state and BLM — but the majority is private. The good news: many of the ranchers we've run into seem open to a courteous request to hop the fence and take a look around. Drive-in requests? Probably not the best idea.

DIRECTIONS
From US 2 just west of Chester, turn north on Whitlash Road (MT 409). The WPA is 30 miles or so out, about a mile west, and 2 miles south of Whitlash (don't blink).

CONTACT
Benton Lake NWR phone: 406-727-7400

CENTRAL MONTANA
#11 Sanford Park

TIBER DAM SOUTH OF CHESTER

KEY BIRD
Bullock's and Baltimore Orioles, Ring-necked Pheasant, Snowy Owl (winter), Spotted Towhee, Bank, Barn, Cliff, Northern Rough-winged, and Tree Swallows, Bald Eagle

BEST SEASONS
Year around; best viewing is spring through fall

AREA DESCRIPTION
River and lake habitat with open grasslands

Lake Elwell, Marias River, trees, shrubs, sagebrush, grasslands, and agricultural lands amid a vast empty landscape attract a variety birds. Gray Partridge, Sharp-tailed grouse, Western Meadowlark, Mountain Bluebird, Yellow-breasted Chat, Say's Phoebe, and Black-headed Grosbeak frequent the area. Raptors abound, such as Prairie Falcon, Great Horned and Western Screech Owls,

Bald Eagle

Merlin, Ferruginous and Swainson's Hawks, Northern Harrier, and Bald and Golden Eagles.

The two campgrounds (above and below the dam) are good places to start. For a more adventurous outing, follow Prospect Road (west of the dam) and turn north on any of the several access roads to the lake. Or continue west on US 2 from the Tiber Dam Road turn-off and take any of the several roads that lead south to the lake.

Roads in the area are mostly good gravel and, of course, dusty as hell in the dry season. Armed with a good map, sojourn possibilities are pretty much unlimited. For example, north of US 2, the Sweet Grass Hills feature rocky buttes, extensive grass, and numerous potholes.

DIRECTIONS
From US 2 about 5 miles west of Chester, turn south on Tiber Dam Road (gravel) and go about 15 miles to the dam.

CONTACT
Bureau of Reclamation, Tiber Field Office phone: 406-759-5077

CENTRAL MONTANA
#12 Fresno Reservoir Wildlife Management Area

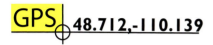

GPS 48.712,-110.139

NORTHWEST OF HAVRE

KEY BIRDS
Northern Harrier, Prairie Falcon, Ferruginous Hawk, Sage and Sharp-tailed Grouse, McCown's Longspur, Marbled Godwit, Northern Shoveler, Vesper and Savannah Sparrows, Sandhill Crane, White-Faced Ibis

BEST SEASONS
Best viewing is spring through fall, whenever there is open water on the lake; river below the dam remains open most of the year

AREA DESCRIPTION
Varied habitat for each WMA – see below

There are two wildlife management areas at this site that comprise a total of 2,700 acres. One is below the dam and the other runs along the upper west side of the lake and continues on along the Milk River. Habitats are very different. Below the dam is typical cottonwood, willow, choke cherry, river bottom. The upper WMA is comprised of grasslands, marshlands, and lake shore with scattered brush and sagebrush.

Local birders have observed about

White-faced Ibis

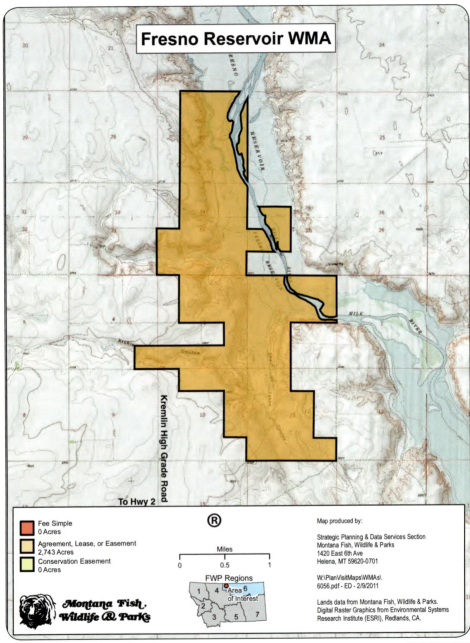

Fresno Reservoir WMA

FRESNO

RESERVOIR

FRESNO RESERVOIR

MILK RIVER

Kremlin High Grade Road

To Hwy 2

Fee Simple
0 Acres

Agreement, Lease, or Easement
2,743 Acres

Conservation Easement
0 Acres

®

Miles

0   0.5   1

FWP Regions

Area of Interest

1 4 6
2
3 5 7

Montana Fish, Wildlife & Parks

Map produced by:

Strategic Planning & Data Services Section
Montana Fish, Wildlife & Parks
1420 East 6th Ave
Helena, MT 59620-0701

W:\PlanVisitMaps\WMAs\
6056.pdf - ED - 2/9/2011

Lands data from Montana Fish, Wildlife & Parks.
Digital Raster Graphics from Environmental Systems
Research Institute (ESRI), Redlands, CA.

70 species of waterfowl, wading birds, shorebirds, raptors, and songbirds. Each year we camp here for several days in early October. Just in and around the campground and the portion of the lake just above the dam, we've listed Chestnut-collared Longspur, Sharp-tailed Grouse, Double-crested Cormorant, Grasshopper Sparrow, Great Blue Heron, Loggerhead Shrike, Willet, Spotted Sandpiper, Forster's Tern, California Gull, Ruddy Duck and Redhead, just to name a few. One of the few neighbors we've had, told us he'd listed 56 species in two days; no record, I'm sure, but still…

Fresno is a pleasant place to camp, especially during October when we've found it all but empty. The Walleyes Unlimited campground above the dam is maintained by the local club. No fee, but donations are accepted. The Havre area is notoriously windy, but the campground sits down below a steep hill, making all but the worst blows tolerable.

DIRECTIONS
From Havre, take US 2 west about 2.1 miles, turn right (north) onto Fresno Road (CR 275) and go about 10 miles to the WMA. The WMA runs north along the reservoir from here. You can get to the top end of the WMA by continuing west on US 2 to Gildford; turn right (north) on Gildford Road (CR 449) to Cottonwood Road, and turn right (west) to the WMA. Main roads are gravel and usually well-maintained; two tracks are high clearance and/or 4x4 and can be impassable when wet.

CONTACT
Al Rosgaard, WMA, phone: 406-265-6177

CENTRAL MONTANA
#13 Wild Horse Lake

GPS 48.975,-110.127

NORTH OF HAVRE

KEY BIRDS
Burrowing Owl, Sprague's Pipit, Baird's and Grasshopper Sparrows (wet years)

BEST SEASONS
Spring

AREA DESCRIPTION
Grasslands, sagebrush, greasewood shrub lands and wetlands (seasonal); water in the lake depends on conditions. Scattered trees and windbreaks mostly at old homestead sites add to the potential bird variety.

A 2001 NRCS Biological Survey listed 43 species (dry year) including waterfowl, Canada Goose, Brant, and Mallard; raptors, Swainson's and Ferruginous Hawks, Golden Eagle, and Prairie Falcon; shorebirds, Killdeer, Willet, Upland Sandpiper, Long-billed Curlew, and Marbled Godwit; Great Horned, Burrowing, and Short-eared Owls; Loggerhead Shrike, Clay-colored, Brewer's, Vesper, and Lark Sparrows; McCown's Longspur and Lark Bunting.

Sage Creek — considered an important bird area in Alberta (wet years) — fuels the creek and wetlands in the area.

This is one of those places a long way off the beaten path; a decent birding opportunity, if you happen to be in the area and in need of a unique bird fix. But before making a long drive, a better idea would be to first check the water situation; except for spring, birding here can be pretty grim during dry years.

DIRECTIONS
From Havre, take MT 232 (Wild Horse Trail) north. About 32 miles out, the road turns sharply left (west); take the next road to the right. Or continue on to the next sharp left and turn north on the first road to the right. If you find yourself being interrogated by a Canadian Customs Agent, beg his pardon and retool.

CENTRAL MONTANA
#14 Holm Waterfowl Production Area

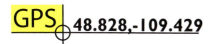 GPS 48.828,-109.429

NORTHWEST OF CHINOOK

KEY BIRDS
Canada Goose, a variety of ducks, Long-billed Curlew, Wilson's Phalarope, Mountain Bluebird, Western Meadowlark, a variety of grassland loving songbirds, upland birds — Sharp-tailed Grouse, Gray Partridge, Ring-necked Pheasant (depending on conditions) — and raptors

BEST SEASONS
Spring and fall migrations; freezes in winter

AREA DESCRIPTION
Three reservoirs, dense natural and tame grasses, and native prairie

The area provides nesting cover for waterfowl, songbirds, shorebirds, and upland birds. Raptors are common.

Not easy to find and all but impassable roads during wet periods, all but insure a peaceful, quiet outing. Water can be a scarce item during drought, except for spring and early summer. Before making a long drive, be sure to check with Bowdoin NWR for current conditions. For the best viewing, be sure to pack along a spotting scope.

The large adjacent state land also has water although, typical of state sections, some of it is grazed almost to dirt…scarcely enough cover to hide a mouse.

North Chinook Reservoir, just south of the Sage Road junction, is also worth a look especially during the spring and fall migrations.

DIRECTIONS
This one requires a good map and some astute navigational skills. Located 20 miles north of Chinook, follow MT 325 (Elloman Road). At the junction with Sage Road, bear left to "T"; turn right (north) trail and the WPA is on the left.

CONTACT
Bowdoin NWR phone: 406-654-2863

Sharp-tailed Grouse

CENTRAL MONTANA

#15 Rookery Wildlife Management Area

GPS 48.576,-109.757

WEST OF HAVRE

KEY BIRDS
American Bittern, Osprey, Northern Harrier, Violet-green Swallow, and Black-billed Magpie

BEST SEASONS
April through early fall; WMA is closed December through May 14.

AREA DESCRIPTION
Cottonwood and shrub bottoms; the uplands (breaks, badlands) are a mix of grass and sagebrush with brushy coulees

Gray Partridge, Ring-necked Pheasant, American Kestrel, Mourning Dove, Common Nighthawk, Killdeer, Spotted Sandpiper, Mallard, Teal, Cliff and Tree Swallows, Robin, Starling, Mountain Bluebird, and Meadowlark are easy to find in this 2,200-acre WMA. Brown Thrasher, American Goldfinch, Lark Sparrow, Least Flycatcher, Western Wood-pewee, and Eastern and Western Kingbirds show up often on our check-off lists.

   Walk-in access is from the county road.

DIRECTIONS
From US 2 in Havre, turn north on 7th Avenue to Wild Horse Trail. Take the overpass over the railroad tracks and Milk River, then head west for about a half mile. Turn left onto Badland Road (aka River Road) which parallels the Milk River on the north side. Continue west for about 5 miles to the WMA.

CONTACT
Al Rosgaard, WMA, phone: 406-265-6177

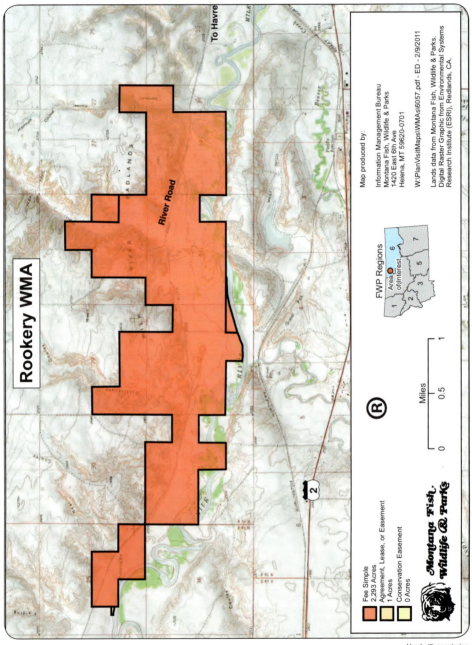

Rookery WMA

River Road

To Havre

Map produced by:

Information Management Bureau
Montana Fish, Wildlife & Parks
1420 East 6th Ave
Helena, MT 59620-0701

W:\PlanVisitMaps\WMAs\6057.pdf - ED - 2/9/2011

Lands data from Montana Fish, Wildlife & Parks.
Digital Raster Graphic from Environmental Systems
Research Institute (ESRI), Redlands, CA.

FWP Regions

Area
of Interest

Fee Simple
2,293 Acres

Agreement, Lease, or Easement
1 Acres

Conservation Easement
0 Acres

Miles

0   0.5   1

Montana Fish,
Wildlife & Parks

CENTRAL MONTANA
Sands Waterfowl Production Area

#16

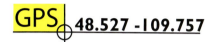

GPS 48.527 -109.757

WEST OF HAVRE

KEY BIRDS
Sandhill Crane, Ring-necked Pheasant, Sharp-tailed Grouse, Gray Partridge, Western Meadowlark, Chipping and Song Sparrows, Northern Harrier, Short-eared Owl, as well as waterfowl and shorebirds

BEST SEASONS
Spring and fall migration offers the best chance for large variety and numbers; freezes in winter.

AREA DESCRIPTION
Shallow lake surrounded by wetlands, grasslands, and agricultural lands

Close to town, Sands Lake offers easy, open water viewing and the associated state school section is also worth a short visit. A good spot to get in that quick bird fix between more pressing obligations…perish the thought, eh?

DIRECTIONS
Located just off US 87, 1 mile south of US 2 junction, just west of Havre.

CONTACT
Benton Lake NWR phone: 406-727-7400

CENTRAL MONTANA

#17 Nez Perce National Historic Park/Bears Paw Battlefield

GPS 48.378,-109.214

SOUTH OF CHINOOK

KEY BIRDS
Mallard, Northern Harrier, Ring-necked Pheasant, Rock Dove, Willow Flycatcher, Eastern Kingbird, Sprague's Pipit

BEST SEASONS
Spring through fall; a ranger is on duty May 1 through Labor Day

AREA DESCRIPTION
Mix of grass and shrub thickets along small creek

Fifty-three species have been observed here. This is a good place to find a variety of sparrows — Clay-colored, Song, Vesper, and Savannah, as well as the occasional Baird's. Western Meadowlarks, Red-winged Blackbirds, and Yellow and Yellow-throated Warblers are common.

The interpretive trail allows access to most of the various bird habitats.

DIRECTIONS
From Chinook (US 2 east of Havre) follow MT 240, 16 miles south.

CONTACT
Nez Perce National Historic Battlefield phone: 406-357-3130

CENTRAL MONTANA
#18 Beaver Creek Park

GPS 48.413,-109.716

SOUTH OF HAVRE

KEY BIRDS
Western and Clark's Grebes, American White Pelican, Yellow-breasted Chat, Lazuli Bunting, Wilson's Warbler, Sora, California Gull

BEST SEASONS
Spring through fall

AREA DESCRIPTION
Lake and creekside habitat with deciduous trees and brush

About a mile wide, this 17-mile long swath along Beaver Creek is one of the largest county parks in the U.S. with about 10,000 acres. A healthy mix of deciduous trees and bushes — alder, aspen, box elder, buffalo berry, cottonwood and willow, lodgepole and ponderosa pine, and Douglas fir — cliffs and grass, all surrounded by endless farm and ranch lands create the sort of diverse habitat birds and birders alike cannot resist.

Look for Long-billed Curlew, Mountain Bluebird, Swainson's and Ferruginous Hawks in the grass; Wilson's Snipe, Baltimore and Northern Orioles, and American Redstart frequent the trees and brush beside the creek. Waterfowl,

California Gull

water birds, and shorebirds frequent the two lakes and the creek.

White-tailed and mule deer, coyote, fox, beaver, mink, Sharp-tailed Grouse, Gray Partridge, and Golden Eagle and other raptors frequent the park and surrounding area.

This is a fee area. Camping is allowed; picnic tables, fire-rings and restrooms; no hunting. Fishing is popular. Bear Paw Nature Trail (about 2 miles) provides an informative hike as well as good birding.

DIRECTIONS
From Havre, follow CR 234 for 10 miles south to the park.

CENTRAL MONTANA
Pah-Nah-To Recreation Park
#19

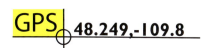

GPS 48.249,-109.8

SOUTH OF HAVRE

KEY BIRDS
Rock Wren, Golden Eagle, Swainson's Thrush, Red Crossbill, Pine Grosbeak, Cooper's Hawk, Sharp-tailed Grouse

BEST SEASONS
June through August

AREA DESCRIPTION
High plains habitat

The Bears Paw Mountains provide a unique, scenic backdrop to the surrounding high plains. Conifer and aspen forest, grassland, and brushy coulees attract a variety birds in this 7,500-acre park.

A fee is required, which can be paid at Jitter Bug's Bar and Café in Box Elder, or the Natural Resources Office, which is 9.5 miles east of US 87 on Agency Road.

Camping is allowed at developed campsites scattered throughout the park. There are tables, grills, and trash containers. No hunting, drugs, or alcohol allowed.

The adjacent tribal lands are open only to enrolled tribal members. Please respect both the tribal land and its people.

DIRECTIONS
From Havre, follow CR 234 past Beaver Creek Park to Pah-Nah-To Park on the Rocky Boy Indian Reservation.

CONTACT
Rocky Boy Department of Natural Resources phone: 800-434-3226

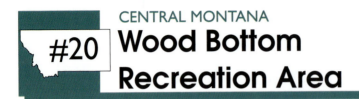

CENTRAL MONTANA
#20 Wood Bottom Recreation Area

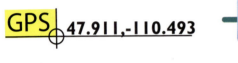

GPS 47.911,-110.493

JUST OUTSIDE LOMA

KEY BIRDS
Yellow-breasted Chat, Spotted and Green-tailed Towhee, Ring-necked Pheasant, Sharp-tailed Grouse, Common Poorwill, Swainson's and Ferruginous Hawks, Osprey, Bald Eagle

BEST SEASONS
Spring through fall

AREA DESCRIPTION
Cottonwood and willow bottoms, native prairie, brushy coulees, sagebrush and grass beside the Missouri River

There are no developed trails other than the short trail at the Lewis and Clark Decision Point Overlook on the way in.

An interesting and productive side trip starts at the fishing access site on the left side of the highway at the bridge and follows the Marias River upstream through some wild and wooly country; all, of course, good birding. To continue all the way upstream to CR 432 requires fording the river, as well as a good map and navigational skills. Should you elect to observe afoot, watch your step — some of this is pretty snaky.

DIRECTIONS
From Great Falls, follow US 87 to just outside Loma. Turn right (east) on Loma Bridge Road for about a mile. Parking, boat launch, and campground are on the right beside the Missouri River. Turn left at the bridge to head upstream along the Marias (many area roads are impassable when wet).

CONTACT
Missouri River Breaks Interpretive Center in Fort Benton – phone: 406-622-4000

Red-tailed Hawk (im)

CENTRAL MONTANA

#21 Kingsbury Lake Waterfowl Production Area

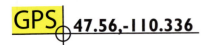 GPS 47.56,-110.336

WEST OF GERALDINE

KEY BIRDS
Grassland birds, raptors and shorebirds (during migration) including Sprague's Pipit, Grasshopper, Vesper, Clay-colored, and Lark Sparrows, Bobolink, Golden Eagle, Ferruginous Hawk, Rock Wren, Burrowing Owl

BEST SEASONS
Spring through fall

AREA DESCRIPTION
Shallow lake (more a marsh and non-existent in dry years) cliffs, brushy coulees, native grasslands, and wetlands (non-existent in dry years) at the edge of the Highwood Mountains

Gray Partridge, Sharp-tailed Grouse, Swainson's Hawk, Prairie Falcon, and Short-eared Owl are common in this 3,700-acre area. In wet years during the spring and fall migration, look for shorebirds such as Avocet, Upland Sandpiper, Willet, Wilson's Phalarope, and Marbled Godwit. Long-billed Curlew and Wilson's Snipe breed here. On the east side of the lake, the prairie dog town houses burrowing owls. Watch for rattlesnakes!
    Walk-in access with restrictions; no camping or fires. Hunting is allowed according to state seasons and regulations.

DIRECTIONS
From Geraldine, turn west on Kingsbury Road and turn left onto Geyser Road for 4 miles to the WPA.

CONTACT
Benton Lake NWR phone: 406-727-7400

CENTRAL MONTANA
#22 Beckman Wildlife Management Area

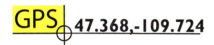

GPS ⊕ **47.368,-109.724**

NORTHEAST OF DENTON

KEY BIRDS
Ring-necked Pheasant, Gray Partridge, Sharp-tailed Grouse, Wild Turkey, Ferruginous and Swainson's Hawks

BEST SEASONS
April through early fall; WMA is closed January through March

AREA DESCRIPTION
Ponderosa pine forest, cottonwood, willow, choke cherry bottoms with sagebrush and grass in consort with the Judith River

Songbirds and raptors are easily found throughout the 6,500 acres. Look for nuthatches, woodpeckers, Veery and Warbling Vireo in the trees. When the berries ripen in late summer Cedar Waxwings, Black-billed Magpies, and Baltimore and Bullock's Orioles are easy to find. Teal frequent the river. Spring through fall expect to see Sandhill Cranes, Western Meadowlarks, and Mountain Bluebirds.

Motorized access is restricted to designated roads and trails; no off road driving. Roads are generally good to the WMA — within, not so hot.

DIRECTIONS
From Denton, follow MT 81 south about 3 miles and turn left (north) on Alton Road, then right onto Bally Dome Road. It is about 10 miles to the southwest entrance of the WMA. The road continues into the property.

The northwest corner of the WMA can be reached by continuing on Alton Road about 4 miles (past Bally Dome) to Bear Springs Road. Turn right (east) to the WMA.

CONTACT
Montana Fish, Wildlife and Parks phone: 406-454-5840

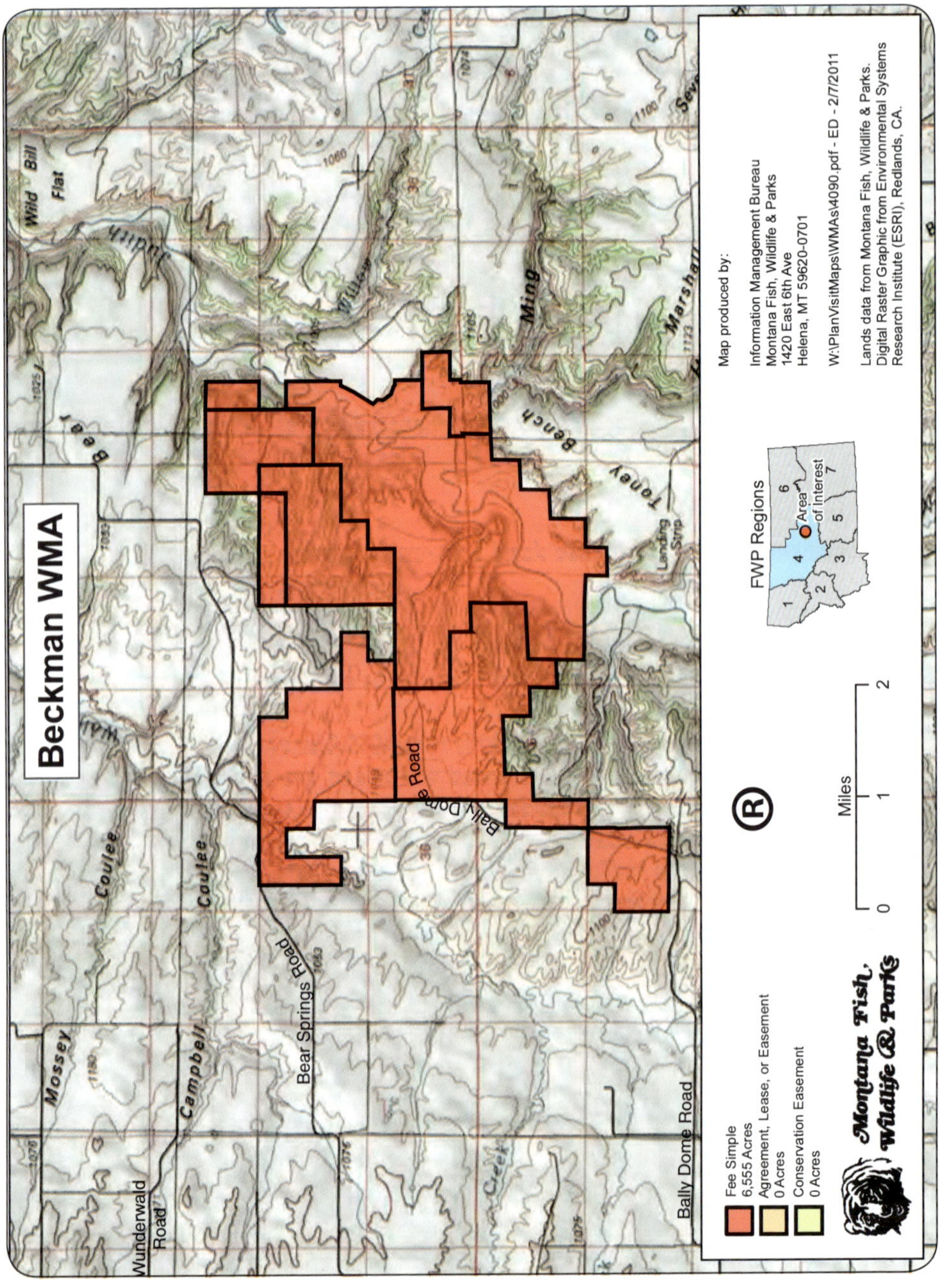

Beckman WMA

Fee Simple
6,555 Acres

Agreement, Lease, or Easement
0 Acres

Conservation Easement
0 Acres

Montana Fish,
Wildlife & Parks

FWP Regions

6

4

1

2

3

5

7

Area
of Interest

Miles

0   1   2

Map produced by:

Information Management Bureau
Montana Fish, Wildlife & Parks
1420 East 6th Ave
Helena, MT 59620-0701

W:\PlanVisitMaps\WMAs\4090.pdf - ED - 2/7/2011

Lands data from Montana Fish, Wildlife & Parks.
Digital Raster Graphic from Environmental Systems
Research Institute (ESRI), Redlands, CA.

Used with permission.

Wild Bill Flat

Beat

Coulee

Coulee

Mossey

Campbell

Bear Springs Road

Wunderwald Road

Bally Dome Road

Bally Dome Road

Ming

Bench

Taney

Marshall

Landing Strip

Creek

CENTRAL MONTANA
#23 Woodhawk Recreation Site

GPS 47.744,-108.95

NORTH OF LEWISTOWN

KEY BIRDS
Sage and Sharp-tailed Grouse, Peregrine and Prairie Falcons, Golden and Bald Eagles, Mountain Plover, Baird's and Le Conte's Sparrows, Long-billed Curlew, Northern Goshawk, Hairy and Three-toed Woodpeckers, Black Tern, Mountain Bluebird

BEST SEASONS
Summer through early fall; spring, late fall, and winter travel tends to be difficult to impossible

AREA DESCRIPTION
Widely varied habitat, from grassland to agricultural land, as well as river and forest habitat

This 36,000-acre recreation area is a mix of state, federal, and private lands in the Missouri Breaks. A rough and tumble mix of grass, sagebrush, ponderosa pine, juniper, and Douglas fir forest, deciduous tree, bare rocky ground, a reservoir, the Missouri River, and cropland — obviously an attractive mix that attracts birds of every sort.

The chance to see both sage and sharp-tailed grouse leks, as well as antelope, elk, mule deer, prairie dogs, bighorn sheep, coyotes, and prairie rattlesnakes add greatly to any birding adventure.

Mountain Bluebird

No fee for the two campgrounds with tables, fire-rings, and vault toilets. Pack-out rules apply. Dispersed camping is allowed anywhere on the public lands. There is no off-road driving. Although the area is open year round, winter and early spring can have difficult to impossible driving conditions. Most roads are impassable when wet anytime of the year.

You need a good map, rugged vehicle, plenty of drinking water, lots of Deet (as Lewis noted often "musketeers are trublesome") and emergency rations are not a bad idea should you become stranded for whatever reasons…like help is <u>real</u> hard to find. Lewistown offers all amenities. Winifred offers limited camping, lodging, food, and gas.

The area is steeped in history dating back to prehistoric times. In 1805, the Corps of Discovery passed through. Later, settlers passed through on steamboats bound for Fort Benton and points farther west. A portion of the Nez Perce Historic Trail also passes through.

DIRECTIONS
From Lewistown, head 38 miles north to Winifred on MT 236. Turn east on Knox Ridge Road. About 12 miles in, the road branches. Head north on Lower Two Calf Road (D Y Trail) or continue east on Knox Ridge. The roads connect in the CMR and a spur road leads to the two campgrounds beside the Missouri River. From one junction to the next, it is 34 miles on Lower Two Calf Road and 23 miles on Knox Ridge Road. The total loop is about 80 miles; allow several hours.

CONTACT
BLM, Lewistown phone: 406-538-7461

CENTRAL MONTANA
#24 Kipp Recreation Area

GPS 47.627,-108.694

NORTH OF LEWISTOWN

KEY BIRDS
Brown Thrasher, Long-eared Owl, Green-tailed Towhee, Western Kingbird

BEST SEASONS
Spring through fall

AREA DESCRIPTION
River habitat with brush and cottonwoods

This 40-acre site beside the Missouri River at Fred Robinson Bridge is a haven for large numbers and variety of birds — songbirds, including numerous neotropical migrants, woodpeckers, and raptors. We have counted over 20 species while eating lunch; double that in a short afternoon and evening. Red-eyed Vireo, Mountain Bluebird, Bullock's Oriole, Great Horned and Long-eared Owls, Brown Thrasher, Common Nighthawk, Green-tailed Towhee, Hairy Woodpecker, Northern Flicker, Western Kingbird, and American White Pelican are common. Pheasants often stroll about the edges.

Should you be lucky enough to be in the area during September, be sure to visit the Slippery Ann Elk Viewing Area (turn-off is signed). Trust me, the rutting bull elk put on a show like no other.

Sort of the southern gateway to the sprawling CMR, be aware that most roads in the area are gumbo — i.e. impassable when wet.

Early 2014 flooding damaged some of the area.

DIRECTIONS
From Lewistown, follow US 191 north to the Missouri River.

CONTACT
Missouri River Breaks Interpretive Center, Fort Benton – phone: 406-622-4000

CENTRAL MONTANA
War Horse
National Wildlife Refuge

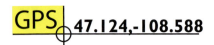 **GPS** 47.124,-108.588

EAST OF LEWISTOWN NEAR GRASS RANGE

KEY BIRDS
Sage Grouse, Golden Eagle, Mountain Plover, Western Meadowlark

BEST SEASONS
Spring through fall; spring is the best chance for finding water.

AREA DESCRIPTION
Sagebrush and grass dominate the uplands; ponderosa and juniper clad hills transition to riparian bottoms, which feature cottonwoods and sandbar willows

To us, some of this site could reasonably qualify as badlands — especially stark and lifeless-looking during dry spells. Water is, of course, the key to finding many species.

Despite many years of wandering about the refuge and nearby hills in the fall, we have never seen water, other than small puddles, in either of the northern lakes. One fall, we found the reservoir all but dried up but, nonetheless, it was wall-to-wall waterfowl and shorebirds. In wet years, all three are said to be productive birding sites; well worth the long drive to get there.

Raptors such as Golden Eagles, Red-tailed Hawks, and Northern Harriers are near givens; as are upland gamebirds — Sage and Sharp-tailed Grouse, Gray Partridge and Ring-necked Pheasant — assuming you are able and willing to sacrifice the shoe leather to find them. Grassland birds such as Vesper and Grasshopper Sparrow, Mountain Bluebird, Western Meadowlark, and Horned Lark are common and easy to find.

Pronghorn antelope, mule deer, and rattlesnakes are also commonly observed, and there is a large prairie dog town located west of the reservoir.

DIRECTIONS
Comprised of three units:

War Horse Lake: From Grass Range, follow MT 200 for 11 miles to the Teigen Ranch. Turn left (north) on Blakeslee Road for about 7 miles; lake will be on your right. At the cement bridge turn right (east) on the dirt trail to the lake.

Wild Horse Lake: From War Horse Lake, continue north on Blakeslee Road about 4 miles to a four-way intersection. Turn right (east) about 2 miles to the lake.

Yellow Water Reservoir: From the junction of MT 200 and MT 244 near the town of Winnett, turn south on MT 244 for about 7 miles to Yellow Water Road. Turn right (west) about 6 miles to the reservoir.

CONTACT
CMR National Wildlife Refuge phone: 406-538-8706

Greater Sage Grouse

CENTRAL MONTANA
#26 Brewery Flats Fishing Access Site

 GPS 47.047,-109.412

UPSTREAM (SOUTH) OF LEWISTOWN

KEY BIRDS
Common Yellowthroat, Baltimore Oriole, Willow Flycatcher, Eastern Kingbird, Great Blue Heron

BEST SEASONS
Year round; creek never freezes

AREA DESCRIPTION
Creekside habitat

This 53-acre site underwent extensive stream channel improvement a few years ago. As part of the project habitat work, tree and bush plantings, seeding, and a trail were completed. Better for trout, of course, but birds profited as well.

This is a pleasant spot to spend a few hours, perhaps enjoy a picnic lunch and check off a surprising number of birds in the bargain. We've counted well over a dozen species just pulling on waders and rigging up for fishing — typical riparian brush-loving species such as Yellow and Yellow-rumped Warblers, Common Yellowthroat, Bluebirds, Catbirds, Bullock's and Baltimore Orioles, dippers, Pacific Wrens, and kingfishers.

On a sad note: the site suffered extensive damage due the record-setting spring 2011 floods. At this writing, repair work is in the works but incomplete. Plan B: Plenty of other birding sites along the creek and in the area.

DIRECTIONS
From Lewistown, follow Upper Spring Creek Road (MT 466) about a mile south.

CONTACT
Montana Fish, Wildlife and Parks phone: 406-454-5840

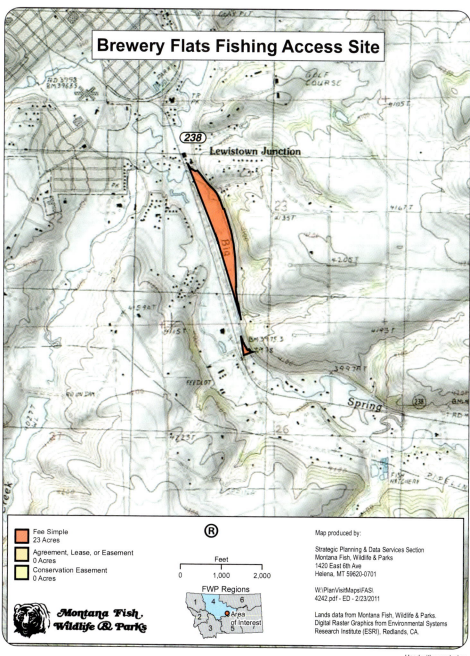

Brewery Flats Fishing Access Site

Fee Simple
23 Acres

Agreement, Lease, or Easement
0 Acres

Conservation Easement
0 Acres

Feet
0   1,000   2,000

FWP Regions

Area of Interest

Montana Fish, Wildlife & Parks

Map produced by:

Strategic Planning & Data Services Section
Montana Fish, Wildlife & Parks
1420 East 6th Ave
Helena, MT 59620-0701

W:\PlanVisitMaps\FAS\
4242.pdf - ED - 2/23/2011

Lands data from Montana Fish, Wildlife & Parks.
Digital Raster Graphics from Environmental Systems
Research Institute (ESRI), Redlands, CA.

CENTRAL MONTANA
#27 Crystal Lake

GPS 46.801, -109.514

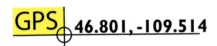

IN THE BIG SNOWY MOUNTAINS SOUTH OF LEWISTOWN

KEY BIRDS
Bald Eagle and Osprey

BEST SEASONS
Fall for fishing eagles and Osprey; late spring through early fall for forest birds

AREA DESCRIPTION
Forested mountain lake habitat

Notwithstanding the early fall main attraction — Bald Eagle and Osprey fishing for planted trout with nowhere to hide in a shrinking lake — good birding ops exist most anytime providing, of course, the way into the snowy Snowies is indeed passable. Forest birds abound — chickadees to Wild Turkeys — and just about every other bird indigenous to the area.

On the road in, keep an eye peeled for Wild Turkey, Ring-necked Pheasant, and Gray Partridge and open country grassland species such Northern Harriers, various sparrows, Mountain Bluebird, Western Meadowlark, Sandhill Crane, and Long-billed Curlew to name just a few.

DIRECTIONS
From Lewistown, take US 87 north about 9 miles to National Forest Access sign; turn left (south) on Crystal Lake Road, and go about 5 miles to a Y intersection. Bear left about 4 miles to Recreation Area sign. Turn left, continuing on Crystal Lake Road for about 13 miles to the lake. Initially the road is well-maintained gravel but (somewhat surprisingly) the last 6 miles are paved; steep and narrow with switch-backs. Please slow down and exercise caution.

From Harlowton on US 191, about 5 miles south of Eddies Corner turn right (east) at the Crystal Lake sign; follow the signs to the lake.

CONTACT
Lewis and Clark National Forest phone: 406-547-3361

Osprey

CENTRAL MONTANA
#28 Ackley Lake State Park

GPS 46.958,-109.941

SOUTHWEST OF HOBSON

KEY BIRDS
Bald Eagle, Osprey, White-crowned Sparrow, Yellow-rumped Warbler

BEST SEASONS
Spring and fall migrations

AREA DESCRIPTION
Wetlands with grasslands and agricultural lands

Lake and surrounding wetlands, farm lands, grasslands, and scattered cottonwoods and willows attract a variety of songbirds, woodpeckers, shorebirds, and waterfowl. Ring-necked Pheasant and Gray Partridge frequent the area. American Robin, Downy Woodpecker, Snipe, Killdeer, Spotted Sandpiper, White-crowned and Song Sparrows, and Yellow and Yellow-rumped Warblers are easy to find around the lakeshore and in the cottonwoods near the campground.

Waterfowl numbers tend to rise and fall with boating activity. The recent jet boat hatch has not helped; hopefully the powers that be will see the light…though I, for one, am not holding my breath.

Camping is free; picnic shelters, vault toilet, no water, pack-in, pack-out rules apply.

Map Key
- Boat Launch
- Picnic Shelter
- FWP Land Ownership
- Other Land Ownership

To Hobson and Route 87

ACKLEY LAKE

Ackley Lake State Park

1/2 Mile

DIRECTIONS
From Hobson follow the signs. The park is about 5 miles south, off of MT 400.

CONTACT
Park Manager phone: 406-454-5858

Used with permission.

CENTRAL MONTANA

#29 Stanford Bluebird Trail

GPS 47.157-110.241

STANFORD

KEY BIRDS
Mountain Bluebird, Mountain Chickadee, Hairy Woodpecker, Gray Catbird, Western Tanager, Lazuli Bunting, Sharp-tailed Grouse, Ring-necked Pheasant, American Dipper

BEST SEASONS
Spring through late summer

AREA DESCRIPTION
Trail through forest, grassland, and wetlands

Known locally as the Bob Niebuhr Trail, it winds through a variety of habitats — grassland, conifer and aspen forest, burned forest, creek bottoms, and wetlands. According to literature, "…since 1992 the trail has fledged over 7,000 bluebirds. Dippers frequent Dry Wolf Creek, especially in the campground area." In our experience, the route is also a great place to view a variety of raptors, and sandhill cranes are common in the open areas.

DIRECTIONS
From Stanford, about a mile west of town on US 87/MT 200, turn south at the National Forest Access sign onto Dry Wolf Road (101); check out Dry Wolf Campground and return to Dry Wolf Road and turn back toward Stanford about 6 miles. Turn right (east) about 5 miles to the "T" intersection. Turn right and follow the widest (best) gravel roads at any junctions until you reach bluebird box #91(about 11miles). Turn back until you reach the sign for Stanford. Follow Running Wolf Road to Stanford (about 11 miles).

CONTACT
Judith Ranger Station, Stanford – phone: 406-566-2292

Lazuli Bunting
Credit: U.S. Fish and Wildlife Service

CENTRAL MONTANA
#30 Judith River Wildlife Management Area

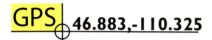

GPS 46.883,-110.325

SOUTHWEST OF UTICA

KEY BIRDS

Golden Eagle, Ferruginous Hawk, Dusky Grouse, Tree Swallow, Vesper and Savannah Sparrows, Sandhill Crane, Clark's Nutcracker, Dark-eyed Junco

BEST SEASONS

April through early fall; WMA is closed December through May 14.

AREA DESCRIPTION

Rolling hills clad in coniferous and deciduous forest and grass, interspersed with brushy creek bottoms and cliffs

During a recent lunch break in this 9,400-acre WMA, we listed American Crow, Raven, Common Nighthawk, Killdeer, Mallard, Mountain Bluebird, Mourning Dove, Flicker, Red-tailed Hawk, Sandhill Crane, Northern Harrier, Black-Capped Chickadee, Red-Breasted Nuthatch, and Kestrel.

Vehicle travel is restricted to designated roads and established trails; no off-road travel. High clearance vehicles are recommended.

During wet years, the spring wildflower display can be spectacular; ditto butterflies from mid-summer through early fall.

Elk, deer, and antelope are common in the area.

DIRECTIONS

From Hobson, follow MT 239 about 10 miles to Utica. Take the main gravel road heading southwest (north side of the Judith River) for 9 miles to Sapphire Village. Just past the village, turn right (west) 1.5 miles to the WMA.

Clark's Nutcracker
Credit: Gary Swant

CONTACT

Adam Grove, WMA, phone: 406-547-2585

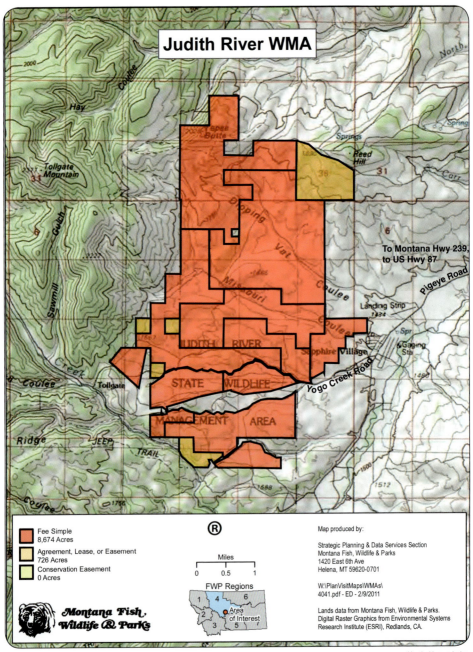

Used with permission.

CENTRAL MONTANA

#31 Haymaker Wildlife Management Area

GPS 46.611,-110.219

NORTHEAST OF MARTINSDALE

KEY BIRDS
Savannah and Vesper Sparrows, Northern Harrier, Golden Eagle, American Kestrel, Red-tailed Hawk

BEST SEASONS
April through early fall; WMA is closed December through May 14.

AREA DESCRIPTION
Wetlands, grasslands, sagebrush and forest

In this 1,300-acre WMA, conifer forest, sagebrush, wetlands, and grasslands combine to create the sort of diverse, edge-filled habitat birds flock to. Upland Sandpiper, Common Raven, American Crow, Yellow Warbler, Common Nighthawk, Black-billed Magpie, Dusky Grouse, and American Goldfinch are common.

Vehicle travel is restricted to designated roads; no off-road travel. Typical of most WMAs, high clearance vehicles are de rigueur.

Elk and mule deer frequent the area, thus birders might consider making blaze orange essential during big game rifle seasons.

DIRECTIONS
From Harlowton, follow US 12 west to Two Dot. Turn north on Haymaker Road. The WMA borders the Lewis and Clark National Forest.

CONTACT
Jay Newell, WMA, phone: 406-323-3170

Red-tailed Hawk (im)

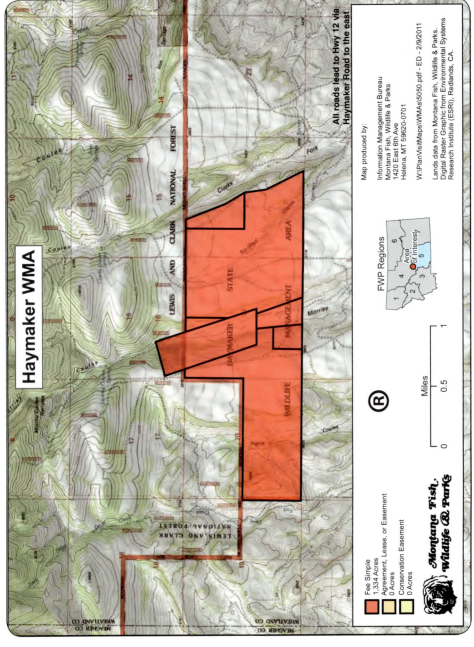

Haymaker WMA

All roads lead to Hwy 12 via
Haymaker Road to the east

Map produced by:

Information Management Bureau
Montana Fish, Wildlife & Parks
1420 East 6th Ave
Helena, MT 59620-0701

W:\PlanVisitMaps\WMAs\5050.pdf - ED - 2/9/2011

Lands data from Montana Fish, Wildlife & Parks.
Digital Raster Graphic from Environmental Systems
Research Institute (ESRI), Redlands, CA.

Used with permission.

FWP Regions

Area
of Interest

Miles
0   0.5   1

Montana Fish,
Wildlife & Parks

Fee Simple
1,334 Acres

Agreement, Lease, or Easement
0 Acres

Conservation Easement
0 Acres

CENTRAL MONTANA
#32 Smith River Wildlife Management Area

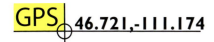 GPS 46.721,-111.174

NORTHWEST OF WHITE SULPHUR SPRINGS

KEY BIRDS
Ruffed Grouse, Bald Eagle, Ferruginous and Red-tailed Hawks, Mountain Chickadee, Red-breasted Nuthatch, Brewer's Blackbird

BEST SEASONS
Mid-May through October; closed to visitation December through mid-May to protect wintering wildlife.

AREA DESCRIPTION
Ponderosa pine forest, riparian shrub, sagebrush, grasslands, and some wetlands

This over 3,000-acre WMA has a mix of habitats that attracts a variety of songbirds — Mountain Bluebird, Western Meadowlark, and Vesper Sparrow to name just three of the more common.

Vehicle access is limited to designated roads and trails; off-road travel is prohibited.

Camping is allowed in designated areas. A popular spot in big game season, so plan your birding trips accordingly.

DIRECTIONS
Follow MT 360 northwest from White Sulphur Springs about 15 miles to Camp Baker/ Smith River Road. Turn right (north) about 3 miles to the WMA entrance.

CONTACT
Adam Grove, WMA, phone: 406-547-2585

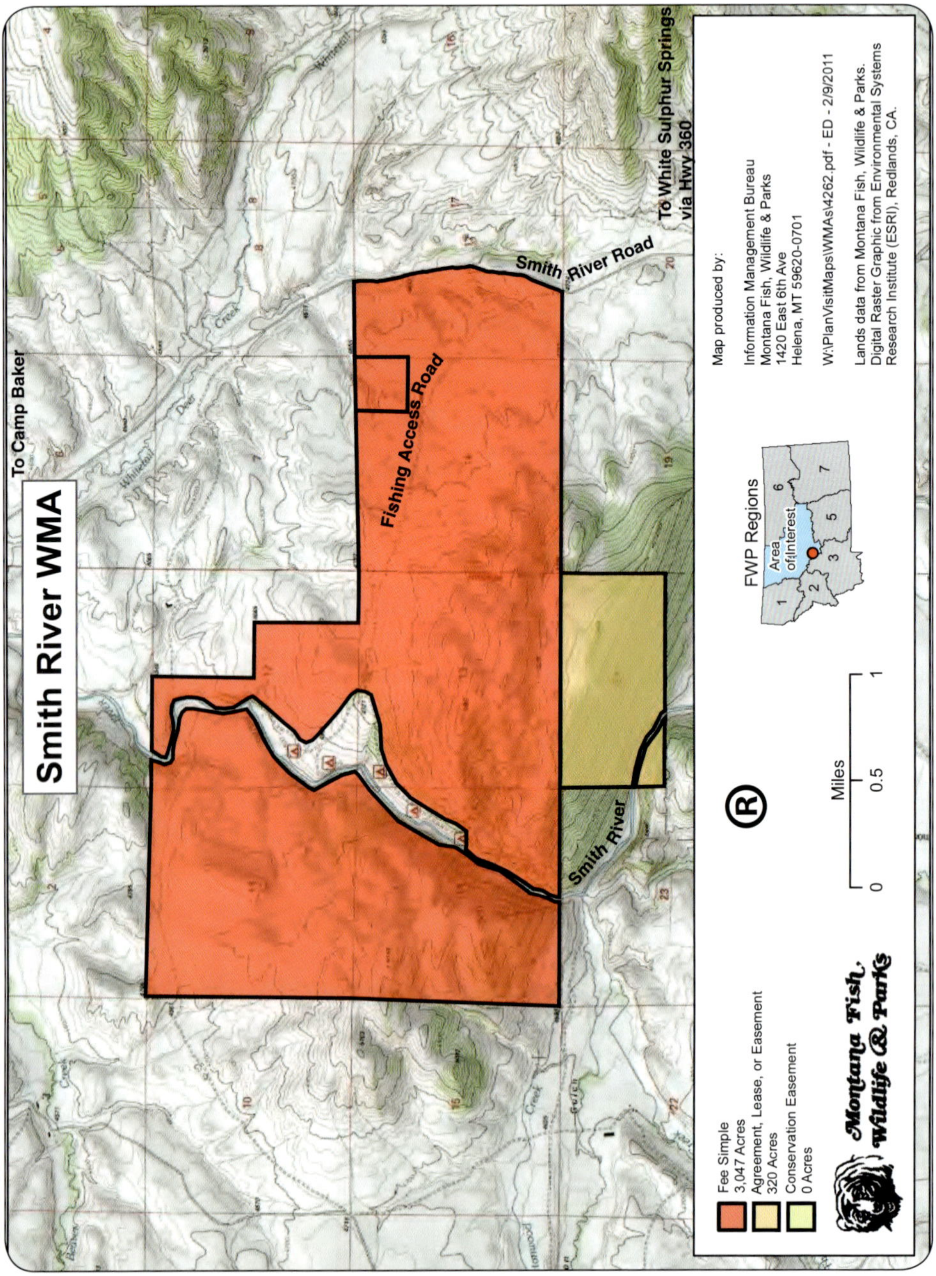

Smith River WMA

To Camp Baker

To White Sulphur Springs via Hwy 360

Smith River Road

Fishing Access Road

Smith River

Map produced by:

Information Management Bureau
Montana Fish, Wildlife & Parks
1420 East 6th Ave
Helena, MT 59620-0701

W:\PlanVisitMaps\WMAs\4262.pdf - ED - 2/9/2011

Lands data from Montana Fish, Wildlife & Parks.
Digital Raster Graphic from Environmental Systems
Research Institute (ESRI), Redlands, CA.

FWP Regions

Area of Interest

Miles
0   0.5   1

Fee Simple
3,047 Acres

Agreement, Lease, or Easement
320 Acres

Conservation Easement
0 Acres

Montana Fish,
Wildlife & Parks

Used with permission.

CENTRAL MONTANA

#33 Newlan Creek Reservoir Fishing Access Site

GPS 46.643,-110.929

NORTH OF WHITE SULPHUR SPRINGS

KEY BIRDS
Sandhill Crane, Common Nighthawk, Spotted Sandpiper, Western Grebe, Mountain Bluebird, American Kestrel

BEST SEASONS
Spring through fall

AREA DESCRIPTION
Reservoir surrounded by forested hills

The reservoir attracts a variety of waterfowl and shorebirds, especially during migration. The site itself attracts the usual forest and water loving songbirds, several raptors, and also woodpeckers.

As time permits, driving any of the roads in the area is worth a shot. In the spring, look for Bald Eagles in the open ranch and farm lands which dominate the landscape around White Sulphur Springs. We have counted over 20 eagles in a single day. Red-tailed and Northern Goshawks and Golden Eagles also frequent the area. Look for Brewer's and Vesper Sparrows in the sagebrush.

American Kestrel

The 430-acre site, nearby state school trust sections, and the Lewis and Clark National Forest allow for plenty of opportunities to get out and stretch your legs.

Fee area; camping is allowed; picnic tables and vault toilet, pack-in, pack-out rules apply. No ATVs, Dirt Bikes, etc. allowed on site, including parking lot and campsites. Hunting is allowed with restrictions.

DIRECTIONS
From White Sulphur Springs, follow MT 360 west to MT 259; turn north about 7 miles to the reservoir.

CONTACT
Fish, Wildlife and Parks phone: 406-454-5840
Beaver Creek Park phone: 406-395-4565

American Goldfinch

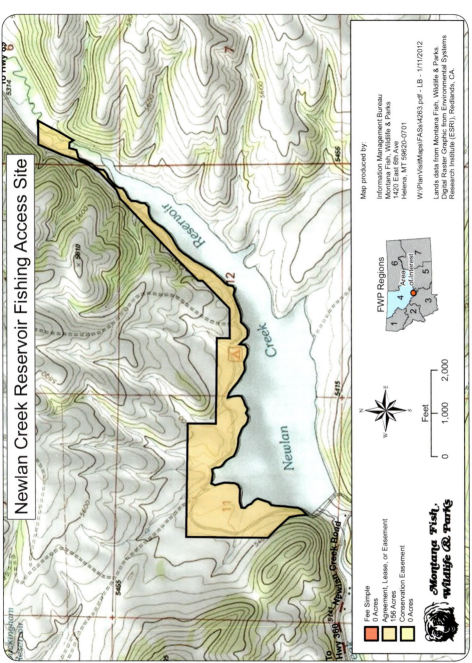

Newlan Creek Reservoir Fishing Access Site

CENTRAL MONTANA
#34 Jumping Creek

GPS 46.766, -110.784

NORTH OF WHITE SULPHUR SPRINGS

KEY BIRDS
American Dipper, Steller's and Gray Jays, Swainson's Hawk, Hermit Thrush, Sandhill Crane

BEST SEASONS
Spring through fall

AREA DESCRIPTION
Mountain creekside habitat with forest

Park at the campground. Several trails both north and south of the highway allow for outings to suit just about any timeframe. Elk, mule and white-tailed deer and black bear frequent the area.

DIRECTIONS
From White Sulphur Springs, follow US 89 north about 20 miles; turn right at campground sign.

CONTACT
Lewis and Clark National Forest phone: 406-547-3361

CENTRAL MONTANA

#35 Kings Hill Pass/ Porphyry Peak Lookout

GPS ⊕ 46.841, -110.695

NORTH OF WHITE SULPHUR SPRINGS

KEY BIRDS
Hairy and Downy Woodpeckers, Steller's and Gray Jays, Clark's Nutcracker, Red-naped Sapsucker, MacGillivray's Warbler, Golden Eagle

BEST SEASONS
Summer through early fall

AREA DESCRIPTION
Forested mountain habitat

The edges in and around Showdown Ski Area attract a variety of birds not easily seen in your typical wall-to-wall forest. Cassin's Finch, Pine Grosbeak, Calliope and Rufous Hummingbirds, and Ruffed Grouse are common.

Mule and white-tailed deer, elk, and the occasional black bear can be expected.

The spring and summer wildflower display can be spectacular, especially so in wet years and/or following heavy winter snowpack. The views from the lookout are equally impressive.

DIRECTIONS
From White Sulphur Springs, follow US 89 to Kings Hill Pass (Showdown Ski Area) and turn left (west) to the lookout.

CONTACT
Lewis and Clark National Forest phone: 406-547-3361

Golden Eagle

CENTRAL MONTANA
#36 Memorial Falls

GPS 46.913,-110.698

SOUTH OF BELT

KEY BIRDS
American Dipper, Lewis's, Hairy, and Downy Woodpeckers, Steller's and Gray Jays, Clark's Nutcracker, Red-naped Sapsucker, MacGillivray's Warbler

BEST SEASONS
Late spring through early fall

AREA DESCRIPTION
Aspen and lodgepole forests with creek and waterfalls

There is a short (about half-mile) round trip hike beside Memorial Creek to two scenic waterfalls. In late spring and early summer, the creek is typically roaring. The falls and the surrounding landscape are a photographer's dream.

Mule and white-tailed deer, elk, and the occasional black bear can be expected.

DIRECTIONS
From the US 87/US 89 junction east of Belt, follow US 89 south about 35 miles to a mile or so south of Neihart; trailhead is signed.

CONTACT
Lewis and Clark National Forest phone: 406-236-5511

CENTRAL MONTANA

#37 Dry Fork Road (AKA Hughesville Road)

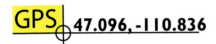

GPS ⊕ **47.096, -110.836**

SOUTH OF BELT

KEY BIRDS
Red-naped Sapsucker, Mountain Chickadee, Ruffed Grouse, Northern Pygmy Owl, Willow and Dusky Flycatchers, MacGillivray's Warbler

BEST SEASONS
Late spring through early fall

AREA DESCRIPTION
Roadside habitat with aspen and pine forests

The road passes through a mosaic of public and private lands (orange-painted fence posts denote private). In the spring, aspen stands beside the road are good places to stop and listen for drumming Ruffed Grouse, woodpeckers, and singing songbirds.

Animal species that may been observed here are mule deer, elk, and the occasional black bear.

The road forks about 11 miles in, and either fork will eventually take you to US 87; a long, often rough and dusty haul either way but nonetheless good birding. The Lewis and Clark National Forest Travel Map is highly recommended, as are high clearance vehicles; 4x4 in wet and/or snow.

DIRECTIONS
From the US 87/US 89 junction east of Belt, follow US 89 south about 21 miles; turn left (east) on gravel road in the community of Monarch.

CONTACT
Lewis and Clark National Forest phone: 406-236-5511

CENTRAL MONTANA
#38 Sluice Boxes State Park

GPS 47.212,-110.935

SOUTH OF BELT

KEY BIRDS
Calliope Hummingbird, White-throated Swift, Mountain Chickadee, Red-naped Sapsucker, Dusky Grouse

BEST SEASONS
Open year around; the best birding is spring through fall.

AREA DESCRIPTION
Creekside habit with towering cliffs and forested hills

A rugged canyon featuring towering limestone cliffs, carved by a cold, swift-flowing creek, conifer forest, a ghost town (Albright), mine and railroad remnants make this one a nostalgic trip back in time with a bit of birding tossed in for good measure. Expect to see typical forest dwelling birds throughout the 1,750-acre state park that includes the canyon and surrounding national forest.

Rich in mining and railroad history, the remains of mines, a railroad, and historic cabins give visitors a rare glimpse into the harsh lives of prospectors searching for precious metals, miners, muleskinners, smelter-men, and railroaders. Interpretive signs spell out the history of

Dusky Grouse (hen)

the Barker Mines and Montana Central Railroad among other interesting tidbits.

A popular and productive trout fishing destination once served by the daily "Fish Train" out of Great Falls.

FYI, about three quarters of a mile in, the trail fords the creek and a short distance beyond it forks; stay right to avoid trespassing.

Mule and white-tailed deer, elk, and the occasional black bear can be expected. Mountain lion, bobcat, coyote, pine marten, red fox and raccoon are common though not often seen.

This is a fee area; Picnic tables and vault toilets, no designated campsites, camping is allowed in the backcountry. Leave no trace, pack-in, pack-out rules apply.

DIRECTIONS
From junction US 87/89 east of Belt, take US 89 south about 10 miles. Follow signs to the park.

CONTACT
Park Manager phone: 406-454-5840

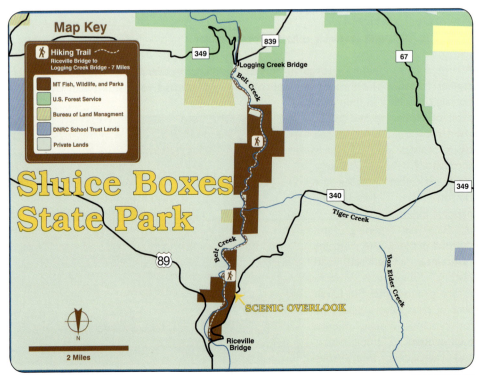

Used with permission

CENTRAL MONTANA
#39 Giant Springs State Park

GPS 47.534,-111.227

GREAT FALLS

KEY BIRDS
Bullock's Oriole, Bald Eagle, Belted Kingfisher, Willow Flycatcher, Barrow's and Common Goldeneyes

BEST SEASONS
Year round; best viewing is spring through fall

AREA DESCRIPTION
Cottonwood forest and shrub riparian habitat with spectacular falls

Tall trees, shrubs, and water that never freezes at the edge of our third largest city attracts a variety of birds — waterfowl, water birds, songbirds, and raptors. So, although spring through fall are the best birding seasons, the fact that the springs and waterfall never freeze make for good birding opportunities year round. Birders report about 80 species have been observed including Black-billed Magpie, Gray Catbird, Swainson's Thrush, Yellow-rumped and Wilson's Warblers, Brown Thrasher, and Common Loon.

Lewis and Clark camped at the springs in 1805. Among the largest freshwater springs in the world (156 million gallons per day) and the site of the Roe River — which by the way is said to be the world's shortest river.

The visitor center (across the road) features bird recognition among other educational programs.

Facilities include tables, fire-rings, toilets (flush), trail (accessible), pack-in, pack-out rules apply. Other activities include fishing, hiking, photography, nature tours, and interpretive programs. No camping.

DIRECTIONS
Located off US 87 in Great Falls, then 1 mile east on (Missouri) River Drive to 4803 Giant Springs Road.

CONTACT
Park Manager phone: 406-454-5840

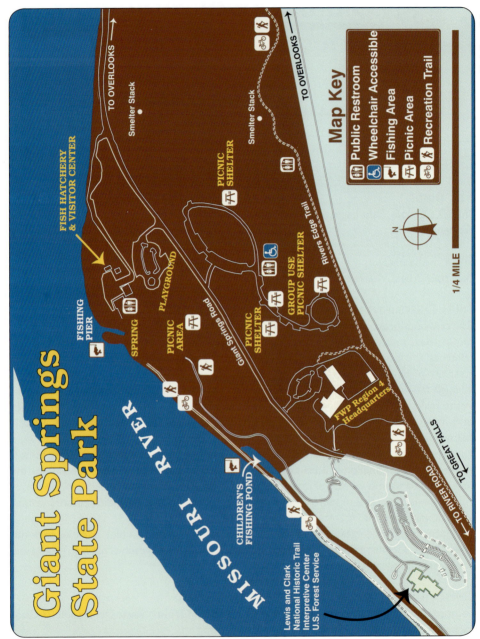

CENTRAL MONTANA
#40 Benton Lake
National Wildlife Refuge

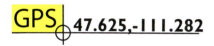

GPS 47.625,-111.282

NORTH OF GREAT FALLS

KEY BIRDS
Chestnut-collared Longspur, Franklin's Gull, Black-necked Stilt, White-faced Ibis, Great Horned Owl, Sharp-tailed Grouse, Eared Grebe

BEST SEASONS
Year around; but the best viewing is from mid-March through October; winter access can be difficult.

AREA DESCRIPTION
Lake, native shortgrass prairie, and seasonal wetlands with shelter belts

The lake is a major stopover and staging site for migrating waterfowl and shorebirds. Waterfowl, shorebirds, wading birds, upland gamebirds, songbirds, and raptors nest here. The 12,000-acre refuge supports several species of conservation concern such as Chestnut-collared Longspur, Black-necked Stilt, White-faced Ibis, and Franklin's Gull.

To date, about 240 species have been observed, including several rarely seen in the state.

Thousands of Snow

Eared Grebe

and Ross's Geese and Tundra Swans show up during migration. Marbled Godwit, Greater and Lesser Yellowlegs, as well as Long-Billed Dowitcher and Long-billed Curlew nest here. In all about 150,000 ducks, 25,000 geese, 5,000 swans, and as many as 50,000 shorebirds use the refuge annually. On average about 20,000 ducks and several thousand pairs of Franklin's Gulls are fledged here.

Animal species abound — mule and white-tailed deer, pronghorn, coyote, badger, porcupine, muskrat, and mink are common.

There is an Auto Tour Route open seasonally. Contact HQ to reserve the sharp-tailed grouse (lek) viewing blind and/or to procure a bird check-off list. No camping. Hunting is allowed with restrictions.

DIRECTIONS
Follow US 87 north about 10 miles and turn left (north) on Bootlegger Trail (signed) to the refuge.

CONTACT
Benton Lake National Wildlife Refuge phone: 406-727-7400

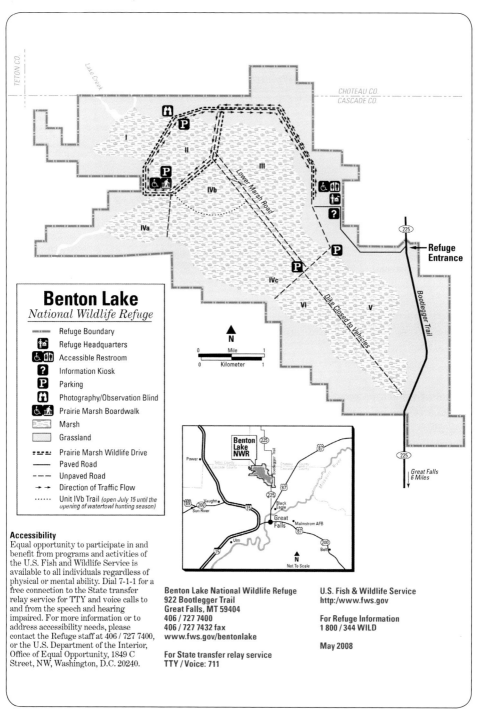

Benton Lake
National Wildlife Refuge

- ▰▰ Refuge Boundary
- 🏠 Refuge Headquarters
- ♿ Accessible Restroom
- ❓ Information Kiosk
- 🅿 Parking
- 📷 Photography/Observation Blind
- ♿ Prairie Marsh Boardwalk
- Marsh
- Grassland
- ▪▪▪ Prairie Marsh Wildlife Drive
- ── Paved Road
- ─ ─ Unpaved Road
- →-→ Direction of Traffic Flow
- ····· Unit IVb Trail *(open July 15 until the opening of waterfowl hunting season)*

Refuge Entrance

Great Falls
6 Miles

Accessibility
Equal opportunity to participate in and benefit from programs and activities of the U.S. Fish and Wildlife Service is available to all individuals regardless of physical or mental ability. Dial 7-1-1 for a free connection to the State transfer relay service for TTY and voice calls to and from the speech and hearing impaired. For more information or to address accessibility needs, please contact the Refuge staff at 406 / 727 7400, or the U.S. Department of the Interior, Office of Equal Opportunity, 1849 C Street, NW, Washington, D.C. 20240.

Benton Lake National Wildlife Refuge
922 Bootlegger Trail
Great Falls, MT 59404
406 / 727 7400
406 / 727 7432 fax
www.fws.gov/bentonlake

For State transfer relay service
TTY / Voice: 711

U.S. Fish & Wildlife Service
http:/www.fws.gov

For Refuge Information
1 800 / 344 WILD

May 2008

CENTRAL MONTANA

#41 Hartelius Waterfowl Production Area

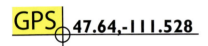

GPS 47.64,-111.528

NORTH OF VAUGHN

KEY BIRDS
Mallard, teal, Canada Goose, Northern Harrier, Long-billed Curlew, Sandhill Crane, Chipping Sparrow

BEST SEASONS
Spring through fall, with restrictions

AREA DESCRIPTION
Grass, wetlands, and marsh lands

Typical of waterfowl production areas, the habitat is maintained to maximize waterfowl production, but of course benefits all sorts of birds. Chipping, Vesper, and Savannah Sparrows, McCown's Longspur, Sprague's Pipit, Western Meadowlark, Golden Eagle, Short-eared Owl, and American Kestrel are common.

Hunting is allowed with restrictions; contact Benton Lake NWR.

DIRECTIONS
From Vaughn, take Frontage Road north and cross under I-15 onto Neuman School Road north for approximately 5 miles. Turn right/east on Wilson Road to the WPA.

CONTACT
Benton Lake NWR phone: 406-727-7400

Chipping Sparrow (im)

CENTRAL MONTANA
#42 First Peoples Buffalo Jump State Park

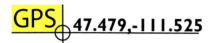

GPS 47.479,-111.525

ULM, SOUTH OF GREAT FALLS

KEY BIRDS
Rock Wren, Burrowing Owl, Say's Phoebe, Long-billed Curlew

BEST SEASONS
Year around; best viewing spring and fall

AREA DESCRIPTION
Sandstone cliffs surrounded by buttes and grasslands

Formerly Ulm Pishkun State Park, the buffalo jump site is a haven for raptors — Ferruginous and Swainson's Hawks, Northern Harrier, Golden Eagle, and Short-eared Owl. Sharp-tailed Grouse and Gray Partridge frequent the grass, as do Vesper and Grasshopper Sparrows. Cliff Swallows nest on the sandstone cliffs and Western Meadowlarks seemingly sing from every perch. Caution: Watch for rattlesnakes.

There is a visitor center and interpretive trail leading up to the top of the butte offering spectacular views in every direction.

DIRECTIONS
From I-15, take the Ulm Exit 270 north and follow signs to the park.

CONTACT
Park Manager phone: 406-866-2217

Used with permission.

CENTRAL MONTANA

#43 Schrammeck Lake Waterfowl Production Area

GPS 47.233,-111.517

SOUTHEAST OF CASCADE

KEY BIRDS
Sandhill Crane, Gray Partridge, Tundra Swan, Blue- and Green-winged Teal, Mallard, Spotted Sandpiper, Killdeer, Marbled Godwit, Northern Harrier

BEST SEASONS
Spring through fall, with restrictions

AREA DESCRIPTION
Shallow lake surrounded by wetlands, grasslands, and agricultural lands

This 400-acre WPA is a great place to view a variety of waterfowl, wading birds, shorebirds, songbirds, and raptors. Best viewing is spring and early summer, and wet years tend to be more productive.

In October, sandhill cranes stage here in ever-growing numbers as departure day nears. With the Big Belt Mountains as backdrop, the scene (and noise) can be quite stunning.

There is no vehicle access and restricted foot travel during the nesting period.

DIRECTIONS
Follow MT 330 for 8 miles east of Cascade and then 1 mile north on a gravel trail. The turn-off is signed.

CONTACT
Benton Lake NWR phone: 406-727-7400

CENTRAL MONTANA
#44 Pelican Point Fishing Access Site

 GPS 47.2,-111.774

BETWEEN HARDY AND CASCADE ON THE MISSOURI RIVER

KEY BIRDS
Gadwall, American Wigeon, Northern Shoveler, Northern Pintail, American White Pelican, Bald Eagle, Osprey, Swainson's Hawk, Double-crested Cormorant, Franklin's and California Gulls, Least and Willow Flycatchers, Tree Swallow

BEST SEASONS
Year around; best variety during spring and fall migrations

AREA DESCRIPTION
River habitat

Montana Audubon lists over 300 species (includes rarely seen and vagrant species) having been observed within the upper Missouri River corridor. For most of us, though, the odds of checking off even half that many during an entire season are long. Still, just about anywhere along the big river is well worthwhile. The many state-owned fishing access sites are good places to start your search.

One of the best ways is to float the river between FAS sites. Birds seem to accept slow-moving, quiet watercraft, making the up-close-and-personal approach a distinct possibility. To get the most out of your float, be sure to glass all levels — on the water, the bushes, the trees, and soaring overhead.

DIRECTIONS
From I-15, take Exit 247 Hardy and follow signs to Pelican Point. The *Fishing Access Field Guide* (fwp.mt.gov/fishing) lists about 300 sites scattered all across the state.

Tree Swallow

Red Rock Lakes National Wildlife Refuge

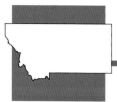

BIRDING TRAILS: MONTANA

SOUTHWEST MONTANA

Southwest Montana is comprised of Beaverhead, Broadwater, Deer Lodge, Granite, Jefferson, Lewis & Clark, Madison, Powell, and Silver Bow Counties. From Red Rock Lakes National Wildlife Refuge in the south and north to Augusta and the Rocky Mountain Front — encompassing numerous mountain ranges, broad valleys including all or part of the Beaverhead, Big Hole, Clark Fork, Jefferson, Red Rock, Ruby, and Missouri River drainages — the region is truly a birder's paradise.

The Blackfoot Valley Important Bird Area (Ovando) lists over 300 bird species observed, and as many as 1,400 nesting pairs of Brewer's Sparrow. The Beaverhead Sage-Steppe IBA (south of Dillon) is home to a thriving Greater Sage Grouse population; about 50 leks have been confirmed within the IBA. Canyon Ferry IBA (Townsend) lists over 60 nesting waterfowl, raptor, and song bird species. Red Rock Lakes NWR (Centennial Valley east of Monida) is one of the most important Trumpeter Swan breeding areas in North America. Peregrine Falcons also nest nearby. Warm Springs WMA (Anaconda), site of the largest Superfund clean-up in North America, boasts over 200 species and counting.

Harrison Reservoir IBA lists 155 species observed while local birders rate it the spot for migrating shorebirds. Madison Valley/Ennis Lake IBA lists over 160 species observed, 14 of which are species of conservation concern. Ennis Lake is a major stopover for migrating loons.

Millions of acres of public land with dozens of private campgrounds make for almost unlimited camping opportunities. Motels, restaurants and cafés abound throughout. Commercial airlines serve Helena, Butte, Bozeman, and Idaho Falls. I-15 and/or I-90 will more or less get you in the ballpark.

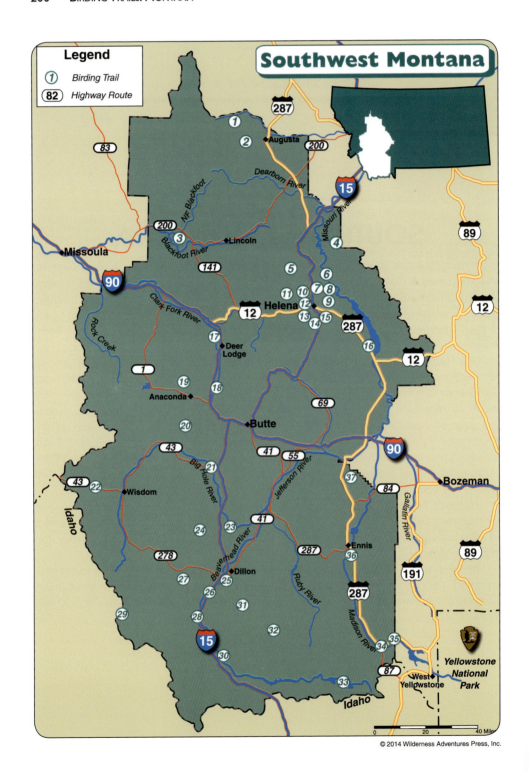

Southwest Montana

Legend

① Birding Trail

82 Highway Route

Missoula

Augusta

Lincoln

Helena

Deer Lodge

Anaconda

Butte

Wisdom

Idaho

Dillon

Ennis

Bozeman

West Yellowstone

Yellowstone National Park

NF Blackfoot

Dearborn River

Missouri River

Blackfoot River

Clark Fork River

Rock Creek

Big Hole River

Beaverhead River

Jefferson River

Ruby River

Madison River

Gallatin River

Idaho

0   20   40 Miles

© 2014 Wilderness Adventures Press, Inc.

Southwest Montana Locations

1. Sun River Wildlife Management Area
2. Sun River Backcountry Loop
3. Blackfoot Valley Important Bird Area
4. Beartooth Wildlife Management Area
5. Little Prickly Pear Creek
6. Lake Helena Causeway
7. Lake Helena Wildlife Management Area
8. Lake Helena Drive /Merritt Lane
9. Helena Valley Regulating Reservoir
10. Floweree Drive /Sierra Road/McHugh Road
11. Lower Skelly Gulch
12. Fairgrounds/Spring Meadow State Park
13. Mount Helena City Park
14. Grizzly Gulch /Orofino Gulch
15. James P. Sunderland Park
16. Canyon Ferry Wildlife Management Area, IBA
17. Grant Kohrs Ranch /Arrow Stone Park
18. Warm Springs Wildlife Management Area
19. Lost Creek State Park
20. Mount Haggin Wildlife Management Area
21. Big Hole River
22. Big Hole Battlefield
23. Burma Road
24. Birch Creek/Thief Creek/French Creek Loop
25. Poindexter Slough Fishing Access Site
26. Beaverhead River
27. Bannack State Park
28. Clark Canyon Reservoir
29. Lemhi Pass
30. Beaverhead Sage-Steppe IBA
31. Blacktail Road
32. Robb-Ledford /Blacktail Wildlife Management Areas
33. Red Rock Lakes National Wildlife Refuge
34. Raynolds Pass Bridge
35. Earthquake Lake Boat Launch
36. Madison Valley IBA
37. Willow Creek Reservoir

SOUTHWEST MONTANA

Sun River Wildlife Management Area

#1

GPS 47.35,-112.40

NORTHWEST OF AUGUSTA

KEY BIRDS
Golden Eagle, Barn Swallow, Calliope Hummingbird, Lazuli Bunting, Sprague's Pipit, Northern Harrier, Brewer's Sparrow, Western Bluebird

BEST SEASONS
Open May 1-December1; winter game range closed to all visitations otherwise.

AREA DESCRIPTION
Grasslands with potholes and riparian habitat

This 20,000-acre WMA is situated amidst one of the state's most spectacular and wildlife rich landscapes; the scenery alone is reason enough for us. The main road — pretty decent except in wet weather — passes through open, rolling grasslands, past potholes and stock ponds, and aspen and willow-lined creeks. There have been 190 species of birds sighted here. Raptors — American Kestrel, Golden Eagle, Ferruginous and Rough-legged (winter) Hawks — Long-billed Curlew, Black-billed Magpie, American Crow, Eastern and Western Kingbirds, and Mountain Bluebird are common. From May on, you can drive well into most corners of the WMA; again, in normal weather the road is pretty good but some of the side roads will test your fillings. As you gain elevation, grasslands give way to grass, rocks, and trees.

Western Bluebird

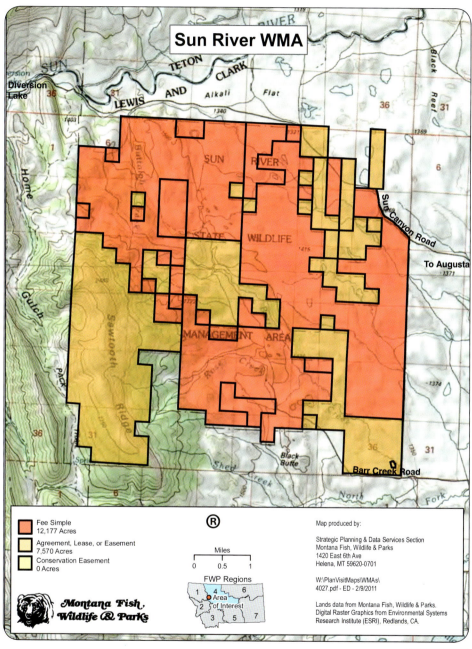

Used with permission.

Intent on witnessing the annual opening day (May 1) circus — better known as "Horn Hunting" — we arrived just in time to watch the plundering mob crash the open gate. As advertised, we found the event lively and entertaining as all get out but...Gale soon lost interest and went off looking for birds. In due time she returned bearing a list; one certainly wouldn't raise an expert's eyebrows but still...Considering the late start, spur of the moment and all, the tally doesn't seem all that shabby, either: Common Yellowthroat, Sprague's Pipit, Pacific Wren, Northern Harrier, Lazuli Bunting, Calliope Hummingbird, Mountain Plover, Bald and Golden Eagles, Mallard, Turkey Vulture, Common Nighthawk, Tree and Barn Swallows, Black-capped Chickadee, Northern Flicker, White-breasted Nuthatch, Red-naped Sapsucker, Mountain Bluebird, Brewer's and Red-winged Blackbirds, Red-tailed Hawk, Brown-headed Cowbird, and American Goldfinch. Meanwhile, considering I failed to find even one shed, damn how I wished I'd gone a birding.

Other activities include: Hiking about in good country, biking, picnicking, camping (with restrictions), fishing, hunting, wildflower viewing, photography, and scenic viewing. Elk, mule and white-tailed deer, occasional bighorn sheep, black and even grizzly bear share the space.

DIRECTIONS
From Augusta, take the Sun Canyon Road about 3 miles. Take the left fork, approximately 5 miles to the southeast corner of the WMA.

CONTACT
Brent Lonner, WMA, phone: 406-467-2488

SOUTHWEST MONTANA
#2 Sun River Backcountry Loop

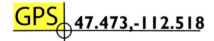

GPS 47.473,-112.518

AUGUSTA

KEY BIRDS
Black-billed Magpie, Bobolink, Mountain Bluebird, American Coot, Golden Eagle, Gadwall

BEST SEASONS
May to October; gates beyond Willow/Beaver Divide to Sun Canyon closed during big game season — late October to the Sunday following Thanksgiving

AREA DESCRIPTION
Varied terrain, from lakeside to open meadows to forests

Starting in Augusta, drive south on the main drag to the edge of town and turn right at the Nilan Lake FAS sign (Benchmark Road) and watch for the usual open country raptors and songbirds until you reach Nilan Lake. Stop there and set up your spotting scope to view the shorebirds and waterfowl — Canada Goose, Coot, Mallard, Wigeon, Gadwall, teal, and Goldeneye are common. In the surrounding marsh and grass we've seen Gray Partridge, Black-billed Magpie, Golden Eagle and Northern Harrier, Upland Sandpiper, Lesser and Greater Yellowlegs, Lazuli Bunting, and Western Meadowlark.

Soon you will pass between several potholes and associated marshland. Be sure to check these out carefully, as often there are more species here than at the lake. Eventually you will come to a fork in the road. The left fork takes you into the mountains, scenic and spectacular in every way, past Wood Lake (another must stop) and then onto, surprise, surprise...for now you've literally reached the proverbial middle of nowhere...of all things an airstrip...a real live, still in use, paved airstrip (Benchmark)...how cool is that?

Just beyond the airstrip the road ends at the South Fork Sun River — a major route into the Bob Marshall Wilderness, by the way. But since this is a bird trip, the best part is the large opening in otherwise dense woods that attracts a lot of birds. Take a hike around and collect your rewards for putting up with a long, often dusty, always rough side trip; about 40-miles round trip, in case you wondered.

Rewind to the fork in the road (16 miles or so from town).

If completing the loop is your intent, take the right fork (past Boy Scout Camp on left). You should now be on Willow/Beaver Road and bouncing steeply uphill, surrounded by mostly open grass and rock on the right and a birdy looking brush, aspen, and grass meadow with a creek running through it on the left. Stop at the first turnout and take a hike around; or set up the spotting scope and have at the raptors and songbirds that are almost always hanging around.

Featuring scenic shots of the mountains, open meadows and lots of aspens interspersed amongst the conifers and a variety birds — woodpeckers, raptors, and forest-loving songbirds — as well as a very good chance of spotting bighorn sheep. The road eventually tops the divide and is all downhill from there to the Sun River (perhaps 15 miles from the Boy Scout Camp).

You are now on Sun Canyon Road just below Gibson Reservoir Dam. Drive up to the boat launch for more waterfowl, water birds, and songbirds. The canyon is a place to observe Bald and Golden Eagles, Osprey, Black-capped Chickadee, Lewis's Woodpecker, Red-naped Sapsucker, Willow Flycatcher, Mountain Bluebird, Western Tanager, American Dipper, and Belted Kingfisher.

Before exiting the canyon, check out Hannan Gulch on the north side and Norwegian and Home Gulches to the south. All three are great places to observe a variety of raptors and songbirds. By the way, it was near the top of Hannan that we spotted our largest ram ever. Part of a sizeable bachelor group of mature rams, he flat out dwarfed the rest.

Beyond the canyon, the road parallels a small brushy creek, open grasslands, several potholes, Willow Creek Reservoir (WMA) and the Sun River WMA most of the way back to Augusta.

Note to the uninitiated: The Rocky Mountain Front is one of the windiest spots in Montana. For example, camped beside Willow Creek Reservoir, suddenly the wind revved from gentle breeze to all out fury. Fearing we'd end up in the lake, at O' Dark Thirty, we chickened, loaded the dogs and headed for town, whereupon for the rest of the night and most of the day, we traded between huddling in the truck and drinking coffee in the local café. When at last the wind died to a dull roar, we headed back to camp, fully expecting to find our little camp trailer in the drink. Lucky us, instead we found it hung on a rock, a mere two yards or so short of drowning.

CONTACT
Augusta Ranger Station phone: 406-562-3247

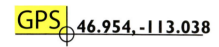

SOUTHWEST MONTANA

#3 Blackfoot Valley (IBA)

GPS 46.954, -113.038

SOUTHEAST OF OVANDO

KEY BIRDS

300+ bird species have been observed; including some 1,400 pairs of Brewer's Sparrow that are thought to nest within the IBA; Bobolink, Ruddy Duck, Long-billed Curlew and Black Tern also nest here.

BEST SEASONS

April-July for nesting waterfowl; June for nesting songbirds; August for shorebirds; spring and fall migration provide best waterfowl viewing

AREA DESCRIPTION

Wetlands, grasslands, agricultural lands, forest, and riparian areas

Encompassing the Blackfoot and Aunt Molly Waterfowl Production Areas, Brown's Lake, Kleinschmidt Lake, and the Blackfoot River, the IBA is a diverse prairie pothole landscape which includes wetlands, intermountain grasslands, sagebrush, agricultural land, riparian aspen and cottonwood bottoms, and dry Ponderosa pine forest. While much of the land is private, decent gravel roads provide ample birding opportunities. A spotting

Ruddy Duck (drake)

Blackfoot Valley IBA

Montana
IMPORTANT BIRD AREAS (IBA) PROGRAM

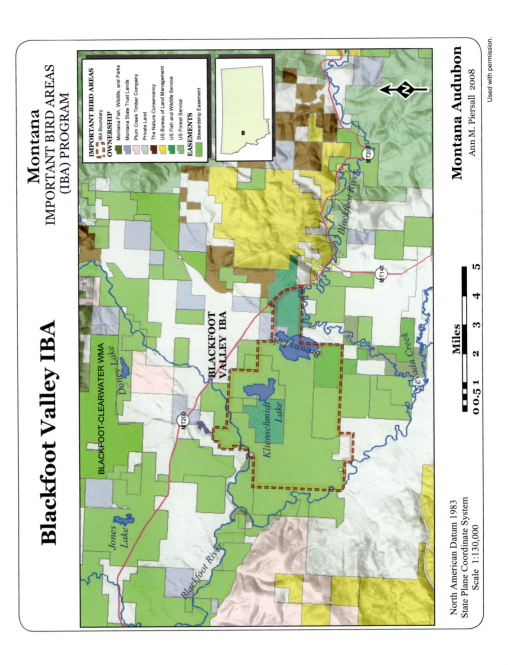

IMPORTANT BIRD AREAS
IBA Boundary
OWNERSHIP
Montana Fish, Wildlife, and Parks
Montana State Trust Lands
Plum Creek Timber Company
Private Land
The Nature Conservancy
US Bureau of Land Management
US Fish and Wildlife Service
US Forest Service
EASEMENTS
Stewardship Easement

BLACKFOOT-CLEARWATER WMA

BLACKFOOT VALLEY IBA

Jones Lake

Doney Lake

Klienschmidt Lake

Browns Lake

Nevada Creek

Blackfoot River

Montana Audubon
Ann M. Piersall 2008

North American Datum 1983
State Plane Coordinate System
Scale 1:130,000

Miles
0 0.5 1 2 3 4 5

scope is helpful. Hot tip: More often than not, a courteous request to one of the area's many friendly landowners works like a charm.

You can access the IBA from Ovando; follow the signs to Brown's Lake. The road crosses the North Fork Blackfoot, a good place to stop and glass the trees and brush for Warbling Vireo, Willow and Least Flycatchers, Kingbirds, Williamson's and Red-naped Sapsuckers, and Bullock's Oriole.

Beyond the bridge, stop and scan the grass and sage for Brewer's and Clay-colored Sparrows, Sandhill Crane, Bobolink, Long-billed Curlew, American Kestrel, Northern Harrier, Red-tailed Hawk and Prairie Falcon.

Soon you will come to an intersection. Stop and glass the pothole on the right before bearing left, which will take you to Brown's Lake. Barrow's Goldeneye, American Coot, Black Tern, Bonaparte's Gull, Common Loon, Red-necked, Eared and Western Grebes, Snow and Ross's Geese, Sora, Bald Eagle, and Osprey are just some of the birds that are common around the lake.

Continue around the lake until you come to the last water before the road turns hard right. This is the best spot on the lake to view waterfowl and water birds. From there it is just a couple miles to the highway (MT 200, 10 miles east of Ovando). On the way out, keep an eye peeled in the trees and brush, a good spot for warblers and other brush-loving songbirds. Also, the pothole on the right almost always holds a surprise or two.

Interesting to note, the highway was once a major Indian trail: "the road to the buffalo" first used by the Kootenai and later the Salish and Pend d' Oreilles. Meriwether Lewis on his return from the Pacific was the first white explorer, camping on July 6, 1806 at the present site of Ovando. He labeled the area "prairie of the knobs", mounds created during the last Ice Age. Ovando, founded in the 1870s, is named for Ovando Hoyt. Descendants of the early settlers remain in the area even today. The McNally brand "MN" is among the original brands registered in Montana. Ranching, lumber, and tourism are the mainstays of the economy.

Brown's Lake Fishing Access Site provides vault toilets, picnic tables, and fire rings; dispersed camping is allowed on the south shore. The lake is a popular and productive rainbow trout fishery.

Gas and limited amenities can be found in Ovando, at Clearwater Crossing on MT 200, and 14 miles north on MT 83 in Seeley Lake.

DIRECTIONS
East of Ovando, west of Lincoln on MT 200, follow the signs.

CONTACT
Montana Audubon Society - Amy Cilimburg, Director of Conservation and Climate Policy
Phone: 406-465-1141
Email: amy@mtaudubon.org

SOUTHWEST MONTANA

#4 Beartooth Wildlife Management Area

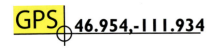

GPS 46.954,-111.934

EAST OF WOLF CREEK

KEY BIRDS
Lazuli Bunting, Western Screech Owl, Baird's Sparrow, Sprague's Pipit

BEST SEASONS
May 15 through September (WMA is closed to visitation December 1-May 15); June is prime time for nesting songbirds

AREA DESCRIPTION
A mosaic of burned and unburned intermountain grasslands, riparian tree and shrub habitats, and ponderosa pine-Douglas Fir forest

Designated roads and trails provide motorized access to this 32,000-acre WMA, though most are poorly maintained or not at all. In the open grasslands, woodlands, and shrub edges look for Turkey Vulture, Northern Pygmy-owl, American Kestrel, Northern Harrier, Red-tailed Hawk, Western Meadowlark, Common Poorwill, Sandhill Crane, Black-billed Magpie, Western and Mountain Bluebirds, Lazuli Bunting, Townsend's Solitaire, Veery, Sprague's Pipit, McCown's Longspur, Western Tanager, Lark, Baird's, White-crowned, and Clay-colored Sparrows, Olive-sided, Hammond's, Dusky, and Cordilleran Flycatchers. Lewis's, Hairy, Downy, and Pileated Woodpeckers, MacGillivray's Warbler, Red-naped and Williamson's Sapsuckers, Great Horned and Western Screech Owls, Gray Jay, and Red-eyed Vireo frequent the burned and unburned timber, while osprey, bald eagle, and a variety of waterfowl are common sights on Holter Lake.

Almost anywhere in the area, along the river, and especially Prickly Pear Creek, hold the potential for good birding.

Other activities include hiking, picnicking, horse-back riding, mountain biking, camping, fishing, hunting (big and small game) and photography.

Wolf Creek provides gas, food, and lodging. Frenchy's Motel is rustic, but clean and friendly. There are developed campgrounds at Holter Lake, while Helena and Great Falls offer everything a traveler needs. Izaack's in nearby Craig, and Prewett Creek Inn a little farther downstream boast top-notch meals, and good service in a friendly atmosphere.

DIRECTIONS

Drive 36 miles north from Helena on I-15 to Wolf Creek (Exit 226). Turn left on the frontage road and, across the bridge, turn right on Beartooth Road for 6 miles.

CONTACT

Cory Loecker, WMA phone: 406-454-5864

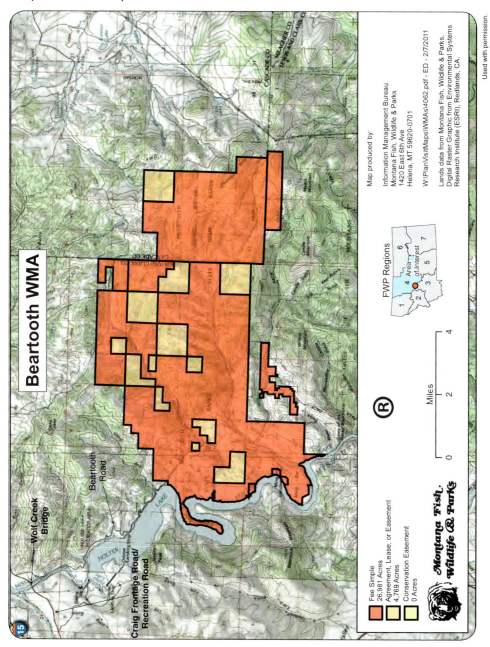

SOUTHWEST MONTANA
Little Prickly Pear Creek

#5

GPS 46.803,-112.196

NORTHWEST OF HELENA

KEY BIRDS
Long-billed Curlew, Willow Flycatcher, Lazuli Bunting, Brewer's Sparrow, Eurasian Collared-dove

BEST SEASONS
Year round, conditions permitting

AREA DESCRIPTION
Mix of wetlands and grasslands

Look for Wilson's Snipe, Common Yellowthroat, Willow Flycatcher, and Bobolink in the grass and wetlands. Also expect to see Gray Catbird, Warbling Vireo, Veery, American Redstart, Black-headed Grosbeak, and a variety of swallows along the way. The road south to Silver City is mostly sagebrush and grass that is attractive to birds such as Northern Harrier, Sage Thrasher, Vesper Sparrow, and Western Meadowlark.

DIRECTIONS
From I-15 north of Helena, Exit Lincoln Road (MT 453, which becomes MT 279), head west about 12 miles and then turn east on Duffy Lane to Chevallier Drive. Here you can turn north to Sieben Ranch and I-15, or south to Silver City.

CONTACT
Last Chance Audubon Society phone: 406-449-1729

Eurasian Collared-dove

SOUTHWEST MONTANA

#6 Causeway (Lake Helena to Hauser Lake)

 **GPS** 46.766,-111.886

NORTHEAST OF HELENA

KEY BIRDS
Bald Eagle, grebes, Common Loon, Common Goldeneye, Yellow-headed Blackbird

BEST SEASONS
Year round; spring and fall migration provides best variety; in winter, waterfowl congregate on open water in the causeway and the river below the dam, both of which never freeze.

AREA DESCRIPTION
Lake and river habitat surrounded by uplands

The causeway, lake, and river attract large numbers of waterfowl and water birds during migration and in winter. Forest and grassland birds nest in ponderosa pine savannah uplands along the way. Bald Eagles and a variety of raptors are common. Be sure to check out the hiking trails at Black Sandy State Park (406-495-3270) and across the dam along the river.

Nearest gas is west of I-15 on Lincoln Road. Helena has everything a traveler needs.

Interesting to note, the Last Chance Audubon Society provides several birding trips throughout the Helena area available to members and non-members. Generally the dates are May, June, August and September.

DIRECTIONS
From I-15 north of Helena, turn east on Lincoln Road to Lake Helena. Turn north on Hauser Dam Road and park at the dam. The trail is on the east side of the Missouri River to Beaver Creek.

CONTACT
Last Chance Audubon Society phone: 406-449-1729

SOUTHWEST MONTANA

#7 Lake Helena Wildlife Management Area (IBA)

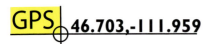 GPS ⊕ 46.703,-111.959

NORTHEAST OF HELENA

KEY BIRDS
170+ species including Long-billed Curlew, Forster's Tern, Franklin's Gull, Bobolink, Bald Eagle and Northern Harrier

BEST SEASONS
Spring and fall migration; year round for raptors and some songbirds

AREA DESCRIPTION
A diverse mix of open-water lake, marshland, riparian cottonwood and willow, native prairie and agriculture

The 5,100-acre IBA is the largest parcel of under-developed marsh and riparian habitat in the Helena Valley. At least 11 species of conservation concern nest here — Long-billed Curlew, Willow Flycatcher, American White Pelican, Bald Eagle, Northern Harrier, Forster's Tern, Wilson's Phalarope, Franklin's Gull, Clay-colored Sparrow, Bobolink, and Yellow-headed Blackbird. Huge flocks of waterfowl gather on the lake during migration. The Lake Helena drive is a good place to set up a spotting scope for a bird's eye view. Be sure to pull far enough off the busy road, though. Check out the grass below the road for songbirds and raptors.

DIRECTIONS
From Helena, travel north on Interstate 15 for approximately 9 miles and exit at the Lincoln Road interchange. Turn right onto Lincoln Road east (MT 453) for approximately 2.5 miles, and turn right (south) onto the Lake Helena WMA. Park at the kiosk.

CONTACT
Montana Audubon Society - Amy Cilimburg, Director of Conservation and Climate Policy
Phone: 406-465-1141
Email: amy@mtaudubon.org

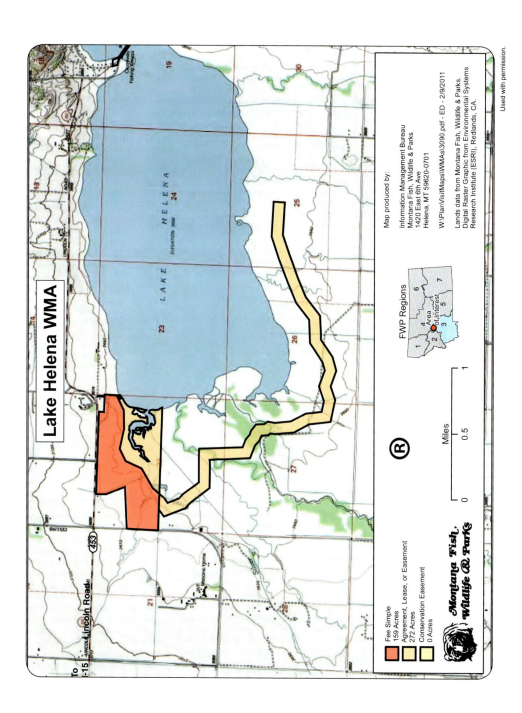

#8 Lake Helena Drive/ Merritt Lane

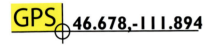

GPS 46.678,-111.894

NORTHEAST OF HELENA

KEY BIRDS
Redhead, Bald Eagle, Sandhill Crane, Marsh Wren, Northern Shoveler

BEST SEASONS
Spring and fall migrations; June for nesting songbirds

AREA DESCRIPTION
Lakeside habitat and marshlands

Lake Helena Drive

In the grass Northern Harriers, Western Meadowlarks, Mountain Bluebirds, and a variety of LBJs are frequently sighted. Once past Merritt Lane and within viewing distance of the lake, pick a spot well off the busy road and set up your spotting scope. Especially during spring and fall migration, waterfowl numbers and variety are sometimes off the charts. Bald Eagles congregate here in March to dine on winter-killed fish and birds.

Merritt Lane

Creek and cattail marsh afford good viewing for Red-winged and Yellow-headed Blackbirds. Mallard and teal are common, as are Great Blue Heron and Black-crowned Night-herons. Sora and Wilson's Snipe frequent the area, but are sometimes difficult to locate.

DIRECTIONS
From Custer Avenue in Helena, take MT 430 east to MT 280 (York Road) and head east. After approximately 6 miles turn north on Lake Helena Drive; Merritt Lane is on your left about 2 miles up. From Townsend, north on US 12/287 to East Helena, turn north on Lake Helena Drive and go approximately 8 miles to the lake.

CONTACT
Last Chance Audubon Society phone: 406-449-1729

Northern Shovelers

SOUTHWEST MONTANA
HELENA AREA

Last Chance Audubon Society provides several birding trips throughout the Helena Area available to members and non-members. Generally the dates are May, June, August, and September.

For information contact: Last Chance Audubon - 406-449-1729

SOUTHWEST MONTANA

#9 Helena Valley Regulating Reservoir

 46.643,-111.881

EAST OF HELENA

KEY BIRDS
Merlin, Forster's Tern, Red-necked Grebe

BEST SEASONS
Ice-out to freeze-up

AREA DESCRIPTION
Water habitat surrounded by grassland

Set up your spotting scope and scan the surrounding grass for sparrows such as Brewer's, Savannah, and Vesper and other grass-loving species such as Western Meadowlark, Sandhill Crane, and Long-billed Curlew. Keep an eye peeled overhead for Bald Eagle, Osprey, Northern Harrier, American Kestrel, Ring-billed and California Gulls, and Caspian Tern. On the lake, expect to see Canada Goose, Eared and Western Grebes, American White Pelican, Double-crested Cormorant, Mallard, Northern Shoveler, American Wigeon, Gadwall, Lesser Scaup, and Ring-necked Duck and Redhead. In August, check the lakeshore for Spotted Sandpiper, Wilson's Phalarope, and American Avocet.

DIRECTIONS
From Custer Avenue in Helena, take MT 430 east to MT 280 (York Road) east approximately 7 miles to the reservoir.

CONTACT
Last Chance Audubon Society phone: 406-449-1729

SOUTHWEST MONTANA

#10 Floweree Drive/Sierra Road /McHugh Drive

GPS 46.655,-112.032

HELENA

KEY BIRDS
Northern Harrier, Bobolink, Western Meadowlark, Swainson's Hawk, Western Tanager, Pinyon Jay

BEST SEASONS
Spring through fall; raptor sightings tend to spike over winter

AREA DESCRIPTION
Roadside habitat with brushy riparian areas

This is a good loop for, say, when you are in town on business and in need of a quick bird fix. Floweree Drive follows Prickly Pear Creek — open field, roadside ditch, and brushy riparian habitats attract a variety songbirds and raptors such as Brewer's Blackbird, Eastern Kingbird, Song and Savannah Sparrows, American Robin, American Crows, Common Raven, and Red-tailed Hawk are common.

The shrubs and trees at Odd Fellows and Forestvale Cemeteries — a sort of oasis in otherwise open country — attract a variety songbirds, woodpeckers, and raptors including Hairy and Downy Woodpeckers, White-breasted Nuthatch, Bullock's Oriole, House Wren, Cedar Waxwing, Pinyon Jay, Black-capped Chickadee, Green-tailed Towhee, American Kestrel, and Great Horned Owl.

Interesting to note, the Last Chance Audubon Society provides several birding trips throughout the Helena Area available to members and non-members. Generally the dates are May, June, August and September.

DIRECTIONS
From Helena east on Custer Avenue, turn north on York Road to Floweree Drive. Turn west (left) on Sierra Road, cross I-15, and turn south (left) on McHugh Drive to the cemeteries.

CONTACT
Last Chance Audubon Society phone: 406-449-1729

Western Tanager

SOUTHWEST MONTANA
Lower Skelly Gulch

#11

GPS 46.657,-112.195

NORTHWEST OF HELENA

KEY BIRDS
Cooper's Hawk, Golden Eagle, Warbling Vireo, Veery, Least Flycatcher, Orange-crowned Warbler

BEST SEASONS
Spring through early fall

AREA DESCRIPTION
Creekside habitat with fir and pine forests and grasslands

Along Skelly and Greenhorn Creeks look for a variety of warblers, flycatchers, Veery, and Mountain Bluebird. Yellow-rumped Warbler, Western Tanager, White-breasted Nuthatch, Hairy and Downy Woodpeckers, and Black-capped Chickadee frequent the Doug fir and ponderosa pine stands. While the uplands and grasslands are a good place to view raptors such as Northern Harrier, American Kestrel, and Swainson's Hawk.

DIRECTIONS
From I-15 north of Helena, Exit Lincoln Road west to Birdseye. Turn south to Austin Road and the gulch.

CONTACT
Last Chance Audubon Society phone: 406-449-1729

SOUTHWEST MONTANA

#12 Fairgrounds/ Spring Meadow State Park/Scratchgravel Hills

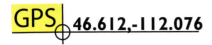

GPS 46.612,-112.076

HELENA

KEY BIRDS
Clay-colored Sparrow, Wilson's Snipe, Sora, Great Blue Heron

BEST SEASONS
Year round; spring and fall migrations for most species

AREA DESCRIPTION
Planned fairground area, spring-fed manmade lake, and low, rocky mountain range

Wood Duck, Mallard, and Canada Goose frequent the fairground pond. The shrub thickets and aspens on the west side of the grounds are a good spot for brush-loving birds such as Clay-colored and Song Sparrows, Wood Warblers, Gray Catbird, and Green-tailed Towhee. Red-winged and Yellow-headed Blackbirds, Marsh Wren, and Black-crowned Night-heron frequent the nearby cattail marsh.

At the state park, follow the trail around the lake to the south and east sides for the best viewing. Summer mornings and evenings are the best times to beat the crowds. The park is a popular stopover for waterfowl and songbirds during migration. Mallard, Wood Duck, Cedar Waxwing, Eastern Kingbird, Red-winged Blackbird, Western Wood-pewee, and Bullock's Oriole are just some of the birds known to nest here. Common Loons are frequently sighted during migration.

The dry, rocky Scratchgravel Hills offer birders the chance to view species not usually seen in the wetter habitats found at the fairgrounds or the park such as Pinyon Jay, Townsend's Solitaire, Horned Lark, and Grasshopper and Lark Sparrows.

Interesting to note, the Last Chance Audubon Society provides several birding trips throughout the Helena area available to members and non-members. Generally the dates are May, June, August and September.

Used with permission.

DIRECTIONS

From US 12 west in Helena, follow signs to Spring Meadow Lake State Park. Just before the park entrance turn north to the fairgrounds (west end of Custer Avenue) or turn northwest on Birdseye Road for several miles and turn north on Echo Drive to the Scratchgravel Hills.

CONTACT

Last Chance Audubon Society phone: 406-449-1729

SOUTHWEST MONTANA

#13 Mount Helena City Park

GPS 46.588,-112.05

HELENA

KEY BIRDS
Vesper Sparrow, Spotted Towhee, Mountain Bluebird, Lazuli Bunting, Mountain Chickadee, Hermit Thrush

BEST SEASONS
Year round; spring and fall migrations for most species; June for nesting songbirds

AREA DESCRIPTION
City park with trails up Mount Helena (5,468 feet)

The 620-acre park has trails that lead up the mountain from the trailhead. In the open grassy areas, look for Western Meadowlark, Mountain Bluebird, Rufous and Calliope Hummingbirds, Green-tailed Towhee, and Chipping Sparrow frequent the brushy areas, while Black-capped Chickadee, Red-breasted and White-breasted Nuthatches, Clark's Nutcracker, Gray and Steller's Jays, Western Tanager, and a variety of warblers inhabit the conifer forest higher up.

DIRECTIONS
From Intersection US 12/I-15, follow US 12 west across town and turn south on Park Avenue to Reeder Village Drive. Follow Reeder Village Drive through the subdivision to the trailhead.

CONTACT
Last Chance Audubon Society phone: 406-449-1729

Mountain Bluebird

SOUTHWEST MONTANA
#14 Grizzly Gulch/Orofino Gulch

GPS 46.578,-112.052

SOUTH OF HELENA

KEY BIRDS
Green-tailed Towhee, Great Horned Owl, Pileated Woodpecker, Rock Wren

BEST SEASONS
Year round; June for nesting songbirds

AREA DESCRIPTION
Brushy willow, choke cherry, cottonwood creek bottoms flanked Douglas fir, ponderosa pine forested hills and dry grasslands

Spotted Towhee, Ruby-crowned Kinglet, Warbling Vireo, Dark-eyed Junco, Yellow-rumped, Yellow and Orange-crowned Warblers, and Calliope and Rufous Hummingbirds inhabit the creek bottoms while Eastern and Western Kingbirds, Mountain Bluebird, Hairy and Downy Woodpeckers, American Kestrel, Northern Pygmy Owl, White-breasted Nuthatch, and Veery are some of the birds to look for in the uplands.

DIRECTIONS
From Highway 12, take Benton Avenue south. Merge left onto Park Avenue after a couple blocks, and follow that to where it forks and becomes either Grizzly Gulch Drive or Orofino Gulch Drive.

CONTACT
Last Chance Audubon Society phone: 406-449-1729

SOUTHWEST MONTANA
#15 James P. Sunderland Park

GPS 46.541,-111.928

SOUTHEAST OF HELENA

KEY BIRDS
American Goldfinch, Yellow-rumped Warbler, Northern Waterthrush, Marsh Wren, Turkey Vulture, Black-billed Magpie

BEST SEASONS
Spring through fall

AREA DESCRIPTION
Established park with riparian trail

Trail (1½ miles) follows Prickly Pear Creek. This is a good spot to hit when time is short. Barn and Tree Swallows, Western Kingbird, Willow Flycatcher, Mountain Bluebird, American Robin, Veery, Gray Catbird, Yellow Warbler, Cedar Waxwing, European Starling, Red-winged Blackbird, Chipping Sparrow, Common Raven, and American Crow are among the more frequent visitors.

The park is free and open year round. Public campgrounds are nearby at Canyon Ferry Campground (Townsend).

DIRECTIONS
From Helena, go south on I-15 and exit at Montana City. Go east on MT 518. From US 12/287 north of Townsend, go north to East Helena and turn west on MT 518. Park is directly across from the Ash Grove Cement Company.

CONTACT
Last Chance Audubon Society phone: 406-449-1729

Black-billed Magpie

SOUTHWEST MONTANA
#16 Canyon Ferry Wildlife Management Area (IBA)

GPS 46.356,-111.535

TOWNSEND

KEY BIRDS
Double-crested Cormorant, Ring-billed Gull, Caspian Tern, Lazuli Bunting, Western Tanager, Bobolink, Bullock's Oriole, Hooded Merganser

BEST SEASONS
Spring and early fall; late summer for shorebirds

AREA DESCRIPTION
Lakeside habitat with grasslands and wetlands

An oasis amid a semi-arid landscape receives annually less than a dozen inches of precipitation. Fed by the Missouri River, the lake forms the centerpiece in a mosaic of agricultural land, upland native prairie, open wetlands, cattail marsh, wooded and herbaceous wetlands, and floodplain forest. Acres of non-native Russian olive provide a nearly limitless source of food and nesting cover for berry- and seed-eating birds.

Four manmade ponds (Pond 4 in the southwest corner, Ponds 1, 2, 3 on the southeast side the lake) are approximately 400 acres each, with over 300 manmade islands that provide nesting habitat for one of only

Hooded Merganser
Credit: U.S. Fish and Wildlife Service

Canyon Ferry Wildlife Management Area

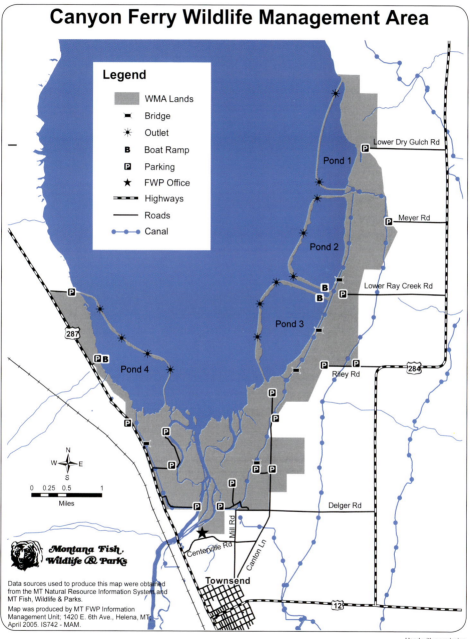

Legend

▨	WMA Lands
⚊	Bridge
✳	Outlet
B	Boat Ramp
P	Parking
★	FWP Office
▱▱▱	Highways
⎯	Roads
•—•	Canal

Lower Dry Gulch Rd

Pond 1

Meyer Rd

Pond 2

Lower Ray Creek Rd

Pond 3

287

284

Riley Rd

Pond 4

N
W   E
S

0   0.25 0.5   1
Miles

Delger Rd

Mill Rd

Canton Ln

Centerville Rd

Montana Fish, Wildlife & Parks

Townsend

12

Data sources used to produce this map were obtained from the MT Natural Resource Information System and MT Fish, Wildlife & Parks.
Map was produced by MT FWP Information Management Unit; 1420 E. 6th Ave., Helena, MT. April 2005. IS742 - MAM.

four nesting colonies of American white pelican in the state. There were 1,800+ nests tallied in 2000. The islands also host large nesting colonies of double-crested cormorants, Ring-Billed gulls, and Caspian Terns.

According to IBA information, an astonishing number of waterfowl, raptors, and songbirds nest here, including American Wigeon, Wood Duck, Canada Goose, Gadwall, Northern Pintail, Horned, Eared and Western Grebes, Gadwall, Redhead, Cinnamon, Green- and Blue-winged Teal, Mallard, Common and Hooded Mergansers, Lesser Scaup, Common Goldeneye, Bufflehead, Lazuli Bunting, Western Meadowlark, Red-winged and Yellow-headed Blackbirds, Bobolink, Bullock's Oriole, Great Horned Owl, Northern Harrier, Osprey, and Sharp-shinned, Cooper's, Swainson's, Ferruginous, and Red-tailed Hawks, as well as Sandhill Crane, American Avocet, Wilson's Snipe, Mourning Dove, Belted Kingfisher, Downy Woodpecker, Red-naped Sapsucker, Northern Flicker, House and Marsh Wrens, Cedar Waxwings, Gray Catbird, Veery, Mountain Bluebird, Western Wood-pewee, Least Flycatcher, Western Kingbird, Tree, Bank, Cliff, Barn and Violet-green Swallows, American Crow, Black-billed Magpie, Raven, American Redstart, Yellow, Yellow-rumped and Common Yellowthroat Warblers and several sparrows.

Directions

West Side: Stay on US 287 north from Townsend. Several access roads (right-hand side) lead to parking areas. All are near water, but three offer good views of Pond 4, the islands, and the lake. Trails lead into the WMA from there. A spotting scope offers the best viewing of the lake and Pond 4. In spring and early summer, ducks and geese with broods in tow are common.

East Side: Turn off US 287 at the stop light in Townsend onto US 12; a couple miles out, turn north on MT 284. Any of several gravel roads to the east will get you into the WMA where trails lead to the ponds and/or the main lake. This has been our best area for checking off the largest number of species, plus it is well off the busy highway (US 287).

Contact
WMA –Tom Carlsen – phone: 406-266-3367

SOUTHWEST MONTANA

#17 Grant Kohrs Ranch/ Arrow Stone Park

GPS 46.421,-112.742

DEER LODGE

KEY BIRDS

About 150 species have been observed, including Horned Lark, Black-capped and Mountain Chickadees, Red-breasted Nuthatch, Bohemian Waxwing (winter), Townsend's Solitaire, American Dipper, Sharp-shinned Hawk

BEST SEASONS

April through October; early morning helps with crowd control.

AREA DESCRIPTION

A diverse mix of hayfields, ponds, wetlands, riparian/stream and short grass prairie

Hike the trails and abandoned railroad bed. The 2010 Christmas Bird count listed Canada Goose, Mallard, Green-winged Teal, Common and Barrow's Goldeneyes, Gray Partridge, Bald and Golden Eagles, Northern Harrier, Sharp-shinned and Rough-legged (winter)

Sharp-shinned Hawk

Hawks, Northern Goshawk, Prairie Falcon, Rock Pigeon, Eurasian Collared-dove, Belted Kingfisher, Downy and Hairy Woodpeckers, Northern Flicker, Northern Shrike (winter), Gray Jay, Clark's Nutcracker, Black-billed Magpie, Common Raven, Horned Lark, Black-capped and Mountain Chickadees, Red-breasted Nuthatch, American Dipper, Townsend's Solitaire, European Starling, Bohemian and Cedar Waxwings, American Tree and Song Sparrows, Dark-eyed Junco, Lapland Longspur, Snow Bunting, Red-winged Blackbird, and House Finch.

Across town, Arrow Stone Park, beside the Clark Fork River is a mix of shrubs — willow, chokecherry, wild rose and water birch, and ponds and wetlands — horsetail, rush, bulrush, and sedge — and non-native grass.

Trails lead to the best birding sites, where you might find Wood Duck, Great Blue Heron, Osprey, Virginia Rail, Sora, Sandhill Crane, Spotted Sandpiper, Long-billed Curlew, Wilson's Snipe, Red-naped Sapsucker, Western Wood-pewee, Willow and Least Flycatchers, Western and Eastern Kingbirds, Gray Catbird, Yellow Warbler, Northern Waterthrush, Common Yellowthroat, Vesper and Savannah Sparrows, Black-headed Grosbeak, Bobolink, Red-winged and Yellow-headed Blackbirds, and Bullock's Oriole.

Interesting to note, Deer Lodge is Montana's oldest registered town. Both Grant Kohrs and the nearby Old Prison are listed in the National Historic Register.

Deer Lodge offers travelers all the amenities.

DIRECTIONS

Grant Kohrs Ranch

Exit I-90 at Exit 184 (Deer Lodge) and follow the signs one-half mile to the ranch.

Stone Arrow Park

Exit I-90 at Exit 187 (Deer Lodge) and turn north on Frontage Road for one-half mile to park.

CONTACT
Grant Kohrs Ranch
266 Warren Lane- Deer Lodge, MT 59722 – phone: 406-846-2070
Arrow Stone Park phone: 406-846-2094

SOUTHWEST MONTANA

#18 Warm Springs Wildlife Management Area/ Anaconda Settling Ponds

GPS 46.179,-112.783

EAST OF DEER LODGE/WEST OF BUTTE

KEY BIRDS

200+ species including Pied-billed Grebe, Long-tailed Duck, Clark's Grebe, American Golden Plover, Red-necked Phalarope, Long-billed Dowitcher, Lesser Yellowlegs, and White-fronted Goose

BEST SEASONS

April through October; spring and fall migrations for waterfowl; August for shorebirds; June for songbirds

AREA DESCRIPTION

Manmade settling ponds surrounded by mudflats, wetlands, grasslands shrub riparian habitat

The ponds were originally constructed by Anaconda Copper to treat mine waste from the Butte Mining District. The first pond was built in 1911; the second in 1916; the third in the late 1950s. Mining in the area resulted in

White-fronted Goose
Credit: U.S. Fish and Wildlife Service

the largest Superfund Site in North America, the massive cleanup of which ARCO is today responsible. Montana Fish, Wildlife and Parks manages the WMA. The entire area encompasses about 6,200 acres.

Collectively labeled "wildlife ponds" the complex comprises 21 ponds…six settling (Arco) ponds, four Jobs Corp ponds, eight Ducks Unlimited ponds, and three sewage lagoons, as well as associated wetlands, sagebrush/grassland uplands, and cottonwood/willow/shrub riparian habitat. Mill, Willow, and Warm Springs Creeks and the Clark Fork River flow through the site. Interesting to note – Gary Swant, a local birder, has documented 213 species at WS WMA.

Walking the dikes of the ARCO ponds and setting up a spotting scope during migration should reveal a good portion of the following: Canada Goose, Tundra Swan, Redhead, Canvasback, Ring-necked Duck, Mallard, American Wigeon, Blue- and Green-winged Teal, Gadwall, Ruddy Duck, Barrow's and Common Goldeneye, Northern Shoveler, Northern Pintail, Bufflehead, Lesser Scaup (Bluebill), and American Coot.

Extensive mudflats attract large numbers of shorebirds. Dave Dziack of the Warm Springs WMA comments, "Typically 20+ species stage here in late summer, including Killdeer, Black-bellied, American Golden and Semipalmated Plover, American Avocet, Wilson's and Red-necked Phalarope, Wilson's Snipe, Long-billed Dowitcher, Long-billed Curlew, Spotted, Baird's, Pectoral, Solitary, Least and Stilt Sandpiper, Greater and Lesser Yellowlegs."

Osprey, Northern Harrier, Sandhill Crane, Bonaparte's and Ring-billed Gulls, Mourning Dove, Common Nighthawk, Northern Flicker, Tree, Northern Rough-winged and Cliff Swallows, Black-billed Magpie, American Crow, Marsh Wren, Yellow Warbler, Vesper and Savannah Sparrows, and Red-winged, Yellow-headed and Brewer's Blackbirds occur on most of our lists.

Warm Springs is a popular and productive trout fishery; trout in excess of 10 pounds have been caught (restrictions apply). Camping is allowed; hunting (in season, with restrictions), hiking and biking are popular activities.

DIRECTIONS
West of Butte and East of Deerlodge on I-90, Exit 201 (Warm Springs) and follow the signs on both sides the Interstate.

CONTACT
Warm Springs WMA
Phone: 406-693-7395
Email: ddziak@mt.gov

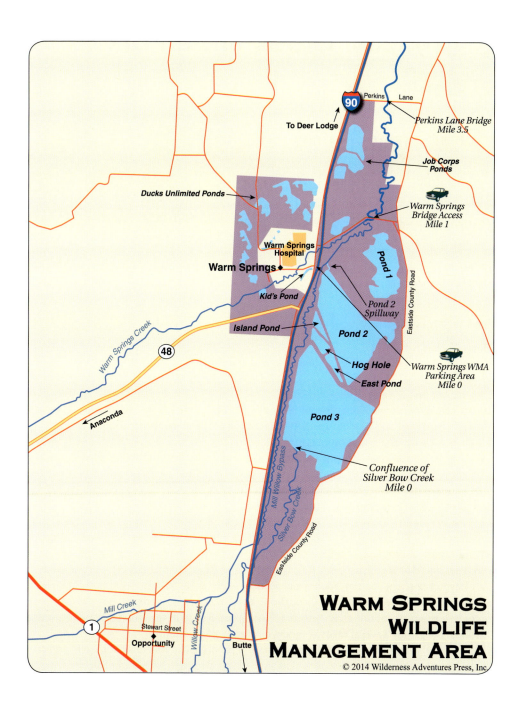

To Deer Lodge

Perkins Lane

Perkins Lane Bridge
Mile 3.5

Job Corps
Ponds

Ducks Unlimited Ponds

Warm Springs
Bridge Access
Mile 1

Warm Springs
Hospital

Warm Springs

Pond 1

Kid's Pond

Eastside County Road

Pond 2
Spillway

Island Pond

Pond 2

Hog Hole

Warm Springs WMA
Parking Area
Mile 0

East Pond

Warm Springs Creek

48

Pond 3

Anaconda

Mill Willow Bypass

Confluence of
Silver Bow Creek
Mile 0

Silver Bow Creek

Eastside County Road

Mill Creek

1

Stewart Street

Willow Creek

Opportunity

Butte

WARM SPRINGS
WILDLIFE
MANAGEMENT AREA

© 2014 Wilderness Adventures Press, Inc.

SOUTHWEST MONTANA
#19 Lost Creek State Park

GPS 46.209, -113.002

Northwest of Anaconda

Key Birds
American Dipper, Dusky Grouse, Golden Eagle, Black-backed Woodpecker, Brown Creeper, Steller's Jay

Best Seasons
April through September

Area Description
Mountain creek and forest with limestone and granite cliffs

Park at the entrance and walk the road through the forest beside Lost Trail Creek. In season Yellow-rumped and Yellow Warblers, Ruby- and Golden-crowned Kinglets, Western Tanagers, and Lincoln's and White-crowned Sparrows move about the greenery. Listen closely for the haunting music of a Hermit Thrush and the distinctive song of the Warbling Vireo. Keep an eye peeled for the Golden Eagles and Red-tailed Hawks soaring high above along the face of the spectacular rock cliffs. Mountain goats and bighorn sheep also frequent the rock escarpments. Winter is the best time to look for Northern Pygmy- and Great Gray Owls and Northern Goshawk.

We've seen Dusky Grouse, Williamson's Sapsucker, American Three-toed Woodpecker, Black-backed Woodpecker, Pileated Woodpecker, Brown Creeper, White-breasted Nuthatch, Steller's Jay and Clark's Nutcracker between the gate and the falls. Pine and Evening Grosbeaks, Red Crossbill, and Pine Siskin also frequent the area.

Beyond the end of the road a paved trail leads to a 50-foot high waterfall. There are interpretive signs scattered throughout that explain the geology. Beyond the park boundary, the trail continues on into the Flint Creek Range in the Beaverhead-Deerlodge National Forest for several miles — good birding in good country.

Summer weekends tend to be noisy so, if possible, plan your visit for early and late in the day and the season. The park season is May 1 through November 30, but you can walk in anytime.

Directions
From I-90 Exit 208, take MT 1 and turn north onto MT 273 for 2 miles, then turn west (sign) 6 miles to park.

CONTACT
Park Manager phone: 406-542-5500

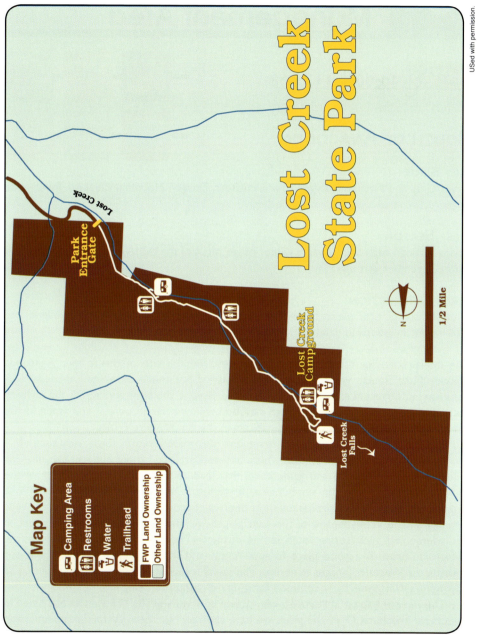

Lost Creek State Park

Lost Creek

Park Entrance Gate

Lost Creek Campground

Lost Creek Falls

N

1/2 Mile

Map Key

- Camping Area
- Restrooms
- Water
- Trailhead
- FWP Land Ownership
- Other Land Ownership

USed with permission.

SOUTHWEST MONTANA
#20 Mount Haggin Wildlife Management Area

GPS ⊕ 46.001, -112.988

SOUTH OF ANACONDA

KEY BIRDS
Great Gray and Northern Pygmy Owls, Western Tanager, Mountain Bluebird, Townsend's Solitaire, Swainson's and Hermit Thrushes

BEST SEASON
Spring through early fall; big game winter range, most of the WMA, is closed to motorized travel December through May 15

AREA DESCRIPTION
Diverse mix of high elevation willow riparian, conifer and aspen forest, wetland and intermountain grassland habitats

The interpretive signs beside the highway describe the site of the former Anaconda Copper Mule Ranch, where mules were pastured for much deserved (needed) R&R between underground stints in the Butte mines. Beyond the signs and across the highway you will discover a diverse mix of high elevation willow riparian, conifer and aspen forest, wetland and intermountain grassland habitats in this 56,000-acre WMA.

Depending on your pleasure, drive the designated roads (high clearance 4X4 recommended) or explore on foot. There are no developed trails, but you can hike for miles on the many cattle and game trails that lead to just about every corner of the WMA and beyond into the surrounding Beaverhead-Deerlodge National Forest. While exploring, keep your eyes peeled for three species of grouse — Dusky, Ruffed, and Spruce (Franklin's). The WMA is one of the best places we know to spot a great gray owl; in late winter and early spring listen for its distinctive deep ten-note hoots. In June, the streamside brush is a good place to spot Yellow and Yellow-rumped Warblers and our favorite, the Western Tanager. American Redstarts frequent the many aspen groves, and Townsend's Warbler is fairly common foraging high atop the Doug firs.

The diverse habitat attracts a wide variety of avian wildlife; 113 species are listed in the official brochure. Over the years we have spotted: Northern Waterthrush, American Dipper, Belted Kingfisher, Eastern Kingbird, Olive-sided and Willow Flycatchers, Yellow,

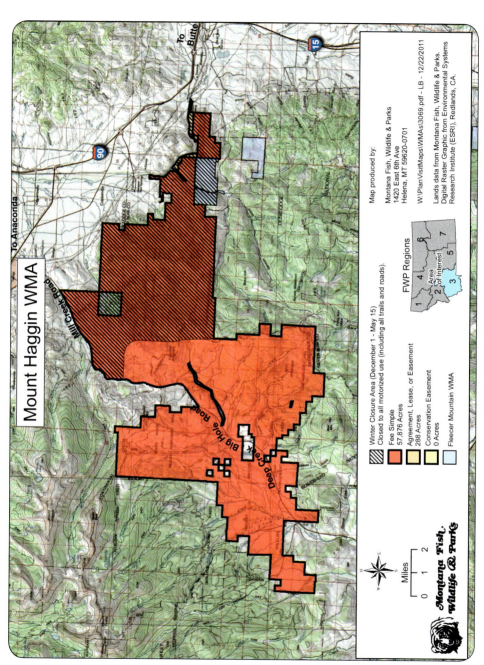

Mount Haggin WMA

Winter Closure Area (December 1 - May 15)
Closed to all motorized use (including all trails and roads).

Fee Simple
57,876 Acres

Agreement, Lease, or Easement
288 Acres

Conservation Easement
0 Acres

Fleecer Mountain WMA

FWP Regions

Map produced by:

Montana Fish, Wildlife & Parks
1420 East 6th Ave
Helena, MT 59620-0701

W:\PlanVisitMaps\WMAs\3069.pdf - LB - 12/22/2011

Lands data from Montana Fish, Wildlife & Parks.
Digital Raster Graphic from Environmental Systems
Research Institute (ESRI), Redlands, CA.

Used with permission.

Common Yellowthroat, Yellow-rumped and Wilson's Warblers, Brewer's Vesper, Savannah and Song Sparrows, Great Horned Owl, Northern Harrier, Lazuli Bunting, Gray and Steller's Jays, Snow Bunting, Red-breasted Nuthatch, Sandhill Crane, Yellow-crowned Kinglet, Clark's Nutcracker, and Ruffed, Dusky, and Spruce Grouse.

With the high peaks of the Pintler Range in the background (Mount Haggin is one) the WMA is both scenic and remote, and boasts an impressive wildlife base which includes moose, elk, mule deer, marten, beaver, mink, coyote, and even the occasional otter. In wet years, the spring and summer wildflower show is spectacular. Hiking, dispersed camping, snow-shoeing, and cross-country skiing are popular activities.

Gas, food, and lodging can be found in Anaconda; limited amenities can be found nearby in Wise River and Wisdom. The Big Hole Crossing in Wisdom is a top-notch eatery, as is the Wise River Club in Wise River. The Hook and Horn in Wisdom serves great coffee and other goodies, as well as a wide variety of trade goods. Check out the Antlers Bar in Wisdom, pizza is "outta this world".

DIRECTIONS
From I-90 Exit 208, take MT I toward Anaconda. Turn left (south) on MT 274 for 10 miles to the WMA. From I-15, Exit 102 south of Butte, take MT 43 approximately 20 miles and turn right (north) on MT 274 for approximately 8 miles to the WMA.

CONTACT
WMA - Vanna Boccadori – phone: 406-494-2082

Northern Pygmy-owl (USFWS photo)

Big Hole River

#21

GPS 45.758,-112.781

SOUTHWEST OF JACKSON TO TWIN BRIDGES

KEY BIRDS
Red-necked Phalarope, Black-crowned Night-heron, Long-eared Owl, Violet-green and Bank Swallows, White-throated Swift, Green-tailed Towhee, Bald Eagle

BEST SEASONS
Spring and fall; June for nesting songbirds

AREA DESCRIPTION
Riparian river habitat with sagebrush and hay meadows

About 175 river miles and born in the Beaverhead Mountains southwest of Jackson (MT 278), the first 15 miles are paralleled by a tooth-rattling Forest Service road through a mix of public and private ranchland. From Jackson north to Wisdom, the river runs through mostly private ranchlands, accessed by several county roads off the highway. The river, bounded by extensive sagebrush, grasslands, willow riparian bottoms, wetlands and hay meadows with scattered aspen and conifer forest, creates the sort of mosaic attractive to all sorts of birds — songbirds, waterfowl, wading birds, raptors, you name it. Stop often and glass your immediate surroundings — you might be surprised at the variety and numbers, especially in spring and fall.

Water, brush, and grass dominate the upper river valley all the way (north) to Wisdom and some days, especially in spring, the number and variety of bird sightings defies description. If you have time, turn left off the highway on any of several roads (often muddy and always rough) and find ducks in the ditches; tree swallows swarming the bridges; and raptors — American Kestrel, Swainson's, and Ferruginous Hawks — Snipe, and kingbirds perching on fence posts. Everywhere you look are Yellow Warblers, Sora, Red-winged and Yellow-headed Blackbirds, Great Blue and Black-crowned Night-herons, Ravens, and Black-billed Magpies. Ospreys, Red-tailed Hawks, and Northern Harriers soar overhead. Coots and Red-necked Phalarope all but cover some of the potholes and, well, by now I'm sure you get the idea.

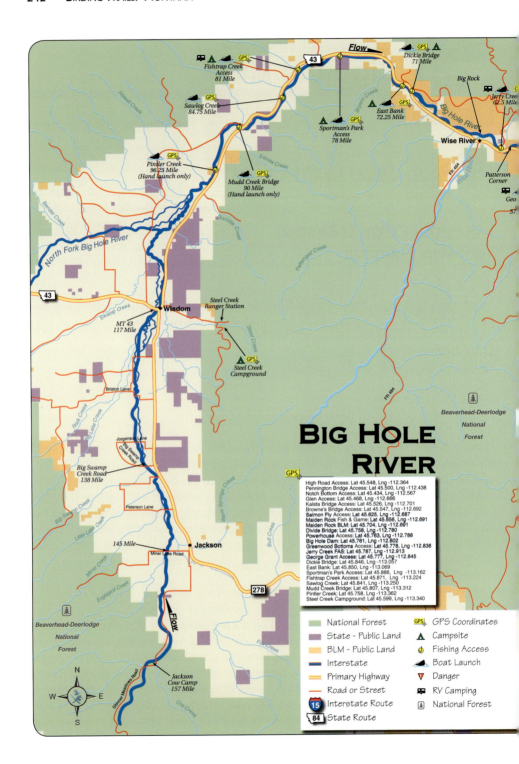

Flow

GPS

Dickie Bridge
71 Mile

Fishtrap Creek
Access
81 Mile

Big Rock

Jerry Cree
62.5 Mile

Sawlog Creek
84.75 Mile

GPS

East Bank
72.25 Mile

Sportman's Park
Access
78 Mile

Wise River

Pintler Creek
96.25 Mile
(Hand launch only)

GPS

Patterson
Corner

Mudd Creek Bridge
90 Mile
(Hand launch only)

GPS

Geo

57

North Fork Big Hole River

Steel Creek
Ranger Station

43

Wisdom

MT 43
117 Mile

Steel Creek
Campground

GPS

Briston Lane

Beaverhead-Deerlodge

National

Forest

Jorgenson Lane

Big Swamp
Creek Road
138 Mile

BIG HOLE
RIVER

GPS

Peterson Lane

145 Mile

Jackson

Miner Lake Road

278

Beaverhead-Deerlodge

National

Forest

Flow

Jackson
Cow Camp
157 Mile

High Road Access: Lat 45.548, Lng -112.364
Pennington Bridge Access: Lat 45.500, Lng -112.438
Notch Bottom Access: Lat 45.434, Lng -112.567
Glen Access: Lat 45.468, Lng -112.666
Kalsta Bridge Access: Lat 45.526, Lng -112.701
Browne's Bridge Access: Lat 45.547, Lng -112.692
Salmon Fly Access: Lat 45.625, Lng -112.687
Maiden Rock Fish & Game: Lat 45.656, Lng -112.691
Maiden Rock BLM: Lat 45.704, Lng -112.691
Divide Bridge: Lat 45.758, Lng -112.780
Powerhouse Access: Lat 45.763, Lng -112.788
Big Hole Dam: Lat 45.761, Lng -112.802
Greenwood Bottoms Access: Lat 45.778, Lng -112.836
Jerry Creek FAS: Lat 45.787, Lng -112.913
George Grant Access: Lat 45.777, Lng -112.845
Dickie Bridge: Lat 45.846, Lng -113.057
East Bank: Lat 45.850, Lng -113.069
Sportman's Park Access: Lat 45.886, Lng -113.162
Fishtrap Creek Access: Lat 45.871, Lng -113.224
Sawlog Creek: Lat 45.841, Lng -113.250
Mudd Creek Bridge: Lat 45.807, Lng -113.312
Pintler Creek: Lat 45.758, Lng -113.362
Steel Creek Campground: Lat 45.599, Lng -113.340

National Forest	GPS	GPS Coordinates
State - Public Land	⛺	Campsite
BLM - Public Land		Fishing Access
Interstate		Boat Launch
Primary Highway	▽	Danger
Road or Street		RV Camping
15 Interstate Route	🏕	National Forest
84 State Route		

N
W ⊕ E
S

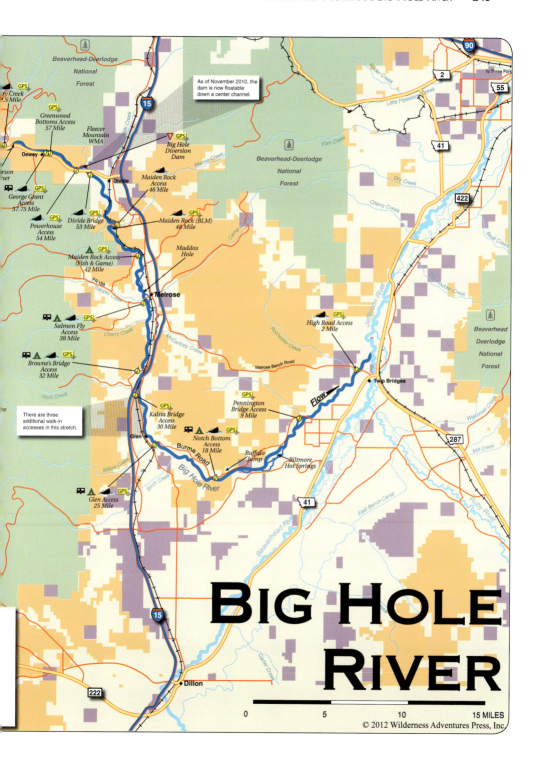

As of November 2010, the dam is now floatable down a center channel.

Beaverhead-Deerlodge
National
Forest

15

Greenwood
Bottoms Access
57 Mile

Dry Creek
.5 Mile

Fleecer
Mountain
WMA

GPS

Big Hole
Diversion
Dam

Dewey

Maiden Rock
Access
46 Mile

Divide

son
ner

George Grant
Access
57.75 Mile

Maiden Rock (BLM)
48 Mile

GPS

Divide Bridge
53 Mile

GPS

Powerhouse
Access
54 Mile

Maddox
Hole

GPS

Maiden Rock Access
(Fish & Game)
42 Mile

FR 188

Melrose

GPS

Salmon Fly
Access
38 Mile

GPS

Browne's Bridge
Access
32 Mile

Rock Creek

There are three
additional walk-in
accesses in this stretch.

GPS

Kalsta Bridge
Access
30 Mile

Glen

Burma Road

GPS

Notch Bottom
Access
18 Mile

Buffalo
Jump

GPS

Glen Access
25 Mile

Big Hole River

GPS

Pennington
Bridge Access
9 Mile

Flow

GPS

High Road Access
2 Mile

Twin Bridges

Beaverhead-Deerlodge
National
Forest

Beaverhead

Deerlodge

National

Forest

Jefferson River

Biltmore
Hot Springs

287

Willow Creek

Birch Creek

15

222

Dillon

Beaverhead River

41

East Bench Canal

BIG HOLE
RIVER

0   5   10   15 MILES

© 2012 Wilderness Adventures Press, Inc

Below Wisdom (MT 43) things start to dry out a bit — wet hay meadows giving way to more arid sagebrush and lodgepole pine-covered foothills; less water, fewer birds, but still well worth a shot. Then a few miles above Wise River the river turns abruptly southeast, changes character yet again as it runs more quickly, and drops through a series of rocky canyons to Divide where, once again, it changes directions, turning south through more canyons and eventually cottonwood-lined banks to Glen (MT 91). There it turns east (more or less paralleling Burma Road) through one of the more arid areas in the state to eventually merge with the Beaverhead River near Twin Bridges.

Access to the canyon stretches is limited to just a few roads unless, of course, you launch a boat at one of the fishing access sites. Dry, rocky, sagebrush-covered for the most part, the canyons support far fewer species than up above, but there is plenty to look for: White-throated Swifts, Flycatchers, Osprey, Golden and Bald Eagles, Red-tailed Hawks, Belted Kingfisher, Common Merganser and Mallard, Violet-green Swallow, Red-naped Sapsucker, and Lewis's Woodpecker.

Each spring, the Big Hole River Foundation members participate in a 12-hour outing — Birding the Big Hole (see contact info below to participate). At each outing, the check-off exceeds 70 species, including American Crow, Bald Eagle, Swallows, Black-capped Chickadee, Black-headed Grosbeak, Bullock's Oriole, sparrows, finches, warblers, ducks, geese, Great Blue Heron, Sora, kinglets, Green-tailed Towhee, White-throated Swift, American Dipper, Western Meadowlark, Sandhill Crane, Red-naped Sapsucker, bluebirds, flycatchers, and on and on.

Productive spots include Salmon Fly (Melrose), Browne's Bridge, Glen, Maiden Rock Divide Bridge, Greenwood Bottoms, Jerry Creek and East Bank Fishing Access Sites, Squaw Creek bridge area, Burma Road, upper Big Hole (Wisdom to Chief Joseph) and side roads off MT 278 between Wisdom and Jackson. Although there is ample public land and access, much of the land is private and requires landowner permission.

Among the state's more popular trout fishing destinations, during the months of June, July, August and early September the fishing access sites tend to be crowded, especially so 8:00am to 5:00pm, e.g. dawn and dusk provide the best birding.

There is gas at Wisdom, Wise River, and Melrose; limited rooms and excellent meals can be had in all three. For groceries and other amenities, Dillon and Butte are about it. Camping is allowed at most of the fishing access sites and dispersed camping is allowed on much of the nearby BLM and Beaverhead National Forest.

CONTACT
Big Hole River Foundation
PO Box 3894, Butte, MT 59702
Website: www.bhrf.org
Email: bhrf@ghrf.org

Violet-green Swallow

SOUTHWEST MONTANA
Big Hole Battlefield/ Surrounding Area

#22

GPS 45.636,-113.644

WEST OF WISDOM

KEY BIRDS
Sandhill Crane, Long-billed Curlew, Sora, Yellow-headed Blackbird, Barn and Cliff Swallows, Snow Bunting

BEST SEASONS
Late spring through early fall; winters tend to be harsh

AREA DESCRIPTION
A mix of sagebrush, grasslands, wetlands, and willow riparian beside the North Fork Big Hole River, plus conifer treed foothills

Huge and relatively lightly populated, the upper Big Hole Valley is a mix of irrigated hay meadows, grass, and sagebrush with numerous willow-choked streams and literally hundreds of miles of irrigation ditches such that water, especially spring through early summer, at times appears to overwhelm the grass. Birds love it.

Experienced birders routinely check off upwards of 75 species a day during the spring and fall migration. At times, the number of birds in and around all that water is truly mind-boggling. Raptors — hawks, owls, and eagles — occupy the fence posts and soar over the vast open landscape. Ducks — Mallard, Cinnamon, Blue- and Green-winged Teal; American Wigeon, Common Merganser and American Coot — dot every puddle. Sandhill Cranes dance in all directions. Warblers and flycatchers of every color flit about the bushes. Bird song rings loud and clear. Every bridge is lined with barn and cliff swallow nests as hundreds soar in the air, obviously doing their damnedest to devastate the valley's infamous "trubelsome mosquiters". By the way, speaking of mosquitoes, just ask the folks in Wisdom: "Yep we enjoy two seasons: one month a skeeters, eleven months a winter."

The battlefield provides picnic tables, developed interpretive trails, and a visitor's center. The valley itself is largely private with some state sections, but the surrounding hills are almost all public. Many ranchers are amenable to a courteous request to walk in, but forget asking to drive.

Elk, mule deer, moose, black bear, and pronghorn (spring through fall), gray wolf, coyote, beaver, river otter, mink, muskrat, pine marten, and ground squirrels galore frequent the area.

Wisdom has gas, excellent dining (Big Hole Crossing), and the best pizza in southwest Montana (Antlers Bar). Beds in the area are limited — e.g. reservations are a good idea. The Hook and Horn serves a great cup-a-joe and other goodies, as well as a wide variety of trade goods. The Mercantile has a surprising variety of local wines.

DIRECTIONS

From I-15 Exit 59 south of Dillon, take MT 278 70 miles to Wisdom. Turn left on MT 43, and go 10 miles west to the battlefield. From I-15 at Divide, take MT 43, 62 miles through Wisdom to the battlefield. From Missoula, take US 93 south through the Bitterroot Valley to Lost Trail Pass. Turn left on MT 43, and go 17 miles to the battlefield.

CONTACT

Big Hole Battlefield phone: 406-689-3155

Dusky Grouse (cock)

SOUTHWEST MONTANA
Burma Road

#23

GPS 45.467,-112.681

NORTH OF DILLON

KEY BIRDS
Wild Turkey, Turkey Vulture, Bald and Golden Eagles, Bank Swallow, Pheasant, Western Tanager

BEST SEASONS
Spring through late fall; ducks and Canada Geese take advantage of open water all winter

AREA DESCRIPTION
Roadside riparian habitat with a mix going from hay meadows to canyon cliffs

From Dillon, take Old Butte Highway, MT 91, north. Look for Swainson's and Ferruginous Hawks (both color phases) and Golden Eagles on the telephone poles and in the fields. Bald Eagles and Prairie Falcons are common, and burrowing owls occasionally show up. In winter, Rough-legged Hawks replace the Swainson's who are on winter holiday in Argentina.

Turn right (20 miles out) at the Glen FAS sign onto Burma Road. Scary, I know, but the county has been known to grade it and barring wet, albeit a bit shaken, you should make it. Anyway, about a

Golden Eagle

mile in, stop at the Glen FAS. The cottonwoods and surrounding brush attract a variety of birds — swallows, warblers, woodpeckers, grackles, Western Tanagers and such. In the spring, listen closely and you might hear Ol' Tom Turkey gobbling. Continue on, keeping your eyes peeled especially on hay meadows. Wild Turkey, American Kestrel and other raptors, Mourning and Eurasian Collared-doves, Turkey Vulture, and various sparrows and buntings are among the possibilities.

In due time — just how long, of course, depends after all on sightings and road conditions — you enter a narrow canyon. Prairie Falcons nest on the canyon walls and songbirds haunt the cottonwoods and brush beside the river. This is also a good spot to surprise a Merganser hen and her brood — their hasty exit always a highlight. Just beyond the canyon is an ancient buffalo jump and then the road rises for a good view of the river. Watch for waterfowl, raptors, and songbirds, especially Cliff and Tree Swallows. Should you decide to commune with nature, watch out for rattlesnakes.

After what might seem many miles but really isn't, arid brown and desert-like habitat suddenly morphs to lush green. Ring-necked Pheasants, Wild Turkey, and a variety of songbirds haunt the fields and ducks, especially teal, swim in ditches. And just when you might think, "Oh my God, lost!" — Voila, behold a real live highway.

Turn right (south) on MT 41. You will pass several ponds that are almost always good for waterfowl and songbirds. Soon Beaverhead Rock will appear (from this angle, doesn't take much imagination, heading north...forget it). Much of the surrounding land here is private, but you can get a look at the wetlands by stopping at the interpretive signs on right just past the bridge. To access the public land, follow the dirt road just before crossing the bridge and check your map closely; landowners here tend to jealously guard their fiefdoms. Waterfowl, water birds, songbirds, and raptors are the main attractions; rattlesnakes are common.

Continue on the highway for about 7 miles south and look for steel corrals on the right. Turn right onto Anderson Lane (gravel). The attractions here are lots of water — ditches, ponds, marshes, sloughs, spring creeks, and the Beaverhead River — along with brush, grass, and croplands. All private. Lacking landowner permission, be sure to stay on the road. However don't despair, there are plenty of opportunities by glassing from the road. Stop often; scan the brush and fields carefully and especially in the sloughs and ditches. Pheasants and white-tailed deer (some really big bucks), puddle ducks, water birds, songbirds, and raptors are common as...well, you know.

At the end of the gravel, turn left (south) and return to Dillon. As I'm sure you will agree, Burma Road notwithstanding, this is one fine birding route.

SOUTHWEST MONTANA

#24 Birch Creek/Thief Creek/ French Creek Loop

GPS 45.413,-112.851

NORTHWEST OF DILLON

KEY BIRDS
Bohemian Waxwing (winter), Great Gray Owl, Northern Goshawk, Spruce Grouse, Steller's Jay

BEST SEASONS
July through October

AREA DESCRIPTION
Riparian habitat with mountain pass and forests

Look for cliff swallow nests beneath the Interstate bridge. Just up Birch Creek Road in the grass around the old homestead on the right side, look for Black-billed Magpie, Long-billed Curlew, Northern Harrier, Raven, Mountain Bluebird, and occasionally Gray Partridge. Beyond the forest boundary fence, check out the ghost town of Farlin and what remains of the copper/ silver smelter. Steeped in its history, be sure to keep one eye peeled on the birds — Clark's Nutcracker, Downy Woodpecker, American Dippers, waxwings, Mountain Bluebird, and Steller's and Gray Jays frequent the area.

Continue on and turn left at the Birch Creek Outdoor Center sign (Thief Creek Road). Stop at the bridge and

Franklin's Grouse

look for American Dipper; Hairy and Downy Woodpeckers, Northern Flicker, Willow Flycatcher, Townsend's Solitaire, and a variety of warblers and sparrows are common. Take a break beside Thief Creek a few hundred yards beyond the center. Watch for birds flying between the open sagebrush on the right and the brushy creek bottom (beaver dams). As you gain altitude, look for more Clark's Nutcrackers and Gray and Steller's Jays. Get lucky and perhaps a Great Gray Owl or a strutting Dusky Grouse cock might show itself. Townsend's Solitaire, Golden Eagle, Northern Goshawk, Spruce Grouse, and Great Horned Owl also frequent the area. The pass features spectacular views and, especially in wet years, wildflowers galore. In winter, the canyon is a good spot to view large concentrations of Bohemian Waxwings dining on juniper berries, which grow profusely in the lower canyon.

In winter, the road to the center is almost always passable, especially in four-wheel or all-wheel drive. Much beyond that, good luck. The 9,000 foot pass between Thief and French Creeks is rarely open December through at least June.

On the French Creek side, you will pass many old mines and what remains of the first smelter in Montana. Openings and the brushy creek bottom afford the best viewing opportunities. Elk and mule deer are common throughout. French Creek Road is impassable once the snow flies, but can be tough to downright impossible during mud season.

Once you reach bottom, turn left and follow Rattlesnake Creek (more good birding ops) through Argenta (rich in mining history) to MT 278. Turn left (east) to I-15 south of Dillon.

DIRECTIONS
From Dillon, take I-15 north 10 miles to Apex Exit (74) and turn left onto Birch Creek Road. High clearance/4X4 vehicles recommended. Allow at least three to four hours to complete the 60-mile loop.

CONTACT
Beaverhead-Deerlodge National Forest phone: 406-683-3900

SOUTHWEST MONTANA

Poindexter Slough Fishing Access Site

#25

GPS 45.182,-112.687

SOUTH OF DILLON

KEY BIRDS
Teal, Sandhill Crane, Osprey, Bald Eagle, Rufous Hummingbird

BEST SEASONS
Spring through fall; ducks take advantage of open water during cold snaps

AREA DESCRIPTION
Creek surrounded by cropland and pasture, thick willows, cattail marsh, ponds, wetlands and grass with scattered cottonwoods

A slough of the Beaverhead River heavily influenced by springs, Poindexter never freezes and is a magnet for birds year round. The three parking areas provide easy access to the state-owned property and about 4 miles of creek, but some ingenuity is required to navigate the private railroad tracks and to a lesser extent the surrounding ranch and farmlands. Be aware the railroad tracks are private, e.g. walk the tracks at your peril.

Dan Block, a retired professor at Western Montana College (now Montana Western University) noted, "Poindexter was a regular stop for my ornithology classes and workshops". Over many years, he figured the average daily count at around 50 species; students attending five-day workshops averaged about 100.

Close to home, and because we like to fish too, Poindexter ranks high on our annual birding bucket list. Like our fishing, check-offs vary depending, of course, on how hot the bite. But it's a rare day we don't see Mallards, Great Blue Herons, Blue-, Green-winged and Cinnamon Teal, Black-billed Magpies, Northern Harriers, Ospreys, Bald Eagles, and Yellow-rumped and Yellow Warblers. Looking back over our lists, Downy and Hairy Woodpeckers, Mountain Bluebird, Northern Flicker, Song and Savannah Sparrows, Long-billed Curlew, Raven, Canada Goose, House Finch and American Goldfinch, Red-winged and Yellow-headed Blackbirds, Marsh Wren, Bullock's Oriole, Western Tanager, Cedar Waxwing, Tree and Barn Swallows, Rock Pigeon, Mourning and Eurasian Collared-doves, and American Kestrel show up enough to not surprise.

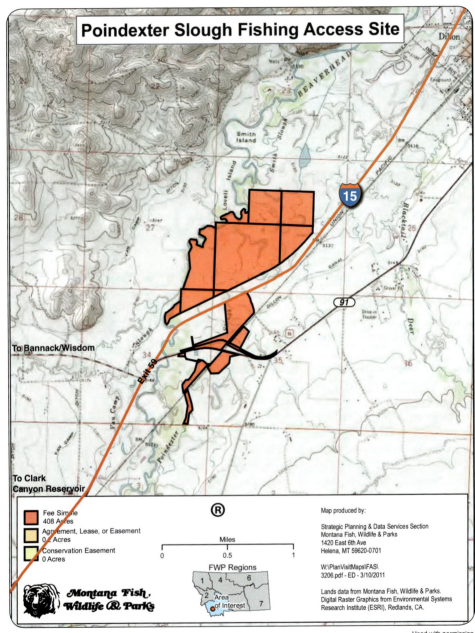

Poindexter Slough Fishing Access Site

Dillon

To Bannack/Wisdom

To Clark
Canyon Reservoir

Fee Simple
408 Acres

Agreement, Lease, or Easement
0.? Acres

Conservation Easement
0 Acres

Ⓡ

Miles

0   0.5   1

FWP Regions

Area
of Interest

Montana Fish,
Wildlife & Parks

Map produced by:

Strategic Planning & Data Services Section
Montana Fish, Wildlife & Parks
1420 East 6th Ave
Helena, MT 59620-0701

W:\PlanVisitMaps\FAS\
3206.pdf - ED - 3/10/2011

Lands data from Montana Fish, Wildlife & Parks.
Digital Raster Graphics from Environmental Systems
Research Institute (ESRI), Redlands, CA.

Over 200 species have been observed in Beaverhead County, Montana's largest county in area and, with around 10,000 permanent residents, one of the state's least populated.

White-tailed deer, beaver, coyote, red fox, muskrat, mink, and raccoon are common; river otters appear on occasion.

DIRECTIONS

From Dillon, take I-15 south to Exit 59 (MT 278). Turn left at the stop sign; go under the Interstate to the stop sign and turn left and cross the Beaverhead River. Three parking lots, one on right and two on left, provide access.

CONTACT

FW&P - Dillon Office phone: 406-683-4258

Rufous Hummingbird

SOUTHWEST MONTANA
Beaverhead River

#26

GPS | CLARK CANYON DAM:
45.003,-112.857

SOUTH OF DILLON, NORTH TO TWIN BRIDGES

KEY BIRDS
Tree Swallow, Yellow-headed Blackbird, teal, Bohemian Waxwing (winter), Osprey, Bald and Golden Eagles

BEST SEASONS
Spring through early fall for songbirds; in winter open water even during the coldest weather attracts large numbers of Mallard and Common Goldeneye

AREA DESCRIPTION
Top to bottom the river flows between willow and cottonwood lined banks, hay meadows, and pasture lands.

Much of the land is private, but there is plenty enough public access: state owned fishing access sites (FAS), state sections, federal BLM, and Bureau of Reclamation lands.

For instance, on a recent visit to the Cattail Marsh Self-Guided Interpretive Trail (paved by the way) below Clark Canyon Dam, we found teal in the spring-fed ponds, American Kestrel and swallows on the sandstone cliffs, a number of LBJs, and watched an Osprey hunting the river just a few yards away; four different butterflies and a similar number of dragon and damsel flies only added to the enjoyment level.

Every so often, I find a guest in my boat more interested in nabbing bird photos than trout. So far Pennsylvanian, Dick Moore, owns the blue-ribbon: a male Yellow-headed Blackbird standing on a stick atop a brown trout munching on hatching mayflies.

Other spots worth checking out: Henneberry Walk-in Fishing Access Site, state-owned Homestead Wetlands, Henneberry, Pipe Organ, and Barretts Fishing Access Sites, Cornell Park (outskirts Dillon on 10-mile Road), Beaverhead Rock area, state school sections between Beaverhead Rock and Twin Bridges, and Twin Bridges Fairground's Area.

White-tailed deer, beaver, coyote, red fox, muskrat, mink, and raccoon are common, and river otters occasionally appear.

CONTACT
FW&P – Dillon phone: 406-683-9310

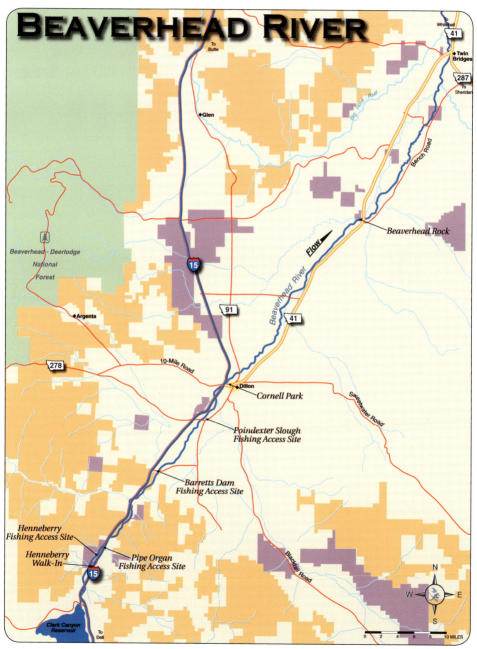

© 2014 Wilderness Adventures Press

SOUTHWEST MONTANA
Bannack State Park

GPS 45.162,-113.000

SOUTHWEST OF DILLON

KEY BIRDS
Cinnamon Teal, Marsh Wren, Mountain Bluebird, Wilson's Snipe, Sage Thrasher, Sage Grouse, Yellow-rumped Warbler

BEST SEASONS
Spring through fall

AREA DESCRIPTION
A mix of cottonwood and willow creek bottom bounded by semi-arid sagebrush/grasslands, with dry lodgepole and Doug fir forest higher up and nearby agricultural lands

The tree and brush lined creek bottom near this well-preserved ghost town beside Grasshopper Creek provides the best viewing opportunities. In the cottonwoods and willows, watch for Least and Gray Flycatchers, Eastern and Western Kingbirds, Hairy and Downy Woodpeckers, Loggerhead Shrike, Marsh Wren, Mountain Bluebird, Common Yellowthroat, Western Tanager, Wilson's Snipe, Gray Catbird, and Wilson's Warbler. Sage Grouse, Sage Thrasher, the occasional Brewer's Sparrow, and McCown's Longspur frequent the sagebrush which extends pretty much unbroken for many square miles. Golden Eagles and Prairie Falcons soar in the canyon below town. While Blue- and Green-winged Teal, Mallard, Common Merganser, and Belted Kingfisher find the brushy confines of the creek attractive.

April and May visits to a Sage Grouse lek off nearby Reservoir Creek Road highlight our annual calendar. To get there: Continue on Bannack Bench Road past the turn-off to the park about a mile. Turn right onto Reservoir Creek Road about 1½-miles; and turn left onto a two-track. About 100 yards in is a large sign with Sage Grouse information and directions to view the lek. The curtain usually rises well before dawn and rarely lasts more than an hour or two after daylight. In other words, get there early or miss it. Please do not approach closer than the end of the two-track and be sure to bring along binoculars; a spotting scope is even better. The area surrounding the park is within the Beaverhead Sage-steppe IBA (Greater Sage Grouse).

Other activities include trout fishing in Grasshopper Creek, hiking, biking, and hunting (outside park).

Bannack was Montana's first territorial capital and is steeped in interesting history. Interpretive programs are conducted weekly during the summer and early fall. Inquire at the park office for further information. There are two small campgrounds in the park and a rental teepee. Dispersed camping is allowed in the surrounding BLM lands, and the nearby Beaverhead National Forest provides both dispersed and developed campgrounds.

Mule deer, antelope, coyote, beaver, muskrat, badger, cottontail and pygmy rabbits, and white-tail jackrabbits are common. Occasionally moose and elk wander by. Watch for rattlesnakes especially in and around the canyon.

Bannack Days, in late July, is a good time to get acquainted with this well-preserved historic ghost town. Snowmobilers flock to the area in winter and hunters pretty much rule the fall. For an interesting and productive side-trip, check out the Pioneer Scenic Byway just up the road off MT 278.

Dillon has everything a traveler needs. The Grasshopper Inn at nearby Polaris (west of Bannack Bench Road off MT 278, follow signs) provides rooms, gas, and diesel fuel, as well as restaurant and bar service.

DIRECTIONS
From I-15, turn off at Exit 59 onto MT 278 west for 17 miles. Turn left at the park sign onto the Bannack Bench Road. Travel 4 miles south and turn left to the park.

CONTACT
Park Manager phone: 406-834-3413
Email: bannack@smtel.com

SOUTHWEST MONTANA

#28 SOUTHWEST MONTANA
Clark Canyon Reservoir

GPS 44.996,-112.855

SOUTH OF DILLON

KEY BIRDS
Great Blue Heron, Canada Goose, American Kestrel, Osprey, Bald and Golden Eagles, Black-billed Magpie, Northern Harrier, Marsh Wren

BEST SEASONS
Spring and fall; June for waterfowl broods; August for shorebirds

AREA DESCRIPTION
Fed by the Red Rock River and Horse Prairie Creek, with 17 miles of shoreline, the lake is surrounded by a diverse mix of dry, rocky limber pine/juniper and grass covered hills, short grass/sagebrush prairie, willow/riparian, wetlands and agriculture fields.

Armed with a spotting scope, numerous access points around the lake provide ample viewing opportunities for a variety of waterfowl and water birds. Shorebirds flock to the lake's edges in August; the drier the year, the wider the exposed mudflats, the more shorebirds.

The Old Armstead Road at the south end parallels the willow-choked Red Rock River, two spring creeks, surrounded by brush and grass, and eventually disappears into the lake. This is a good place to check off multiple species of songbirds, waterfowl, wading birds, and raptors.

At the west end, where Horse Prairie Creek enters, the willows attract a variety of water-loving songbirds. Raptors, Black-billed Magpie, Gray Partridge, Northern Flicker, Mountain Bluebird, Western Kingbird, Common Raven, and American Crow are common in the Wildlife Management Area just west of the lake. Look closely and you might see Sage Grouse, which frequent the sagebrush in the surrounding foothills.

Below the dam, hike the paved Cattail Marsh Nature Trail. Teal frequent the spring-fed ponds and Kestrel and swallows nest on the sandstone cliffs while Ospreys hunt the Beaverhead River. The river harbors large numbers of Common Goldeneye and Mallard. Some days it seems there is a Common Merganser hen with brood in tow around every bend.

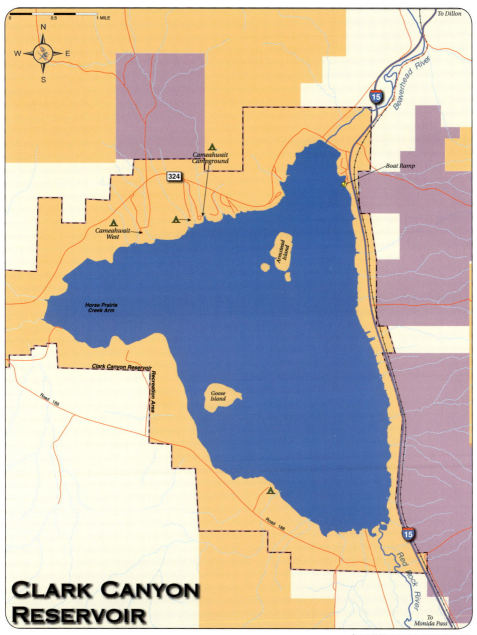

CLARK CANYON
RESERVOIR

The 2010 Christmas Bird Count listed 37 species: Canada Goose, Gadwall, American Wigeon, Mallard, Green-winged Teal, Ring-necked Duck, Bufflehead, Common and Barrow's Goldeneye, Common and Hooded Mergansers, Gray Partridge, Bald and Golden Eagles, Northern Harrier, Red-tailed and Rough-legged Hawks, American Kestrel, American Coot, Wilson's Snipe, Rock Pigeon, Belted Kingfisher, Northern Flicker, Northern Shrike, Black-billed Magpie, Common Raven, Horned Lark, Black-capped and Mountain Chickadees, American Dipper, Townsend's Solitaire, European Starling, American Tree, Harris's and Song Sparrows, Dark-eyed Junco, and House Sparrow.

In dry years, irrigation drawdown exposes extensive mudflats which, in August, draw legions of shorebirds such as American Avocet, Willet, Marbled Godwit, Wilson's Phalarope, and several sandpipers.

Mule and white-tailed deer, moose, elk, pronghorn and coyote are common.

Interesting to note: The site of Camp Fortunate is nearby. It is where Sacagawea's long lost brother, Chief Cameahwait, met up with the Lewis and Clark expedition and subsequently furnished horses, allowing the expedition to continue.

The reservoir is one of the best rainbow trout fisheries in the state.

Camping is free, first come, first served. Dillon and Dell offer the nearest gas. The Calf-A-Dell is a primo breakfast stop. Dillon offers just about everything a traveler needs.

DIRECTIONS
From Dillon, go 18 miles south on I-15, to Exits 44 & 37. From Idaho, go north on I-15 to Exits 37 & 44. Armstead Road and MT 324 circle reservoir.

CONTACT
Bureau of Reclamation, Clark Canyon Field Office phone: 406-683-6472

Marsh Wren

SOUTHWEST MONTANA

#29 Lemhi Pass

GPS 44.975,-113.445

WEST OF GRANT
(BEAVERHEAD COUNTY)

KEY BIRDS
Pine Siskin, Clark's Nutcracker, Golden Eagle, Townsend's Warbler, White-breasted Nuthatch, Northern Flicker

BEST SEASONS
June to October; the wildflower display in early summer is spectacular

AREA DESCRIPTION
High mountain pass with forests, grasslands and creeks

Meriwether Lewis described Lemhi Pass well, "*the road took us to the most distant fountain of the waters of the Mighty Missouri in surch of which we have spent so many toilsome days and wristless nights. thus far I had accomplished one of those great objects on which my mind has been unalterably fixed for many years, judge then of the pleasure I felt in all[a]ying my thirst with this pure and ice-cold water . here I halted a few minutes and rested myself. two miles below McNeal had exultingly stood with a foot on each side of this rivulet and thanked his god that he had lived to bestride the mighty & heretofore deemed endless Missouri. after refreshing ourselves we proceeded on to the top of the dividing ridge from which I discovered immence ranges of high mountains still to the West of us with their tops partially covered with snow ... here I first tasted the water of the great Columbia river*"

Sitting atop the Beaverhead Mountains (elevation 7,200 feet) the pass is a designated National Historic Monument. The site is situated in mature Douglas fir forest surrounded by large sagebrush and grass parks, several small creeks, and numerous spring seeps. In other words, the sort of diverse habitat attractive to a wide variety of birds.

Served by a well-maintained but narrow and twisty gravel road, access is easy except, of course, during periods of extreme wet or snow. No trailers or RVs.

No camping on site, but dispersed camping is possible in the surrounding Beaverhead-Deerlodge and Salmon-Challis National Forests.

DIRECTIONS
From I-15 south of Dillon, turn west on MT 324 (Clark Canyon Dam) for about 20 miles. Turn right to Lemhi Pass (turn is signed). There is a developed parking area on the left side of the highway for trailers and RVs.

SOUTHWEST MONTANA

#30 Beaverhead Sage-Steppe (IBA)

GPS 44.731,-112.705 (NEAR DELL, MONT.)

SOUTH OF DILLON

KEY BIRDS
Greater Sage Grouse, Golden Eagle, Snowy Owl (winter), Swainson's and Ferruginous Hawks

BEST SEASONS
Sage Grouse leks are most active in April and the first half of May; June for nesting songbirds; raptors anytime

AREA DESCRIPTION
A mix of high elevation (6,000-9,000 feet) sagebrush-steppe, intermountain grasslands, with scattered brushy draws and spring seeps

The 560,000-acre IBA embodies the largest intact sagebrush habitat in southwestern Montana and supports at least 3 percent of the state's Greater Sage Grouse population. More than 24 active leks are found within the IBA. Largely public lands (BLM and state),

Greater Sage Grouse

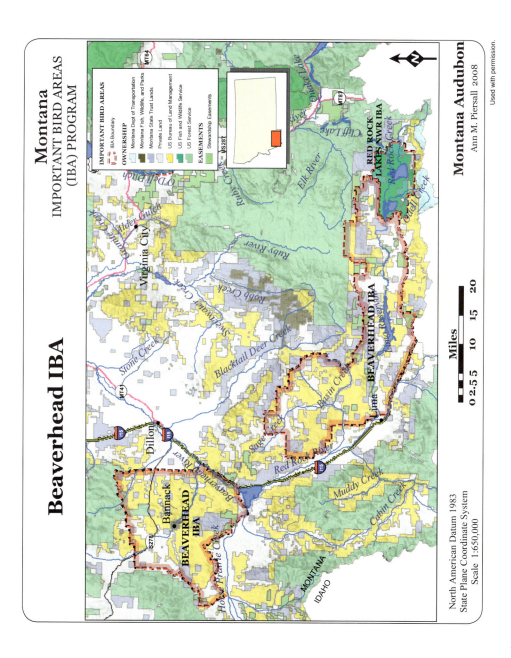

numerous roads and trails (too many in my opinion) provide nearly unlimited motorized access. (Please note: Most are non-maintained, rough and/or gumbo laden, impassable when wet, e.g. high clearance, 4x4 vehicles are highly recommended.)

Sage Grouse and sagebrush are the main focus. But water is key to bagging the most species. Numerous brushy, aspen, willow and cottonwood stream bottoms, grasslands, wetlands, and scattered timber attract legions of songbirds, woodpeckers, wading birds, and raptors. Especially during spring and fall migration, numerous stock ponds, Clark Canyon and Lima Reservoirs and, farther south, the Red Rock Lakes NWR, attract major concentrations of waterfowl, water birds, and shorebirds.

With the IBA practically in our backyard, notwithstanding our "thing" for sage hens, we go there often year round. Especially in April and May to look in on strutting Sage Grouse, but we've found almost anytime is a good time. Over the years in early spring and winter, we've been lucky enough to spot every raptor species indigenous to the area. Golden Eagles are common anytime. One day last winter, we spotted a Great Gray and a Snowy Owl on the same day. In the warmer months, Raven, Mallard, Goldeneye, American Wigeon, Cinnamon, Blue- and Green-winged Teal, Canada Goose, Horned Lark, Great Blue Heron, Sora, Cedar Waxwing, Red-winged and Yellow-headed Blackbirds, American Goldfinch, Sandhill Crane, White-faced Ibis, American Coot, Wilson's Snipe, Wilson's Phalarope, White-throated Swift, Common Nighthawk, Bullock's Oriole, Common Yellowthroat, Yellow-rumped Warbler, Mountain Bluebird, Eastern and Western Kingbirds, Western Tanager, and countless LBJs are as common as Black-billed Magpies, which are nearly as common as Mourning and Eurasian Collared-doves and Starlings and…well you name it. Bohemian Waxwings show up in great numbers once the snow flies. Really no surprise, considering 232 species have been observed at Red Rock Lakes NWR. So, considering the NWR is within the IBA, there is no reason to believe most if not all show up across the entire area at one time or another.

Largely public you can hike, bike, camp, fish, hunt, feast your eyes on wildflowers and butterflies, and shoot photos to your heart's content.

Elk, mule and white-tailed deer, moose, badger, coyote, cottontail and pygmy rabbits, and white-tail jackrabbits are common. Occasionally we jump a black-tail jack and scattered beaver dams and prairie rattlesnakes (at lower elevations mostly) add spice to the adventure.

Gas and food are available in Dillon, Dell, and Lima; motels in Lima and Dillon; camping is available at Clark Canyon Reservoir (nine campgrounds; no fee); at Bannack State Park (fee) and dispersed camping is allowed most everywhere on BLM. We give high marks to the Calf-A-Dell in Dell, and The Bus (Mexican) and Lion's Den Steak House in Dillon.

DIRECTIONS
I-15 south of Dillon separates the east and west units. MT 278 gets you to the Bannack side. Off I-15, numerous gravel and dirt roads and trails will get you into the IBA.

CONTACT
Montana Audubon Society - Amy Cilimburg, Director of Conservation and Climate Policy
Phone: 406-465-1141
Email: amy@mtaudubon.org

Blacktail Road

GPS 45.203, -112.642

SOUTH OF DILLON TO CENTENNIAL VALLEY

KEY BIRDS

Golden Eagle, Black-billed Magpie, Common Raven, Red-naped Sapsucker, Sandhill Crane, Swainson's Hawk, Mourning and Eurasian Collared-doves, Eastern and Western Kingbirds, Western Meadowlark, Red-winged and Brewer's Blackbirds, Mountain Bluebird

BEST SEASONS

Late spring through early fall; road is usually passable by mid-June, but check locally first

AREA DESCRIPTION

Mix of sagebrush and grasslands with creeks and mountain foothills

Approximately 10 miles south of Dillon, the road changes to gravel with signs of human habitation limited to just a few widely scattered ranch buildings. For the next 40 miles or so, the road carves its rough and dusty way through a mix of open grasslands and sagebrush bordered by Blacktail Deer Creek and Sweet Grass Hills to the east and the grass, sagebrush, and forested Blacktail Range to the west; eventually gaining elevation in the foothills of the Gravelly Range before topping Clover Divide and dropping into the Centennial Valley.

Last July, we checked off Golden Eagle, Sage Grouse, Long-billed Curlew, Mountain Bluebird, Western Tanager, White-faced Ibis, Tundra Swan, Northern Goshawk, Northern Harrier, Peregrine and Prairie Falcons, a variety of sparrows including (we think?) Brewer's, Sage, and Savannah Sparrows, Black-billed Magpie, Common Raven, Red-naped Sapsucker, Sandhill Crane, Swainson's Hawk, Mourning and Eurasian Collared-doves, Eastern and Western Kingbirds, Western Meadowlark, Red-winged and Brewer's Blackbirds, Brown-headed Cowbird, Great-tailed Grackle, Red-tailed Hawk, American Kestrel, Great Horned Owl, a bunch of distinctly different — though alas beyond our birding skills — LBJs and shorebirds, Cinnamon, Blue- and Green-winged Teal, Mallard, American Wigeon, and American Coot. And we turned around at the Red Rock River and retraced our route, missing out on who knows how many check-offs at the refuge and/or Lima Reservoir. Allow at least a half-day, include the Centennial Valley and you can easily eat up an entire day, no matter how you choose to complete the journey — out to Idaho, Monida, back to Dillon, whatever.

Moose, elk, white-tailed and mule deer, pronghorn, coyote, red fox, Richardson's ground squirrel, badger, porcupine, bobcat, and mountain lion frequent the area.

Interesting to note, for much of the way the road passes through the sprawling (250,000 acres) Matador Ranch, an integral cog in the multi-state Matador Cattle Company. The Matador is the largest parcel left of the million-acre cattle empire founded in 1865 by Phillip Poindexter and William Orr, who registered the Square and Compass, the first registered brand in Montana Territory.

DIRECTIONS
From Dillon, follow Atlantic Street south to Sparky's Garage Restaurant just past the University. Turn left onto old MT 91 and take the first left onto Blacktail Road. Continue on to the Centennial Valley, where you can either return via the same route and go east to Lima, or Monida and I-15, or west to RT 87 at Henry's Lake, Idaho.

Alternate Route #1

Follow Blacktail Road over Clover Pass to the intersection with North Valley Road. Instead of continuing on to Red Rock Lakes NWR, turn left on North Valley Road and go approximately 2 miles to Centennial Divide Road and turn left (north). The road crosses over Centennial Divide and drops down into the upper Ruby River Valley. You will eventually (about 50 miles) come out in Alder. Turn left to Twin Bridges and south on MT 41 back to Dillon. The route passes through some of the most scenic country imaginable, including Ted Turner's Snowcrest Ranch. Good birding the entire way; pretty good fishing too. Moose, elk, and mule and whitetail deer are common.

Alternate Route #2

About 5 miles downstream of Snowcrest Ranch HQ, turn left on Sweetwater Road; about 30 miles to Dillon. Parts of the road can be impassable when wet.

Alternate Route # 3

About 3 miles below the turn-off to Sweetwater Road, turn left on Cottonwood Creek Road (just prior to reaching Ruby Reservoir). The road crosses Stone Creek Divide and a big open pit talc mine before dropping down along Stone Creek to MT 41; turn left back to Dillon.

All of the above are impassable and/or closed in winter; check snow conditions before leaving Dillon.

CONTACT
Beaverhead-Deerlodge National Forest phone: 406-683-3900
Dillon BLM phone: 406-683-8023

SOUTHWEST MONTANA

#32 Robb-Ledford/Blacktail Wildlife Management Areas

BLACKTAIL WMA:
44.904,-112.354
GPS ROBB-LEDFORD WMA:
44.915,-112.194

SOUTHEAST OF DILLON AND SOUTH OF ALDER

KEY BIRDS
Gray Partridge, Northern Harrier, Swainson's and Ferruginous Hawks, Golden Eagle

BEST SEASONS
Spring through early fall; closed to visitation December 1- through May 15

AREA DESCRIPTION
The rolling foothills leading up to scenic Snowcrest Mountains are a mix of intermountain grassland and sagebrush with scattered dark timber — lodgepole and limber pine, Douglas fir, curl-leaf mountain mahogany, and juniper — wetlands and willow, aspen, and cottonwood riparian areas

The roads and designated two-tracks tend toward rough and rougher, but don't let that stop you for these 47,000 acres are one of the more remote, scenic, and productive birding sites in southwest Montana. Lacking in open water, there are no doubt better spots for waterfowl, shorebird, and wading bird viewing but beyond those, just about every other of the 200+ species listed at Red Rock Lakes NWR (sort of just over the hill) shows up here one time or another.

Last spring in just a few hours, we watched a golden eagle hunting; spied on a small flock of Sage Grouse gleaning an ant hill; hiked up into the woods where we photographed a pair of strutting Dusky Grouse cocks; flushed a pair of Gray Partridge no doubt thinking about setting up housekeeping in the grass; glassed a bunch of hawks (sorry we failed to agree on pedigree), a flock of Long-billed Curlews and several foraging Mountain Bluebirds; thrilled to the melodious singing of Western Meadowlarks; checked off our first Sage Thrasher of the young season; laughed at the courtship antics of a pair of show-off Sandhill Cranes; watched a Great Blue Heron fishing; as usual, we scratched our noggins

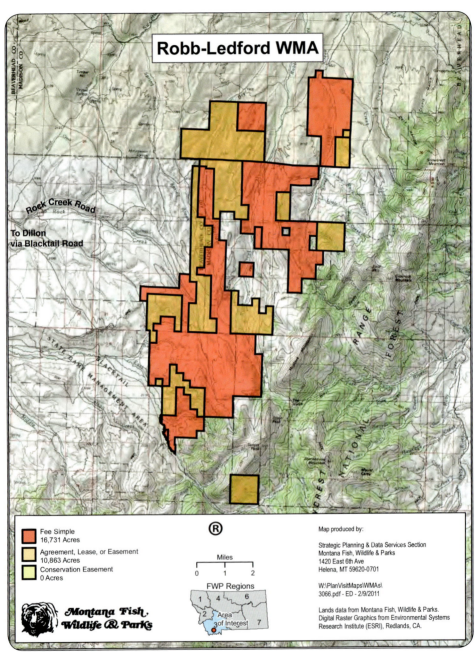

Robb-Ledford WMA

BEAVERHEAD CO.
MADISON CO.

Rock Creek Road

To Dillon
via Blacktail Road

STATE PARK MANAGEMENT AREA

BLACKTAIL

BEAVERHEAD

RANGE

CREST

NATIONAL

FOREST

Fee Simple
16,731 Acres

Agreement, Lease, or Easement
10,863 Acres

Conservation Easement
0 Acres

®

Miles

0   1   2

FWP Regions

1   4   6

2   Area   7
3 of Interest

Montana Fish,
Wildlife & Parks

Map produced by:

Strategic Planning & Data Services Section
Montana Fish, Wildlife & Parks
1420 East 6th Ave
Helena, MT 59620-0701

W:\PlanVisitMaps\WMAs\
3066.pdf - ED - 2/9/2011

Lands data from Montana Fish, Wildlife & Parks.
Digital Raster Graphics from Environmental Systems
Research Institute (ESRI), Redlands, CA.

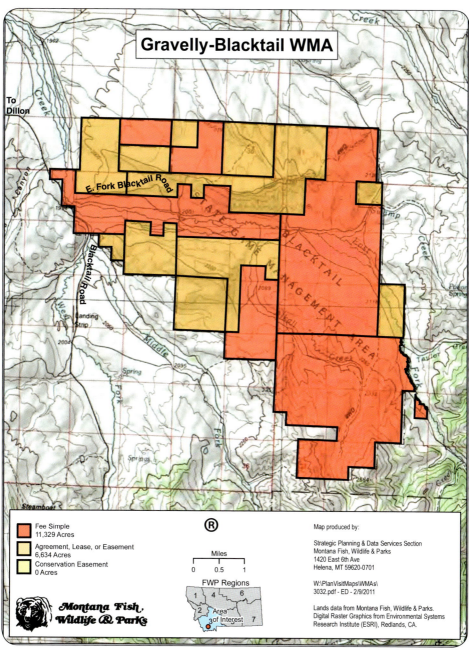

Gravelly-Blacktail WMA

To
Dillon

E. Fork Blacktail Road

Blacktail Road

Fee Simple
11,329 Acres

Agreement, Lease, or Easement
6,634 Acres

Conservation Easement
0 Acres

®

Miles
0   0.5   1

FWP Regions

Area
of Interest

Map produced by:

Strategic Planning & Data Services Section
Montana Fish, Wildlife & Parks
1420 East 6th Ave
Helena, MT 59620-0701

W:\PlanVisitMaps\WMAs\
3032.pdf - ED - 2/9/2011

Lands data from Montana Fish, Wildlife & Parks.
Digital Raster Graphics from Environmental Systems
Research Institute (ESRI), Redlands, CA.

Montana Fish,
Wildlife & Parks

at LBJs that just would not hold still long enough, although one we both agreed on just had to be a Sage Sparrow; let mom Killdeer lead us astray and in the creek counted coup on Mallard, Cinnamon, Blue- and Green-winged Teal...And those are just the highlights; all told, we checked off 46 species.

Popular for big game hunting September through November, the WMA is an important big game winter range closed to all visitation from December 1 to May 15. Elk, mule and white-tailed deer, moose, pronghorn, coyote, and the occasional black bear frequent the area. Brushy and difficult casting Ledford and Blacktail Deer Creeks and the larger and more open upper Ruby River provide excellent small stream trout fishing. In addition to wildlife viewing, hunting, camping, hiking, biking, and photography are popular.

Camping is allowed just about anywhere. There are campgrounds at Vigilante Station and Cottonwood Creek on the upper Ruby River, at the entrance to the Blacktail WMA, and 12 miles in at end of the main road.

Nothing fancy, vault toilets, picnic tables, first come, first served and pack-in, pack-out rules apply. Dillon and Sheridan offer all the amenities a traveler needs.

DIRECTIONS

Robb Creek WMA

Follow MT 287 south from Sheridan to Alder and turn south on Upper Ruby Road forapproximately 25 miles to Ledford Creek Road.

Blacktail WMA

In Dillon, follow Atlantic south and turn left at Sparky's Garage Restaurant. Go a block or so, and turn left onto Blacktail Road (sign) for approximately 30 miles

CONTACT
WMA - Bob Brannon phone: 406-842-5233

Peregrine Falcon

SOUTHWEST MONTANA

#33 Red Rock Lakes National Wildlife Refuge

GPS⊕ 44.593,-111.729

EAST OF MONIDA, MT/ WEST OF HENRY'S LAKE, ID

KEY BIRDS
Trumpeter Swan, Peregrine Falcon, Sage Grouse, Long-billed Curlew, Prairie Falcon, Golden Eagle, Red Crossbill, Western Tanager, Yellow-headed Blackbird

BEST SEASONS
Depending on conditions, mid- to late June through October

AREA DESCRIPTION
A diverse mix of large expanses of relatively shallow water, extensive sagebrush grass and treed uplands, mudflats, willow and marsh wetlands all surrounded by high mountains

Perhaps the most diverse bird habitat in southwest Montana, the refuge comprises some 25,000 acres. Refuge staff point to the Upper Red Rock Lake Campground as one of the best spots to check off multiple species. Refuge literature lists Lower Structure, Idlewild, Odell Creek to Sparrow Pond, between Shambo Pond and the Upper Lake Campground, along Elk Lake Road, and Pintail Ditch West as potential hotspots. According to the literature, "To date 232 species have been observed, 53 of which are considered rare or vagrants. In the past two years rare birds such as great egret, whooping crane, wood duck, turkey vulture, dunlin, northern mockingbird, northern parula, black-and-white warbler, northern oriole, rose-breasted grosbeak, and grasshopper sparrow have been seen."

Set up your spotting scope and scan the wet areas for Sora, American Avocet, Killdeer, Marbled Godwit, Willet, Spotted Sandpiper, Wilson's Phalarope, Marsh Wren and Yellow-headed Blackbird. Trumpeter Swans are heard (and seen) almost anytime. Open water, especially during spring and fall migrations, attract legions of waterfowl such as Lesser Scaup, Redhead, Canvasback, Ruddy Duck, teal, and Northern Pintail. In the trees and bushes, look for Western Wood-pewee, Olive-sided Flycatcher, Ruby- and Golden-crowned Kinglets, Warbling Vireo, Western Tanager, Red Crossbill, Cassin's Finch, and White-crowned Sparrow. Long-billed Curlew, Sandhill Crane, and Western

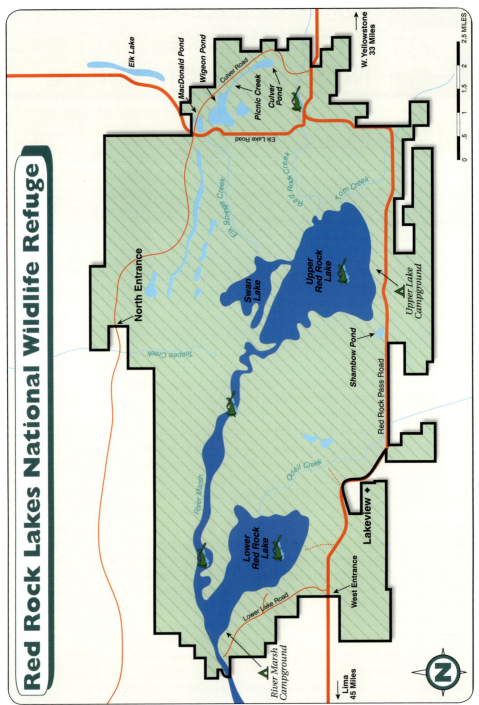

Red Rock Lakes National Wildlife Refuge

Elk Lake

MacDonald Pond

Wigeon Pond

Culver Road

Picnic Creek

Culver Pond

Elk Lake Road

W. Yellowstone 33 Miles

2.5 MILES

0 .5 1 1.5 2

Red Rock Creek

Tom Creek

Elk Springs Creek

North Entrance

Swan Lake

Upper Red Rock Lake

Upper Lake Campground

Teepee Creek

Shambow Pond

Red Rock Pass Road

Odell Creek

River Marsh

Lakeview

Lower Red Rock Lake

West Entrance

Lower Lake Road

River Marsh Campground

Lima 45 Miles

N

© 2014 Wilderness Adventures Press, Inc.

Meadowlark are common, as are raptors such as Short-eared Owl, Red-tailed and Swainson's Hawks, American Kestrel, and Northern Harrier. Peregrine Falcons and Golden Eagles nest in the cliffs of the Centennial Range while Bald Eagles and Ospreys can be seen hunting the lakes and numerous streams. Sage Grouse, Sage Thrasher, and Vesper and Brewer's Sparrows frequent the sagebrush.

The Centennial is one of the most remote valleys in the Lower 48. Elevations range from 7,000 feet on the valley floor to 10,000 feet on the Continental Divide to the south — the peaks of the Centennial Range.

Established in 1939, today the refuge is one of the most important Trumpeter Swan breeding areas in North America. At Red Rock Lakes the Trumpeter Swan population has rebounded from a low of only 69 birds in 1932 to more than 500 in recent years. Joined each winter by Trumpeters from Canada, the flock swells to around 2,500. Through a process called "hacking" Peregrine Falcons once again nest on the refuge. Several hundred Sandhill Crane pairs nest in the valley.

Gravel roads more or less encircle the refuge, affording nearly unlimited viewing ops. Motorized travel is restricted throughout to designated roads and trails. There are no developed interpretive trails, but there are two primitive trails to Sparrow Ponds and to Odell Creek that penetrate the interior. Boat launches to Lower Lake (no ramp; no motors allowed) at the end of Idlewild Road, at River Marsh Campground, and mid-lake between the two add to the birding ops. Boat access (no ramp, no motors) to Upper Lake is found at the campground. Otherwise, hiking cross-country and/or game trails is about it. Seasonal closures are in effect to protect nesting trumpeter swans. Mosquitoes are thick from early spring through late summer.

Beds, meals, and full bar service is available year round at nearby Elk Lake Resort — 406-276-3282.

Keep an eye peeled for moose, elk, mule and white-tailed deer, pronghorn, the occasional gray wolf, and many small mammals in and around the refuge. Grizzly and black bears roam the Gravelly and Centennial Mountains. Bear country rules apply, and spray comes highly recommended for any off-road excursions.

DIRECTIONS

From I-15 south of Lima, turn east at Monida and follow the gravel road 28 miles to Lakeview, Refuge Headquarters. From MT 87 just north of Henry's Lake, turn west on Red Rock Lake road and go 35 miles to Lakeview. Both roads are impassable in winter and difficult to impossible when wet.

Last chance for gas is either Lima, MT or Henry's Fork, ID.

CONTACT

Refuge HQ phone: 406-276-3536
Web site: www.fws.gov/redrocks

SOUTHWEST MONTANA
Raynold's Pass Bridge

#34

GPS 44.826,-111.485

NORTHWEST OF WEST YELLOWSTONE

KEY BIRDS
Osprey, Bald and Golden Eagles, Cliff Swallow, Spotted Sandpiper, Belted Kingfisher, Broad-tailed Hummingbird

BEST SEASONS
May through October

AREA DESCRIPTION
Just downstream of where the Madison River roars out of Quake Lake, surrounded by extensive sagebrush bordered on the west by Sheep Mountain (10,311 feet) and the foothills of the Gravelly Range to the east.

Fishermen trails lead up and down river. American Dipper, Belted Kingfisher, Cliff Swallow, Osprey, Bald Eagle, and Spotted Sandpiper frequent the river corridor. Scan the sagebrush for Mountain Bluebird, Brewer's Sparrow, and Western Meadowlark and look toward Sheep Mountain for soaring Prairie Falcon and Golden Eagle.

Bighorn sheep, mountain goat, and elk and mule deer frequent the hills. Good binos or a spotting scope greatly enhance the viewing ops.

For a lung-busting hike, scenic views of Quake Lake amid a stunning landscape, and the chance to view a variety of wildlife and forest-dwelling birds, follow Sheep Mountain Road (just south of the bridge) to the trailhead.

DIRECTIONS
From West Yellowstone, follow US 191 north to the junction with US 287. Turn left to the junction with MT 87 and turn left (south) to the bridge.

Broad-tailed Hummingbird

SOUTHWEST MONTANA

#35 Earthquake Lake Boat Launch

GPS ⊕ 44.855,-111.388

NORTHWEST OF WEST YELLOWSTONE

KEY BIRDS
Osprey, Bald and Golden Eagles, Double-crested Cormorant, American White Pelican, and numerous duck and water bird species

BEST SEASONS
May through October

AREA DESCRIPTION
Mountain lake habitat

Bald Eagle, Osprey, and Double-crested Cormorant nest here. Common Loons are widespread during migration as are a variety of waterfowl species — Canada Goose, Tundra Swan, Common Merganser, and Ring-necked Duck to name just a few. A spotting scope is highly recommended.

Beaver, elk, mule deer, and moose are common. Mountain goats and bighorn sheep frequent the cliffs on the south side of the lake. Wildflowers are abundant in the spring and summer, and the early fall aspen display can be spectacular. Early mornings offer the best viewing ops.

Please exercise caution when entering and exiting the highway, especially during the busy tourist season in high summer.

Quake Lake has excellent fishing.

DIRECTIONS
From West Yellowstone, follow US 191 north to the junction with US 287, turn left and go about 16 miles (about 2miles past the Campfire Lodge turnoff, see Ghost Village Road). Turn left (south) onto the gravel road to Quake Lake.

CONTACT
Hebgen Lake Ranger District phone: 406-823-6961

SOUTHWEST MONTANA
#36 Madison Valley IBA

GPS | **ENNIS BRIDGE:**
45.347,-111.722

MADISON RIVER CORRIDOR
UPSTREAM OF BEAR TRAP CANYON TO VARNEY BRIDGE

KEY BIRDS
170+ species have been observed of which about 70 are known to nest within the IBA, including Trumpeter Swan, Common Loon, Redhead Duck, Northern Pintail, Red-naped Sapsucker, Gray Partridge, and Bald Eagle.

BEST SEASONS
April through November; June for nesting songbirds

AREA DESCRIPTION
Riparian and grassland habitat along the river

Bald and Golden Eagles and Osprey are common throughout. American Dipper and Belted Kingfisher ply the tumbling waters of Bear Trap Canyon. Ennis Lake is the place to look for ducks, geese, and swans including Mallard, Common and Barrow's Goldeneyes, Trumpeter and Tundra Swans, Redhead, American Wigeon, Northern Pintail, and American Coot.

In the grasslands look for Pheasant, Gray Partridge, Sprague's Pipit, Northern Harrier,

Trumpeter Swan

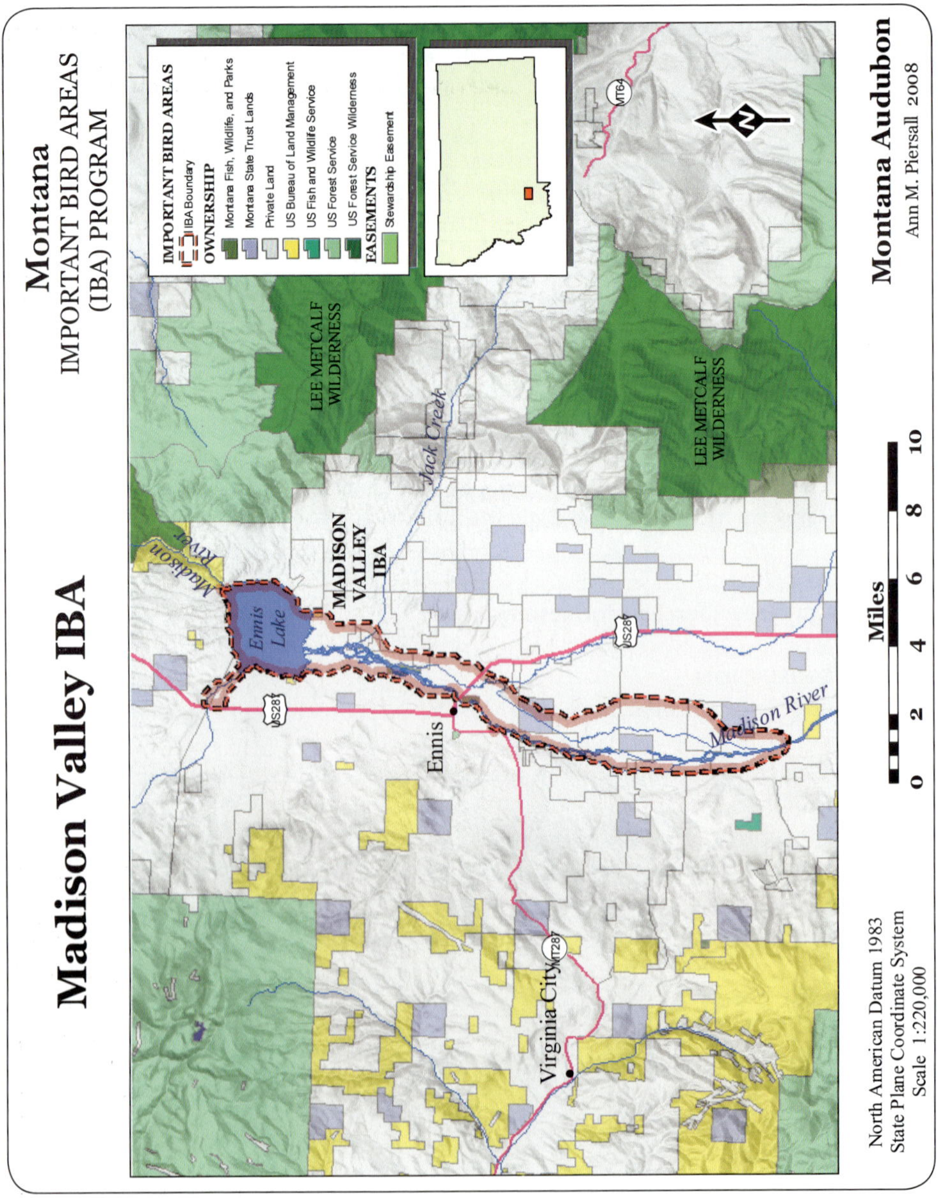

Madison Valley IBA

Montana
IMPORTANT BIRD AREAS (IBA) PROGRAM

Montana Audubon
Ann M. Piersall 2008

IMPORTANT BIRD AREAS

IBA Boundary

OWNERSHIP

Montana Fish, Wildlife, and Parks
Montana State Trust Lands
Private Land
US Bureau of Land Management
US Fish and Wildlife Service
US Forest Service
US Forest Service Wilderness

EASEMENTS

Stewardship Easement

LEE METCALF WILDERNESS

LEE METCALF WILDERNESS

Jack Creek

MADISON VALLEY IBA

Madison River

Ennis Lake

Madison River

US287

US287

MT64

Ennis

Virginia City MT287

Miles

0   2   4   6   8   10

North American Datum 1983
State Plane Coordinate System
Scale 1:220,000

Ferruginous and Rough-legged Hawks (winter). The willows and cottonwoods beside the Madison River are the best place to view Bohemian Waxwing (winter), American Tree Sparrow, Black-capped and Mountain Chickadees, Northern Pygmy and Great Horned Owl, Western Tanager, Red-naped Sapsucker, American Redstart, Veery, Least and Willow Flycatchers, and Yellow Warbler.

Other good birding spots include the state fishing access sites: Valley Garden, Ennis Bridge, Burnt Tree, Eight Mile Ford, and Varney Bridge as well as Odell Creek and associated private lands, but be sure to get landowner permission on the private lands first.

On occasion, the fall migration features some rarely seen birds passing through, such as Surf Scoter, Red Phalarope, Long-tailed Duck, White-fronted Goose, Fox and White-throated Sparrows, and Blue Jay. As many as 200 loons can be seen in a single day on Ennis Lake in late October.

According to Montana Audubon, 14 species of conservation concern are known to use the IBA, including Downy Woodpecker, Warbling Vireo, Gray Catbird, Song Sparrow, Ferruginous Hawk, Sprague's Pipit, Bald Eagle, Common Loon, Red-breasted Merganser (spring migration), Red-naped Sapsucker, American Restart, Veery, Least and Willow Flycatchers, Yellow Warbler, Lazuli Bunting, American White Pelican, Trumpeter Swan, and Sandhill Crane as well as large numbers of American Wigeon, American Coot, and Redheads during fall migration.

There is public camping at Ennis and Varney Bridge Fishing Access Sites, and Ennis has gas, food, and lodging.

DIRECTIONS

Exit I-90 at Exit 274 (Three Forks). Follow US 287 south through Norris to Rainbow Point Road just north of Ennis, and then follow the signs to Bear Trap Canyon. After viewing, turn around and follow Ennis Lake Road (along east side of lake) to US 287. Turn south through Ennis to MT 249. Turn left (south) for about 10 miles to Varney Bridge Road. Follow Varney Bridge (east) until it connects back with US 287.

CONTACT

Montana Audubon Society - Amy Cilimburg, Director of Conservation and Climate Policy
Phone: 406-465-1141
Email: amy@mtaudubon.org

SOUTHWEST MONTANA
#37 Harrison Reservoir (IBA)
(Willow Creek Reservoir FAS)

SOUTHWEST OF THREE FORKS

KEY BIRDS
American Avocet, Spotted Sandpiper, Greater Yellowlegs, Willet, Long-billed Curlew, Ruddy Duck

BEST SEASONS
Spring through fall for waterfowl; August for shorebirds; raptors anytime

AREA DESCRIPTION
Lake habitat with surrounding grasslands and agricultural lands

Local birders say this is "*the* place for shorebirds". Set amid rolling crop lands, grasslands, and a rocky, snaky canyon, the lake has to be among the windiest spots on the planet. I cannot recall ever spending a day there that the wind did not rage at least part of the afternoon. Built for irrigation, except for the odd extreme wet year, by late summer extensive mudflats and heretofore unseen islands draw huge numbers and variety of shorebirds; many state and local rarities have been documented here. Later, the lake serves as a major staging area

Ruddy Duck (hen)

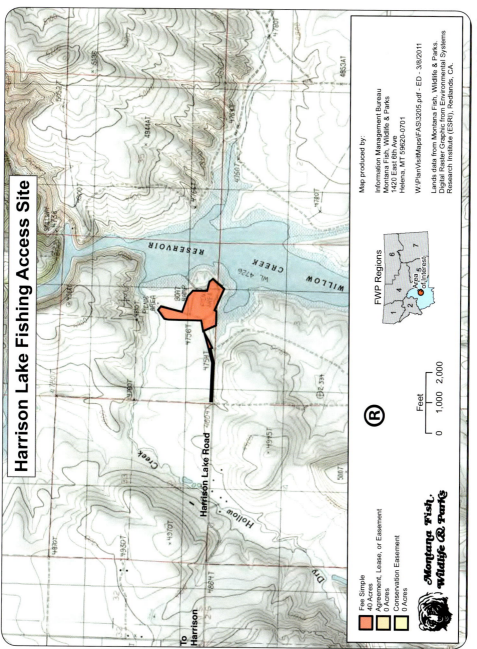

Harrison Lake Fishing Access Site

Map produced by:

Information Management Bureau
Montana Fish, Wildlife & Parks
1420 East 6th Ave
Helena, MT 59620-0701

W:\PlanVisitMaps\FASI3205.pdf - ED - 3/8/2011

Lands data from Montana Fish, Wildlife & Parks.
Digital Raster Graphic from Environmental Systems
Research Institute (ESRI), Redlands, CA.

Used with permission.

FWP Regions

Feet

0   1,000   2,000

Fee Simple
40 Acres

Agreement, Lease, or Easement
0 Acres

Conservation Easement
0 Acres

Montana Fish,
Wildlife & Parks

for Sandhill Cranes and a stopover for migrating waterfowl. The bad news is that most congregate at the south end of the lake, where access is at the landowner's discretion. Summer weekends tend to be circus-like so...

One day in September, we arrived to yet another off the charts blow. No birds anywhere in sight; we decided, instead of scrapping the operation, to check out a more secluded Jefferson River slough nearby. Turns out it was a good move as we found the slough wall-to-wall waterfowl, water birds, and shorebirds — Tundra Swan, Mallard, American Wigeon, teal, American Coot, Gadwall, Canada Goose, Great Blue Heron, shorebirds galore, several Bald Eagles, countless Red-winged and Brewer's Blackbirds, American White Pelican, Common Merganser, and Common Goldeneye — covering just about every square inch of water.

DIRECTIONS

From I-90 turn, south at the Three Forks Exit (US 287) and follow US 287 approximately 20 miles to Harrison. Turn at the Willow Creek Reservoir FAS sign; and go 4 miles east to the lake.

Western Meadowlark

YELLOWSTONE COUNTRY

Yellowstone Country is comprised of Carbon, Gallatin, Park, Stillwater, and Sweet Grass Counties; the area generally north and east of Yellowstone National Park to the Bighorn River and south of US 12 and the Musselshell River including the Gallatin National Forest and parts of the Beaverhead-Deerlodge, Custer, and Lewis and Clark National Forests. While not as large as some of the other tourism regions, what it lacks in size is more than made up for in diverse bird habitats — riparian, alpine, badland, short grass prairie, conifer and hardwood forest, you name it, Yellowstone Country has it.

Bridger Sage-Steppe IBA (Bridger) supports roughly 3 percent of the male sage grouse surveyed in the state. Bear Canyon IBA (Bridger) is generally regarded as *the* spot in Montana to check off the *rare* blue-gray gnatcatcher.

Bozeman and Billings offer commercial air service and I-90 cuts a swath through the region. US routes 12, 89, 191, 212, and 287 provide reasonable driving access to most of the region. Amenities vary, but good food and reasonable beds can be found throughout. Paradise Valley is on just about every visitor's bucket list, as is Yellowstone National Park — a must-do birding site in its own right.

Beartooth Mountains

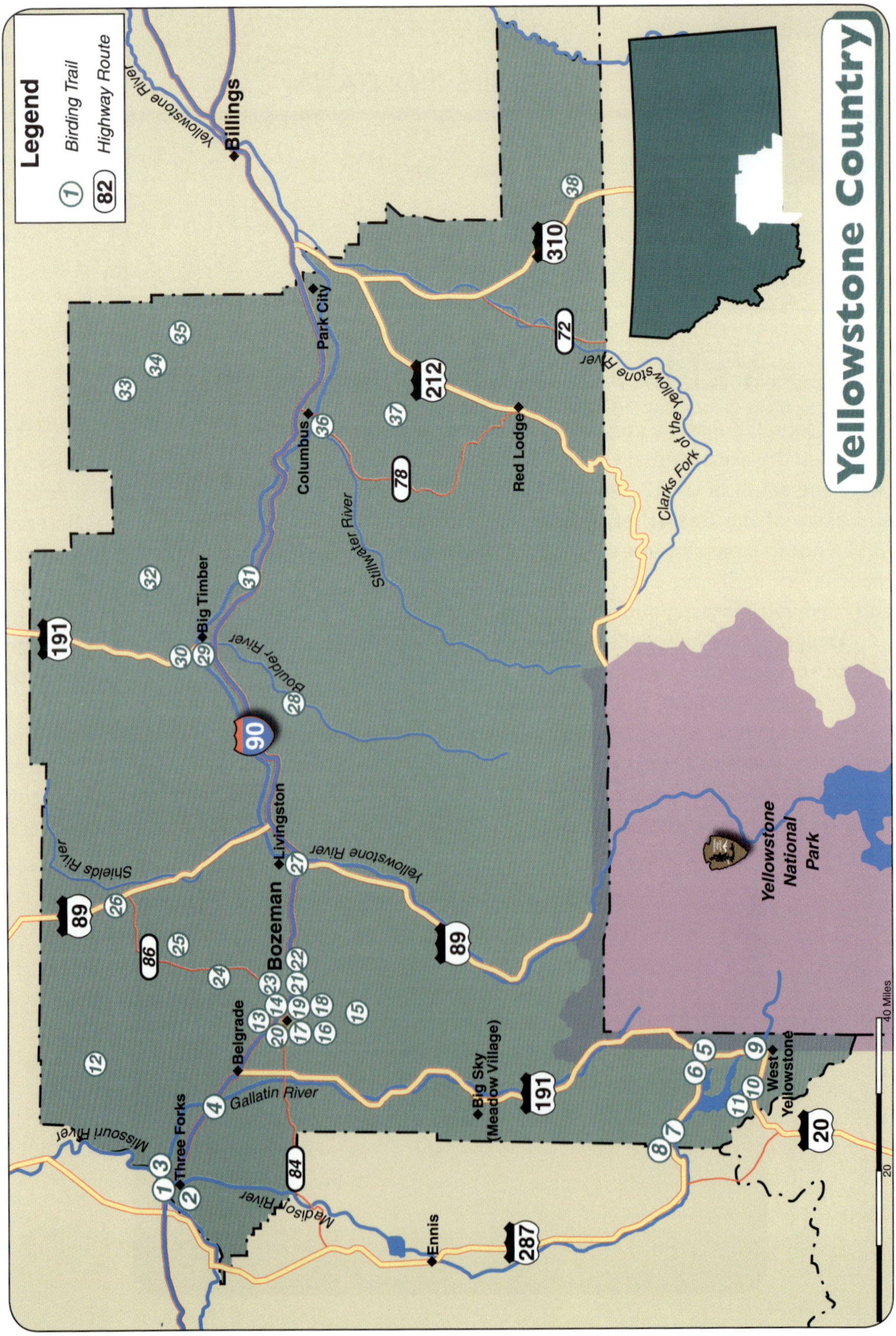

Legend

① Birding Trail

82 Highway Route

Yellowstone Country

Billings

Yellowstone River

310

36

72

Clarks Fork of the Yellowstone River

Park City

212

35

34

33

37

Columbus

36

78

Red Lodge

Stillwater River

32

31

Big Timber

30

29

Boulder River

191

90

Shields River

Livingston

21

Yellowstone River

Yellowstone National Park

89

26

25

24

89

Bozeman

86

23

20 14 13

19 21 22

18

17

16

15

Belgrade

12

Gallatin River

4

Big Sky (Meadow Village)

6 5

9

191

Three Forks

Missouri River

1 3

2

84

Madison River

Ennis

287

10

11

8 7

West Yellowstone

20

40 Miles

20

© 2014 Wilderness Adventures Press, Inc.

Yellowstone Country Locations

1. Old Town Road
2. Bench Road
3. Headwaters State Park
4. Central Park Pond
5. Fir Ridge Cemetery
6. Whit's Lake Road
7. Ghost Village Road
8. Beaver Creek Viewing Site
9. Baker's Hole Campground
10. South Fork of the Madison River
11. Hebgen Lake Road
12. Springhill Road/Dry Creek Road Loop
13. Cherry River Fishing Access Site
14. East Gallatin Recreation Area
15. Hyalite Canyon
16. Kirk Hill
17. Sourdough Nature Trail
18. Triple Tree Trail
19. Lindley Park
20. Bozeman Trail System
21. Mount Ellis
22. Trail Creek Road
23. Fish Hatchery /M Trail
24. Bridger Raptor Festival
25. Battle Ridge Campground
26. Cottonwood Reservoir
27. Livingston Parks
28. Boulder River
29. Big Timber City Parks
30. Otter Creek
31. Pelican Fishing Access Point
32. Sweet Grass Road Loop
33. Hailstone National Wildlife Refuge
34. Halfbreed National Wildlife Refuge
35. Molt /Big Lake Complex
36. Itch-Kep Park
37. Cooney Reservoir
38. Bear Canyon Important Bird Area

YELLOWSTONE COUNTRY
#1 Old Town Road

GPS 45.903,-111.533

NORTH OF THREE FORKS

KEY BIRDS
Sage Thrasher, Clay-colored Sparrow, American Kestrel, Northern Flicker

BEST SEASONS
Spring through fall

AREA DESCRIPTION
Roadside habitat with river and sagebrush

A good spot for a brief bird fix. Probably not worth a long drive, but worth checking out should you be in the area with time to spare. The road starts just outside of town, crosses the Jefferson River, and continues on through mostly sagebrush to merge with US 287. Especially during the spring and early summer, a variety of water birds and water-loving songbirds frequent the river bottoms. Out in the open, look for Northern Harriers, Mountain Bluebirds, and Western Meadowlarks.

Animals that might be seen are pronghorn, mule deer, badger, coyote, and prairie rattlesnake.

DIRECTIONS
From I-90, Exit 278 (Three Forks, MT 2) turn north on Frontage Road and then turn left onto Old Town Road.

Northern Flicker

YELLOWSTONE COUNTRY
Bench Road

#2

GPS 45.881,-111.555

SOUTH OF THREE FORKS

KEY BIRDS
Golden Eagle, Short-eared Owl, Sandhill Crane, Sage Thrasher, Cinnamon Teal, Virginia Rail, Mountain Bluebird, Northern Harrier

BEST SEASONS
Year round; winter and spring for raptors; spring and fall migrations for waterfowl and shorebirds

AREA DESCRIPTION
Roadside habitat with agricultural lands and wetlands

This route (loop) passes through farming and ranching country and past creeks and ponds, allowing for numerous opportunities to view grassland, marshland, waterfowl, and water birds. Mostly private, so be sure to pack enough glass to view birds from the road. Pronghorn, deer, and coyote are common.

Come prepared for hot, dry, and dusty and don't be surprised to find yourself mixed up in a cattle drive. Take a break in the Willow Creek Café, which serves great food and some of the best pies on the planet…hint, hint.

DIRECTIONS
From the main drag in Three Forks, turn south on 2nd Avenue W to Bench Road. Turn right on Baseline Road to Old Yellowstone Trail and then turn right and return through Willow Creek to Three Forks.

#3 Missouri Headwaters State Park (IBA)/Three Forks Area

GPS 45.920,-111.499

NEAR THREE FORKS

KEY BIRDS
At least nine species of conservation concern nest within the park — Red-naped Sapsucker, Least Flycatcher, Gray Catbird, Veery, Warbling Vireo, Song Sparrow, Bald Eagle, and Clay-colored Sparrow; also Sandhill Crane

BEST SEASONS
Best viewing April to September; June for nesting songbirds

AREA DESCRIPTION
Riparian habitat

In these 530 acres, more than 100 species have been observed in the riparian cottonwood, willow and water birch forest, ponds, and wetlands found at the confluence of the Gallatin, Madison, and Jefferson Rivers.

Drive the paved road and stop at the designated parking areas. Walk the 4 miles of trails or simply wander about cross-country. White-throated Swift, Spotted and Solitary Sandpipers, American White Pelican, Double-crested Cormorant, Osprey, and Bald Eagle are common around the water. Raptors such as Prairie and Peregrine Falcons, Northern Harrier, Red-tailed hawk, American Kestrel, and Rough-legged Hawk (winter) hunt the grass and forest edges. Long-billed Curlew, Western Wood-pewee, Least Flycatcher, Eastern and Western Kingbirds, Canyon and Rock Wrens, Bullock's Oriole, Gray Catbird, Tree and Violet-green Swallows, Yellow Warbler, American Tree, and Vesper and Savannah Sparrows are common all summer.

The trail leading east from the parking area a half-mile or so north of the campground leads to Lewis's Rock, which is a good spot for viewing the waterfowl using the confluence of rivers. Ladies, those whistles you hear are not "low-life cat-calls" but yellow-bellied marmots not all that happy at your intrusion. On down the road, around the interpretive center, is one of the best birding sites in the park — songbirds in the brush and trees, and waterfowl, water birds, wading and shorebirds in the Missouri River. A trail leads to nearby Indian pictographs and, of course, more chances to bird along the way.

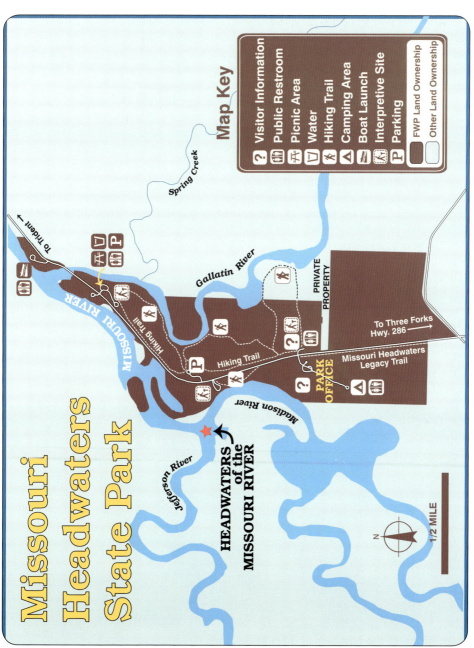

Used with permission.

Note also a threatened species of orchid, Ute Ladies' Tresses, which blooms in the park.

A short drive from the park, the Three Forks Ponds at the edge of town attract a variety of waterfowl, water birds, and songbirds including Caspian Terns. Old Town Road passes through riparian cottonwood habitat along the Jefferson River, a good place to see Western Wood-pewee and Bullock's Oriole, and the sagebrush beyond is a good place to spot Sage Thrasher and Clay-colored and Brewer's Sparrows.

The Three Forks area is steeped in history. On July 28, 1805 Meriwether Lewis noted *"... we called the S.W. fork, that which we meant to ascend, Jefferson's River in honor of that illustrious personage Thomas Jefferson. [the author of our enterprize.] the Middle fork we called Madison's River in honor of James Madison, and the S.E. Fork we called Gallitin's River in honor of Albert Gallitin. ... the beds of all these streams are formed of smooth pebble and gravel, and their waters perfectly transparent; in short they are three noble streams."*

And it was here, several years later that free trapper, John Colter, stripped naked and barefoot began the race for his life. He somehow out distanced several hundred angry Crow warriors intent on claiming his scalp.

There is a campground in the park. In Three Forks, check out the historic Sacajawea Hotel (rooms and fine dining). We have enjoyed excellent meals at the Cattlemen's Café (Three Forks), the Land of Magic (Logan), and the Willow Creek Saloon (in Willow Creek just down the road).

DIRECTIONS
From I-90, Exit 278 (Three Forks) follow signs 2 miles to the park.

CONTACT
Park Manager phone: 406-285-3610

Sandhill Cranes

YELLOWSTONE COUNTRY
Central Park Pond

#4

GPS 45.830,-111.285

WEST OF BELGRADE

KEY BIRDS
Blue- and Green-winged Teal, Wigeon, Mallard, Canada Goose, Great Blue Heron

BEST SEASONS
Year round; spring and fall migration offer the best variety

AREA DESCRIPTION
Spring-fed pond in old gravel pit

Local Audubon members rate the 16-acre pond, "the best spot in Gallatin County for waterfowl."

Once hunting season opens, we've seen the pond literally wall-to-wall ducks and geese, especially since there is no hunting allowed in this area as this is a designated waterfowl protection area.

Spring-fed, it remains at least partially open year round. During migration and over winter, more than a dozen species and up to 3,000 Common and Barrow's Goldeneye have been observed in a single day. We have seen both Tundra and Trumpeter Swans in the fall.

Mallard, Gadwall, and Wigeon are frequent visitors. Wilson's Snipes frequent the marshy edges, as do Sandhill Cranes and Long-billed Curlews; shorebird numbers peak in late summer.

DIRECTIONS
From I-90, Exit 298 (Belgrade) turn north on MT 85; turn left (west) on the Frontage Road for 6 miles and turn left on Heeb Road under the Interstate to the pond.

YELLOWSTONE COUNTRY

#5 # Fir Ridge Cemetery

GPS 44.796,-111.104

NORTH OF WEST YELLOWSTONE

KEY BIRDS
Northern Goshawk, Swainson's Hawk, Sandhill Crane, Long-billed Curlew, Clark's Nutcracker

BEST SEASONS
July through September; trails are closed March 10 through June 30 due to high bear activity.

AREA DESCRIPTION
Old growth Douglas fir and aspen forest, willows, sagebrush, wet meadows, and grasslands

About a half-mile in, the trail splits. Gneiss Trail turns north, and a mile farther enters the park for about a mile to Campanula Creek before continuing on to the southeast. Park Boundary Trail leads south to Duck Creek.

Beaver ponds attract a variety of raptors, songbirds, and waterfowl such as Northern Harrier, teal, Rufous Hummingbird, Yellow Warbler, Warbling Vireo, Savannah Sparrow, Lazuli Bunting, and Mountain Bluebird. In the forest and wet meadows look for a variety of woodpeckers, songbirds, and, during the warm months, the area is a haven for neotropical migrants.

This is major bear country, so please Be Bear Aware; never hike alone, avoid stealthy behavior, and be alert for bear sign: droppings, tracks, etc. When in doubt, leave and, above all, keep bear spray handy and know how to use it. Beware also of Mrs. Moose who tends to get particularly ornery with calf in tow.

The wildflower display is spectacular in late spring and early summer, and the aspens turn smoky gold in September and are equally stunning. Be sure to keep an ear peeled in September for bugling bull elk. Keep one eye peeled anytime for wandering grizzlies.

DIRECTIONS
From West Yellowstone, follow US 191/287 north 9 miles (6-miles north of Baker's Hole Campground) to the Gneiss Creek Trailhead on the east side of the highway (signed).

CONTACT
Hebgen Lake Ranger District phone: 406-823-6961

YELLOWSTONE COUNTRY
#6 Whit's Lake Road (FR 971)

GPS 44.798,-111.157

NORTH OF WEST YELLOWSTONE

KEY BIRDS
Northern Harrier, Red-tailed Hawk, Dusky and Ruffed Grouse, Red-naped Sapsucker, Olive-sided Flycatcher, Clark's Nutcracker, Black-headed Grosbeak, Hermit Thrush, Black-capped Chickadee, Mountain Chickadee

BEST SEASONS
Late May through early August

AREA DESCRIPTION
Rolling sagebrush, open meadows and aspen stands give way to Doug fir and lodgepole pine forest higher up

Two signed trailheads along the road lead into the Gallatin National Forest backcountry. Elk, mule deer, moose, and black bear are frequently sighted, as is the occasional gray wolf pack and grizzly bear. Mountain goats can sometimes be seen on the cliffs. Look for otters and beavers in the river.

This is a popular big game hunting area, so be sure to wear blaze orange during fall hunting seasons.

DIRECTIONS
From West Yellowstone take US 191 north and turn left on US 287. Travel 2.5miles and turn right (north) on Whit's Lake Rd. NOTE: Not for passenger cars except when dry.

CONTACT
Hebgen Lake Ranger District phone: 406-823-6961

Black-capped Chickadee

YELLOWSTONE COUNTRY
Ghost Village Road (FR 989)

#7

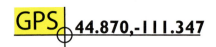

GPS 44.870,-111.347

NORTHWEST OF WEST YELLOWSTONE

KEY BIRDS
Osprey, Bald Eagle, Peregrine Falcon, American Dipper, American White Pelican

BEST SEASONS
June through early August; snow often renders the road impassable for passenger cars

AREA DESCRIPTION
The road is a bit rough in spots but doable, sans snow

The trail follows the Madison River to Quake Lake and is easy walking. Ghost Village (the result of the 1959 magnitude 7.5 earthquake, the largest to hit Montana in recorded history) offers extensive wildflowers, abundant wildlife, and good fishing which all but overshadow what is really a great birding spot. Most of our visits result in multiple check-offs including raptors, songbirds, and water birds.

Beaver, elk, mule deer, moose, and black bear are frequently sighted, as are the occasional grizzly bear and otter.

Anglers flock to this section of the Madison (between the lakes) for good reason, so be sure to pack along the rod…you know, just in case.

There are a kiosk and vault toilet/picnic tables at the trailhead. No motorized access beyond the trailhead.

DIRECTIONS
From West Yellowstone, follow US 191 north to the junction with US 287. Turn left for about 12 miles and turn at the Campfire Lodge sign, with about a mile more to the trailhead.

CONTACT
Hebgen Lake Ranger District phone: 406-823-6961

YELLOWSTONE COUNTRY
#8 Beaver Creek Viewing Site

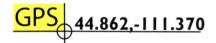

GPS 44.862,-111.370

NORTHWEST OF WEST YELLOWSTONE

KEY BIRDS
Green-winged Teal, Ring-necked Duck, Common Goldeneye, Clark's Nutcracker, Sandhill Crane, Sora

BEST SEASONS
June through August; ponds are typically frozen from November through May

AREA DESCRIPTION
Beaver ponds and associated wetlands, with aspen and coniferous forest

A spotting scope is highly recommended for this site, which is an attractive site for raptors, waterfowl, songbirds, and water birds.

Beaver, elk, mule deer, and moose are also common. Mountain goats frequent the cliffs north and west of the site during spring and early summer. Wildflowers are abundant and the early fall aspen display can be spectacular. Early mornings offer the best viewing ops.

Please exercise caution entering the busy highway, especially during the busy tourist season in high summer.

DIRECTIONS
From West Yellowstone, follow US 191 north to the junction with US 287. Turn left for about 14 miles (about 1.5 miles past Campfire Lodge turnoff, see Ghost Village Rd.). There are turnoffs on either side of the highway.

CONTACT
Hebgen Lake Ranger District
phone: 406-823-6961

Common Goldeneye (hen)

YELLOWSTONE COUNTRY
Baker's Hole Campground

#9

GPS 44.703,-111.102

NORTH OF WEST YELLOWSTONE

KEY BIRDS
Osprey, Bald Eagle, Cinnamon Teal, Red-breasted Nuthatch, Brown Creeper, Pine Grosbeak, Steller's and Gray Jay, Belted Kingfisher

BEST SEASONS
May through October

AREA DESCRIPTION
Borders Madison River; campground is largely lodgepole pine forest surrounded by grass, wetlands, and willows

The Yellowstone Park boundary is immediately east of the campground. Birders can park in the parking areas outside the campground.

The marshy area beside the river is a good place to spot Wilson's Snipe, Sora, and the occasional American Bittern. Ruby-crowned Kinglets, Hairy and Downy Woodpeckers, and Mountain and Black-capped Chickadees are easy to find in the campground and surrounding forest.

Belted Kingfisher
Credit: U.S. Fish and Wildlife Service

Elk, bison, moose, coyote, black bear, and the occasional grizzly are frequently sighted in the area. At times, the frog music is deafening.

Baker's Hole is one of the river's more popular fishing holes, especially in October when the big browns run up from nearby Hebgen Lake on their annual spawning runs.

West Yellowstone offers all the amenities. There is good public camping at Baker's Hole and off US 20 west of town at Lonesomehurst Campground on Hebgen Lake's Madison Arm.

DIRECTIONS
From West Yellowstone, follow US 191 north for 3 miles. The campground is on the east side of the highway (signed).

CONTACT
Hebgen Lake Ranger District phone: 406-823-6961

BIRDING THE WEST YELLOWSTONE AREA

Aside from being one of the more scenic and wildlife-friendly spots in Montana; to say nothing of sitting on the doorstep of America's favorite National Park, local birders report observing as many as 50 to 60 species a day; enough variety to keep all but our most jaded grinning.

YELLOWSTONE COUNTRY
#10 South Fork Madison River

GPS 44.677,-111.186

WEST OF WEST YELLOWSTONE

KEY BIRDS
Wilson's Warbler, Northern Waterthrush, Bald Eagle, Osprey, Lincoln's Sparrow, Great Blue Heron

BEST SEASONS
May through October

AREA DESCRIPTION
Riparian habitat with thick willows

The Madison Arm Road follows the river to the north. Upstream of the highway, private lands make access tricky but not impossible. The Madison Arm Road provides easy, seat-of-the-pants birding. Much of the land along the Madison Arm is public, allowing foot access but there are no developed trails.

Much of the river is guarded by thick, extensive willows and upstream of the bridge (left of highway) there is little motorized access. Should you decide to commune with nature, keep a wary eye peeled for moose and grizzly bears, both of which frequent the area and neither of which are especially fond of surprises. We have never endured an actual encounter, but two sojourns uncovered enough fresh grizzly sign to seriously consider that birding elsewhere might be the better idea.

DIRECTIONS
From West Yellowstone, follow US 20 west about 5 miles and turn right at the sign.

CONTACT
Hebgen Lake Ranger District phone: 406-823-6961

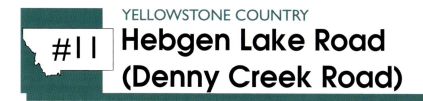

YELLOWSTONE COUNTRY

#11 | Hebgen Lake Road (Denny Creek Road)

 44.688,-111.241

WEST OF WEST YELLOWSTONE

KEY BIRDS
Red-naped Sapsucker, Dusky Grouse, Bald Eagle, Osprey, Trumpeter Swan, Northern Goshawk, Northern Harrier, Red-tailed Hawk, Sora, Hooded Merganser, Great Blue Heron

BEST SEASONS
May through October

AREA DESCRIPTION
A diverse habitat comprised of open ranch land, sagebrush, marsh, wet meadows, grassland, aspen and conifer forest, willows and cottonwood bottoms and the big lake itself

The diverse habitat attracts just about all of 200+ plus species indigenous to the area at one time or another.

Several trailheads lead into the Gallatin National Forest, allowing for almost unlimited foot travel and, of course, birding opportunities.

With so many birding ops nearby, we usually HQ at Lonesomehurst Campground (about 4 miles in on the lake) and fan out from there.

DIRECTIONS
From West Yellowstone, follow US 20 west about 8 miles and turn right (north) on Hebgen Lake Road. The road parallels the lake and eventually (20 miles or so in) ends at a locked gate; return to the highway via the same route.

CONTACT
Hebgen Lake Ranger District phone: 406-823-6961

Hooded Merganser

YELLOWSTONE COUNTRY
#12 Springhill-Dry Creek Loop

GPS 46.101,-111.168

NORTH OF BELGRADE

KEY BIRDS
Golden Eagle, Prairie Falcon, Rough-legged Hawk (winter), Northern Harrier, Wild Turkey, Mountain Bluebird, Horned Lark, Lapland Longspur, Snow Bunting (winter)

BEST SEASONS
Year around; winter and spring for raptors

AREA DESCRIPTION
A 60-mile loop through grass, pasture and cropland, juniper and cottonwood habitats

Local birders list, "Bald and Golden Eagles, Northern Harrier, Prairie Falcon, Red-tailed and Rough-legged Hawks as winter and early spring residents along this loop. In summer, both Swainson's and Ferruginous Hawks show up. Horned Lark, Mountain Bluebird, Vesper and Savannah Sparrows, and Western Meadowlark are common. Lapland Longspurs and Snow Buntings sometimes show up over winter as does the occasional Gyrfalcon." Ring-necked Pheasants can be thick at times.

While birding in this area, you may also come across mule and white-tailed deer, pronghorn, and coyote.

DIRECTIONS
From I-90, Exit 305 (19th Avenue in Bozeman) and turn north to Springhill Road. Continue north on Springhill, which becomes Rocky Mountain Road, to Bremer Creek Road (impassable when wet) to Dry Creek Road and then turn south to Belgrade.

Wild Turkey

YELLOWSTONE COUNTRY

#13 Cherry River Fishing Access Site

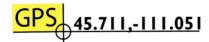 GPS 45.711,-111.051

NORTH OF BOZEMAN

KEY BIRDS
Mallard, Willow Flycatcher, Yellow-rumped and Yellow Warblers, Barn, Tree, Violet-green, and Northern Rough-winged Swallows

BEST SEASONS
Early mornings during spring and fall migrations

AREA DESCRIPTION
Riparian river habitat surrounded by grasslands

The site attracts a variety of songbirds, water birds and waterfowl. Look for Song Sparrows, Marsh Wrens, and Yellow-headed Blackbirds. Chipping and Savannah Sparrows are easy to find, as are Red-winged Blackbirds, Blue-winged, Green-winged, and Cinnamon Teal, and Eastern and Western Kingbirds. Gray Catbirds and Cedar Waxwings are frequently sighted.

Located on the banks of the East Gallatin River, the site features an interpretive trail, vault toilet and picnic tables; pack-in, pack-out rules apply.

DIRECTIONS
From I-90, Exit 305 turn north on 19th Avenue, and turn right (east) on Frontage Road. Turn left at FAS sign.

CONTACT
MTFW&P phone:
406-994-4042

Mallard (drake)

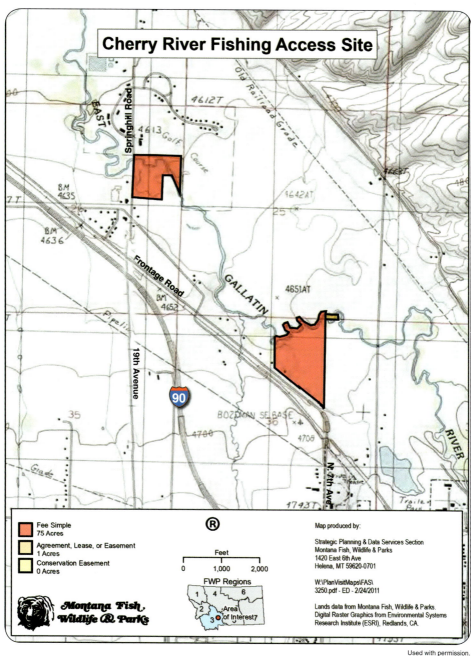

Cherry River Fishing Access Site

Fee Simple
75 Acres

Agreement, Lease, or Easement
1 Acres

Conservation Easement
0 Acres

®

Feet

0   1,000   2,000

FWP Regions

Area
of Interest

Montana Fish,
Wildlife & Parks

Map produced by:

Strategic Planning & Data Services Section
Montana Fish, Wildlife & Parks
1420 East 6th Ave
Helena, MT 59620-0701

W:\PlanVisitMaps\FAS\
3250.pdf - ED - 2/24/2011

Lands data from Montana Fish, Wildlife & Parks.
Digital Raster Graphics from Environmental Systems
Research Institute (ESRI), Redlands, CA.

YELLOWSTONE COUNTRY
#14 East Gallatin Recreation Area

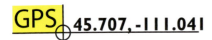

GPS 45.707, -111.041

BOZEMAN

KEY BIRDS
Western Meadowlark, Song Sparrow, Violet-green Swallow, Gray Catbird, Green-winged Teal, Western Bluebird, Northern Waterthrush

BEST SEASONS
Year around; spring and fall migration offers the best chance for viewing large numbers of waterfowl.

AREA DESCRIPTION
Cottonwoods and shrub thickets, Glen Lake and associated grass

The area provides an attractive mix to attract a variety birds — waterfowl, wading birds, water birds, songbirds, and raptors. Trails allow easy access. Set up a spotting scope to view the lake.

Featuring picnic tables, trails, restrooms, potable water, garbage collection, sand beach and more, this one is a popular spot during the summer; the rest of the year is relatively quiet. Donation requested to help defray maintenance costs.

Violet-green Swallow

DIRECTIONS
From I-90, take Exit 309 and turn north to Frontage Road. Turn right on Frontage Road and turn left (east) on West Griffin Avenue, and turn left (north) on Manley Road to the access sign.

YELLOWSTONE COUNTRY

#15 | Hyalite Canyon

GPS | 45.563,-111.072

SOUTH OF BOZEMAN

KEY BIRDS
Bohemian Waxwing, Common Redpoll, Western Tanager, Mountain Chickadee, Red-naped Sapsucker, Hairy and Downy Woodpeckers, American Dipper, Canada Jay

BEST SEASONS
May through October offers the best chance for a variety species; but the canyon is accessible year round. Late winter through early spring is a good time to listen for owls.

AREA DESCRIPTION
Rugged, forested canyon with some small meadows and a reservoir

Several trails lead into the Gallatin National Forest. Said to be the most used canyon in the state, right out the backdoor of perhaps the state's fastest growing city, avoiding a crowd means getting up early and don't even think about being alone on weekends. There is no parking anywhere along the road except at designated pull-offs.

But, with miles of trails and a big, largely empty forest to explore, birding ops are limited only by your ability to get around. You may also come across white-tailed and mule deer, moose, black bear, coyote, and bobcat.

There is trout fishing in the reservoir and creek, and three developed campgrounds as well as mountain biking, cross country skiing, and ice climbing…you know, just in case the birds prove elusive.

DIRECTIONS
From Bozeman, take 19th Avenue south about 7 miles. Turn left on Hyalite Canyon Road for about 10 miles to the reservoir.

CONTACT
Gallatin National Forest phone: 406-587-6701

YELLOWSTONE COUNTRY

#16 Kirk Hill

GPS 45.592,-111.063

SOUTH OF BOZEMAN

KEY BIRDS
Western Tanager, Warbling Vireo, Mountain Bluebird, Red-breasted Nuthatch, Steller's Jay, Western Screech Owl

BEST SEASONS
Spring through fall offers the best variety; keep an eye and ear peeled in late winter for Great Gray Owls.

AREA DESCRIPTION
Mountain foothills with mixed forest and grasslands

Local birders say, "Kirk Hill is one of the most accessible spots to bird the foothills transition zone. A single trail leads from the parking area which soon divides, leading to several loops of varying distances and steepness through a mix of willow, aspen, and Douglas fir forest. Typical forest dwelling birds such as nuthatches, warblers, vireos, woodpeckers, Brown Creeper, Veery, Steller's Jay, Long-eared Owl, Cooper's Hawk, Northern Goshawk and Western Screech Owl and even Great Gray Owls are possible."

DIRECTIONS
Take 19th Avenue south out of Bozeman. When the road takes a hard turn to the right, the trailhead parking area is on the left.

Red-breasted Nuthatch

YELLOWSTONE COUNTRY

#17 Sourdough Nature Trail

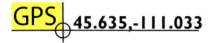 GPS 45.635,-111.033

BOZEMAN

KEY BIRDS
Rufous and Calliope Hummingbirds, Black-headed Grosbeak, MacGillivray's, Orange-crowned, Yellow-rumped, and Yellow Warblers, Warbling Vireo, Western Wood-pewee

BEST SEASONS
Year round; spring through fall for best variety

AREA DESCRIPTION
Fairly level trail through wooded area surrounded by homes

Deciduous woods with a brushy understory, the trail beside Bozeman Creek (aka Sourdough) affords easy viewing for a variety of songbirds, raptors, and woodpeckers despite its close proximity to the hustle and bustle of town life.

DIRECTIONS
From I-90, Exit 309 on US 191 (Main Street); turn left (south) on Church Avenue and continue on Sourdough Road to Goldstein Lane. Turn right (west) to the trailhead.

Calliope Hummingbird
Credit: Gary Swant

YELLOWSTONE COUNTRY

#18 Triple Tree Trail

GPS 45.613,-111.022

SOUTH OF BOZEMAN

KEY BIRDS
Red-naped Sapsucker, Fox, Savannah, Song, Vesper, and Clay-colored sparrows, Mountain Bluebird, Northern Harrier

BEST SEASONS
May through October

AREA DESCRIPTION
Developed hiking trail that crisscrosses a creek and heads steeply uphill

The trail (about a 3-mile loop) begins in grass, crosses Limestone Creek, and continues uphill, traversing the northwest slope of Mount Ellis. Grass, brushy bottoms, and coniferous forest attract a variety of birds. For the hale and hearty and/or young at heart, summiting (steep) is rewarded by spectacular views of the city and the surrounding valley and mountains.

The spring wildflower show can be equally spectacular, especially in wet years.

DIRECTIONS
From I-90, Exit 309, follow US 191 (Main Street) to South Church Avenue (Sourdough Road after crossing Kagy Boulevard) to the parking area (signed).

YELLOWSTONE COUNTRY
#19 Lindley Park

GPS 45.679,-111.025

BOZEMAN

KEY BIRDS
Great Horned Owl, nuthatches, woodpeckers, warblers

BEST SEASONS
Year round; spring through fall for best variety

AREA DESCRIPTION
City park with old-growth trees

Old-growth Douglas fir and spruce trees in the park and in the nearby cemetery attract a variety of coniferous forest-dwelling birds.

DIRECTIONS
From I-90, Exit 309 on US 191 (Main Street). Turn left onto Buttonwood Avenue and go approximately ¼ mile to the park.

Great Horned Owl

YELLOWSTONE COUNTRY
#20 Bozeman Trail System

GPS **Gallagator Trail:**
45.678,-111.027

Bozeman

Key Birds
Green-tailed Towhee, American Redpoll, Bullock's Oriole, Western Tanager, Mountain Bluebird

Best Seasons
Year round; spring through fall for best variety

Area Description
Developed trail system through urban and suburban area

The 45 miles of trails — Pond, Chris Boyd, Gallagator, Highland Ridge, Painted Hills, and Story Mill Spur — allow birders confined to the city for whatever reasons, to get out there no matter how hectic their other schedule obligations might be.

Set amid a bustling city, the trail system winds through just about every sort of habitat imaginable and attracts birds like bees to honey. As you might imagine, the trails attract the usual thundering herd — hikers, joggers, mountain bikers, cross-country skiers, and dog walkers. In other words, the best viewing typically occurs *early* on weekday mornings.

The Gallatin Valley Land Trust produces a map that is available at many local retailers for $2, that shows many of these trails and other public land.

YELLOWSTONE COUNTRY
#21 Mount Ellis

GPS ⊕ **45.652,-110.960**

SOUTHEAST OF BOZEMAN

KEY BIRDS
Hairy, Downy, and Lewis's Woodpeckers, Common Raven, White-breasted Nuthatch, Mountain Bluebird, Northern Harrier, Savannah and White-crowned Sparrows

BEST SEASONS
Spring through fall

AREA DESCRIPTION
Hiking trail that climbs slowly into forest

The trail begins in grass for about a mile before climbing to forested foothills. Rough two-track offers wheeled options. Meadows break up the forest, creating the sort of edges and mosaic habitat attractive to a variety of birds.
  The spring and early summer wildflower display and the scenic views higher up can be spectacular.

DIRECTIONS
Follow Kagy Blvd. east to Bozeman Trail, to Mt. Ellis Lane. Turn right (south) to the trailhead. Or take Bozeman Trail to Bear Canyon Road south. Park at the New World Gulch Trailhead.

Common Raven

YELLOWSTONE COUNTRY
Trail Creek Road
#22

GPS 45.646,-110.886

EAST OF BOZEMAN

KEY BIRDS
Hammond's and Cordilleran Flycatchers, Western Tanager, Yellow and Yellow-rumped Warblers, Warbling Vireo, Ruby-crowned Kinglet, Sharp-shinned Hawk

BEST SEASONS
Spring through fall

AREA DESCRIPTION
Mountain pass road cutting between two valleys with forests and meadows

The best viewing is along the willow-choked creek. Despite the busy interstate nearby, a surprising variety of birds thrive here. Songbirds of every sort — thrushes, finches, hummingbirds, sparrows — you name it. The Chestnut Mountain Trail provides access to the foothills.

DIRECTIONS
From I-90, Exit 316, Trail Creek Road; turn right onto Trail Creek Road.

YELLOWSTONE COUNTRY
#23 Fish Hatchery/"M" Trail

GPS 45.709,-110.978

NORTHEAST OF BOZEMAN

KEY BIRDS
Lazuli Bunting, Orange-crowned Warbler, Green-tailed and Spotted Towhees, Mountain Bluebird, Northern Harrier

BEST SEASONS
Spring through fall offers the best variety

AREA DESCRIPTION
Steep climb up mountain with forest habitat and grassy areas

Birds such as Vesper Sparrow, Horned Lark, and Western Bluebird frequent the grassy areas. In the brush and trees, look for Townsend's Solitaire, Brown Thrasher, and Mountain Chickadee. Bridger Creek offers the best chance of checking off birds such as American Dipper, MacGillivray's Warbler, Northern Waterthrush, Gray Catbird, and Black-headed Grosbeak.

To beat the crowds, plan on getting out early and late, both in the season and in the day.

DIRECTIONS
From I-90, Exit 306 turn north on N. 7th Avenue. Turn right on Griffin Drive and then turn left onto Bridger Canyon Road. It's about 4 miles to the trailhead (on the left).

Northern Harrier

YELLOWSTONE COUNTRY

#24 Bridger Raptor Festival

GPS 45.817,-110.884

BRIDGER BOWL SKI AREA NORTH OF BOZEMAN

KEY BIRDS
Golden Eagle and 18 other raptor species have been observed.

BEST SEASONS
Mid-October for peak eagle numbers although dates vary, see contact info below.

AREA DESCRIPTION
Developed ski area with grassy areas and forest

Hosted annually by Bridger Bowl Ski Area since 1995, the main draw is the largest known golden eagle migration in the country. Access is free and visitors can enjoy wildlife films, a keynote speaker, guided nature walks, and educational and entertaining programs suited to folks of all ages.

According to festival literature: "The Bridger Ridge first gained national recognition among raptor specialists as a major migratory flyway in the early 1980's. Raptor enthusiast Fred Tilly first discovered the Bridger site in 1979. Observers monitor the Bridger migration daily from 27 August through 31 October each year. On average the annual count includes more than 1,500 golden eagles and between 2,500 and 3,000 raptors overall. Since 1991 observers have sighted 18 species. October is the peak activity period for both Golden and Bald Eagles, with Rough-legged Hawk activity mostly confined to the latter half of October. In contrast, the migrations of a few other species, such as Ospreys, Broad-winged Hawks, and Swainson's Hawks, are generally confined to September. For most other species, however, activity begins to pick up markedly in mid-September and generally peaks during the period spanning the last 10 days of September and first 10 days of October. Weather permitting, late September and early October are therefore the most productive times for visiting the site to see many species, with mid-October the best time for seeing lots of eagles. Peak daily activity periods vary with weather conditions, but generally extend from late morning to mid-afternoon."

DIRECTIONS
From Bozeman, take Route 86 north of Bozeman, also known as Bridger Canyon Road to sign on the left side of the road for Bridger Ski Area. Take a left and park in the parking lot.

CONTACT
Bridger Raptor Festival / Phone: 406-586-1518 or 800-223-9609 /
Website: www.bridgerraptorfest.org

YELLOWSTONE COUNTRY
#25 Battle Ridge Campground

GPS 45.883,-110.882

BRIDGER MOUNTAINS
NORTHEAST OF BOZEMAN

KEY BIRDS
Williamson's Sapsuckers, Lincoln's Sparrow, Black-backed Woodpecker, Hammond's and Cordilleran Flycatchers, MacGillivray's Warbler

BEST SEASONS
June to October

AREA DESCRIPTION
Developed campground in national forest

Situated in the Gallatin National Forest (elevation 6,500 feet) the campground and surrounding forest is home to an interesting variety of birds such as Steller's and Gray Jays, Clark's Nutcracker, and Mountain Chickadee. Trails and designated forest roads allow easy access to the surrounding area.

As the story goes, Battle Ridge got its name in 1878 after a brief battle between local cowboys and a band of "horse thieving" Indians; probably Flatheads who frequently passed through the area on their way to and from buffalo hunts farther east.

Camping, hiking, mountain biking, and picnicking are popular. There are 13 campsites, vault toilet and picnic tables; pack-in, pack-out rules apply.

DIRECTIONS
From I-90, Exit 306 and turn north on N. 7th Avenue. At light, turn right on Griffin Drive and then turn left onto Bridger Canyon Road (MT 86). It's approximately 18 miles to the campground.

YELLOWSTONE COUNTRY

#26 Cottonwood Reservoir

GPS 46.037,-110.683

NORTHWEST OF LIVINGSTON

KEY BIRDS
Grebes, American White Pelican, Barn Swallow, raptors including Golden Eagle and Ferruginous Hawk, Trumpeter Swans during migration

BEST SEASONS
Early mornings during spring and fall migrations offer the best variety

AREA DESCRIPTION
Reservoir surrounded by grasslands and sagebrush

Amid a wide, farm and ranch valley with the stunning Crazies to the east and the Bridgers to the west, the reservoir serves as a watering hole for dozens of birds of several types. Typical of Montana reservoirs built for irrigation, water levels fluctuate widely — brimming in spring, a bit grimmer later on — exposing extensive mudflats attractive to large numbers and variety of shorebirds during the late summer (August) migration. Large flocks of waterfowl use the reservoir during spring and fall migrations. Sandhill cranes nest in the valley and large numbers can be seen staging in October prior to the annual fall exodus. Open country loving songbirds are easy to find.

DIRECTIONS
From I-90, east of Livingston Exit 340, turn north on US 89. The reservoir is about 3 miles or so north of Wilsall.

Barn Swallow

YELLOWSTONE COUNTRY
#25 Livingston County Parks and Surrounding Area

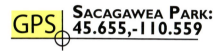

GPS | SACAGAWEA PARK:
45.655,-110.559

LIVINGSTON

KEY BIRDS
Wood Duck, Barrow's Goldeneye, Bald and Golden Eagles, Rough-legged hawk, Eurasian Collared-dove, Belted Kingfisher, Mourning Dove, Black-capped and Mountain Chickadees, Townsend's Solitaire, Swainson's Thrush

BEST SEASONS
Year round

AREA DESCRIPTION
Mixed habitat from urban to country roads

Several-time winner of the Tree City USA award from the National Arbor Foundation, as you might expect almost anywhere in town is a potential bird hotspot. For starters, check out the 11 city parks — our favorite is Sacagawea Park beside the Yellowstone River, where it seems just about every bird indigenous to the area shows up at one time or another.

Area roads worth checking out include: Mission Creek, Swingley, Willow Creek, Old Yellowstone Trail, Convict Grade and Duck Creek. Up toward Clyde Park, Cottonwood Creek Road is also a productive drive.

DIRECTIONS
Armed with a good map — DeLorme Atlas is one — just about any street in Livingston or road in the surrounding area is worth a shot. There are three exits from I-90.

CONTACT
Livingston Chamber of Commerce
303 E. Park St.
Livingston, MT
Phone: 406-222-0850
Website: www.livingston-chamber.com

Osprey

YELLOWSTONE COUNTRY
#28 Boulder River

GPS | BOULDER FORKS FAS:
45.657,-110.109

SOUTH OF BIG TIMBER

KEY BIRDS
Bald Eagle, Osprey, Wild Turkey, American Dipper, Western Tanager, Least Flycatcher, Yellow Warbler

BEST SEASONS
Spring through fall

AREA DESCRIPTION
Roads following river through diverse mountain habitat

Leaving Big Timber, take the less traveled Old Boulder Road, instead of the main highway, where it's easier to pull off and look around. About 10 miles out, the road merges with the highway; continue on to McLeod and turn left to the Boulder Forks Fishing Access Site and Campground, a good place to view a variety of songbirds and watch for dippers in the tumbling river.

South of McLeod, if you have time, take the signed East Boulder Road which winds its way into the mountains through a variety of habitats, offering some spectacular views of the peaks of the Absaroka-Beartooth Wilderness and the chance for plentiful check-off ops.

Continuing south of McLeod on MT 298, a mile or so out of town the West Boulder Road is another interesting and worthwhile side trip. FYI, you can eventually connect with Swingley Road and work your way back to Livingston; a long and often rough sojourn but offering lots of birding ops along the way.

About 10 miles south of McLeod, the paved road ends at spectacular Natural Bridge. Enjoy the view, look for dippers and a variety of forest dwelling birds. For you more adventurous souls, the gravel and rock Main Boulder Road continues on upriver (south) for over 20 miles; all spectacular, all good bird habitat, all good fishing…you know, just in case.

Not all of this is public, please respect private ownership rights; access requires written landowner permission.

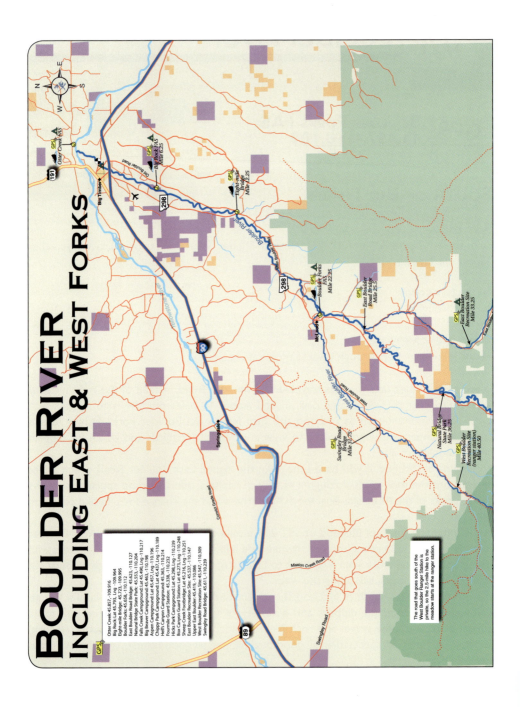

BOULDER RIVER
INCLUDING EAST & WEST FORKS

Otter Creek: 45.857, -109.916
Big Rock: Lat 45.793, Lng -109.964
Eight-mile Bridge: 45.723, -109.995
Boulder Forks: 45.58, -110.112
East Boulder Road Bridge: 45.623, -110.127
Natural Bridge State Park: 45.553, -110.204
Falls Creek Campground: Lat 45.490, Lng -110.217
Big Beaver Campground: 45.463, -110.198
Aspen Campground: Lat 45.457, Lng -110.196
Chippy Park Campground: Lat 45.437, Lng -110.189
Hell's Canyon Campground: 45.363, -110.214
Fourmile Guard Station: 45.338, -110.232
Hicks Park Campground: Lat 45.296, Lng -110.239
Box Canyon Guard Station: Lat 45.273, Lng -110.248
Sheep Creek Footbridge: Lat 45.216, Lng -110.251
East Boulder Recreation Site: 45.537, -110.147
Upper East Boulder: 45.419, -110.088
West Boulder Recreation Site: 45.547, -110.309
Swingley Road Bridge: 45.611, -110.239

The road that goes south of the
West Boulder Ranger Station is
private, so the 2.5-mile hike to the
meadow starts at the ranger station.

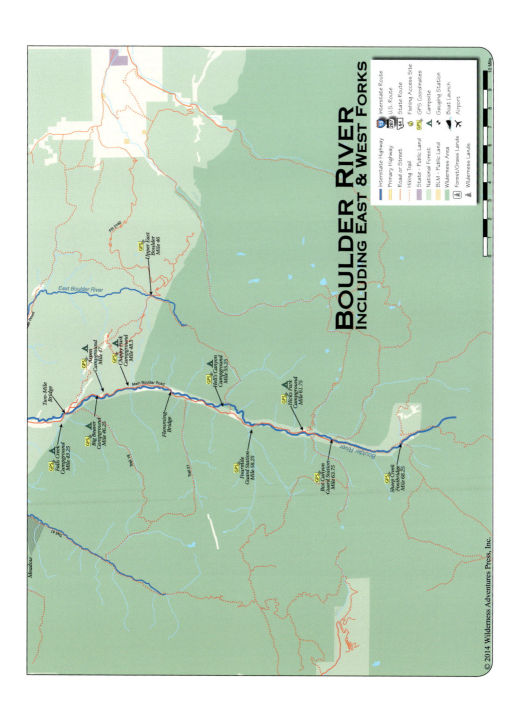

BOULDER RIVER
INCLUDING EAST & WEST FORKS

Legend:
- Interstate Route
- U.S. Route
- State Route
- Primary Highway
- Road or Street
- Hiking Trail
- State – Public Land
- National Forest
- BLM – Public Land
- Wilderness Area
- Forest/Grass Lands
- Wilderness Lands
- Fishing Access Site
- GPS Coordinates
- Campsite
- Gauging Station
- Boat Launch
- Airport

Upper East Boulder Mile 46

East Boulder River

FR 2140

Big Spring Road

Two-Mile Bridge

Aspen Campground Mile 47

Chippy-Park Campground Mile 48.5

Main Boulder Road

Hell's Canyon Campground Mile 55.25

Falls Creek Campground Mile 63.25

Big Beaver Campground Mile 46.25

Flemming Bridge

Trail 18

Trail 21

Fourmile Guard Station Mile 58.25

Boulder River

Hicks Park Campground Mile 61.75

Box Canyon Guard Station Mile 63.75

Sheep Creek Footbridge Mile 68.25

Meadow

Trail 41

© 2014 Wilderness Adventures Press, Inc.

Contact
Gallatin National Forest phone: 406-587-6701

Yellow Warbler

YELLOWSTONE COUNTRY
#29 Big Timber City Parks

GPS **DORNIX PARK:**
45.839,-109.934

BIG TIMBER

KEY BIRDS
Brewer's Blackbird, Common Grackle, Sandhill Crane, Lark Sparrow, Wood Duck, Turkey Vulture

BEST SEASONS
Spring through fall

AREA DESCRIPTION
Undeveloped park along river confluence

Trails wind through Dornix Park (50-acres) near the confluence of the Boulder and Yellowstone Rivers, allowing easy access. Local birders say, on average, about 60 species are observed annually; about 40 of which can be observed within the park.

Osprey are common (Yellowstone Bridge and Lion's Club Park). During spring migration, look for Audubon Warbler and Pine Siskin. Chickadees are common most anytime.

While hardly what you call a park by any stretch, the sewage lagoon is still one of the best spots to check off a few waterfowl species.

Once known as Dornix, in 1883 the town's name was changed to Big Timber by railroad officials in St. Paul, Minnesota.

CONTACT
Big Timber Chamber of Commerce
1350 Hwy 10 W
Big Timber, MT
Phone: 406-932-5161
Website: www.bigtimber.com

YELLOWSTONE COUNTRY
#30 Otter Creek Road

GPS 45.871,-109.946

NORTH OF BIG TIMBER

KEY BIRDS
Sage Grouse, Wild Turkey, Say's Phoebe, Savannah and Vesper Sparrow, Western Meadowlark, Mountain Bluebird, Ruby-crowned Kinglet, Sharp-shinned Hawk, Swainson's Hawk

BEST SEASONS
Spring through fall

AREA DESCRIPTION
Raptors abound all along the route — Golden Eagles, Northern Harriers, Prairie Falcons, and Great Horned Owls are common. Although dwindling in numbers, Sage Grouse show up on occasion. Western Meadowlarks and Mountain Bluebirds are easy finds, as are Yellow-headed Blackbirds in the marshy areas. Lavold Reservoir, just off Otter Creek Road, and Lower Glaston Lake, just off Glaston Lake Road, sometimes host a surprising variety of waterfowl and water birds — especially during migration.

You may also come across animals such as pronghorn, deer and coyote.

DIRECTIONS
From Big Timber, follow US 191 approximately 4 miles north and turn right on Otter Creek Road. Otter Creek Road circles back around to US 191 just a few miles north of Melville. The full loop is about 45 miles round trip.

Swainson's Hawk

YELLOWSTONE COUNTRY

#31 Pelican Fishing Access Site

GPS 45.758,-109.771

EAST OF BIG TIMBER
ON THE YELLOWSTONE RIVER

KEY BIRDS
American White Pelican, Tundra Swan, Song Sparrow, Tree and Violet-green Swallows, Burrowing Owl (nearby Greycliff State Park)

BEST SEASONS
Year round; spring through early fall offer the best viewing ops.

AREA DESCRIPTION
Mix of developed golf course, open grassland, river habitat

On the way to the fishing access, look for Sandhill Crane, Northern Harrier, Western Meadowlark, Mourning Dove, and Ring-necked Pheasant, along with waterfowl, gulls, and Killdeer that are frequent visitors at the overland golf course.

Also stop at the Greycliff Prairie Dog

Tundra Swan

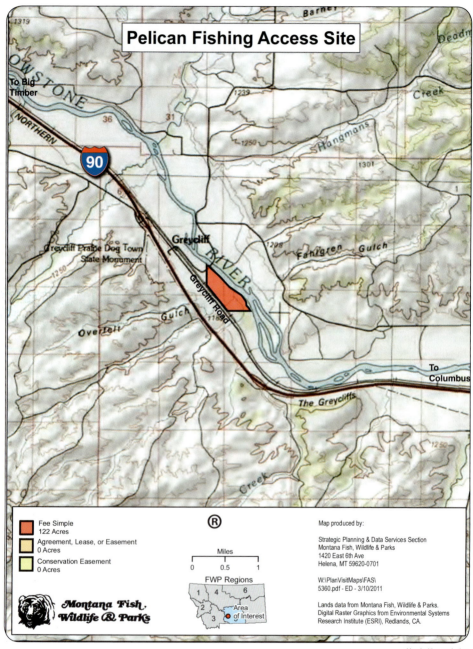

Pelican Fishing Access Site

Fee Simple
122 Acres

Agreement, Lease, or Easement
0 Acres

Conservation Easement
0 Acres

Miles
0   0.5   1

FWP Regions

Area of Interest

Montana Fish,
Wildlife & Parks

Map produced by:

Strategic Planning & Data Services Section
Montana Fish, Wildlife & Parks
1420 East 6th Ave
Helena, MT 59620-0701

W:\PlanVisitMaps\FAS\
5360.pdf - ED - 3/10/2011

Lands data from Montana Fish, Wildlife & Parks.
Digital Raster Graphics from Environmental Systems
Research Institute (ESRI), Redlands, CA.

Used with permission.

Town State Park for the chance to view Burrowing Owls and black-tailed prairie dogs; you do know, rattlesnakes love prairie dogs…of course, you do.

Continue on to the 123-acre Pelican FAS (aka, Greycliff Road) where Bald Eagles, Ospreys, pelicans, a variety of ducks and geese, and songbirds are common sightings.

Hunting is allowed, and this is a popular launch site for fishing and boating the Yellowstone River.

DIRECTIONS
From Big Timber, follow Interstate 90 east to Exit 377; the turn-offs to the State Park and Fishing Access Site are signed.

CONTACT
Montana Fish, Wildlife and Parks phone: 406-247-2940

YELLOWSTONE COUNTRY
#32 Sweet Grass Creek Loop

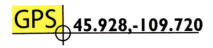

GPS 45.928,-109.720

EAST OF BIG TIMBER

KEY BIRDS
Wild Turkey, Western Meadowlark, Mountain Bluebird, Golden Eagle, Vesper and Savannah Sparrow, Yellow-headed and Red-winged Blackbirds

BEST SEASONS
Spring through early fall offer the best viewing ops

AREA DESCRIPTION
Cottonwood and willow riparian habitat surrounded by often dry land

The riparian zone in this section attracts a wide variety of bird life in an otherwise dry and often dusty landscape. Look for songbirds and water birds along the creek and watch for wild turkeys which frequent the ranch and farm land margins and sparsely treed rocky hills. The gravel road roughly parallels Sweet Grass Creek to Rapelje Road.

Sweet Grass Creek is born in the Crazy Mountains (Gallatin National Forest), runs northeast and then turns southeast past Melville to eventually merge with the Yellowstone River, all good birding, as well as a chance to see pronghorn, deer, and coyote.

DIRECTIONS
From I-90, Greycliff, Exit 377 turn east on Frontage Road (aka Greycliff Road, US 10) to Pelican Fishing Access. Cross the river and follow Lower Sweetgrass Road north to Rapelje Road (MT 478). Turn left and return to Big Timber via Rapelje Road.

YELLOWSTONE COUNTRY

#33 Hailstone National Wildlife Refuge

GPS 45.993,-109.171

NORTHEAST OF RAPELJE

KEY BIRDS
Redhead, Canvasback, American Avocet, Phalaropes, American White Pelican, several grebe and gull species

BEST SEASONS
Spring and fall waterfowl migration; late summer shorebird migration are highlights

AREA DESCRIPTION
Reservoir surrounded by wheat fields

Once surrounded by native prairie, the landscape now features mostly wheat, making the 300-acre reservoir the prime attraction for the thousands of waterfowl, shorebirds, and other water-loving birds that visit here during migration. Sharp-tailed Grouse, Baird's Sparrows, and Golden Eagles frequent the dry land portion of the refuge and surrounding farm and ranch lands. Northern Harriers and Short-eared Owls frequent the area and the occasional Peregrine Falcon shows up in the mix.

Rattlesnakes are common anywhere in the area, so watch your step. There is a black-tailed prairie dog town on the lake's east side; a good place to view Burrowing Owls, and pronghorn, deer, and coyote are also common at this site.

Hailstone Basin was the location of an 1865 gun battle between the Piegen (alleged horse thieves) and victimized Crow Indians and area ranchers. Two ranchers and one Piegen were killed in the ensuing gun battle.

The refuge is open to hunting according to state regulations.

Like its nearby cousin, Halfbreed NWR, drought negatively impacts use. When in doubt, contact refuge managers before making a long drive. FYI, Rapelje is pronounced Rap'-I-jay.

DIRECTIONS
From Rapelje, follow Molt Road about 4 miles; turn north at the refuge sign.

CONTACT
Hailstone NWR phone: 406-538-8706

Red-necked Grebe

YELLOWSTONE COUNTRY

#34 Halfbreed National Wildlife Refuge (IBA)

 GPS 45.973,-109.111

EAST OF RAPELJE

KEY BIRDS
Western, Eared, Pied-billed, and Western Grebes, American White Pelican, Lesser Scaup and Redhead, Sandhill Crane, Long-billed Curlew, Pectoral Sandpiper, American Bittern, Franklin's Gull

BEST SEASONS
Spring waterfowl migration and late summer shorebird migration offer the best viewing ops. Dry years can be grim.

AREA DESCRIPTION
Seasonal lake fed by small creeks and surrounding wetlands with extensive native-grass uplands

More than 100 species have been observed here. During wet years, waterfowl numbers often soar beyond 20,000 individuals; shorebirds in excess of 5,000 have been observed, and during the late summer, post breeding period as many as 3,000 Franklin's Gulls have been counted.

When Halfbreed (4,200 acres) like its nearby cousin Hailstone (2,800 acres) experiences drought conditions, bird numbers are negatively impacted. When in doubt, contact refuge managers before making a long drive.

Animals that are common here are pronghorn, deer, coyote, black-tailed prairie dog, and rattlesnakes.

DIRECTIONS
From Rapelje, follow Molt Road about 6 miles; entrance to refuge is signed.

CONTACT
Halfbreed NWR phone: 406-538-8706

Semipalmated Sandpiper

YELLOWSTONE COUNTRY
#35 Molt/Big Lake Complex

 GPS 45.916,-109.064

WEST OF BILLINGS

KEY BIRDS
Four grebes, American White Pelican, Canvasback, Northern Pintail and Redhead, American Wigeon, Gray Partridge, Sharp-tailed Grouse, bittern, American Avocet, Greater and Lesser Yellowlegs, Black-necked Stilt, Short-eared Owl, Lark Bunting, Gray-crowned Rosy Finch, Wild Turkey, Pinyon Jay, Pine Siskin

BEST SEASONS
Year round; spring for largest numbers and variety; winter for viewing raptors, wild turkeys, and songbirds

AREA DESCRIPTION
Comprising Hailstone and Halfbreed National Wildlife Refuges, and state-owned and managed, Big Lake Wildlife Management Area — the Complex — is one of the best spots in the area to view waterfowl, shorebirds, raptors, upland game birds, and songbirds. Water is of course paramount and thus, wet years are far better than dry years. Still, especially winter and spring, our visits have proved rewarding.

Hailstone NWR is about 2,000 acres. Open water, short-grass prairie, and rocky outcrops provide a diverse habitat for a variety species. The big draw is waterfowl and shorebirds, but many other birds use the refuge. There is a black-tailed prairie dog town on the east side of the lake.

Halfbreed NWR is about 4,000 acres. Open water, wetlands, and uplands attract more migrants than its two sisters combined. Access is walk-in only, from the north boundary, and restricted to hiking and wildlife viewing only. Animals that are common are pronghorn, deer, and coyote.

Big Lake WMA is about 3,000 acres. During wet years, the lake is about 2,800 acres and attracts as many as 20,000 ducks and geese and countless shorebirds. Hunting is allowed, so birders would do well to be sure that they are visible to others.

DIRECTIONS
From Billings, follow MT 302 west to Molt and follow the signs.

Contact
Hailstone and Halfbreed NWRs phone: 406-538-8706
Big Lake WMA Justin Paugh — phone: 406-932-5012

American Wigeon (male non-breeding)

YELLOWSTONE COUNTRY
#36 Itch-Kep-Pe Park and the Stillwater River

GPS ⊕ **45.630,-109.253**

SOUTH OF COLUMBUS

KEY BIRDS
Rufous, Broad-tailed, Calliope, and occasional Black-chinned Hummingbirds, Bald Eagle, Belted Kingfisher, American Dipper, Osprey

BEST SEASONS
Spring and fall migrations

AREA DESCRIPTION
Cottonwood riparian zone

Before continuing south along the Stillwater River stop at Itch-Kep-Pe Park, beside the Yellowstone River, just south of town; a good place to view a variety of songbirds including Bullock's and the occasional Baltimore Orioles, as well as warblers, flycatchers, and woodpeckers busily foraging the tall cottonwoods. Common Merganser hens with broods in tow provide summer-long entertainment.

At Absarokee, the Stillwater River Road leads into the foothills of Custer National Forest where trails take off into the high-country Absaroka-Beartooth Wilderness, affording birders enough territory to last several lifetimes. Typical forest-dwelling birds abound all along the route.

Bearing left on MT 78 in Absarokee will eventually take you to Red Lodge. Interesting side roads lead up Fishtail, East and West Rosebud, and Rosebud Creeks. It should go without saying, but birding opportunities pretty much depend on how-adventurous-are-you?

Regardless the scenery is spectacular; the river in spots is awesome and not too shabby fishing.

DIRECTIONS
I-90, Exit 405 (Columbus) and follow MT 78 south through town to the Yellowstone River. Turn left into the park. Continue on across the river and follow MT 78 upriver.

CONTACT
Custer National Forest phone: 406-255-1400

STILLWATER RIVER

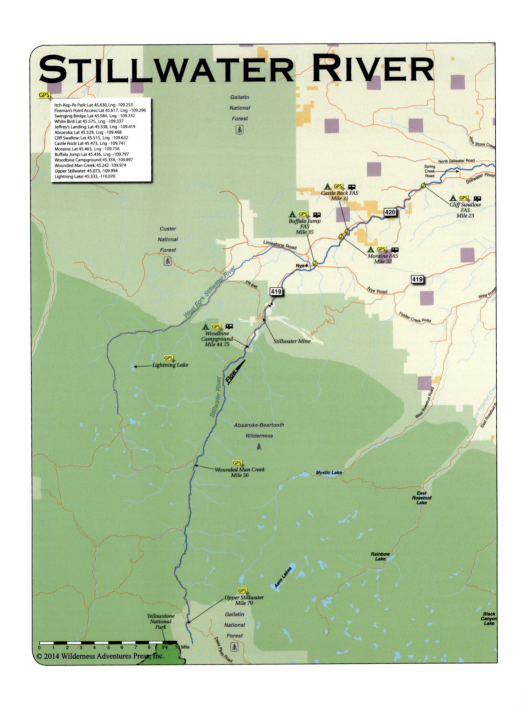

GPS

Itch-Kep-Pe Park: Lat 45.630, Lng -109.253
Fireman's Point Access: Lat 45.617, Lng -109.296
Swinging Bridge: Lat 45.584, Lng -109.332
White Bird: Lat 45.575, Lng -109.337
Jeffrey's Landing: Lat 45.538, Lng -109.419
Absaroka: Lat 45.529, Lng -109.468
Cliff Swallow: Lat 45.515, Lng -109.632
Castle Rock: Lat 45.473, Lng -109.741
Moraine: Lat 45.463, Lng -109.756
Buffalo Jump: Lat 45.436, Lng -109.797
Woodbine Campground: 45.354, -109.897
Wounded Man Creek: 45.242 -109.974
Upper Stillwater: 45.073, -109.994
Lightning Lake: 45.333, -110.070

Gallatin
National
Forest

North Stillwater Road

Spring
Creek
Road

Stillwater River

Castle Rock FAS
Mile 31

Cliff Swallow
FAS
Mile 23

420

Custer
National
Forest

Buffalo Jump
FAS
Mile 35

Limestone Road

Moraine FAS
Mile 32

419

Nye

Nye Road

419

419

Woodbine
Campground
Mile 44.75

Stillwater Mine

Lightning Lake

Stillwater River Flow

West Fork Stillwater River

Absaroka-Beartooth

Wilderness

Mystic Lake

East
Rosebud
Lake

Wounded Man Creek
Mile 56

Rainbow
Lake

Arro Lakes

Upper Stillwater
Mile 70

Yellowstone
National
Park

Gallatin
National
Forest

Black
Canyon
Lake

0 1 2 3 4 5 6 7 8 9 10 Mile

© 2014 Wilderness Adventures Press, Inc.

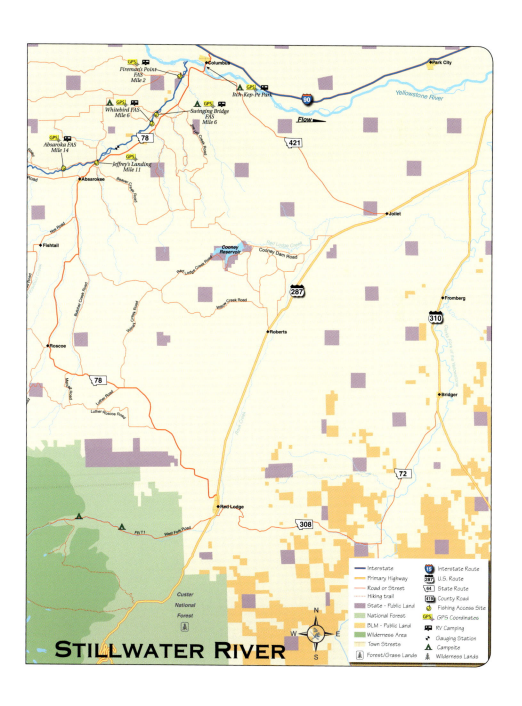

STILLWATER RIVER

Fireman's Point FAS Mile 2
Columbus
Park City
Itch-Kep-Pe Park
Whitebird FAS Mile 6
Swinging Bridge FAS Mile 6
Yellowstone River
Flow
Absaroka FAS Mile 14
Jeffrey's Landing Mile 11
78
421
Absarokee
Beaver Creek Road
Joliet
Fishtail
Cooney Reservoir
Cooney Dam Road
Red Lodge Creek
287
Willow Creek Road
Fromberg
310
Roberts
Roscoe
78
Luther Road
Luther-Roscoe Road
Rock Creek
72
Red Lodge
308
FR 71
West Fork Road
Custer National Forest

Legend:
- Interstate
- Primary Highway
- Road or Street
- Hiking trail
- State - Public Land
- National Forest
- BLM - Public Land
- Wilderness Area
- Forest/Grass Lands
- Interstate Route
- U.S. Route
- State Route
- County Road
- Fishing Access Site
- GPS Coordinates
- RV Camping
- Gauging Station
- Campsite
- Wilderness Lands

YELLOWSTONE COUNTRY
#37 | Cooney Reservoir State Park

GPS 45.440,-109.229

SOUTH OF COLUMBUS

KEY BIRDS
Vesper, White-crowned and Lark Sparrows, American Avocet, Western and Eared Grebes, Common Loon, Horned Lark, Chestnut-collared Longspur, Eastern and Western Kingbirds, Yellow Warbler, American White Pelican

BEST SEASONS
Spring and fall migrations offer the best variety

AREA DESCRIPTION
Developed state park surrounded on two sides with the reservoir

The west end of the lake, in and around the campground, offers the best viewing ops. A spotting scope is useful for viewing the lake.

The 309-acre park has 72 camping sites in its five campgrounds, with 13 available with electricity. Cooney is a popular spot so get out early and avoid summer weekends and holidays if possible.

DIRECTIONS
From Laurel, follow US 212 for 22 miles to Boyd. Turn north to the lake; turnoff is signed. Or south of Columbus, on MT 78, go 4 miles to Shane Creek Road; the lake is 14 miles farther.

White-crowned Sparrow

CONTACT

Montana Fish, Wildlife and Parks phone: 406-445-2326

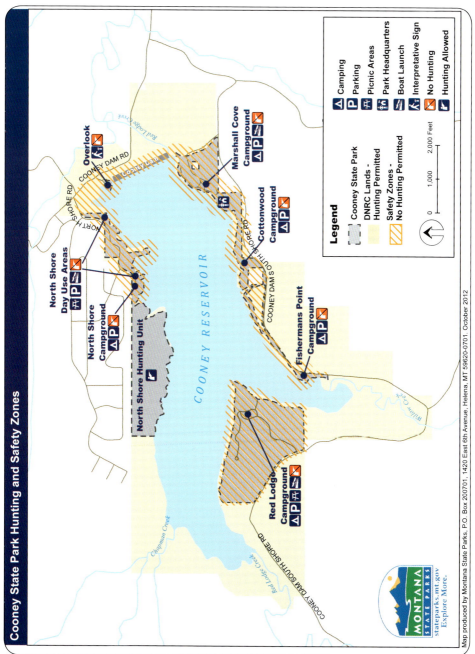

Cooney State Park Hunting and Safety Zones

Legend

- Cooney State Park
- DNRC Lands – Hunting Permitted
- Safety Zones – No Hunting Permitted

0   1,000   2,000 Feet

Camping
Parking
Picnic Areas
Park Headquarters
Boat Launch
Interpretive Sign
No Hunting
Hunting Allowed

Overlook

Marshall Cove Campground

Cottonwood Campground

North Shore Day Use Areas

North Shore Campground

North Shore Hunting Unit

Fishermans Point Campground

Red Lodge Campground

COONEY RESERVOIR

COONEY DAM RD
NORTH SHORE RD
SOUTH SHORE RD
COONEY DAM S
COONEY DAM SOUTH SHORE RD

Red Lodge Creek
Chapman Creek
Willow Creek

Map produced by Montana State Parks, P.O. Box 200701, 1420 East 6th Avenue, Helena, MT 59620-0701. October 2012

Used with permission.

MONTANA STATE PARKS
stateparks.mt.gov
Explore More.

YELLOWSTONE COUNTRY
#38 Bear Canyon
Important Bird Area (IBA)

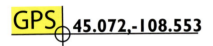

GPS 45.072,-108.553

PRYOR MOUNTAINS,
SOUTH OF BILLINGS

KEY BIRDS
Rock and Canyon Wrens, Blue-gray Gnatcatcher, White-throated Swift, Loggerhead Shrike, Calliope Hummingbird, Brown Thrasher

BEST SEASONS
Late spring through early fall

AREA DESCRIPTION
Canyon changing from sagebrush to cottonwood riparian zone to conifer forest

In one of the driest areas in the state, the number of bird species sometimes seen here is remarkable. Audubon groups have observed 40 or more species in a single outing. An Important Bird Area, the canyon supports breeding populations of more than a dozen species of conservation concern, including Downy Woodpecker, Common Poorwill, Cooper's Hawk, Warbling Vireo, Green-tailed Towhee, MacGillivray's Warbler, Lazuli Bunting, Cassin's Finch, Brewer's, Chipping and Lark Sparrows, Loggerhead Shrike, Pinyon Jay, Greater Sage Grouse, Sage Thrasher, and Clark's Nutcracker. It also boasts the highest known number of nesting Blue-gray Gnatcatchers among the handful of foothill canyons in the area that constitute the entire range of the species in Montana.

The canyon mouth is surrounded by sagebrush; a good place to spot Sage Thrasher, Common Poorwill, Loggerhead Shrike, Green-tailed Towhee and Pinyon Jay. Greater Sage Grouse are common, though sometimes hard to find.

As you head up canyon, the habitat changes to cottonwood riparian and up top conifer forest takes over. The natural progression of habitats greatly enhances the diversity of birds found here.

Alas, cattle and off-road driving continue to degrade the habitat. Hopefully the powers that be — BLM and USFS — get a handle on before it's too late.

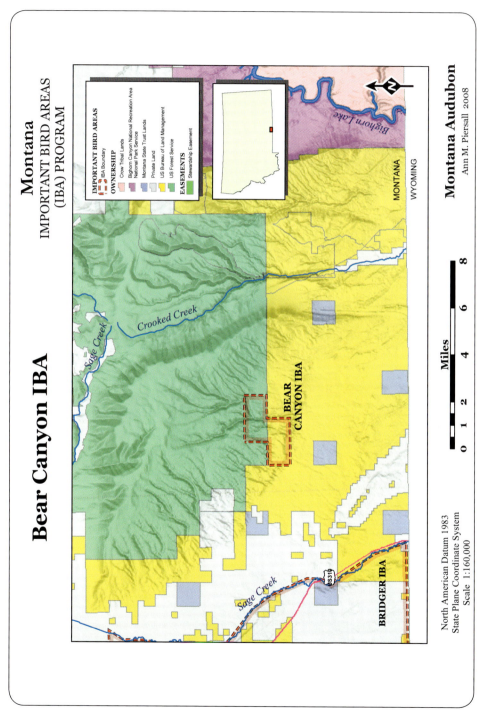

Montana
IMPORTANT BIRD AREAS
(IBA) PROGRAM

Bear Canyon IBA

IMPORTANT BIRD AREAS
IBA Boundary
OWNERSHIP
Crow Tribal Lands
Bighorn Canyon National Recreation Area
National Park Service
Montana State Trust Lands
Private Land
US Bureau of Land Management
US Forest Service
EASEMENTS
Stewardship Easement

Bighorn Lake

MONTANA
WYOMING

Crooked Creek

Sage Creek

BEAR
CANYON IBA

Sage Creek

US310

BRIDGER IBA

Miles

0   1   2   4   6   8

North American Datum 1983
State Plane Coordinate System
Scale 1:160,000

Montana Audubon
Ann M. Piersall 2008

The site supports the state's only stands of Utah juniper. The scenery and views are spectacular, often compared to the Desert Southwest, and make the visit well worthwhile, regardless of the number of bird sightings.

While the Bear Canyon itself was not included in a recent 24-hour study of the area's flora and fauna, wildlife abounds here. The following mammals show up from time to time: deer and white-footed mice, kangaroo rat, least chipmunk, red squirrel, yellow pine chipmunk, bushy-tailed woodrat, desert cottontail, white-tailed jackrabbit, red fox, coyote, black bear, mule deer, bighorn sheep and, of course, the infamous Pryor Mountain's wild horses.

DIRECTIONS
From I-90, Exit 434 (Laurel) follow US 212 to Rockvale; turn left onto US 310. Approximately 25 miles south of Bridger, turn left onto Bear Canyon Road and go about 6 miles to the canyon.

CONTACT
Custer National Forest; 406-255-1400

BIRDING TRAILS: MONTANA

SOUTHEAST MONTANA

Big Horn, Carter, Custer, Dawson, Fallon, Golden Valley, Musselshell, Powder River, Prairie, Rosebud, Treasure, Wibaux and Yellowstone Counties make up the vast and largely unpopulated Southeast Region.

Musselshell Sage-steppe IBA (roughly three million acres northeast of Roundup) is the largest of Montana's five greater sage grouse IBAs. Twenty-one species of conservation concern can be found on the Tongue River IBA (Ashland). The Powder Carter Sage-Steppe IBA is home to about 10 percent of Montana sage grouse. Isaac Homestead WMA and nearby Howrey Island (Hysham) top our list of Southeast Montana favorites. Visiting Billings or Miles City? Don't miss the great birding ops in and around both. Makoshika State Park (Glendive) and Terry Badlands (Terry) are home to a surprising variety of birds for…well, you know…badlands.

Makoshika State Park

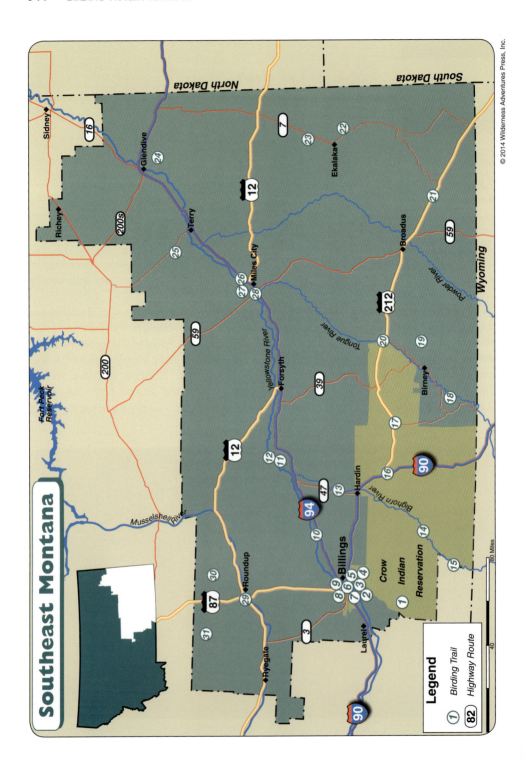

Southeast Montana

Legend

① Birding Trail

㉘ Highway Route

© 2014 Wilderness Adventures Press, Inc.

Southeast Montana Locations

1. Chief Plenty Coups State Park
2. Audubon Center
3. Mystic Island Park
4. Pictograph Cave State Park
5. Four Dances Natural Area
6. Earl Guss Park
7. Norm Shoenthal Island
8. Two Moon Park
9. Lake Elmo State Park
10. Pompey's Pillar National Monument
11. Howrey Island Recreation Area
12. Isaac Homestead Wildlife Management Area
13. Grant Marsh Wildlife Management Area
14. Afterbay Dam
15. Bighorn Canyon National Recreation Area
16. Little Bighorn National Monument
17. Tongue River Birding Route
18. Tongue River Reservoir State Park
19. Black's Pond
20. Tongue River IBA
21. Powder Carbon Sage-Steppe IBA
22. McNab Pond
23. Medicine Rocks State Park
24. Makoshika State Park
25. Terry Badlands Wilderness Study Area
26. Matthews Recreation Area
27. Pirogue Island State Park
28. Miles City Parks
29. Roundup RiverWalk Heritage Trail
30. Musselshell Sage-Steppe IBA
31. Lake Mason National Wildlife Refuge

SOUTHEAST MONTANA
Chief Plenty Coups (Alek-Chea-Ahoosh) State Park

#1

GPS 45.425,-108.550

SOUTH OF BILLINGS

KEY BIRDS
Spotted Towhees, Bullock's Oriole, Western Wood-pewee, Eastern and Western Kingbird, American Crow, Kestrel, Golden Eagle

BEST SEASONS
Year round; spring and fall, early and late in the day offer the best birding ops

AREA DESCRIPTION
Mixed habitat surrounding the chief's homestead comprised of short-grass prairie, cottonwoods, sagebrush, shrubs, and grassland

Best birding ops involve walking, so dress appropriately and bring good glass.

Interpretive and self-guided tours, restrooms, picnic tables, store, tipi, museum, and a variety of programs on site; camping, lodging, food, and fuel nearby. Visitors should be aware this is Crow Indian Tribal Land; please respect the land and the native people.

DIRECTIONS
From I-90 Exit 447 South on MT 416 (Blue Creek Rd.) to Pryor Creek Road, then turn right and go about 17 miles to Pryor. Turn right and go 1 mile to the park; route is signed south of the Interstate.

Eastern Kingbirds

CONTACT
Park Manager phone: 406-252-1289

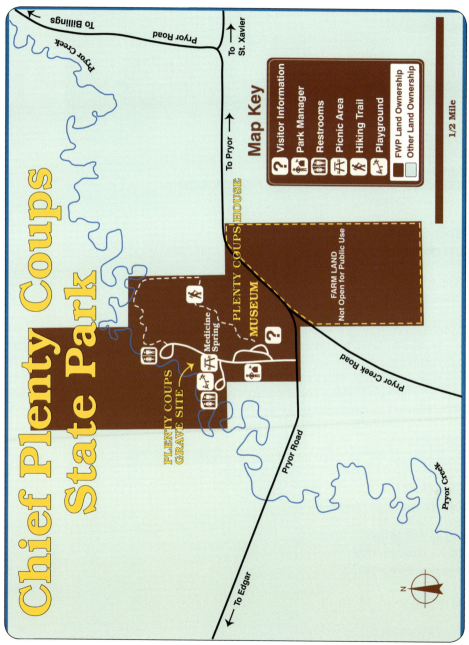

Chief Plenty Coups State Park

Map Key

? Visitor Information
Park Manager
Restrooms
Picnic Area
Hiking Trail
Playground

FWP Land Ownership
Other Land Ownership

1/2 Mile

To Billings
To St. Xavier
To Pryor
To Edgar

Pryor Creek
Pryor Road
Pryor Creek Road

PLENTY COUPS HOUSE
PLENTY COUPS GRAVE SITE
Medicine Spring
MUSEUM
?

FARM LAND
Not Open for Public Use

N

SOUTHEAST MONTANA
Audubon Center

GPS 45.743,-108.539

BILLINGS

KEY BIRDS
Townsend's Solitaire, Tree Sparrow, Pine Siskin, House Finch, American Goldfinch, Northern Flicker

BEST SEASONS
Spring and fall migrations, but something to see year round

AREA DESCRIPTION
Developed bird area along Yellowstone River

Formerly a barren gravel pit, since 1998, the Yellowstone River Parks Association in partnership with Yellowstone Valley Audubon and Montana Audubon have since transformed the site into a model bird habitat. Some 65,000 trees and shrubs and three ponds, in conjunction with the 200-plus acres within the Riverfront Park system afford birds of every sort nesting and brood rearing habitat so vital in an otherwise bustling urban setting. Montana Audubon holds a 99-year lease to conduct educational programs.

DIRECTIONS
From I-90, Exit 447, go south on S. Billings Blvd. to Riverfront Park.

CONTACT
Yellowstone River Parks Association
2409 2nd Ave. N
Billings, MT 59101
Phone: 406-248-1400
Website: www.yrpa.org

House Finch
Credit: Gary Swant

SOUTHEAST MONTANA
Mystic Island Park

#3

GPS 45.770, -108.479

BILLINGS

KEY BIRDS
Waterfowl, wading birds, raptors, and a variety of songbirds

BEST SEASONS
Spring and fall migrations, but something to see year round

AREA DESCRIPTION
Undeveloped parkland beside Yellowstone River

Approximately 100 acres, this park has no designated trails, no "Keep off the Grass" signs, and no restricted areas. Feel free to wander about, observing birds to your heart's content. The park also provides public access to Big Sky Island.

DIRECTIONS
From I-90 East, Exit 450, take 27th Street South (right) to Belknap Avenue to the park.

CONTACT
Yellowstone River Parks Association
2409 2nd Ave. N
Billings, MT 59101
Phone: 406-248-1400
Website: www.yrpa.org

SOUTHEAST MONTANA
Pictograph Cave State Park

#4

GPS **45.737,-108.433**

SOUTHEAST OF BILLINGS

KEY BIRDS
Bald and Golden Eagles, Lark and Lazuli Buntings, Mountain and Western Bluebirds, Rock, Canyon and House Wrens, Peregrine and Prairie Falcons, Cliff Swallow, White-throated Swift

BEST SEASONS
Open year round

AREA DESCRIPTION
Ponderosa pine, shrubs, sagebrush, grass and sandstone bluffs around the caves

The main draw is, of course, the three caves — Pictograph, Middle, and Ghost — which are accessed by paved trails. The best birding is off trail at the tail ends of the day and season. Be sure to pack along binoculars and keep one eye peeled for snakes.

According to state park literature, the caves were used by prehistoric hunters as long as 10,000 years ago; leaving behind some 100 pictographs and 30,000 artifacts which have been recovered by archaeologists over the years.

Interpretation, picnic area, and restrooms are on site; lodging, camping, and fuel can be found nearby.

Golden Eagle

DIRECTIONS
I-90 Exit 452, take US 87 South. Turn right on Coburn Road to the park. The turn is signed.

CONTACT
Park Manager phone: 406-247-2955 or 406-245-0227

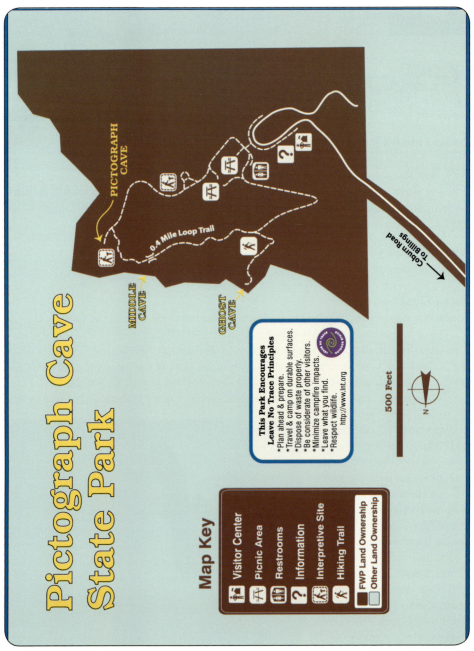

Pictograph Cave State Park

PICTOGRAPH CAVE

0.4 Mile Loop Trail

MIDDLE CAVE

GHOST CAVE

Coburn Road
To Billings

This Park Encourages
Leave No Trace Principles
*Plan ahead & prepare.
*Travel & camp on durable surfaces.
*Dispose of waste properly.
*Be considerate of other visitors.
*Minimize campfire impacts.
*Leave what you find.
*Respect wildlife.
http://www.lnt.org

500 Feet

N

Map Key
Visitor Center
Picnic Area
Restrooms
Information
Interpretive Site
Hiking Trail

FWP Land Ownership
Other Land Ownership

SOUTHEAST MONTANA
Four Dances Natural Area

#5

GPS ⊕ **45.777,-108.467**

BILLINGS

KEY BIRDS
Peregrine Falcon, Rock Wren (rare), Rock Pigeon, Pinyon Jay, Brown Creeper, Ruby-crowned Kinglet

BEST SEASONS
Spring and fall migrations; something to see year round

AREA DESCRIPTION
Pine and cottonwood riparian zone with grasslands, sagebrush, and cliffs

Thanks to landowners, the Yellowstone River Parks Association, and the BLM the 750-acre area was purchased in 1999. Birders can enjoy this rugged piece of natural terrain within sight of Montana's largest city. Habitat consists of rock outcrops, cliffs, sagebrush, native grassland, and ponderosa pine and cottonwood riparian forest (along the river). Hiking trails lead to the Will James Cabin, through the area, along the cliffs, and down to the river. The area is open year round; walk-in only. Activities include hiking, picnicking,

Ruby-crowned Kinglet

cross-country skiing, and wildlife viewing — with restrictions. Watch for rattlesnakes.

According to BLM literature, "The area was named Four Dances Natural Area after Chief Four Dances, an important religious and military figure in Crow Indian History. The name in the Crow language is 'Annishi Shopash', translated as 'Place of Four Dances'. The cliff is traditionally recognized as a fasting site used by Four Dances in the 1830s, during the heyday of the Rocky Mountain fur trade and the intertribal plains wars. Four Dances took his name from the vision he received while fasting at this place."

Interesting to note Will James, the famous artist and writer, divided many of the last years of his life between his ranch in the Pryor Mountains (Montana) and here in Billings at the cabin in Four Dances.

DIRECTIONS
From I-90 East, Exit 452 and take US 87 south. Turn south on Coburn Road to Four Dances.

CONTACT
BLM Billings phone: 406-896-5013

Cedar Waxwing

SOUTHEAST MONTANA
Earl Guss Park

#6

GPS 45.804,-108.476

BILLINGS

KEY BIRDS
MacGillivray's Warbler, Chipping Sparrow, Gray Catbird, Ovenbird, Cedar Waxwing

BEST SEASONS
Spring and fall migrations; something to see year round

AREA DESCRIPTION
Heavily vegetated creekside park

The park, complete with manmade waterfall (looks almost natural), is something of an anomaly in that it attracts a wide variety of songbirds, yet lies so close to the hustle and bustle of Montana's largest city. Trails wind through the greenery offering end-to-end birding opportunities.

Day use only with picnic shelters and restrooms.

DIRECTIONS
From I-90 East, Exit 450 and take 27th Street North to 1st Avenue North. Turn right go to where Main Street forks to the left (US 87 & 312) and follow Main Street to the park at the intersection with Airport Road.

CONTACT
Yellowstone River Parks Association
2409 2nd Ave. N
Billings, MT 59101
Phone: 406-248-1400
Website: www.yrpa.org

SOUTHEAST MONTANA
#7 Norm Shoenthal Island

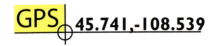

BILLINGS

KEY BIRDS
Canada Goose, (occasionally Greater White-fronted and Snow Goose), Bald Eagle, American Tree Sparrow, House Finch, American Goldfinch, Osprey, American Crow

BEST SEASONS
Floods in spring; open rest of the year

AREA DESCRIPTION
Cottonwood riparian island

The island floods each spring, a classic example of how flood plain ecology works. Comprised of city, state, and private lands, there are numerous trails, a couple of ponds, and the river channel itself to offer birders the chance to view a variety of birds: songbirds, woodpeckers, waterfowl, shorebirds, raptors, and wading birds. The Yellowstone River Parks Association is in the process of eradicating invasive Russian olive trees to help enhance the native cottonwoods.

DIRECTIONS
I-90, Exit 447, take S. Billings Blvd. to Riverfront Park. There is a parking lot and bridge leading to the island.

CONTACT
Yellowstone River Parks Association
2409 2nd Ave. N
Billings, MT 59101
Phone: 406-248-1400
Website: www.yrpa.org

SOUTHEAST MONTANA

Two Moon Park

#8

GPS 45.809, -108.462

BILLINGS

KEY BIRDS
Cedar Waxwing, Townsend's Solitaire, White- and Red-breasted Nuthatches, White-crowned and American Tree Sparrows, Northern Flicker

BEST SEASONS
Spring and fall migrations, but something to see year round

AREA DESCRIPTION
Open meadows and cottonwoods with a steep, wooded bluff

The park is named for the Northern Cheyenne chief who fought at the Battle of the Little Bighorn.

Bordering the Yellowstone River and "a steep, forested bluff" the park features several trails winding through meadows and trees. The Weeping Wall "shot through with seeping springs, attracts a great variety of birds and mantles the cliffside with sheaths of ice in winter," according to Yellowstone River Parks Association literature.

Facilities include restrooms and benches scattered along the trails. The park is open year round for day use only.

DIRECTIONS
From I-90 East, Exit 450, take 27th Street North (left) to 4th Avenue North. Turn right and travel east to Main Street (US 87). Take first right on Bench Boulevard to the park.

CONTACT
Yellowstone River Parks Association
2409 2nd Ave. N
Billings, MT 59101
Phone: 406-248-1400
Website: www.yrpa.org

SOUTHEAST MONTANA
Lake Elmo State Park

GPS 45.845, -108.481

BILLINGS

KEY BIRDS
Loggerhead Shrike, Red-headed Woodpecker, House Wren, Common and Yellow-billed Loons, Eared, Western, and Horned Grebes

BEST SEASONS
Open year round

AREA DESCRIPTION
Open water, trees, shrubs, and grass set in a bustling urban setting

There are paved trails, picnic tables, and restrooms in this 64-acre park. Busy spot in the summer for swimming and fishing, the best time to beat the crowds is early and late in the day and season.

DIRECTIONS
I-90 Exit 452, take US 87 North (Old Highway 312) to Pemberton Lane; turn west (left) to the park. The turn is signed.

CONTACT
Park Manager phone: 406-247-2955

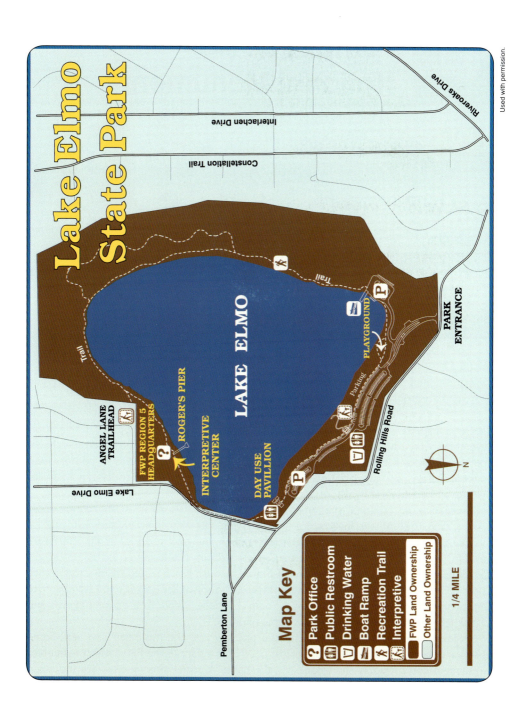

Used with permission.

Lake Elmo State Park

Riveroaks Drive

Interlachen Drive

Constellation Trail

LAKE ELMO

Trail

Trail

PARK ENTRANCE

PLAYGROUND

Parking

Rolling Hills Road

ANGEL LANE TRAILHEAD

FWP REGION 5 HEADQUARTERS

ROGER'S PIER

INTERPRETIVE CENTER

DAY USE PAVILLION

Lake Elmo Drive

Pemberton Lane

Map Key

- Park Office
- Public Restroom
- Drinking Water
- Boat Ramp
- Recreation Trail
- Interpretive
- FWP Land Ownership
- Other Land Ownership

N

1/4 MILE

SOUTHEAST MONTANA

#10 Pompey's Pillar National Monument

GPS 45.988,-108.002

EAST OF BILLINGS

KEY BIRDS
Peregrine Falcon, Blue Jay, Brown Thrasher, Lazuli Bunting, Bullock's Oriole, Loggerhead Shrike, Ferruginous Hawk, Northern Goshawk, Franklin's Gull, Forster's Tern, Hairy Woodpecker

BEST SEASONS
May through October; early and late in the day

AREA DESCRIPTION
Sandstone bluff and cliffs, cottonwood, green ash and willow riparian forest, and short-grass prairie

This area attracts a surprising variety of birds, including many neoptropicals in migration. Several fairly common birds in the area — Peregrine Falcon, shrikes, Northern Goshawk, Franklin's Gull, and Forster's Tern for example — are listed as species of conservation concern. Peregrines have been released in the area since 1996 and today are a familiar sight up and down river.

According to National Monument literature, "Pompeys Pillar is one of the most famous sandstone buttes in America. It bears the only remaining physical evidence of the Lewis and Clark Expedition, which appears on the trail today as it did 200 years ago. On the face of the 150-foot butte, Captain William Clark carved his name on July 25, 1806, during his return to the United States through the beautiful Yellowstone Valley. Captain Clark named the Pillar 'Pompeys Tower' in honor of Sacagawea's son Jean Baptiste Charbonneau, whom he had nicknamed 'Pomp'. Nicholas Biddle, first editor of Lewis and Clark's Journals, changed the name to 'Pompeys Pillar.'"

Native Americans called the Pillar 'the place where the mountain lion lies'. Some observers suggest that a sandstone formation, that is a part of the Pillar, which resembles a mountain lion's head, is the reason for the name. Another theory cites live mountain lions being spotted in the area.

There is an accessible interpretive center, restrooms, and day use area, as well as a 1,000-foot long, 200 step boardwalk to the top of the mesa, and a concrete walkway along river. No camping. Vehicle access is available from May through October; walk-in from gate access the rest of year during daylight hours only. Fee area.

DIRECTIONS
From Billings via I-94, approximately 30 miles east, take Exit 23, Pompey's Pillar.

CONTACT
Interpretive Center phone: 406-875-2400

Hairy Woodpecker
Credit: Gary Swant

SOUTHEAST MONTANA

#11 Howrey Island Recreation Area

GPS ⊕ 46.252,-107.341

NEAR HYSHAM

KEY BIRDS
Bald Eagle (largest concentration in winter), Red-headed Woodpecker, Wild Turkey, Spotted Towhee, and a variety of warblers and flycatchers

BEST SEASONS
Open year round; spring and fall offers best chance for checking off migrants

AREA DESCRIPTION
Large cottonwoods, green ash and willows with a dense shrub under-story interspersed with wet meadows and cattail sloughs

This 592-acre recreation area is closed to waterfowl hunting, so it attracts large concentrations of ducks and geese once the shooting starts. A surprising variety birds can be found here most anytime.

Whitetails, fox squirrel, beaver, and red fox are common.

There is undeveloped camping plus a boat ramp, picnic tables, fire pits, and restrooms; motorized access with restrictions; walk-in access is allowed anytime. The area features a nature trail with 10 interpretive stops. Brochure is available on site or from Miles City BLM Office (see below).

DIRECTIONS
From Billings, take I-94 east to the Hysham exit and take MT 311 west. The recreation area is just across the Myers Bridge.

CONTACT
BLM, Miles City phone: 406-233-2800

SOUTHEAST MONTANA

#12 Isaac Homestead
Wildlife Management Area

GPS 46.279,-107.332

NEAR HYSHAM

KEY BIRDS
Ring-necked Pheasant, Sharp-tailed Grouse, Wild Turkey, Wood Duck, Blue Jay, Baltimore Oriole, Loggerhead Shrike

BEST SEASONS
Open year round; spring and fall offers best chance for checking off migrants

AREA DESCRIPTION
Cottonwood riparian area crop fields, grasslands, and sagebrush

Like many of our favorite birding spots, we first visited Isaac Homestead hoping to find Pheasants, Sharptails, and perhaps a Wood Duck or two to entertain our German wire-haired pointers and, of course, maybe get lucky and bag a meal or two. Tired from the long drive, instead of hunting that first evening we grabbed binoculars and took a hike. Two hours later the dogs had not only found the pheasants we were hoping for but we had checked off a pretty impressive (for us) songbird list including a few birds we don't usually see around Dillon: Blue Jay, Wood Duck, Baltimore Oriole, and Brown Thrasher.

The 1,200-acre WMA is sharecropped (alfalfa and corn, part for the farmer, part left for wildlife). Large cottonwoods line the Yellowstone River, interspersed with Russian olive, sagebrush, grasslands, and dense underbrush — including wild grape and other indigenous fruit bearing plants — all told a lush and diverse habitat which attracts not only upland game birds and waterfowl but shorebirds, wading birds, and over 100 songbird species.

Driving is allowed on designated roads and trails; primitive camping is allowed, although there are no facilities.

Whitetails, raccoons, and striped skunk add spice to an already tasty cake.

Hysham is a typical small and friendly Montana farming and ranching community. The town takes its name from Charlie Hysham who once ramrodded the huge Flying E Ranch — one of Montana's largest cattle operations. Back in the day, the Great Northern Railroad served Hysham and surrounding area. Passing through town, the supplies were simply tossed out and waiting townsfolk then distributed them.

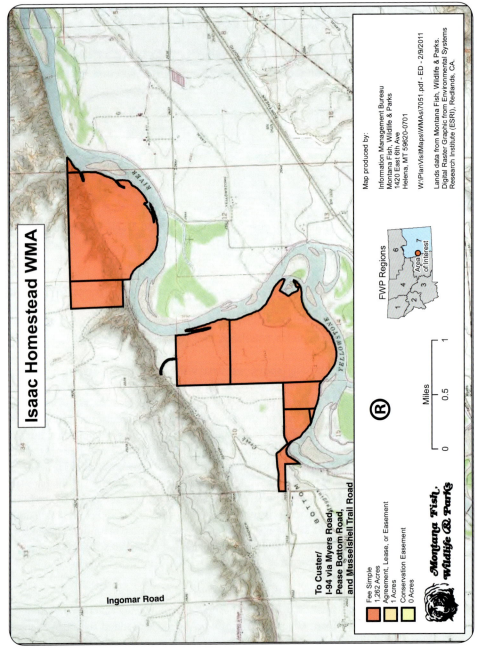

Isaac Homestead WMA

River
Yellowstone

To Custer/
I-94 via Myers Road,
Pease Bottom Road,
and Musselshell Trail Road

Ingomar Road

Fee Simple
1,262 Acres

Agreement, Lease, or Easement
1 Acres

Conservation Easement
0 Acres

FWP Regions

Area of Interest

Miles
0   0.5   1

Montana Fish,
Wildlife & Parks

Map produced by:

Information Management Bureau
Montana Fish, Wildlife & Parks
1420 East 6th Ave
Helena, MT 59620-0701

W:\PlanVisitMaps\WMAs\7051.pdf - ED - 2/9/2011

Lands data from Montana Fish, Wildlife & Parks.
Digital Raster Graphic from Environmental Systems
Research Institute (ESRI), Redlands, CA.

Today, Hysham's main claim to fame is the historic Yucca Theater — a Santa Fe art deco style building complete with white buffalo and Lewis and Clark statues. A real head-turner, it draws curious onlookers from all over.

DIRECTIONS
From Billings, take I-94 east to the Hysham exit and follow MT 311 west approximately 7 miles. Follow signs (which by the way do not show up until nearly there).

CONTACT
WMA, Scott Denson phone: 406-234-8176

Wild Turkey

SOUTHEAST MONTANA

#13 Grant Marsh Wildlife Management Area

GPS 45.844,-107.591

NORTH OF HARDIN

KEY BIRDS
Ring-necked Pheasant, Sharp-tailed Grouse, Mourning Dove, Bald Eagle, Mallard, Canada Goose, Western Meadowlark, Kestrel, Barn and Cliff Swallows

BEST SEASONS
Spring and fall migration, early and late in the day

AREA DESCRIPTION
Deciduous tree and shrub bottomland, interspersed with grass and wet meadows

Part of the WMA is an island accessible by boat or wading at low water levels. Facilities include a boat ramp and vault toilet; primitive camping; pack-in, pack out rules apply. Hunting is allowed in season with no weapon restrictions. NOTE: birders should wear blaze orange during hunting seasons.

DIRECTIONS
From I-94 East, Exit 49 (MT 47) south and go approximately 20 miles to the WMA (signed). From I-90, take Exit 495 (MT 47) north and go approximately 8 miles.

CONTACT
WMA, Scott Denson phone: 406- 234-8176

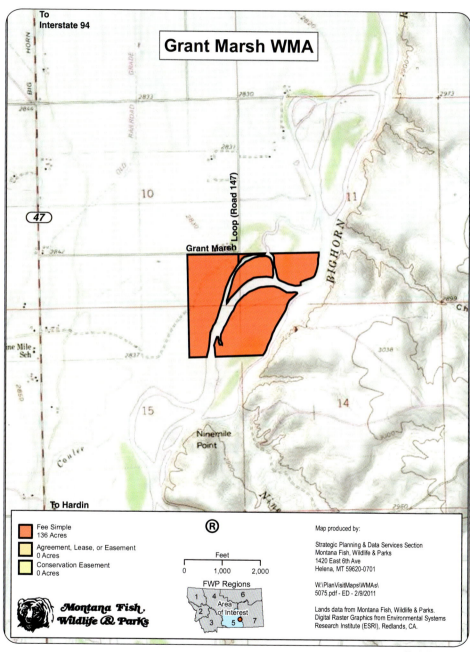

Grant Marsh WMA

To Interstate 94

Loop (Road 147)

Grant Marsh

BIGHORN

To Hardin

Ninemile Point

Fee Simple		136 Acres
Agreement, Lease, or Easement		0 Acres
Conservation Easement		0 Acres

®

Feet

0   1,000   2,000

FWP Regions

Area of Interest

Montana Fish, Wildlife & Parks

Map produced by:

Strategic Planning & Data Services Section
Montana Fish, Wildlife & Parks
1420 East 6th Ave
Helena, MT 59620-0701

W:\PlanVisitMaps\WMAs\
5075.pdf - ED - 2/9/2011

Lands data from Montana Fish, Wildlife & Parks.
Digital Raster Graphics from Environmental Systems
Research Institute (ESRI), Redlands, CA.

SOUTHEAST MONTANA
#14 Afterbay Dam

GPS 45.317, -107.921

FORT SMITH, ON THE BIGHORN RIVER

KEY BIRDS
Long-tailed Duck (Oldsquaw), Northern Pintail, Lesser Scaup, Redhead, Ruddy and Ring-necked Ducks, Hooded Merganser, Horned and Western Grebes, American Dipper, Northern Shrike, Song Sparrow, Wild Turkey, Ring-necked Pheasant, Rough-legged Hawk

BEST SEASONS
Year round; spring through fall for largest numbers and variety; winter for waterfowl and raptors

AREA DESCRIPTION
Mouth of Bighorn Canyon, surrounded by rolling grass and sage covered hills

Afterbay Dam is about 2 miles downstream of Yellowtail Dam on the Bighorn River. Armed with binoculars and/or a good spotting scope, the pool offers easy viewing for a large variety of water birds. All along the highway and the river below Hardin is a great place to view upland game birds, waterfowl, raptors, and songbirds. Some of the best viewing is at the Fishing Access Sites along the way. Be aware that this is Crow Indian Reservation; please respect tribal lands and avoid trespass.

Food, gas, and lodging is available in Fort Smith. The Bighorn National Recreation Area offers campsites, picnic tables, and toilets. The Bighorn River is one of the best trout streams around, just in case you wondered.

DIRECTIONS
I-90 east of Billings, exit at Hardin and drive south on MT 313 and 463 to Fort Smith and the dam.

CONTACT
Bighorn National Recreation Area phone: 406-666-2412

Song Sparrow

SOUTHEAST MONTANA

#15 Bighorn Canyon National Recreation Area

BARRY'S LANDING:
45.096,-108.211
PARK HEADQUARTERS:
GPS 45.309,-107.920

SOUTH OF HARDIN

KEY BIRDS
Bald and Golden Eagles, Peregrine and Prairie Falcons, American Kestrel, Lazuli Bunting, White-throated Swift, Cliff and Rough-winged Swallows, Northern Oriole

BEST SEASONS
Year round; the water in Afterbay Lake below the dam and the river never freeze. Early spring, late fall and winter are relatively quiet times.

AREA DESCRIPTION
River with sheer cliffs surrounded by forest and upland prairie

At least 231 species have been observed; as many as 75 species in a single outing is a distinct possibility for the experienced birder; including Song, Vesper and Tree Sparrows, Common Yellowthroat, Yellow Warbler, Lark Bunting, Lazuli Bunting, Mountain Bluebird, Northern Oriole, Canyon and House Wrens, Western Meadowlark, Brewer's and Red-winged Blackbirds, Rough-legged Hawk, Turkey Vulture, and Great Horned Owl.

Waterfowl, shorebirds, and water birds abound. Pied-billed, Eared and Western Grebes, Black-crowned Night-heron, Great Blue Heron, American White Pelicans, Forster's Tern, Sandhill Crane, Mallard, Gadwall, Northern Shoveler, Blue-winged Teal, American Wigeon, Lesser Scaup, Canada Goose, Wilson's Phalarope, Spotted Sandpiper, Killdeer, Black-necked Stilt, American Coot, and Belted Kingfisher are just a sampling of the more common sightings.

The Bighorn River is, of course, high on most angler's must-do list. Camping is available year around. Motel space is limited and hard to come by, especially during the spring, summer, and fall.

The canyon is surrounded by Crow Indian Reservation lands, please respect private landowner rights.

DIRECTIONS
From Fort Smith, take 313 to Route 12 and go right; the park headquarters is immediately on the left. From Lovell, Wyoming, take US Hwy 14 east to Route 37 and go north 24 miles to Barry's Landing.

CONTACT
Bighorn Canyon National Recreation Area phone: 406-666-2412

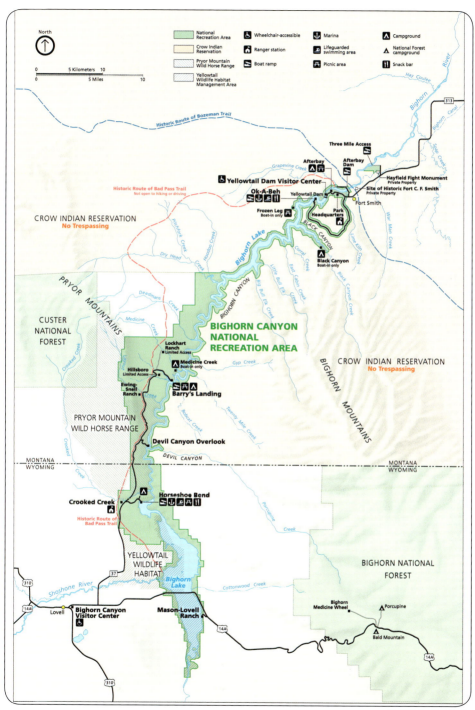

North

National Recreation Area
Crow Indian Reservation
Pryor Mountain Wild Horse Range
Yellowtail Wildlife Habitat Management Area

Wheelchair-accessible
Ranger station
Boat ramp
Marina
Lifeguarded swimming area
Picnic area
Campground
National Forest campground
Snack bar

0   5 Kilometers   10
0   5 Miles   10

Historic Route of Bozeman Trail

Bighorn River
Hay Coulee
313
Bighorn Canal

Three Mile Access

Grapevine Creek
Afterbay
Afterbay Dam

Hayfield Fight Monument
Private Property

Yellowtail Dam Visitor Center
Ok-A-Beh
Yellowtail Dam

Site of Historic Fort C. F. Smith
Private Property
Fort Smith

Historic Route of Bad Pass Trail
Not open to hiking or driving

CROW INDIAN RESERVATION
No Trespassing

Frozen Leg
Boat-in only

Park Headquarters

BLACK CANYON

War Man Creek
Lime Kiln Creek

Pitchfork Creek
Hoodoo Creek
Dry Head

Deadmans Creek

Medicine

PRYOR MOUNTAINS

CUSTER NATIONAL FOREST

Crooked Creek

BIGHORN CANYON

Coral Creek
Little Bull Elk Creek
East Cabin Creek
Big Bull Elk Creek

Black Canyon Creek

Black Canyon
Boat-in only

BIGHORN CANYON
NATIONAL
RECREATION AREA

CROW INDIAN RESERVATION
No Trespassing

BIGHORN MOUNTAINS

Lockhart Ranch
Limited Access

Medicine Creek
Boat-in only

Gyp Creek

Hillsboro
Limited Access

Ewing-Snell Ranch

Barry's Landing

PRYOR MOUNTAIN
WILD HORSE RANGE

Twenty Mile Creek

Devil Canyon Overlook

DEVIL CANYON

MONTANA
WYOMING

MONTANA
WYOMING

Bobcat Creek

Crooked Creek

Horseshoe Bend

Historic Route of
Bad Pass Trail

Porcupine

Creek

YELLOWTAIL
WILDLIFE
HABITAT

Bighorn
Lake

310

Shoshone River

37

Cottonwood Creek

BIGHORN NATIONAL

FOREST

Bighorn
Medicine Wheel

Porcupine

14A

Lovell

Bighorn Canyon
Visitor Center

Mason-Lovell
Ranch

14A

Bald Mountain

310

14A

Credit: National Park Service

SOUTHEAST MONTANA
#16 Little Bighorn National Monument

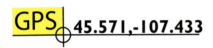
GPS 45.571,-107.433

CROW AGENCY

KEY BIRDS
Horned Lark, Lark Sparrow, Wild Turkey, Red-tailed Hawk, Turkey Vulture, Mourning Dove

BEST SEASONS
Open year round; closed Thanksgiving, Christmas, and New Year's Day. Best birding in spring and fall.

AREA DESCRIPTION
Often referred to as "Custer's Last Stand", most visitors come here to experience the eerie aftermath of the infamous trooper's dramatic defeat. But don't let that stop you from discovering the birds and wildlife that call these rolling, hilly open grasslands with brushy coulees home. Most diverse bird habitat is along the river. The short auto tour route and walking trails afford the best birding ops.

Look for pronghorn, coyotes, and prairie dogs, and don't be surprised to hear the warning buzz of a disturbed rattler.

DIRECTIONS
Drive east of Billings on I-90 to Crow Agency and follow signs.

SOUTHEAST MONTANA

#17 Tongue River Birding Route

GPS | **HWY 314:**
45.529,-106.990

CROW AGENCY/TONGUE RIVER ROAD/BIRNEY/LAME DEER LOOP

KEY BIRDS
Sharp-tailed Grouse, Say's Phoebe, Turkey Vulture (summer), Wild Turkey, Belted Kingfisher, Western Kingbird

BEST SEASONS
Spring, summer, and fall

AREA DESCRIPTION
Paved and good gravel roads (Tongue River Road) pass through mostly empty country

Diverse habitat attracts a wide variety of birds and wildlife. Traffic, except for summer weekends is largely non-existent. It is a long way between light bulbs, so be sure to gas up. Summer is typically hot and dry; though blizzards and extreme cold are common in winter and early spring. Side roads can be impassable when wet. Within the loop is mostly Northern Cheyenne Indian Reservation; please respect both the land and its people.

DIRECTIONS
From Crow Agency, follow US 212 east about 20 miles and turn right on MT 314 for about 20 miles. Turn right into the Rosebud Battlefield State Park; or continue on MT 314 about 10 miles to Tongue River Road (Tongue River State Park). Follow Tongue River Road about 40 miles to Birney. Turn north on Lamedeer Divide Road (NCIR 4) about 30 miles to Lame Deer. Turn left on US 212 back to Crow Agency (44 miles). For the best of it, start early, arrive back late.

Western Kingbird

SOUTHEAST MONTANA
#18 Tongue River Reservoir State Park

GPS 45.109, -106.788

SOUTH OF BUSBY

KEY BIRDS
Eastern Kingbird, Mourning Dove, Redpoll, Horned Lark, Western Meadowlark, Common Nighthawk, Bald Eagle and a variety of waterfowl and shorebirds

BEST SEASONS
Spring and fall migration

AREA DESCRIPTION
Water with shrubs and grasslands surrounded by juniper and pine clad coulees and canyons

The 700 acres in this state park attract a surprising number and variety of birds. The best birding is found on the reservoir and river and in the surrounding areas. Be aware, many of the roads in the area are impassable when wet. Watch for rattlesnakes.

Best to bird early and late in the day, since this is a popular fishing and camping spot. Off season actually provides the best birding ops.

Nearby Rosebud Battlefield State Park offers much the same birding ops (without the water) on a somewhat smaller scale.

Mule and white-tailed deer, coyote, red fox, wild turkey, and upland game birds frequent the area.

DIRECTIONS
From I-90 East, Exit 510 (US 212 East) just past Crow Agency, follow US 212 to MT 314. Turn south and go approximately 22 miles to the Rosebud Battlefield turnoff (signed); continue on MT 314 for 10 miles to the Tongue River State Park.

Horned Lark

CONTACT

Park Manager phone: 406- 234-0900

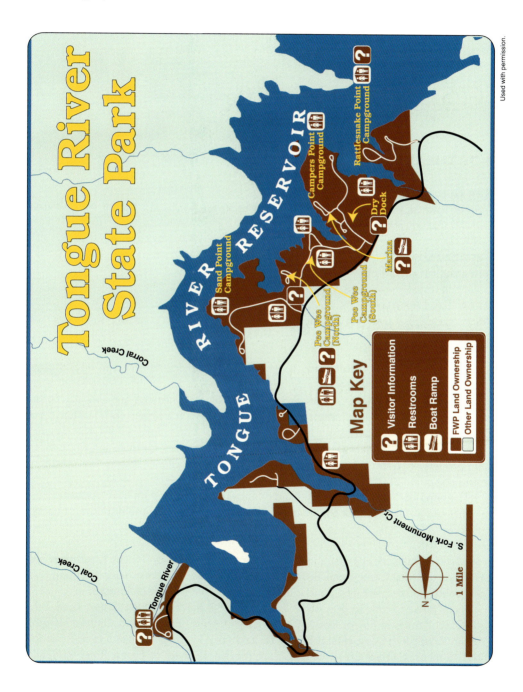

Used with permission.

SOUTHEAST MONTANA
#19 Black's Pond

GPS 45.347,-106.286

SOUTHEAST OF ASHLAND

KEY BIRDS
Spotted Towhee, Western Meadowlark, Warbling Vireo, Swainson's Thrush, Marsh Wren, Gadwall, Mallard, and Wild Turkey

BEST SEASONS
Spring and fall migrations

AREA DESCRIPTION
Water, ponderosa pine, cottonwood, green ash, choke cherry, cattails, sagebrush and grassland

A variety of waterfowl, water birds, songbirds, woodpeckers, raptors, and upland game birds are attracted to this area.

Originally called Black's Sawmill Pond, in 1989 Ducks Unlimited and the U.S. Forest Service combined to build a manmade dam which resulted in a larger, more attractive site for both waterfowl and indigenous birds and wildlife.

On a Custer National Forest Watchable Wildlife route, look for mule and white-tailed deer, pronghorn, bobcat, coyote, fox, badger, and the occasional beaver and scattered prairie dog colonies.

The pond harbors black bullhead and rainbow trout; largemouth bass, maybe?

Facilities are limited to a couple of picnic tables, an outhouse, and primitive camping.

DIRECTIONS
From Ashland: take US 212 east about a mile; turn right (south) on Tongue River Road and go 8 miles to Odell Creek Road. Turn left (east) for 7 miles to Forest Road 4021 and turn right (south) to the pond. The pond is approximately 17 miles out of Ashland.

From Birney: From Tongue River Road north 13 miles to Odell Creek Road. Turn right (east) 7 miles to Forest Road 4021 turn right (south) to the pond. Or take Hanging Woman Creek Road east out of Birney to East Fork Hanging Woman Creek Road for about 15 miles to Odell Creek Road. Go left (north) 2.5 miles to Forest Road 4021, and turn left. The pond is quickly on the right.

CONTACT
Custer National Forest phone: 406-784-2344

Western Meadowlark

SOUTHEAST MONTANA
#20 Tongue River (IBA)

GPS 45.591, -106.298

WEST OF ASHLAND

KEY BIRDS
Yellow-breasted Chat, Lazuli Bunting, Red-eyed and Warbling Vireos, Redstart, Bald Eagle, Red-tailed Hawk, Red-headed Woodpecker, Eastern Screech Owl, Ovenbird

BEST SEASONS
Spring through fall offers best viewing ops.

AREA DESCRIPTION
Cottonwood riparian area

The 7,100 acres surrounds 40 miles or so of the Tongue River, all of which lies within the Northern Cheyenne Indian Reservation. The IBA was created in cooperation with the reservation's Natural Resource Department. Mostly cottonwood forest habitat, surveys have identified over 100 species using the IBA; 21 of which are species of conservation concern.

Biologists fear coal bed methane extraction could degrade water quality and thus negatively affect the cottonwood forest on which most of the species depend.

As for mammals, mule deer, elk, coyote, red and swift fox, white-tailed jackrabbit, and mountain cottontail are common. Less common are white-tailed deer, badger, bobcat, otter, beaver, mink, and black bear.

DIRECTIONS
The IBA is located along the Tongue River, upstream and down from Ashland (for specific directions and entry info, contact the reservation's Dept. Natural Resources, see below).

CONTACT
Northern Cheyenne Department Natural Resources phone: 406-477-6503
Montana IBA Information can be found at http://www.audubon.org/bird/iba; follow links to Montana.

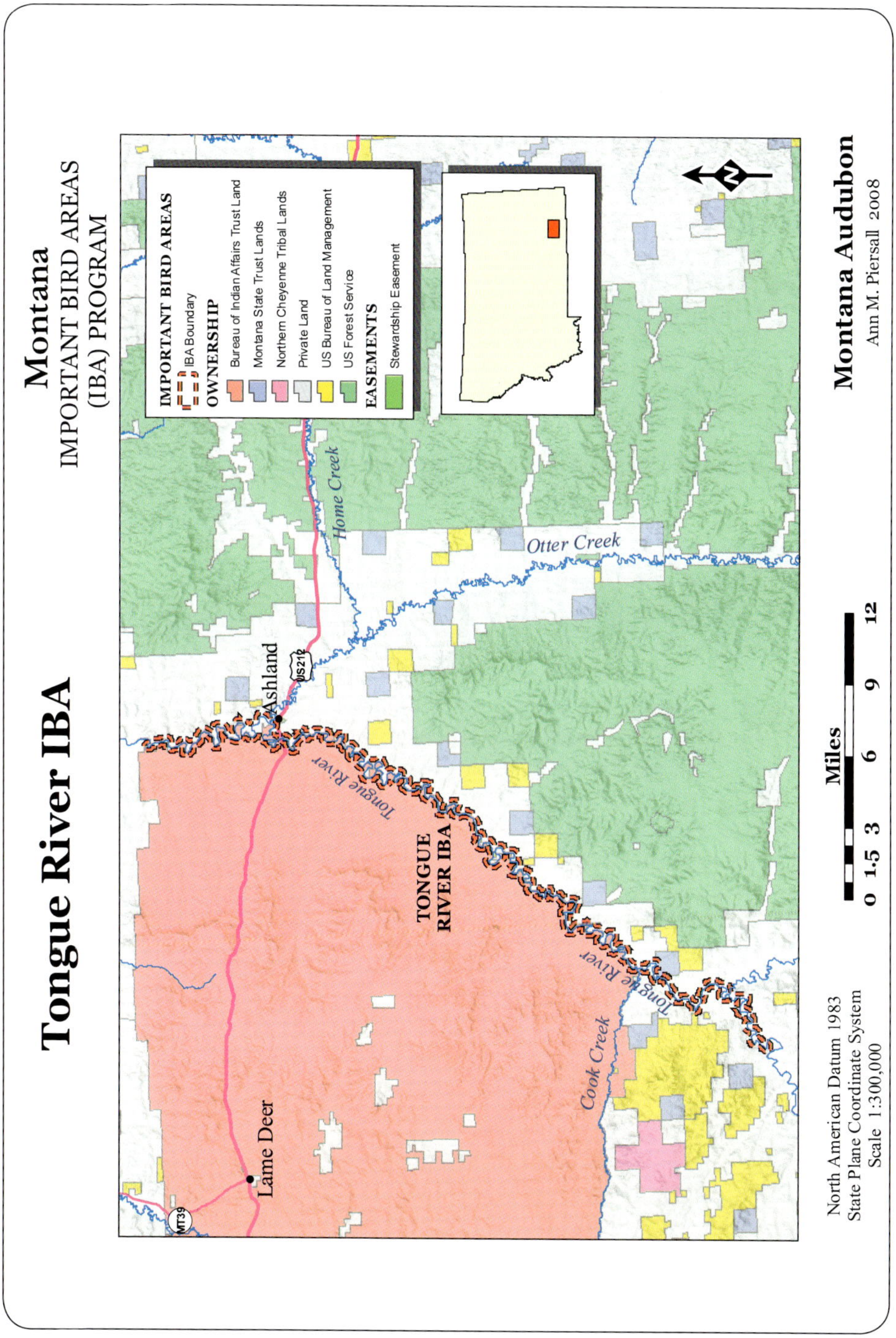

Tongue River IBA

Montana
IMPORTANT BIRD AREAS (IBA) PROGRAM

IMPORTANT BIRD AREAS

IBA Boundary

OWNERSHIP

Bureau of Indian Affairs Trust Land
Montana State Trust Lands
Northern Cheyenne Tribal Lands
Private Land
US Bureau of Land Management
US Forest Service

EASEMENTS

Stewardship Easement

Home Creek

Otter Creek

Ashland

US212

Tongue River

TONGUE RIVER IBA

Tongue River

Cook Creek

Lame Deer

MT39

North American Datum 1983
State Plane Coordinate System
Scale 1:300,000

Miles

0 1.5 3 6 9 12

Montana Audubon
Ann M. Piersall 2008

SOUTHEAST MONTANA
#21 Powder Carter Sage-Steppe (IBA)

GPS | BOYES: 45.269,-105.032

EAST OF BROADUS

KEY BIRDS
Sage and Sharp-tailed Grouse, Wild Turkey, Burrowing Owl

BEST SEASONS
Spring through fall

AREA DESCRIPTION
Numerous creeks surrounded by grasslands and high quality sagebrush

This IBA consists of one million acres plus in the southeast corner of the state, one of the state's least populated. Comprised of a mix of BLM, state, and private lands, some enrolled as stewardship easements. Private lands are mostly cattle and sheep ranches and dryland wheat farms. The best bird habitat consists of high quality sagebrush and native grass carved by numerous creeks. The IBA supports a thriving sage grouse population, at least 10% of the state population. However, West Nile Virus has reduced numbers somewhat in recent years. Coal bed methane and other energy development is also a concern.

Sparsely populated, many roads are impassable when wet; high clearance (4x4) vehicles and a good set of maps are imperative. A fascinating spot to explore, the area is rich in history, and wildlife abounds — antelope, mule and white-tailed deer are everywhere and coyotes serenade nightly. The night sky is...well, flat out awesome... among the blackest, star-studded night skies anywhere on the planet. In other words, like there's more to fishing than catching...

DIRECTIONS
Follow US 212 east of Broadus for approximately 20 miles to Boyes. From there, for the next 30 miles or so, the IBA is roughly northeast and southwest of the highway.

CONTACT
Montana IBA Information can be found at http://www.audubon.org/bird/iba; follow links to Montana.

Burrowing Owl
(Keith Szafranski photo)

SOUTHEAST MONTANA
McNab Pond

#22

GPS 45.836,-104.433

NEAR EKALAKA

KEY BIRDS
Sage and Sharp-tailed Grouse, Wild Turkey, Burrowing Owl, Long-billed Curlew, Western Tanager, and a whole host of waterfowl and water birds, especially during migration

BEST SEASONS
Spring and fall migrations

AREA DESCRIPTION
Ponderosa pine, cottonwood, willow, choke cherry, sagebrush, and grasslands

With the above terrain, toss in cattails in the pond and no wonder so many different bird species flock to what is really an oasis in a dry land.

Small campground (first come, first served) and picnic area, fire pits and vault toilet, pack-in, pack-out rules apply. Motorized access to the surrounding BLM and Custer National Forest is restricted to designated roads and trails. This is a popular spring turkey and fall big game hunting area. The pond is stocked with crappie, largemouth bass, and rainbow trout.

Two other nearby sites — **Camp Needmore** and **Ekalaka Park** — on the right (west) side of the highway are worth a shot. Look for forest-dwelling birds: woodpeckers, songbirds, and Wild Turkey. The **Chalk Buttes** (southwest of Ekalaka) and **Capitol Rock** (southeast of Ekalaka) are great places to view raptors and a variety of songbirds and woodpeckers, as well as Sharp-tailed Grouse and Wild Turkey. Should you have a little time to kill, take a stroll about **Ekalaka**; not only an interesting Old West town but a variety of birds live and nest in the town's tall trees and shrubs.

As far as animals, mule and white-tailed deer, pronghorn, coyote, red fox, may be seen as well as the occasional badger, beaver, bobcat, and scattered prairie dog colonies.

DIRECTIONS
From Ekalaka, follow MT 323 south about 8 miles and turn left onto Prairie Dale Road. Turn left again at the first gravel road and it's about 1 mile to the pond.

CONTACT
Custer National Forest phone: 605-797-4432

SOUTHEAST MONTANA
#23 Medicine Rocks State Park

GPS 46.045,-104.458

NEAR EKALAKA

KEY BIRDS
Sage and Sharp-tailed Grouse, Rock Wren, Golden Eagle

BEST SEASONS
Spring through fall

AREA DESCRIPTION
Sandstone buttes, ponderosa pine forest, sagebrush and mixed short- and long grass prairie

This 330-acre state park is one of our favorite stops in southeast Montana and not just for the birds. Indians considered this spot sacred "Big Medicine" and so do we. All those "Swiss-cheese-like" sandstone buttes, sort of like misplaced monuments in an otherwise sea of rolling grass…as I say, BIG Medicine. There is a pretty active Sharp-tailed Grouse lek nearby.

Camping, picnicking, hiking, wildlife viewing, and photography are popular. Fee area; facilities include drinking water, picnic tables, fire rings and grills, and restrooms. Motorized access on designated roads only; pack-in, pack-out rules apply.

DIRECTIONS
From Miles City, follow US 12 west to Baker and turn south on MT 7 for approximately 25 miles to the park.

CONTACT
Park Manager phone: 406-377-6256

Rock Wren

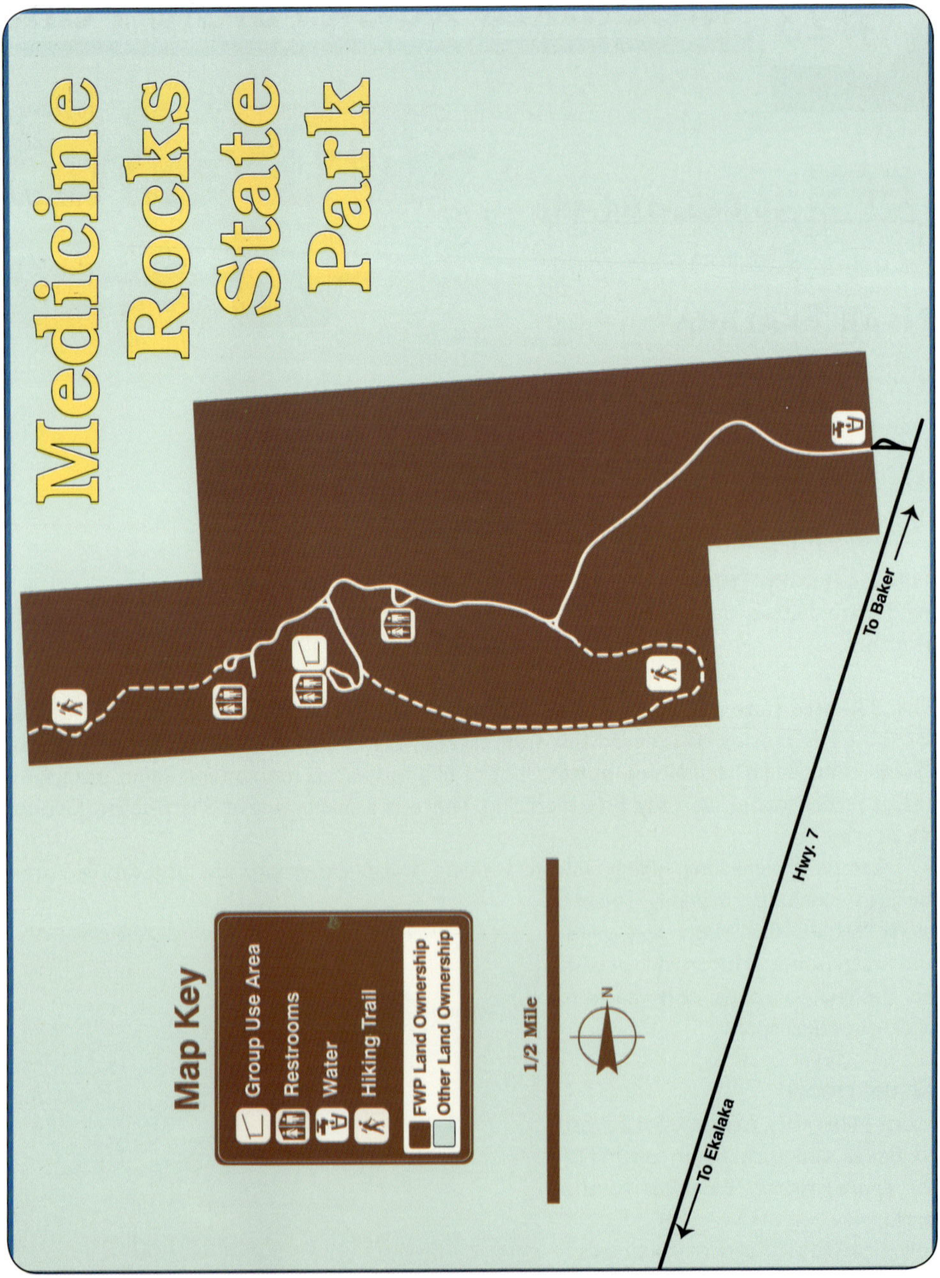
Medicine Rocks State Park
Map Key
Group Use Area
Restrooms
Water
Hiking Trail
FWP Land Ownership
Other Land Ownership
1/2 Mile
N
Hwy. 7
To Baker
To Ekalaka

Used with permission.

SOUTHEAST MONTANA
#24 Makoshika State Park

GPS 47.089,-104.707

GLENDIVE

KEY BIRDS
Turkey Vulture, Rock Wren, Prairie Falcon, Golden Eagle

BEST SEASONS
Spring through fall

AREA DESCRIPTION
Clay and sandstone outcroppings surrounded by grasslands and juniper covered hillsides

Park literature notes, "Habitat types include dissected sedimentary plains; bare, exposed clay, shale and sandstone outcrops, grassland mesas, forested (juniper) hillsides on northern exposures and coulees with seasonal water."

On our first visit, the aim was solely to experience the park's Annual Buzzard Day (early June, contact the park for specific date). I don't recall knowing much, if anything, about Makoshika only that it was our largest state park and... Really now, who are these folks to celebrate the return of "buzzards" no less? Were we in for a big surprise? You bet. Not only was the

Turkey Vulture

event fun and enlightening but the badlands…Well, ever since, we've been fans of badlands everywhere. And who would have imagined all those birds and dinosaurs even!

Makoshika (Ma-ko'-shi-ka) stems from a Lakota Indian phrase meaning "land of bad spirits or badlands." The 11,500 acres of this park fit perfectly with that description.

According to park literature: "200+ species have been observed; a 1982 evaluation study revealed 60 species ranging from riparian to badlands species, 16 of which were species of conservation concern."

Beyond birds, the park is a popular spot for hiking, biking, camping, picnicking, disc golf, wildlife viewing, and photography. There is a wonderful interpretive center, a public rifle range, and a private archery range (contact Jim Thompson; 406-687-3412 within the park).

Fee area; open all year.

Directions

From Glendive, follow Merrill Avenue south and turn left at E. Barry Street across the railroad tracks. Turn right on S. Peterson Avenue and go 6 blocks, then turn left on Snyder Street to the park. Route is signed.

Contact

Park Manager phone: 406-377-6256

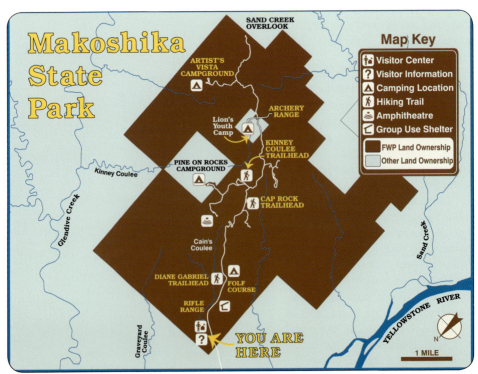

SOUTHEAST MONTANA
#25 Terry Badlands Wilderness Study Area

GPS⊕ 46.897,-105.419

TERRY

KEY BIRDS
Blue and Steller's Jays, Mountain Bluebird, Prairie Falcon, Red-tailed Hawk, Golden Eagle, Turkey Vulture, American Kestrel, Cooper's Hawk, Burrowing, Long-eared, and Great Horned Owls, Sage and Sharp-tailed Grouse

BEST SEASONS
Spring thru fall; many roads are impassable when wet.

AREA DESCRIPTION
Badlands, ponderosa and limber pines, juniper, sagebrush, and native short-grass prairie

The topography in this 44,000-acre Wilderness Study Area create a unique and, to me, surprising birding adventure. In a landscape more like what I imagine the moon than the sort of lush, wet bottomlands birds are obviously drawn to, badlands harbor a remarkable number and variety of avian birdlife. While I've never seen a Terry Badlands bird list, the nearby Makoshika State Park (Glendive) list exceeds 200 birds and counting. As I say, remarkable.

In 1806, William Clark on his return from the Pacific noted in passing,...*here the river*

Red-tailed Hawk (im)

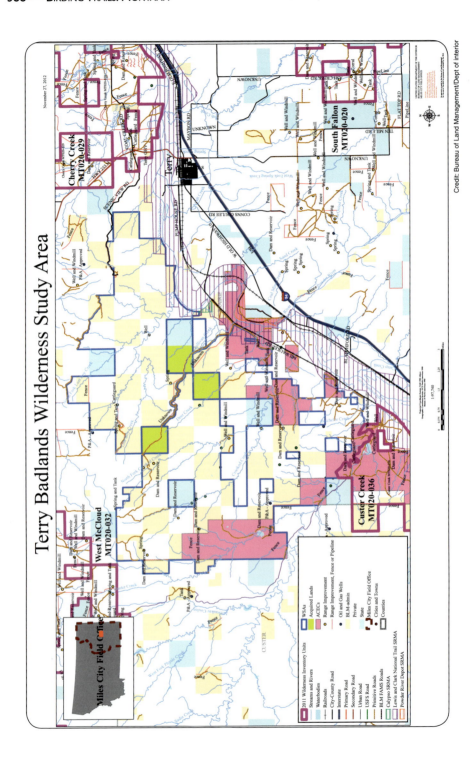

Terry Badlands Wilderness Study Area

November 27, 2012

Credit: Bureau of Land Management/Dept of interior

approaches the high mountainous country on the N W. Side. those hills appear to be composed of various Coloured earth and Coal without much rock. I observe Several Conical pounds which appear to have been burnt. this high Country is washed into Curious formed mounds & hills and is cut much with reveens. The high Country is entirely bar of timber. great quantities of Coal or carbonated wood is to be seen in every Bluff and in the high hills at a distance on each Side.

Visitors today, might word it somewhat differently but in reality the view remains much the same.

Pronghorn, mule deer, coyote, white-tailed jackrabbit, and desert cottontail are common; white-tailed deer, porcupine, and badger less so.

Motorized access is restricted to designated roads and trails. Camping is allowed just about anywhere; pack in-pack-out rules apply. There are no facilities or developments within the WSA.

Hunting is allowed according to state seasons and regulations.

Directions
From Terry, follow Old MT 10 west to Milwaukee Road and turn north (left) to Calypso Trail. The trail ends at a gate about 7 miles in. Or follow MT 253 north from town for about 3 miles, turn west (left) on Scenic View Road to the overlook. Or continue north on MT 253 to Cherry Creek Road and turn west (left) into the WSA; roads and trails lead off in every direction.

Contact
BLM Miles City phone: 406-233-2800

SOUTHEAST MONTANA
#26 Matthews Recreation Area

GPS 46.503,-105.735

MILES CITY

KEY BIRDS
Greater and Lesser Yellowlegs, Belted Kingfisher, Cedar Waxwing, Lazuli Bunting, Cooper's Hawk, Osprey

BEST SEASONS
May through October

AREA DESCRIPTION
Cottonwood, green ash, willow riparian forest interspersed with grassy meadows beside the river

Level, the site is easy walking. Picnic tables, fire rings, standing grills, covered picnic pavilion, interpretive kiosk, handicap accessible fishing platform and cement walkway; pack-in, pack out rules apply. Camping is allowed.

DIRECTIONS
From Miles City, follow Valley Drive east about 7 miles and take a left on Tusler Road. The area is a short drive east, on the north side of the road.

CONTACT
BLM Miles City phone: 406-233-2800

SOUTHEAST MONTANA
#27 Pirogue Island State Park

GPS 46.440,-105.823

MILES CITY

KEY BIRDS
Mourning Dove, American Kestrel, Bald Eagle, Northern Flicker, Belted Kingfisher, Eastern and Western Kingbirds, Yellow-breasted Chat, Eastern Screech Owl

BEST SEASONS
Open all year; spring and fall migrations are best.

AREA DESCRIPTION
Tall cottonwoods tower above green ash, Russian olive, and willow interspersed with wet meadows, all carved by narrow river channels

This 269-acre park is an attractive environment for a wide variety of birds: waterfowl, water birds, woodland- and grassland-loving birds, raptors and well, you name it, are likely to show up here. During migration look for birds that are normally found in central and eastern U.S. — such as indigo bunting, scarlet tanager, and a number of neotropicals which show up occasionally according to local birders.

Grabbing your binos and taking a hike is the most productive way we know to view birds here. Except perhaps at the height of 'skeeter season, this is a pleasant spot to spend quality time with the birds, to soak up a bit of fresh air and history and, if you get lucky, to pick up a moss agate or two.

Mule and white-tailed deer, fox squirrel, mink, muskrat and raccoon also frequent the park.

The park features an interpretive trail, picnic tables, benches, and restrooms; no motorized access, pack-in, pack-out rules apply. Be careful when wading the channels during even modest flows. Hunting is allowed with restrictions.

DIRECTIONS
From Miles City, go north on MT 22 (59) and turn right (east) on Kinsey Road (MT 489). After about 2 miles, turn right to the park. Turns are signed.

CONTACT
Park Manager phone: 406-234-0900

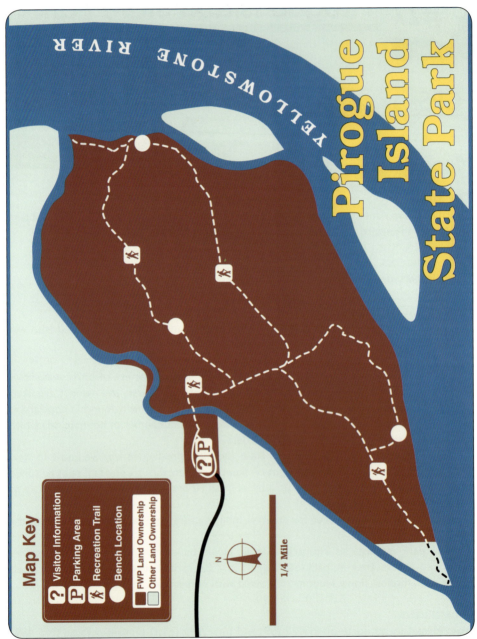

YELLOWSTONE RIVER

Pirogue Island State Park

Map Key

? Visitor Information
P Parking Area
🏃 Recreation Trail
● Bench Location

◼ FWP Land Ownership
◻ Other Land Ownership

N

1/4 Mile

SOUTHEAST MONTANA
#28 Miles City Parks

GPS
RIVERSIDE PARK:
46.405,-105.854

MILES CITY

KEY BIRDS
Wood Duck, Great Horned Owl, Orchard and Bullock's Orioles, Common Grackle, Hairy, Downy, and Red-headed Woodpeckers, Yellow-rumped Warbler

BEST SEASONS
Year round; best birding is early spring and late fall

AREA DESCRIPTION
Lots of trees — deciduous and conifer — shrubs and water

The city parks create diverse, if a bit noisome at times, areas that attract a variety of species. Spotted Eagle Recreation Area is a good spot to view waterfowl and shorebirds, especially during migration.

Once the summer season starts, earlier and later in the day are better for birding. Riverside Park tends to be especially noisy on summer weekends; Pumping Plant and Spotted Eagle Recreation Area not so much.

The Miles City Bucking Horse Sale is held annually the third weekend in May.

DIRECTIONS

Riverside Park

I-94 East, exit at MT 59 north (Business Route) and turn right on Dike Street just across the Tongue River Bridge to the park.

Pumping Plant Park

I-94 East, exit at MT 59 north (Business Route) and turn left on Waterplant Road to the park.

Spotted Eagle Recreation Area

I-94 East, exit at MT 59 north (Business Route) and turn right on Garryowen Road. Bear left onto Pacific Avenue, turn right onto Spotted Eagle Road, and turn right to the recreation area.

CONTACT
Miles City Chamber of Commerce
511 Pleasant Street
Miles City, MT 59301
Phone: 406-234-1639
Website: www.milescitychamber.com

Common Grackle

SOUTHEAST MONTANA

#29 Roundup River-Walk Heritage Trail

GPS 46.440,-108.532

ROUNDUP

KEY BIRDS
Great Horned Owl, Yellow-breasted Chat, Lazuli Bunting, Bullock's Oriole, Belted Kingfisher, Yellow, Orange-crowned, Yellow-rumped and MacGillivray's Warblers

BEST SEASONS
Spring and summer

AREA DESCRIPTION
Developed trail along cottonwood and green ash forested river and up into pine and juniper forest

According to local birders: "Great Horned Owl, Yellow-breasted Chat, Lazuli Bunting, Yellow, Orange-crowned, Yellow-rumped and MacGillivray's Warbler, Belted Kingfisher, Bullock's Oriole, Yellow-headed, Red-winged and Brewer's Blackbird nest here; Blue Jay and Ferruginous Hawks are common in winter; Northern Goshawk, Snowy Owl and even a single Mountain Bluebird, though rare, have over-wintered here."

The trail follows the Musselshell River and continues into the sandstone bluffs and uplands. Cottonwood and green ash forest dominates the river section, while uphill the trail winds through ponderosa pine and juniper forest. The Annual Bird Walk (morning of July 4th) is quite popular amongst locals and is a great way for visiting birders to get acquainted with the area. The Christmas Bird Count tally usually exceeds 100 species.

DIRECTIONS
From I-90 exit in Billings, take US 87 North to Roundup — approximately 45 miles.

CONTACT
Roundup Chamber of Commerce phone: 406-248-1400

Bullock's Oriole

SOUTHEAST MONTANA
#30 | Musselshell Sage-Steppe (IBA)

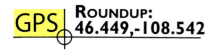

GPS ⊕ **ROUNDUP:**
46.449,-108.542

NORTH OF ROUNDUP/SOUTH OF THE MISSOURI RIVER

KEY BIRDS
Sage Grouse, Poorwill, Pinyon Jay, Sage Thrasher, Golden Eagle, Burrowing Owl

BEST SEASONS
Open year round; spring and fall offer best chance for checking off migrants

AREA DESCRIPTION
Sagebrush, wooded bottoms, upland forest, native prairie, and badlands interspersed with extensive crop and ranch lands

Once native prairie, woodlands, and badlands, the ongoing threat to the welfare of Sage Grouse is the continued loss of intact, healthy sagebrush thanks to overgrazing, wild fire, oil and gas development, and invasive plants. Still a lot of Sage Grouse habitat remains in this three million acre area — the portion of the Charles M. Russell NWR south of the Missouri River, the rugged breaks of the Musselshell River, tens of thousands of acres of BLM lands, and numerous state sections largely covered in sagebrush.

In my experience, the key to finding sage grouse in spring through early fall are large tracts of sagebrush with a good grass understory, relatively near water with succulent greens nearby. Native forbs and, where it occurs, dandelion leaves seem to dominate the warm

Sage Grouse (cock)

season diet. Sage Grouse country is by definition semi-arid; in the driest years, birds often concentrate around the tiniest seeps. Later in the fall and over winter, water seems less of a concern and studies have shown sagebrush leaves make up nearly 100 percent of the diet. I have seen hundreds of birds in areas of deep snow, but if there is a wind-blown bare ridge nearby, we almost always find birds using it.

Animals that might been seen here are pronghorn, mule deer, elk, coyote, swift fox, bobcat, white-tailed jackrabbit, desert cottontail, prairie dog, porcupine, and badger.

DIRECTIONS
Bounded on the north by the Missouri River and to the south by Musselshell River, the IBA sprawls across parts of five counties; access from US 12, 87, and 191 and MT 200.

CONTACT
Montana IBA Information can be found at http://www.audubon.org/bird/iba; follow links to Montana.

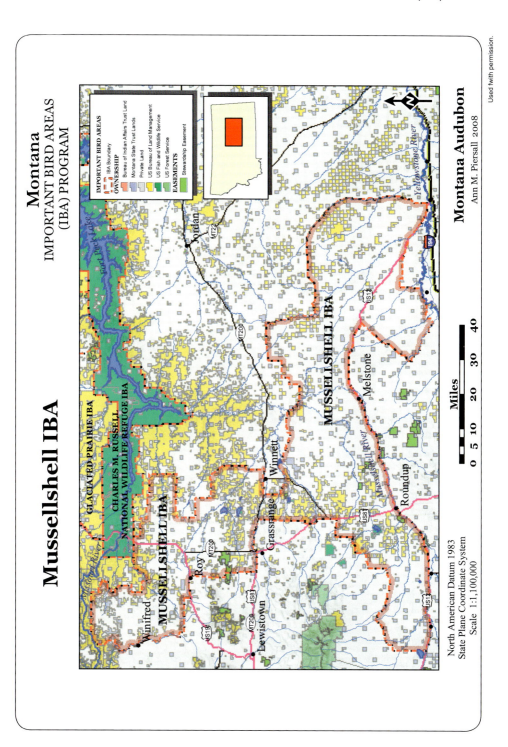

Montana
IMPORTANT BIRD AREAS
(IBA) PROGRAM

Mussellshell IBA

IMPORTANT BIRD AREAS
- IBA Boundary

OWNERSHIP
- Bureau of Indian Affairs Trust Land
- Montana State Trust Lands
- Private Land
- US Bureau of Land Management
- US Fish and Wildlife Service
- US Forest Service

EASEMENTS
- Stewardship Easement

Montana Audubon
Ann M. Piersall 2008

North American Datum 1983
State Plane Coordinate System
Scale 1:1,100,000

Miles
0 5 10   20   30   40

SOUTHEAST MONTANA

#31 Lake Mason National Wildlife Refuge

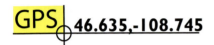 GPS 46.635,-108.745

NORTHEAST OF ROUNDUP

KEY BIRDS
Long-billed Curlew, Upland Sandpiper, Sage Grouse, Mountain Plover, Baird's and Grasshopper Sparrows, Burrowing Owl

BEST SEASONS
Spring; wet years are best.

AREA DESCRIPTION
Mixed habitats in the various units, see below

The 8,700-acre NWR is comprised of three units: North, Willow Creek, and Lake Mason itself which, in reality, is more a marsh than a bona fide lake. The North Unit is comprised of grasslands, sagebrush, sandstone bluffs, and grassy meadows beside Jones Creek. Wide spots in the creek provide limited waterfowl habitat in wet years. The Willow Creek Unit is primarily native short-grass prairie, while the Lake Mason Unit is mostly marsh; only in the wettest years does the lake resemble a lake. Obviously the more water, the more waterfowl.

Local birders point to "Long-billed Curlew, Upland Sandpiper, Sage Grouse, Baird's and Grasshopper Sparrows, Mountain Plover and Burrowing Owl along with a variety of neotropicals and raptors as pretty much givens." Obviously, waterfowl numbers and species ebb and flow with water abundance or lack thereof.

Animals that might be seen are pronghorn, mule deer, the occasional elk, coyote, red fox, and prairie dogs in the surrounding grasslands.

DIRECTIONS
From Roundup, follow Golf Course Road to Lake Mason Road; follow the signs.

CONTACT
Lake Mason NWR phone: 406-538-8706

Long-billed Curlew (nest)

Fort Peck Lake

BIRDING TRAILS: MONTANA

MISSOURI RIVER COUNTRY

In Daniels, Garfield, McCone, Phillips, Sheridan, Richland, Roosevelt and Valley Counties, birds and wildlife far outnumber people. In tiny (1-acre) Westby Town Park, for example, the bird list includes over 200 species observed, including 29 warbler species. In Glasgow, during the 2006 three-day Montana Bird Festival, 139 species were observed, of which significant numbers were observed within the nearby Little Beaver Creek IBA. The Charles M. Russell (CMR), Bowdoin, and Medicine Lake NWRs list 276, 232, and 270 species respectively. Bitter Creek WSA (Hinsdale), Manning Lake IBA (west of Froid), and Westby Prairie-Wetland IBA should be on every birder's bucket list.

Perhaps most unique is the sprawling (270,000 acres and counting), remote American Prairie Reserve (south of Malta) which lists 130 bird species, as well as free roaming bison and the black-footed ferret, North America's most endangered mammal. Threatened species such as Greater Sage Grouse, Piping and Mountain Plovers, Baird's Sparrow, Sprague's Pipit, and Burrowing Owl are relatively common throughout the region. I know of no place in the lower 48 with the potential to see such a variety of birds and mammals.

Closest commercial air service is Billings or Great Falls. All of the larger towns offer decent meals and clean, reasonable rooms.

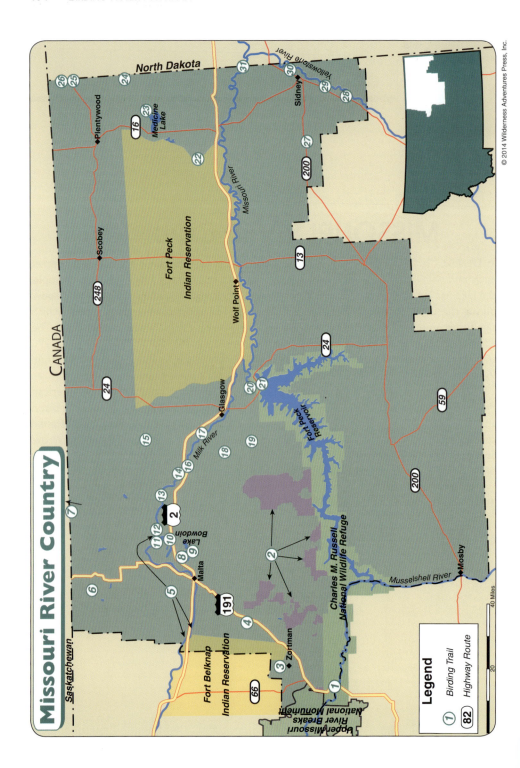

Missouri River Country

CANADA

Saskatchewan

North Dakota

Yellowstone River

Missouri River

Milk River

Musselshell River

Fort Peck Indian Reservation

Fort Peck Reservoir

Charles M. Russell National Wildlife Refuge

Fort Belknap Indian Reservation

Upper Missouri River Breaks National Monument

Plentywood
Scobey
Medicine Lake
Sidney
Wolf Point
Glasgow
Malta
Zortman
Mosby

Legend

1 Birding Trail
82 Highway Route

40 Miles
20

Missouri River Country Locations

1. Charles M. Russell National Wildlife Refuge
2. American Prairie Reserve
3. Camp Creek Campground/Little Rockies)
4. Korsbeck Waterfowl Production Area
5. Milk River Wildlife Management Area
6. Dyrdahl/Webb Waterfowl Production Areas
7. Grasslands National Park (Canada)
8. Bowdoin National Wildlife Refuge
9. Beaver Creek Waterfowl Production Area
10. Nelson Reservoir
11. McNeil Slough Waterfowl Production Area
12. Cole Ponds
13. Bjornberg Bridge Fishing Access Site
14. Hinsdale Wildlife Management Area
15. Bitter Creek Wilderness Study Area
16. Vandalia Wildlife Management Area
17. Faraasen Park Recreation Site
18. Paulo Reservoir
19. Little Beaver Creek IBA
20. Fort Peck Dredge Cut Pond
21. Fort Peck Campground (Downstream Recreation Area)
22. Manning Lake Wetland Complex IBA
23. Medicine Lake National Wildlife Refuge
24. Brush Lake State Park
25. Westby City Park
26. Westby Prairie Wetland Complex IBA
27. Fox Lake Wildlife Management Area
28. Elk Island Fishing Access Site
29. Seven Sisters Fishing Access Site
30. Dlamond Willow Fishing Access Site
31. Fort Union Trading Post/ Fort Buford National Historic Site

MISSOURI RIVER COUNTRY
Charles M. Russell National Wildlife Refuge (IBA)

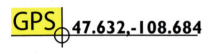

GPS 47.632,-108.684

North of Lewistown

Key Birds
Sage Grouse, Mountain Plover, Burrowing Owl, Bald and Golden Eagles, Ferruginous Hawk, Green-tailed and Spotted Towhees, Lazuli Bunting, Loggerhead Shrike

Best Seasons
Year round; spring through fall for largest variety and numbers.

Area Description
Dramatic mix of badlands, forested coulees, sagebrush-steppe grasslands, native grass prairies, and cottonwood river bottoms

The vast CMR sprawls across over one million acres. It straddles the Missouri River, including Fort Peck Reservoir, for over 125 miles, which makes where to start birding rather vexing.

For starters, drive the 19-mile long Auto Tour route. Unlike most roads within the refuge which are impassable when wet, the AT is more or less passenger car friendly. With 13 interpretive stops along the way, it's a good way to jump start the check-offs and learn what the CMR is all about. Probe a bit deeper and pretty soon you begin to realize how unique, how special birding the CMR is — like where else might you find 276 bird species in one area?

Birds are everywhere, but the largest numbers and variety are always found near water. We have spent entire days searching the trees and brush in and around the campground at Fred Robinson Bridge, and not once felt we might have spent our time better elsewhere. There is an accessible hunting/viewing blind at Hell Creek (first come, first served basis). Sage and Sharp-tailed Grouse leks are scattered about the refuge; contact staff for directions. Best time is April.

Motorized access is restricted to established roads and trails but don't despair, there are literally hundreds of miles of road access.

Camping is allowed just about anywhere within 100 yards of established roads and trails. Beyond that, camping is by foot or horseback only. There are few developed hiking trails (contact staff for directions and maps), but countless game trails afford hikers limitless opportunities. Developed campgrounds are scattered about the refuge, mostly around Fort Peck Reservoir and the Missouri River. Facilities vary; request a guide map at HQ in Lewistown. Potable water is scarce to non-existent. Bring your own and in warm weather, bring plenty — summer and early fall tend to be hot, dry, and dusty. There are no gas stations or restaurants, so plan accordingly. A popular hunting spot, in season blaze orange is highly recommended.

Other wildlife to look for includes black-footed ferret, mountain lion, pronghorn, mule and white-tailed deer, elk, bighorn sheep, black-tailed prairie dog, prairie rattlesnake, bull snake, coyote, and bobcat.

In September, be sure to check out Slippery Ann Elk Viewing Area (just around the corner from Fred Robinson Bridge) where a couple hundred elk show up each year to participate in the annual rut.

The CMR is steeped in history. Indians once lived and hunted here evidenced by teepee rings and a buffalo jump. Lewis and Clark paved the way for white settlement. The refuge is named for the "cowboy artist" Charlie Russell whose paintings documented the Great Plains in the 19th century — the so-called Wild, Wild West before bison vanished and railroads, barbed wire fences, and sodbusters carved up the Plains. Old homesteads and cemeteries remain as testament to the broken dreams of the many that came and largely failed.

Greater Sage Grouse

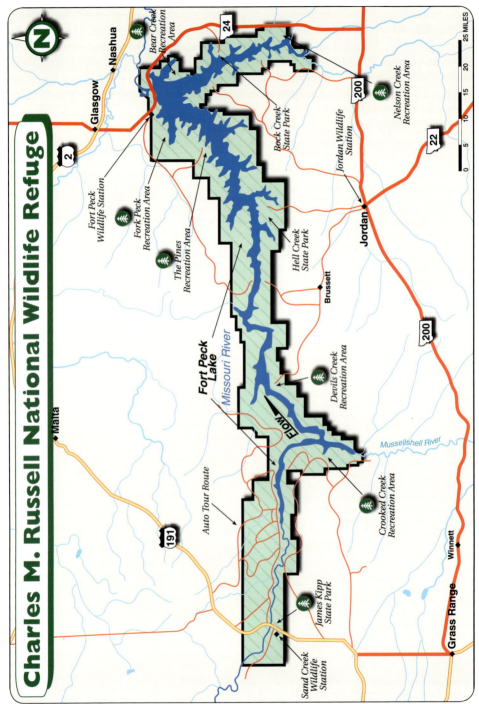

Charles M. Russell National Wildlife Refuge

© 2014 Wilderness Adventures Press, Inc.

The UL Bend National Wildlife Refuge occupies 200,000 acres within the CMR, at UL Bend in the Missouri River. Same landscape, same birds; spring through fall is the best time for birding.

One of the more remote spots within the CMR; plan accordingly. Gumbo rules, so be sure to check with refuge staff for current conditions.

Black-footed ferret re-introduction is in its eighth year, and some of the largest bighorn rams on the planet reside at UL Bend.

UL Bend was named for the UL Ranch which was part of the U.L. Cattle Company, Great Falls circa 1900.

DIRECTIONS
From Lewistown, drive north on US 191. From Malta, go south on US 191.

CONTACT
CMR Headquarters, Lewistown phone: 406-538-8706
Sand Creek Field Station phone 406-464-5181
Jordan Field Station phone: 406-557-6145
Fort Peck Field Station phone: 406-526-3464

MISSOURI RIVER COUNTRY
American Prairie Reserve

#2

GPS | 47.763,-107.773

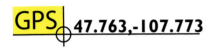

SOUTH OF MALTA

KEY BIRDS
Greater Sage Grouse, Sharp-tailed Grouse, Burrowing Owl, Baird's Sparrow, Mountain Plover, Long-billed Curlew, Sandhill Crane, Eastern Screech Owl, Sprague's Pipit, Golden Eagle, Western Meadowlark

BEST SEASONS
Open year round. Grouse breeding late March thru early May; Burrowing Owl chicks most visible in July; spring and fall migration for waterfowl and shorebirds.

AREA DESCRIPTION
Native mixed-grass prairie

Over 130 bird species have been observed here. At this time, the reserve comprises 274,000 acres in five locations: Sun Prairie, Burnt Lodge, White Rock, Dry Fork, and Timber Creek. This includes 57,972 acres of private land with the balance in leased land from the BLM and the State of Montana.

The American Prairie Reserve is in the process of assembling the largest wildlife park in the United States. About as remote as it gets anywhere in the Lower 48, the plan is to eventually connect and conserve some 3 million acres of native mixed-grass prairie. It is perhaps the "last best place" to observe both birds and wildlife in a landscape as Lewis and Clark and Native Americans originally experienced it. Exploring the Reserve afoot, on horseback, or by automobile is unique; truly a step back in time.

Unlike our national parks, the reserve offers no amenities, save a primitive campground and interpretive signage. Gas is available in Zortman, Lewistown, Glasgow, and Malta. Be prepared for a long, tedious drive on unimproved, mostly unmarked, often difficult roads. Many are gumbo and impassable when wet. High clearance, 4x4 vehicles are de rigueur. There is limited to no cell phone service and no potable water. There are no friendly rangers to lend a helping hand or, perish the thought, usher you to safety should you P.O. mama bison or, perhaps worse, step on an angry rattler (common). Mosquitoes are sometimes thick, especially in spring and early summer.

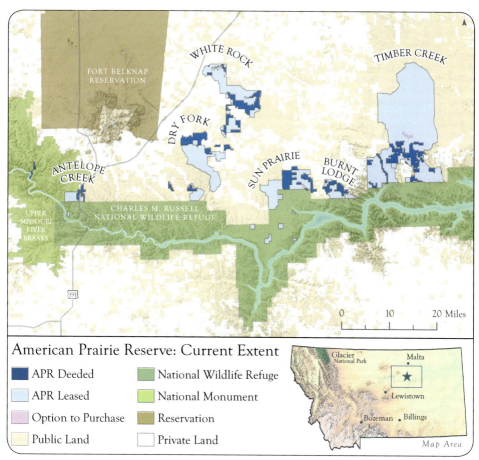

American Prairie Reserve: Current Extent

- APR Deeded
- APR Leased
- Option to Purchase
- Public Land
- National Wildlife Refuge
- National Monument
- Reservation
- Private Land

Map Courtesy of American Prairie Reserve. APR is growing every year, so please visit americanprairie.org for the most current property map or for more information.

Look for bison, elk, mule deer, pronghorn, prairie dog, coyote, kit fox, black-footed ferret (North America's most endangered mammal – though never released or recorded on the Reserve, they have been released at the adjacent UL Bend NWR and CMR NWR) and best keep one eye peeled for rattlesnakes. Prairie Union one-room schoolhouse, numerous abandoned homesteads, and Plains Indian rock art sites relate the area's long and interesting human history. Wildflowers peak in mid- to late May. Free visitor maps are located throughout the Sun Prairie region of the reserve and can be requested online.

Hunting is permitted, according to state seasons and regulations. Much of the deeded property is enrolled in the Block Management program. Hiking, biking, camping, horseback riding, and wildlife watching are popular. No off-road driving is allowed.

There is an eleven-site (four tent and seven camper) primitive camping area at the Buffalo Camp site in the Sun Prairie section, which also provides non-potable water and vault toilets.

DIRECTIONS

From Lewistown, head north on US 191. About 20 miles north of the Missouri River at MM 109 (sign for Zortman) turn right (east) and bear left on Dry Fork Road about 25 miles to the T intersection. Turn left (north) about 4 miles to the fork, bear right about 13 miles to sharp bend in the road. Turn right, about 6 miles to Buffalo Camp. Some of the route is signed. Travel time is approximately three hours.

From Malta, drive south on Central Avenue, cross the canal, go past 12th Street and turn left onto MT 364 (unmarked). About 4 miles in, the road turns to gravel and forks a few hundred yards farther on. Bear right and follow Regina Road about 30 miles to the T intersection. Turn left, past First Creek Hall (waste transfer station) and go about 6 miles to a bend in the road. Turn right and it's about 6 miles to Buffalo Camp. Part of the route is signed. Travel time from Malta is one hour.

CONTACT

American Prairie Preserve
Phone: 877-273-1123
Email: mail@americanprairie.org
Website: www.americanprairie.org

Sandhill Crane (colt)

MISSOURI RIVER COUNTRY
#3 Camp Creek Campground /Little Rockies

GPS 47.916,-108.511

ZORTMAN

KEY BIRDS
Clark's Nutcracker, Pinyon Jay, Mountain Chickadee, Dusky Grouse, Wild Turkey, Gray-crowned Rosy Finch, Sage Grouse, White-throated Swift

BEST SEASONS
Year round; spring through fall for largest variety and numbers.

AREA DESCRIPTION
Mountain meadows and forests

The campground itself offers astute birders plenty of opportunities but the real appeal is the relative solitude and the chance to explore one of Montana's best kept secrets, the Little Rockies.

The area was once heavily mined, and many of the best birding spots are privately-owned mountain meadows surrounded by BLM lands. The best way to view birds and other wildlife on private land is to set up a spotting scope.

In the past, natural wild fires maintained a mosaic of mountain meadows and forests. Fire suppression efforts of the past century have led to pine forests encroaching on meadows, which translated to less habitat for wildlife. Thanks to ongoing restoration efforts, many meadows are once again attracting everything from songbirds and butterflies to elk and bighorn sheep.

There are no developed trails and no auto tour route, but don't let that stop you. Take a hike, perhaps to the top of Old Scraggy Peak — mostly trail-less so allow at least two to three hours. Or follow one of the old mining roads. Since most are rough and minimally maintained, high clearance vehicles (4x4) are highly recommended. Joining in on the annual Christmas Bird Count (406-327-0405) is a good way to get acquainted. In winter, any open water is likely to attract a variety of birds.

Nearby Azure Cave is the largest bat winter roost in the area. Bighorn sheep, mule deer, and mountain lion (good luck, spotting these elusive critters) frequent the area.

DIRECTIONS

From Malta, follow US 191 south for approximately 38 miles and turn right (west) onto Bear Gulch Road to Zortman. Turn right onto the gravel entrance road and follow the signs to the campground. From Lewistown or Billings, take the Seven Mile Road (gravel) from US 191 straight into the campground.

CONTACT

BLM, Malta Field Station phone: 406-654-5100

Canada Goose

MISSOURI RIVER COUNTRY
Korsbeck Waterfowl Production Area

#4

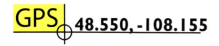 GPS 48.550, -108.155

SOUTH OF DODSON

KEY BIRDS
Blue-winged Teal, Northern Shoveler, Northern Pintail, Mallard, American Wigeon, Gadwall, Baird's Sparrow, McCown's and Chestnut-collared Longspurs, Sage Grouse

BEST SEASONS
Year round; spring through fall for largest variety and numbers.

AREA DESCRIPTION
Reservoirs and wetlands

Two large reservoirs offer good waterfowl, shorebird, songbird, and raptor ops, especially in wet years. Sage Grouse can be found in the surrounding sagebrush.

A variety of animals can also be seen at this site: pronghorn, mule and white-tailed deer, coyote, badger, swift fox, and white-tailed jackrabbit.

DIRECTIONS
From Dodson, take MT 204 south about 21 miles and turn left (east) onto Hog Farm Road. Ester Lake is located at the northwest corner of the state section 2 miles in. Wild Horse Reservoir is a few miles to the northeast. You can also get there by following US 191 south from Malta about 20 miles and turn right (west) at KRM Ranch gate to Wild Horse. Continue south on US 191 to Hog Farm Road and turn right (west) and go about 4 miles and turn right on trail to Ester.

CONTACT
Bowdoin NWR phone: 406-654-2863

MISSOURI RIVER COUNTRY
#5 Milk River Wildlife Management Areas

DODSON DAM UNIT:
48.417,-108.308
DODSON CREEK UNIT:
48.378,-108.246
SLEEPING BUFFALO UNIT:
 48.517,-107.472

EAST OF MALTA NEAR NELSON RESERVOIR

KEY BIRDS
Sage and Sharp-tailed Grouse, Ring-necked Pheasant, Pied-billed Grebe, American Avocet, Greater Yellowlegs, Black Tern, Western Screech Owl, Sprague's Pipit, Baltimore Oriole

BEST SEASONS
Year round; spring thru fall for best variety.

AREA DESCRIPTION
Grasslands, open water, cattail marsh, wetlands, and sagebrush, with agricultural lands nearby

This 1,300-acre WMA attracts a variety of songbirds, raptors, waterfowl, shorebirds, and game birds. Local birders report having seen as many as 36 bird species in a single short day.

There is walk-in access from designated roads and two-tracks. There are no developed trails within the WMA. Ground cover tends to be thick and uncivil, so dress accordingly. Mosquitoes are thick during warm season. Waterfowl and shorebird numbers are greatest during migration.

White-tailed deer and antelope are common throughout the area. Coyote, striped skunk and red fox frequent the area. Blaze orange is recommended during the fall hunting season. No camping; no facilities.

DIRECTIONS
From Malta, take US 2 east about 17-miles and turn left (north) at Sleeping Buffalo. Bear right at the "Y" intersection (toward Saco) for about 2 miles. Units are on both sides of the road.

Two other units — **Dodson Dam** and **Dodson Creek —** are located west of Malta off US 2. Contact FWP (below) for specifics.

CONTACT
MT FW&P - Mark Sullivan phone: 406-654-1183

American Avocet

MISSOURI RIVER COUNTRY
#6 Dyrdahl/Webb Waterfowl Production Areas

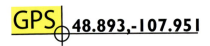 **GPS** 48.893,-107.951

NORTH OF MALTA

KEY BIRDS
Mallard, Northern Shoveler, Northern Pintail, American Wigeon, Wilson's Phalarope, Loggerhead Shrike, Golden Eagle

BEST SEASONS
Year round; spring through fall for largest variety and numbers. Wet years are far better than dry.

AREA DESCRIPTION
Wetlands and potholes with native prairie

The 1,327-acre Dyrdahl WPA is made up of natural wetlands and potholes, some of which are deep enough to hold water year round, except for the driest years. About half of the WPA is uplands consisting mostly of native prairie grasses.

The 500-acre Webb WPA consists of wetlands with dense nesting cover and native prairie.

Walk-in access only; no camping; no facilities. Roads in the area are difficult when wet.

Mule deer, antelope and coyote are common.

DIRECTIONS
From Malta follow, US191 north about 34 miles to Loring, then go 2 miles north of Loring and turn left (west) on Sunny Slop Road for 8 miles to the WPA. Impassable when wet.

CONTACT
Bowdoin NWR phone: 406-654-2863

MISSOURI RIVER COUNTRY
#7 Grasslands National Park (Canada)

GPS 49.246,-107.732

NORTH OF MALTA AND OPHEIM IN SASKATCHEWAN

KEY BIRDS
Mountain Plover, Baird's and Grasshopper Sparrows, Sprague's Pipit, Golden Eagle, Ferruginous Hawk, Burrowing Owl, Long-billed Curlew, Marbled Godwit, Gray Partridge

BEST SEASONS
May through August for grassland breeders; September for migrating songbirds

AREA DESCRIPTION
Native prairie with river and wetlands

Technically out of bounds but oh so close and great birding besides, why not? Widespread native prairie and lots of water attract threatened and endangered grassland-loving birds, some of which have all but vanished elsewhere. Riparian areas, such as the Frenchman River corridor, harbor extensive aspen groves, attracting a variety of birds not necessarily associated with grasslands.

The Frenchman River Valley Ecotour is a 2½ hour interpretive auto tour route in the West Block. There are marked hiking trails for birders wishing a more intimate look.

In the East Block, you are on your own. A clone of the Bitter Creek WSA on the US side, the area is remote, much of it difficult to get around, so be sure to come prepared… do the research, good map, high clearance vehicle, full gas tank, plenty of water, ample food just in case. Impassable when wet, check for current conditions.

Mammals that might be seen are bison, black-footed ferret, coyote, prairie dog, mule and white-tailed deer, and rattlesnakes frequent the area. Snake gaiters can be rented at the West Block Visitors Center.

Gas, food, and lodging are <u>only</u> available in the larger towns. Camping is allowed with restrictions, check with park staff.

Check with Grasslands National Park staff or the Rodeo Ranch Museum staff (summer only) in the Wood Mountain Regional Park to obtain information on the access routes and road conditions. Port of Entry times vary, so check first before making the long drive.

DIRECTIONS

To reach the West Block, from Malta follow US 191 and CA 4 to Val Marie. The park visitor center is located at the junction of CA 4 and Centre Street.

To reach the East Block, follow MT 24 north from Opheim to the border. Continue on CA 2 and follow the signs. Access is limited, with only a small portion of the East Block accessible in dry weather.

CONTACT

Grasslands National Park of Canada
Phone: 306-298-2257
Email: grasslands.info@pc.gc.ca

Gray Partridge

MISSOURI RIVER COUNTRY

#8 Bowdoin National Wildlife Refuge (IBA)

GPS 48.393,-107.735

EAST OF MALTA

KEY BIRDS

Baird's Sparrow, Sprague's Pipit, Ring-necked Pheasant, Sharp-tailed Grouse, Black-necked Stilt, Long-billed Curlew, American White Pelican, Great Egret, Bald Eagle, Peregrine Falcon

BEST SEASONS

Year round; spring through fall for largest variety and numbers. Wet years are far better than dry.

AREA DESCRIPTION

Lake and wetlands surrounded by native prairie

The large alkali lake is the center of this 15,500-acre NWR. Several smaller impoundments bordered by extensive bulrush and cattail marsh, and numerous shelterbelts (many primarily Russian olive in various stages of eradication — non-native species) surrounded by short-grass prairie provide outstanding nesting, brood rearing, and protective cover for a large number of birds and mammals — 232 bird species and 26 mammals have been observed.

As many as 100,000 migrants visit here in the fall, with spring counts not far behind. Bowdoin is host to one of only five American White Pelican colonies in Montana.

Interesting to note, Lake Bowdoin was once an oxbow of the Missouri River which now flows 70 miles to the south. The refuge derives its water from various sources: the Milk River, Beaver Creek, irrigation returns, and rain and snowmelt. On average, the area receives about 12 inches of precipitation annually.

Hunting is allowed for waterfowl and upland game birds; whitetail deer are common though off-limits to hunters. There are seasonal restrictions, so check with refuge staff (Visitor Center) before making a long drive. Blaze orange is recommended during the fall hunting seasons.

Driving is allowed only on designated roads, including a 15-mile long Auto Tour route with interpretive signs. A refuge bird list is available at headquarters or online at www.fws.gov/bowdoin.

Hiking is allowed on the refuge with restrictions. A handicap-accessible trail and blind is available on a first come, first served basis at nearby Pearce WPA. No camping allowed on the refuge. Camping and all amenities including some good places to eat — Great Northern Hotel, Stockman, Hitchin' Post Café — in Malta. Free camping is available at nearby Nelson Reservoir.

DIRECTIONS

Follow US 2 east of Malta about 5 miles and turn right (south) at the sign. Follow Old Highway 2 to the refuge.

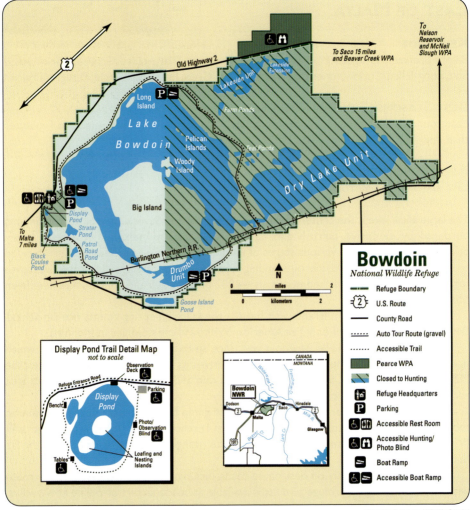

Credit: U.S. Fish and Wildlife Service

CONTACT
Bowdoin National Wildlife Refuge phone: 406-654-2863

Great Egret

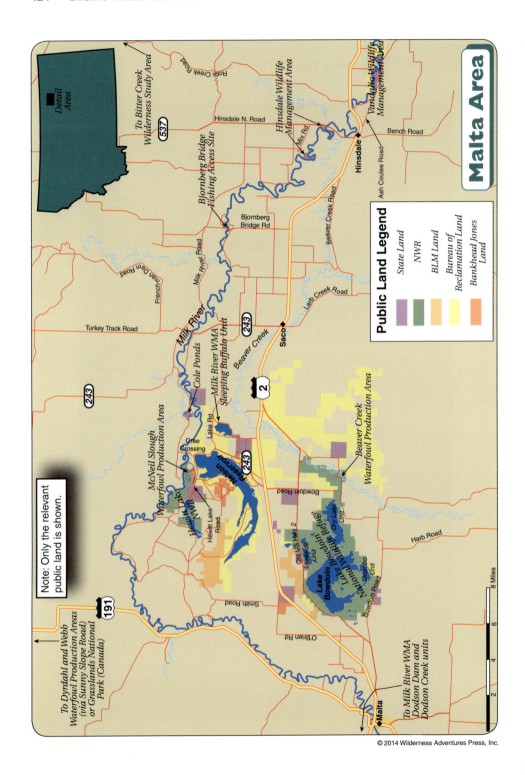

Malta Area

Public Land Legend
State Land
NWR
BLM Land
Bureau of Reclamation Land
Bankhead Jones Land

Note: Only the relevant public land is shown.

© 2014 Wilderness Adventures Press, Inc.

MISSOURI RIVER COUNTRY

#9

Beaver Creek Waterfowl Production Area

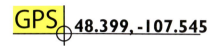

GPS 48.399, -107.545

EAST OF BOWDOIN NATIONAL WILDLIFE REFUGE

KEY BIRDS
Wood Duck, Cinnamon Teal, Ring-necked Pheasant, Sharp-tailed Grouse, Piping Plover, Black-necked Stilt

BEST SEASONS
Year round; spring through fall for largest variety and numbers. Wet years are far better than dry.

AREA DESCRIPTION
Wetlands, creek, cattail marsh, and a mix of native and domestic grasses

This 2,200-acres WPA is managed for waterfowl and upland game birds. The WPA is a unique partnership involving USFWS, Ducks Unlimited, and the Gallatin County Pheasants Forever Chapter.

Thanks in large part to DU and GCPFC, extensive habitat improvement work is ongoing within the WPA. Habitat being key to all wildlife — birds and mammals — Beaver Creek is on the fast track to becoming a destination wildlife viewing spot. Animals that might be seen are pronghorn, mule and white-tailed deer, coyote, and porcupine.

Access beyond the parking areas is by foot travel only. Much of the area is covered in dense vegetation, so dress accordingly. Mosquitoes can and often are troublesome, even well into October barring killing frosts. Blaze orange is recommended during the fall hunting season. No camping; no facilities.

DIRECTIONS
From Malta, take US 2 east about a half mile and turn right (east) on Old US Hwy 2. After about two miles, take a right on Bowdoin Road. In about 5 miles, turn left (sign) to the WPA.

CONTACT
Bowdoin NWR phone: 406-654-2863

MISSOURI RIVER COUNTRY
#10 Nelson Reservoir

GPS 48.489,-107.538

EAST OF MALTA

KEY BIRD
Black-crowned Night-heron, Osprey, Virginia Rail, Sora, Pied-billed and Eared Grebes, Mallard, Gadwall, Redhead, Ruddy Duck, Blue-winged, Cinnamon, and Green-winged Teal, American White Pelican, Bald Eagle (winter), Pheasant, Sharp-tailed Grouse, Gray Partridge

BEST SEASONS
Year round, spring thru fall offers the greatest variety. Winters can be harsh and travel difficult.

AREA DESCRIPTION
Lake surrounded by native prairie

Gravel roads and two-tracks afford easy access to the lake and the surrounding uplands (7,700 acres of public and private lands which require landowner permission). Managed by the Bureau of Reclamation, the recreation area encompasses about 290 acres.

A campground (no fee, first come, first served) is available offering several tent and trailer camping spots and the basic facilities, including restrooms and drinking water.

Fishing and hunting are popular, so plan accordingly.

Look for a variety of ducks (especially grebes which tend to congregate at the southern end of the lake), geese, and swans. Songbirds frequent the marshes and shorelines in spring, summer, and fall. Pheasant, Sharp-tailed Grouse, and Gray Partridge also frequent the area. Yellow-headed, Red-winged, and Brewer's Blackbirds nest here. Consider bringing along a spotting scope, as large numbers of waterfowl tend to raft up offshore.

Mammals that might be seen are pronghorn, white-tailed deer, coyote, and porcupine.

Malta offers all the basic amenities, including clean and comfortable motels and excellent dining at the Great Northern and Stockman restaurants and the Hitchin' Post Café (our favorite breakfast spot).

DIRECTIONS
Approximately 17 miles east of Malta on US 2, turn north at the Sleeping Buffalo to the reservoir.

CONTACT
Bureau of Reclamation phone: 406-759-5077

American White Pelican

MISSOURI RIVER COUNTRY

#11 McNeil Slough Waterfowl Production Area

GPS 48.531,-107.539

NORTHEAST OF MALTA, A FEW MILES BEYOND NELSON RESERVOIR

KEY BIRDS
Dabbling and diving ducks, Bald and Golden Eagles, Harlan's and Cooper's Hawks, Peregrine Falcon

BEST SEASONS
Year round, spring thru fall offers the greatest variety.

AREA DESCRIPTION
Wetlands, open water, cattail marsh, cropland, grassland, and cottonwood bottoms

The slough is bordered on the north for 4 miles by the Milk River, Big McNeil Slough to the south, and Hewitt Lake NWR to the west. Pheasant, Sharp-tailed Grouse, and puddle ducks are easy to find. Woodpeckers, songbirds, hawks, and owls frequent the large cottonwoods bordering the river. Great Blue Herons and Sandhill Cranes frequent the edges of the open water and associated wetlands and grasslands and Snowy Owls are occasionally sighted. You might want to join the annual Christmas bird count, a good way to get acquainted.

Deer and antelope are common throughout the area. A popular hunting area, blaze orange is recommended during hunting seasons.

A good gravel road leads to the main gate. Walk-in access only with seasonal restrictions, check Bowdoin NWR for specifics. There are no developed trails and some of the ground cover is thick and uncivil, so dress accordingly. Mosquitoes are thick during the warm season.

DIRECTIONS
From Malta, follow US 2 east, 17 miles; turn at the sign to Nelson Reservoir (Sleeping Buffalo intersection) and follow the road to the dam. Turn west on Hewitt Lake Road and then turn right to the slough (signed turn-off).

CONTACT
Bowdoin NWR phone: 406-654-2863

MISSOURI RIVER COUNTRY
#12 Cole Ponds

GPS 48.539,-107.465

EAST OF MALTA

KEY BIRDS
Red-necked Grebe, Black-crowned Night-heron, Cinnamon Teal, Wood Duck, Least Flycatcher, Tree Swallow, Belted Kingfisher

BEST SEASONS
Open year round; spring and fall offers best chance for checking off migrants.

AREA DESCRIPTION
Two ponds surrounded by sagebrush, trees, brush, and croplands

With the Milk River a short distance south and Whitewater Creek a short distance north the 200-acre area serves as a convenient stopover for waterfowl and songbirds. Raptors and pheasant are easy to find.

Access is by well-maintained gravel roads that are suitable for passenger cars in all but the worst weather. We find the ponds a great place to set up camp; though spaces are limited. Popular amongst anglers and hunters, off seasons are the best times to visit. With Nelson Reservoir, the Milk River Wildlife Management Area, several waterfowl production areas, and Hewitt and Bowdoin National Wildlife Refuges in the area, birding ops are pretty much unlimited.

DIRECTIONS
From US 2 east of Malta, turn north at Saco on MT 243; about 6 miles in, turn left (west) on Milk River Road for about 4 miles.

Cinnamon Teal

MISSOURI RIVER COUNTRY

#13 Bjornberg Bridge Fishing Access Site

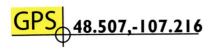 GPS 48.507,-107.216

NORTH OF SACO

KEY BIRDS
Baltimore Oriole, Gray Catbird, Bank Swallow, American Goldfinch

BEST SEASONS
Open year round; spring and fall offers best chance for checking off migrants.

AREA DESCRIPTION
River habitat with shrubs, trees, and grasslands

A small but productive spot comprised of shrubs, trees and grassland beside the Milk River and surrounded by cropland the area is attractive to a variety of songbirds, waterfowl, raptors, and wading birds.

Too small to warrant a long drive, still, we find it a good spot to stop for lunch, perhaps make a couple casts while keeping one eye peeled on the birds.

DIRECTIONS
East of Malta via US 2, turn north at Saco for 4 miles on MT 243.

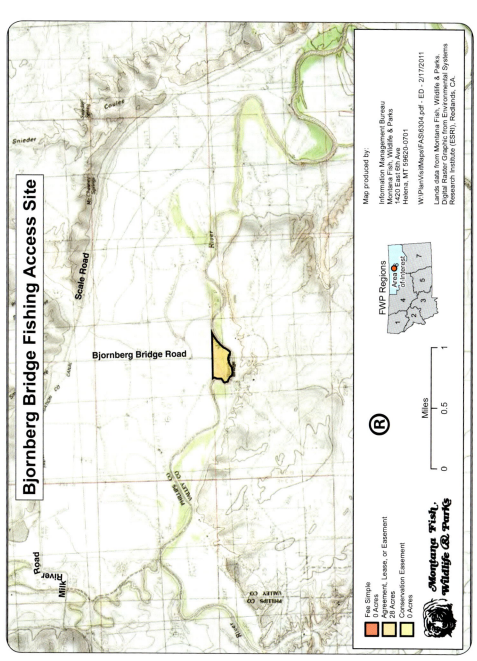

Bjornberg Bridge Fishing Access Site

Bjornberg Bridge Road

Scale Road

Snieder

Coulee

River

Milk River Road

Fee Simple
0 Acres

Agreement, Lease, or Easement
28 Acres

Conservation Easement
0 Acres

Montana Fish, Wildlife & Parks

FWP Regions

Area of Interest

1 2 3 4 5 6 7

Miles
0   0.5   1

Map produced by:

Information Management Bureau
Montana Fish, Wildlife & Parks
1420 East 6th Ave
Helena, MT 59620-0701

W:\PlanVisitMaps\FAS6304.pdf - ED - 2/17/2011

Lands data from Montana Fish, Wildlife & Parks.
Digital Raster Graphic from Environmental Systems
Research Institute (ESRI), Redlands, CA.

Used with permission.

MISSOURI RIVER COUNTRY
#14 Hinsdale Wildlife Management Area

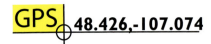 GPS 48.426,-107.074

HINSDALE

KEY BIRDS
American Kestrel, Spotted Towhee, Wild Turkey, Ring-necked Pheasant, Baltimore Oriole, Northern Rough-winged Swallow, Gray Catbird, Eastern Kingbird

BEST SEASONS
Spring through early fall

AREA DESCRIPTION
Cottonwood, willow, green ash river bottoms, with grassland and cropland

Only 250 acres, the habitat attracts a surprising variety of waterfowl, wading birds, songbirds, raptors, and upland game birds. We have checked off as many as 20 species over lunch in early fall.

Animals that can be seen are pronghorn, white-tailed deer, coyote, and porcupine.

The WMA is comprised of two parcels: one just north of Hinsdale, and the other is a short distance farther north; look for the signs. Access to the lower unit (a pleasant spot to hike around) is by foot off the main access road. Access to the upper unit is across private land (landowner permission required) or by boat; no overnight camping allowed.

DIRECTIONS
On US 2 east of Malta, turn north at Hinsdale on MT 537; lower unit is on your left just north of town.

CONTACT
WMA, Kelvin Johnson phone: 406-228-1709

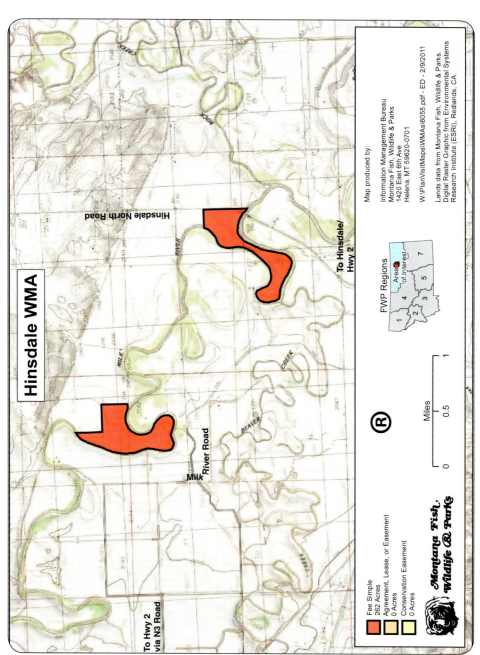

Hinsdale WMA

Fee Simple
262 Acres

Agreement, Lease, or Easement
0 Acres

Conservation Easement
0 Acres

Montana Fish,
Wildlife & Parks

FWP Regions

Area of Interest

Miles
0   0.5   1

Map produced by:

Information Management Bureau
Montana Fish, Wildlife & Parks
1420 East 6th Ave
Helena, MT 59620-0701

W:\PlanVisitMaps\WMAs\6055.pdf - ED - 2/9/2011

Lands data from Montana Fish, Wildlife & Parks.
Digital Raster Graphic from Environmental Systems
Research Institute (ESRI), Redlands, CA.

MISSOURI RIVER COUNTRY
Bitter Creek
Wilderness Study Area

GPS 48.630, -106.888

NORTHEAST OF HINSDALE

KEY BIRDS
Mountain Plover, Ferruginous Hawk, Red-tailed Hawk, Sage Grouse, Long-billed Curlew, Burrowing Owl, Loggerhead Shrike, Sprague's Pipit, Baird's, Brewer's, and Grasshopper Sparrows, Lark Bunting, McCown's Longspur

BEST SEASONS
Year round; spring through fall for largest variety and numbers. Wet years are far better than dry.

AREA DESCRIPTION
Grasslands and badlands

This 60,000-acre wilderness study area is remote, with lots of grass and extensive badlands. Water is scarce, though wet weather travel can be difficult to impossible — in other words, when wet, best pick another day. High clearance vehicles are de rigueur. The WSA boundary is largely unsigned, so be sure to bring a good map; better yet, get someone to mark it up. Both are available at the BLM office in Glasgow. Obviously at 60,000 acres, birding ops are limited only by how adventurous your soul.

Rough-legged Hawk

BLM literature interestingly notes, "Unlike much of the Great Plains, where native prairie has largely given way to agriculture, within Bitter Creek (including nearby Frenchman Creek/Dry Fork Creek areas) large intact prairie communities can still be found. It is the largest remaining intact grassland north of the Hi-Line and stands out as one of the most extensive naturally functioning glaciated plains grasslands in North America."

Swift fox, black-tailed prairie dog, mule deer, and antelope are found here; rattlesnakes frequent the area, especially the badlands.

April 1 through July 1, no driving or other human disturbance is allowed within a quarter mile of a nesting plover. Camping is allowed most anywhere. No facilities, and help is a long way off, so come prepared. Blaze orange is recommended during fall hunting seasons.

DIRECTIONS
From Hinsdale on US 2 east of Glasgow, follow Rock Creek Road north; the WSA is located east of the road. You can also access the WSA from MT 24 north of Glasgow by turning left on Kerr Road (aka Baylor) and looking for two-tracks leading into the area. To enter the WSA from the north, follow Theony Road west from Opheim; numerous unmarked trails lead south into the area.

CONTACT
BLM, Glasgow Field Station phone:406-228-3750

MISSOURI RIVER COUNTRY
#16 Vandalia Wildlife Management Area

GPS 48.373,-107.005

HINSDALE

KEY BIRDS
Mourning Dove, Wild Turkey, Western Wood-pewee, Downy Woodpecker, Vesper Sparrow, Least Flycatcher

BEST SEASONS
Spring through early fall

AREA DESCRIPTION
Cottonwood and shrub bottomland, with grassland, sagebrush, and agricultural land

This 310-acre WMA borders the Milk River and features a mix of waterfowl, upland birds, wading birds, songbirds, woodpeckers, and raptors.

Animals of note here are pronghorn, white-tailed deer, coyote, and porcupine.

Walk-in access, no camping, no facilities. A popular hunting spot, so dress appropriately.

DIRECTIONS
A mile east of Hinsdale on US 2, turn south on Furrason Road and then turn left along the railroad tracks.

CONTACT
WMA, Kelvin Johnson phone: 406-228-1709

Downy Woodpecker

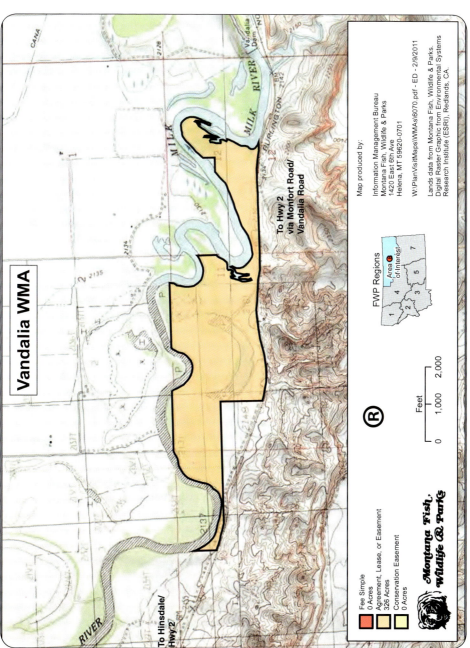

Vandalia WMA

To Hinsdale/Hwy 2

To Hwy 2 via Monfort Road/Vandalia Road

Fee Simple
0 Acres

Agreement, Lease, or Easement
326 Acres

Conservation Easement
0 Acres

FWP Regions

Area of Interest

Feet
0   1,000   2,000

Map produced by:

Information Management Bureau
Montana Fish, Wildlife & Parks
1420 East 6th Ave
Helena, MT 59620-0701

W:\PlanVisitMaps\WMAs\6070.pdf - ED - 2/9/2011

Lands data from Montana Fish, Wildlife & Parks.
Digital Raster Graphic from Environmental Systems
Research Institute (ESRI), Redlands, CA.

Montana Fish, Wildlife & Parks

MISSOURI RIVER COUNTRY
#17 Faraasen Park Recreation Site

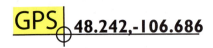

GPS 48.242,-106.686

WEST OF GLASGOW

KEY BIRDS
Belted Kingfisher, Northern Rough-winged and Bank Swallows, Eastern and Western Kingbirds, Alder, Least and Willow Flycatchers

BEST SEASONS
April thru October. Summer and early fall are best times to find largest variety of flycatchers

AREA DESCRIPTION
Native prairie, trees, and brush beside the Milk River

The park attracts a large number of grass- and water-loving birds. Walk-in access only. There are no developed trails, but you can hike anywhere, any time.

No fee area, open year round with vault toilets and picnic tables; no overnight camping. Fishing and hunting are popular activities.

Glasgow offers all the amenities a traveler might need, including several pretty good eateries. For starters, check out the Cottonwood Inn, Sam's Supper Club, and Duram's… all three serve a mean steak. PS…Sources tell me the Cottonwood is _the_ spot for miles around to quench a hankering for genuine single malt scotch.

DIRECTIONS
From Glasgow take US 2 west 3miles and turn west on Riverside Drive. The park is 3 miles in (turn-offs signed).

CONTACT
BLM, Glasgow Field Office phone: 406-228-3750

MISSOURI RIVER COUNTRY
#18 Paulo Reservoir

GPS 48.176,-106.873

SOUTHWEST OF GLASGOW

KEY BIRDS
Blue-winged Teal, Mallard, Northern Shoveler, American Coot, Great Blue Heron, Killdeer, Swainson's Hawk

BEST SEASONS
April through October. Summer and early fall are best times to find largest variety flycatchers.

AREA DESCRIPTION
Open water reservoir surrounded by low bushes and grasslands

Depending on the season, this is a good spot for viewing waterfowl, shorebirds, wading birds, and grass-loving songbirds. Mammals that can be seen here are pronghorn, mule deer, and coyote.

No fee, open all year round; a popular fishing spot for largemouth bass, camping, and picnicking.

DIRECTIONS
From Glasgow, take 2nd Avenue south toward Tampico, across the Milk River bridge. Turn south (left) on Bentonite (impassable wet) Road and travel 10 miles to the Paulo Reservoir sign.

CONTACT
BLM, Glasgow Field Office phone: 406-228-3750

American Coot

MISSOURI RIVER COUNTRY
#19 Little Beaver Creek (IBA)

GPS 48.044,-106.908

SOUTHWEST OF GLASGOW

KEY BIRDS
Mountain Plover, Greater Sage Grouse, Ring-necked Pheasant, Long-billed Curlew, Burrowing Owl, Brewer's Sparrow, Chestnut-collared and McCown's Longspur

BEST SEASONS
Spring and fall

AREA DESCRIPTION
Hardpan areas in and around Little Beaver Creek, plus surrounding grassland and sagebrush

This 25,000-acre IBA site includes mountain plover habitat that is characterized by extremely low vegetation and large amounts of bare bentonite (gumbo) soils and native prairie. All of the above key birds are listed as species of conservation concern.

In June 2006, Glasgow hosted the Montana Audubon Annual Bird Festival; 139 species were observed during the three-day event, and significant numbers were observed within the IBA.

Ring-necked Pheasant

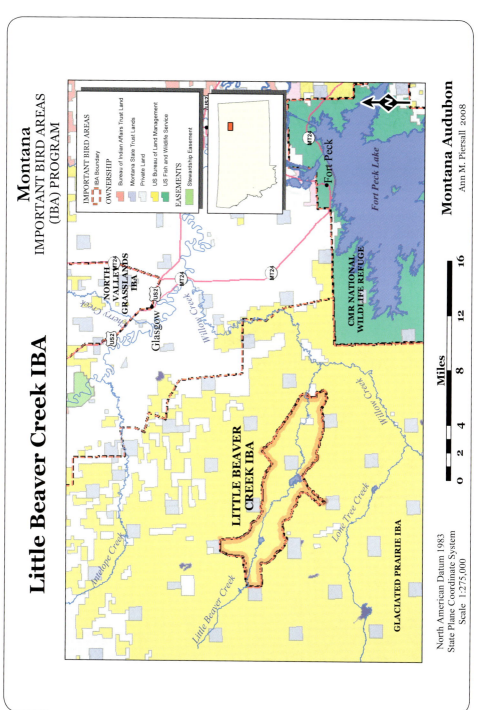

Little Beaver Creek IBA

Montana
IMPORTANT BIRD AREAS
(IBA) PROGRAM

IMPORTANT BIRD AREAS
IBA Boundary
OWNERSHIP
Bureau of Indian Affairs Trust Land
Montana State Trust Lands
Private Land
US Bureau of Land Management
US Fish and Wildlife Service
EASEMENTS
Stewardship Easement

Montana Audubon
Ann M. Piersall 2008

North American Datum 1983
State Plane Coordinate System
Scale 1:275,000

Miles
0   2   4   8   12   16

NORTH VALLEY GRASSLANDS IBA

Glasgow

LITTLE BEAVER CREEK IBA

CMR NATIONAL WILDLIFE REFUGE

Fort Peck

Fort Peck Lake

GLACIATED PRAIRIE IBA

Little Beaver Creek

Antelope Creek

Lone Tree Creek

Willow Creek

Remote, be sure to come prepared: full gas tank, ample food and water, good map, suitable vehicle for backcountry travel. Motor vehicle access is limited to designated roads and trails; no off-road driving. There are no formal hiking or interpretive trails; no auto tour trail. Nearest gas is in Glasgow. Primitive camping is allowed on public lands unless otherwise noted. The area is open year round, though roads can be and often are impassable when wet.

Summers are typically hot and dry; best birding is usually early and late in the day, and near water.

Expect to see mule deer, antelope, and coyote; the prairie rattlesnake is common, and elk frequent the nearby Larb Hills.

Other activities include hunting, photography, camping, hiking, biking, and wildlife watching.

Glasgow offers any and all amenities a traveling birder might want or need; including excellent dining at the Cottonwood Inn, Sam's Supper Club, and Johnnies Café.

DIRECTIONS
From Glasgow, turn south onto MT 42 and then turn south on 3rd Avenue S. Turn right on 6th Avenue. S. to Aitiken Road, to Little Beaver Road. The IBA is approximately 14 miles out.

CONTACT
Montana Fish, Wildlife and Parks; Glasgow phone: 406-228-9347

MISSOURI RIVER COUNTRY
#20 Fort Peck Dredge Cut Ponds

GPS 48.056,-106.438

NORTHEAST OF FORT PECK

KEY BIRDS
Ring-billed, Glaucous, California, Thayer's, and Franklin's Gulls, Common Merganser, Caspian Tern, Bullock's and Baltimore Orioles, Ovenbird, Northern Waterthrush

BEST SEASONS
Open year round; spring and fall offers best chance for checking off migrants

AREA DESCRIPTION
Large ponds surrounded by cottonwood, shrub, and juniper forest, grasslands, wetlands, and cattail marsh

The large ponds in this 123-acre site were created during the building of Fort Peck Dam.

You can easily spend a week or more birding and exploring the historic town-site, the dam, the interpretive center, fish hatchery, the lakeshore, and the Missouri River corridor. Over 230 birds have been observed in the area. We have checked off as many as three dozen species in a single morning in and around the ponds.

Check out the Fort Peck Campground, one of the best in our opinion. Nearby Glasgow offers gas, lodging, food, and shopping.

Common Merganser (drake)

DIRECTIONS

The ponds are two miles northeast of Fort Peck via MT 117.

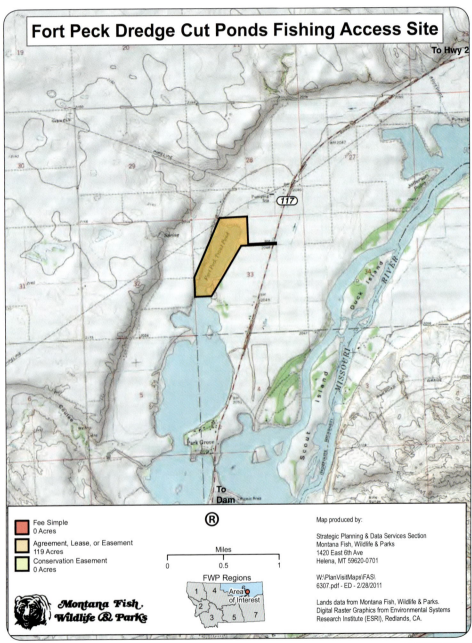

MISSOURI RIVER COUNTRY
#21 Fort Peck Campground (Downstream Rec. Area)

GPS 48.008,-106.429

FORT PECK DAM

KEY BIRDS
Baltimore, Bullock's, and Orchard Orioles; Blackpoll, Bay-breasted, Canada, Mourning, and Tennessee Warblers; Glaucous, Thayer's, Franklin's, and California Gulls; Ovenbird, House Sparrow

BEST SEASONS
Year round; spring through fall for largest variety and numbers

AREA DESCRIPTION
Developed area with trees, cattail marsh and water

This is a large, developed campground beside the Missouri River just below the dam with a wonderful lighted night-time view of the turbine towers. Trees, cattail marsh, dense brush, and water combine to attract a wide variety of birds, including many eastern species. A favorite campsite, we have checked off as many as 40 species in a three-day stay. Paved roads and an accessible trail make for easy viewing.

House Sparrow

Be sure to stop by the interpretive center which features Peck's Rex, dam history, and other educational exhibits. The nearby fish hatchery is also worth a visit, as is Fort Peck itself, home of the Fort Peck Summer Theatre. The sign in front of the theatre reads as follows:

A JEWEL OF THE PLAINS

Standing majestically atop the rolling prairies of Eastern Montana, the Fort Peck Theatre is one of the state's most magnificent treasures. Originally built in 1934 as only a temporary structure, its beauty and sound construction have weathered an incredible 75 years. Today it is a vibrant, vital part of community and culture for residents and visitors alike. Design and construction of the Theatre was carried out by the United States Army Corps of Engineers. It was a labor-intensive project which integrated the New Deal arts and crafts tradition with a Swiss chalet motif. Many elaborate, decorative appointments can be found both inside and out.

On Friday, November 16, 1934, only 9 short months after construction was begun, the Fort Peck Theatre opened its doors as a movie house, showing The Richest Girl in the World, starring Miriam Hopkins and Joel McCrea. During The Dam Days, movies ran 24 hours a day, seven days a week, often with every one of the 1,209 seats filled. People sometimes stood in lines seven blocks long to purchase tickets. The adult admission price was 40 cents on the main floor, 30 cents in the balcony. Children attended for a dime. During this time, the population of the area in and around Fort Peck was over 50,000 and an evening at the movies was a special event for young and old alike.

DIRECTIONS
From Glasgow, take US 2 east about a mile or so; turn south on MT 24 to Fort Peck.

CONTACT
Corps of Engineers phone: 406-526-3411

MISSOURI RIVER COUNTRY

#22 Manning Lake Wetland Complex (IBA)

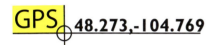

GPS 48.273,-104.769

FORT PECK INDIAN RESERVATION NORTHWEST OF CULBERTSON

KEY BIRDS
One of only five breeding colonies of Franklin's Gulls in Montana. Other colonials include Eared Grebe, Forster's and Black Tern, and White-faced Ibis. Marbled Godwit, Long-billed Curlew, Upland Sandpiper, Willet, Wilson's Phalarope, Sprague's Pipit, Lark Bunting, Grasshopper, Nelson's Sharp-tailed and Le Conte's Sparrows and Chestnut-collared Longspur also nest here.

BEST SEASONS
Spring thru fall; high water years attract the largest numbers and variety

AREA DESCRIPTION
Lake, floodplain with wetlands and grasslands

The Big Muddy Creek floodplain, Manning Lake, and associated wetlands and grasslands comprise the 21,000-acre IBA which lies within the Fort Peck Assiniboine and Sioux Indian Reservation.

In 2004, the tribes, USFWS, NRCS, and MTFWP formed the Manning Lake Working Group to protect and restore bird habitat within the area. In 2005, the tribes granted the Working Group a Landowner Incentive Program Grant to help merge land ownership and develop a conservation plan to manage the site as a Tribal Wildlife Refuge.

Open water, bulrush marsh, wetland and native prairie is an attractive mix for all sorts of birds and mammals. Animals that can be viewed here are coyote, badger, red fox, mink, muskrat, skunk, and porcupine.

DIRECTIONS
Because the complex is comprised of a mix of private and tribal lands, roads leading to the area are impassable when wet visitors are asked to contact the refuge staff for directions and road conditions.

CONTACT
Manning Lake Wetlands Tribal Wildlife Refuge staff phone: 406-768-2329

MISSOURI RIVER COUNTRY

#23 Medicine Lake National Wildlife Refuge (IBA)

GPS 48.479,-104.497

NORTH OF CULBERTSON

KEY BIRDS
Piping Plover, Baird's, Brewer's, Le Conte's and Nelson's Sharp-tailed Sparrows, American White Pelican, Franklin's Gull, Long-billed Curlew, Burrowing and Short-eared Owls

BEST SEASONS
May through August for grassland breeders; September for migrating songbirds

AREA DESCRIPTION
A rich mix of grass, lakes, potholes and wetlands with extensive sand dunes tossed in for good measure

There have been 270 species observed here, including 22 species of conservation concern. Black ducks occasionally show up during migration.

The North Tract (11,000 acres of which are designated wilderness) includes the 8,200-acre Medicine Lake, 17 potholes, extensive grasslands, wetlands, and sand dunes. The nearby smaller Homestead Tract includes Homestead Lake and surrounding grasslands and wetlands. In addition, refuge staff manages 45 Waterfowl Production Areas. All in all, enough birding to sate the appetite of even the most jaded.

In an area devoid of even mid-size towns, as you might expect, birds and other wildlife far outnumber people. While many come to witness such rarities as the threatened piping plover (30 breeding pairs fledge about 80 percent of the state's annual crop), the diminutive Baird's, Le Conte's, or Nelson's Sharp-tailed Sparrows are also specialties. Perhaps the best show in town are the large breeding colonies of American White Pelican (10,000 plus), Double-crested Cormorant, California and Ring-billed Gulls, and Great Blue Heron.

The refuge produces about 40,000 waterfowl annually and hosts in excess of 100,000 migrants each spring and fall. As many as 30,000 birders show up in spring; many hoping to check off rarities such as Baird's Sparrow and Piping Plover from the life list. On occasion, the rare endangered Whooping Crane drops in for a visit. Given Sandhill Cranes are fair game during hunting season, whoopers get much the same protection as, say, a visiting President might.

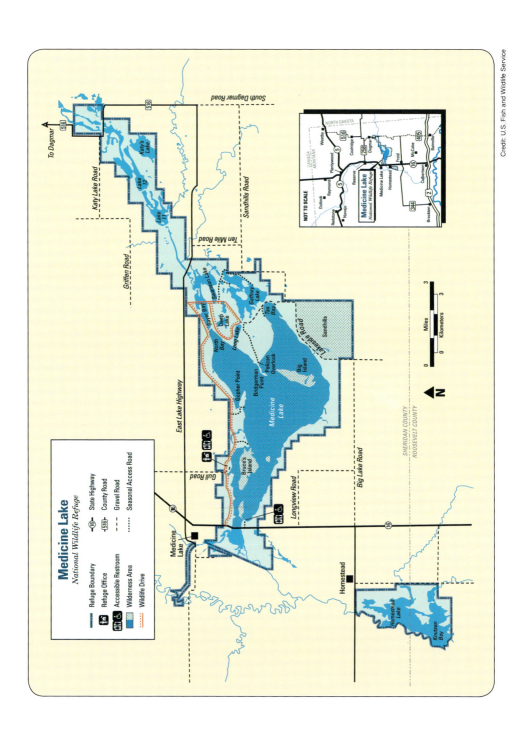

Animals that might be seen here are white-tailed deer, coyote, badger, red fox, mink, muskrat, skunk, and porcupine.

There is a 14-mile interpretive Auto Tour route and a 99-foot tall observation tower. Foot travel is allowed with restrictions. Hunting and fishing are also allowed with restrictions. No motorized travel (water or land) is allowed within the Wilderness Area.

Limited lodging, camping, gas, and food are available in Medicine Lake; no camping is allowed on the refuge and public land camping ops are few and far between, so plan your visits accordingly.

DIRECTIONS
From US 2, turn north on MT 16 at Culbertson. The refuge is approximately 25 miles.

CONTACT
Medicine Lake NWR phone: 406-789-2305

Franklin's Gull

MISSOURI RIVER COUNTRY
#24 Brush Lake State Park

GPS 48.606,-104.102

NORTHEAST OF MEDICINE LAKE

KEY BIRDS
Sharp-tailed Grouse, Northern Harrier, Mallard, Wigeon, American Avocet, Black-necked Stilt, Black-crowned Night-heron

BEST SEASONS
Year round; spring and fall migration attracts largest variety and numbers

AREA DESCRIPTION
Extensive grass and croplands surrounding lake

The 280-acre lake is too alkali to support fish. This is a popular summer destination for locals, so the best birding is early and late in the day and season. Camping is allowed; fee area.

Fall migration attracts a variety of birds not usually seen in Montana, including such rarities as Connecticut Warbler, Philadelphia Vireo, Scarlet Tanager, and Yellow-bellied Flycatcher.

DIRECTIONS
From Medicine Lake, follow MT 515 east and turn north on MT 516 through Dagmar. Turn right on Brush Lake Road to the park.

Black-crowned Night-heron

CONTACT

Brush Lake State Park phone: 406-483-5455

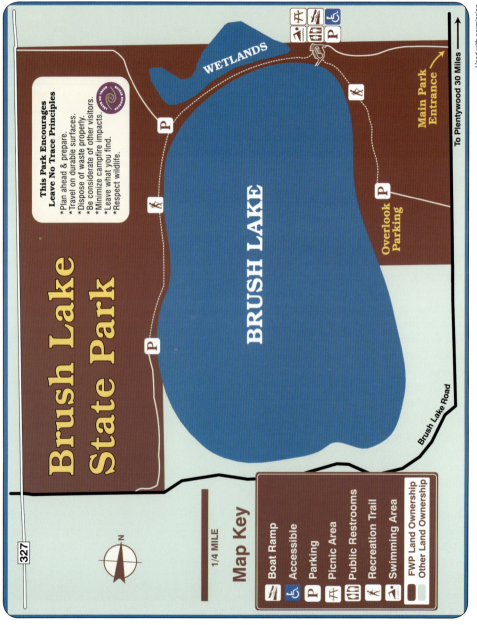

MISSOURI RIVER COUNTRY
#25 Westby City Park

GPS 48.868,-104.053

WESTBY

KEY BIRDS
Warblers (29 species have been observed), Philadelphia and Blue-headed Vireos, Gray-cheeked Thrush, Yellow-bellied Flycatcher, Scarlet Tanager (rare)

BEST SEASONS
April-October; May and September best of migrating songbirds. Fall migration offers best chance to view migrating birds that tend to linger longer than in spring.

AREA DESCRIPTION
Small developed city park

"A forested oasis in the prairie that's smack dab in the middle of a migration corridor where eastern and western bird species overlap makes this park a birder's dream. More than 200 species of birds have been seen in the one-acre park, including 29 species of warblers!"… according to literature from Northeastern Plains Birding and Nature Trail.

Some migrate between the Yukon and Mexico's Yucatan Peninsula. That so many stop over in a tiny city park surrounded by endless treeless prairie to me is, well, simply mind boggling.

Restroom, picnic tables, and limited camping hook-ups are available in the park. The town boasts a grocery store, gas station, and restaurant. Limited lodging and camping, food, and gas are available in Plentywood. Plan ahead.

Interesting to note, Montana Birding and Nature Trail literature states, "In 1909, Danish settlers established Westby just over the North Dakota line. Largely because Montana allowed sales of alcohol while North Dakota prohibited liquor, many of the early settlers soon packed up and moved west. The final blow came when the railroad located on the Montana side. By 1914, Westby, ND was all but empty."

DIRECTIONS
From US 2 at Culbertson, turn north on MT 16. About 1 mile south of Plentywood, turn east on MT 5. It's approximately 25miles to Westby.

Contact
Westby City Hall phone: 406-385-2445

Scarlet Tanager

MISSOURI RIVER COUNTRY

#26 Westby Prairie-Wetland Complex (IBA)

GPS 48.894,-104.060

NORTH AND EAST OF WESTBY

KEY BIRDS

Piping Plover, Yellow Rail, Sprague's Pipit, Sedge Wren, Chestnut-collared Longspur, Baird's, Nelson's Sharp-tailed and Le Conte's Sparrows, Semipalmated, White-rumped, Baird's, and Stilt Sandpipers, Sanderling, Wilson's Phalarope, Yellow-headed Blackbird

BEST SEASONS

April thru October; spring and fall migrations are best for shorebirds which often exceed 20,000 individuals.

AREA DESCRIPTION

Lush mix of native prairie, alkali wetlands, and prairie potholes surrounded by wheat and domestic grasslands

The first eight of the Key Birds listed above are species of conservation concern. To date, 26 shorebird species have been observed here.

Ownership in this 1,295-acre site is a combination of federal waterfowl production areas, state school trust lands, and private lands, some of which are under conservation easement. No motorized access to the public lands; access to private lands requires written landowner permission.

Hunting is allowed on WPAs with restrictions; check with Medicine Lake NWR. Birders should wear blaze orange during the fall hunting seasons.

Food, gas, lodging, and camping are available on a limited basis in Westby.

DIRECTIONS

Stop at Medicine Lake NWR for a map. Continue on MT 16 toward Plentywood and turn right (east) on MT 5 to Westby. Take Main Street north until you cross the railroad tracks, and continue north to W Northern Avenue. Take a left on to Northern and follow it north (it becomes Westby Road). Take the first gravel road (Flowing Well Road) north of Round Lake. The state line and WPA border this road.

Westby Prairie-Wetland Complex IBA

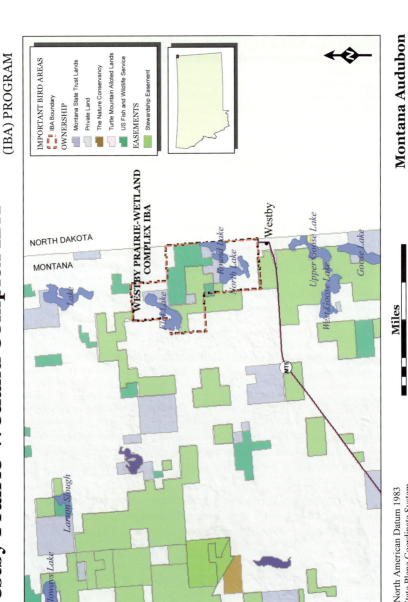

Montana
IMPORTANT BIRD AREAS (IBA) PROGRAM

IMPORTANT BIRD AREAS

IBA Boundary

OWNERSHIP

Montana State Trust Lands

Private Land

The Nature Conservancy

Turtle Mountain Alloted Lands

US Fish and Wildlife Service

EASEMENTS

Stewardship Easement

WESTBY PRAIRIE-WETLAND COMPLEX IBA

NORTH DAKOTA

MONTANA

Galloway's Lake

Larson Slough

Flat Lake

Lake

Round Lake

North Lake

Westby

Upper Goose Lake

West Goose Lake

Goose Lake

Miles

0   1   2   3   4

North American Datum 1983
State Plane Coordinate System
Scale 1:100,000

Montana Audubon
Ann M. Piersall 2008

Contact
Medicine Lake NWR phone: 406-789-2305

Yellow-headed Blackbird

MISSOURI RIVER COUNTRY
#27 Fox Lake Wildlife Management Area

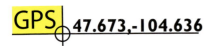

GPS 47.673,-104.636

SOUTH OF SIDNEY

KEY BIRDS
Ferruginous Hawk, Northern Harrier, Burrowing Owl, Virginia Rail, Sora, Marbled Godwit, Greater Yellowlegs, Willet, Sandhill Crane, Loggerhead Shrike

BEST SEASONS
April through October; August for largest numbers and variety of shorebirds

AREA DESCRIPTION
Lake with cattail and bulrush marsh, wetlands, native prairie

The 1,546-acre WMA attracts large numbers and varieties of songbirds, waterfowl, wading birds, shorebirds, and raptors. Sharp-tailed Grouse and Ring-necked Pheasant also frequent the area. The key is, of course, water. We have visited here during drought years and found very little; on the other hand, 2011's record water attracted legions.

You can drive to the north and south boundaries of the WMA; no motorized access beyond the parking areas. Camping is allowed in the parking areas, though no facilities are offered. Limited food and gas are available in Lambert. The closest lodging is in Sidney.

This is a popular hunting site; be sure to wear blaze orange during the fall hunting seasons. Bugs tend to be especially thick spring through early fall.

White-tailed and mule deer, antelope, red fox, coyote, raccoon, and thirteen-lined ground squirrel are common.

According to the historic sign in Lambert, "Lambert was founded in 1914, thanks to a Great Northern Railroad spur line built to haul the million or so bushels of wheat produced here annually in the 1920s. A 1927 fire leveled part of the town precipitating a gradual decline in the population which today is around 350."

DIRECTIONS
From Sidney, follow MT 200 for 21 miles west. Turn into Lambert and drive straight through town. A half mile south of town, turn right (west) onto CR 325. The south entrance to the WMA is on the right. Continue on MT 200 a mile or so to the north entrance.

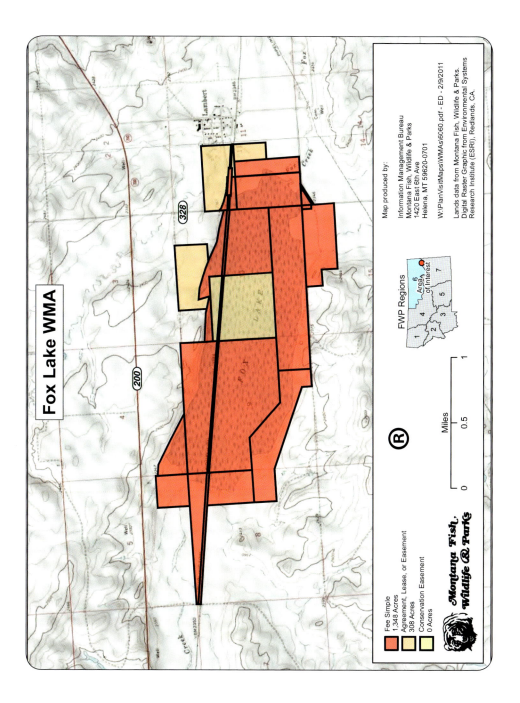

Fox Lake WMA

Map produced by:

Information Management Bureau
Montana Fish, Wildlife & Parks
1420 East 6th Ave
Helena, MT 59620-0701

W:\PlanVisitMaps\WMAs\6060.pdf - ED - 2/9/2011

Lands data from Montana Fish, Wildlife & Parks.
Digital Raster Graphic from Environmental Systems
Research Institute (ESRI), Redlands, CA.

FWP Regions

Area of Interest

Miles
0   0.5   1

Fee Simple
1,348 Acres

Agreement, Lease, or Easement
308 Acres

Conservation Easement
0 Acres

Montana Fish,
Wildlife & Parks

Contact
MT FW&P phone 406-228-3700

Willet

MISSOUR RIVER COUNTRY

#28 Elk Island Fishing Access Site

GPS 47.465,-104.313

SOUTH OF SIDNEY ON THE YELLOWSTONE RIVER

KEY BIRDS
Bobolink, Eastern Screech Owl, Eastern Bluebird, Ovenbird, American Redstart, Yellow-breasted Chat, Northern Oriole, Wild Turkey, Ring-necked Pheasant

BEST SEASONS
May through September; June for woodland nesters

AREA DESCRIPTION
River habitat with cottonwood forest, dense shrub understory, cattail marsh, and grass

The 1,200 acres along the Yellowstone River attract a variety of songbirds, woodpeckers, waterfowl, wading birds, upland birds, and raptors.

No auto tour; no developed trails, no motorized access. Area is open year round, but birders are advised to wear blaze orange during fall and spring (turkey) hunting seasons.

Lots of wood ticks especially in spring and early summer; mosquitoes can be troublesome even well into October, e.g. dress appropriately and don't forget the DEET.

Expect to see whitetails and painted turtles; raccoons, beavers, and several bat species also frequent the area.

Primitive camping is allowed; restrooms and a boat launch (usable only during high water) are available. Fishing and hunting are popular.

DIRECTIONS
Located 19 miles south of Sidney off MT 16. Turn east at MP 32 (signed) for 2 miles.

CONTACT
MT FW&P phone: 406-234-0900

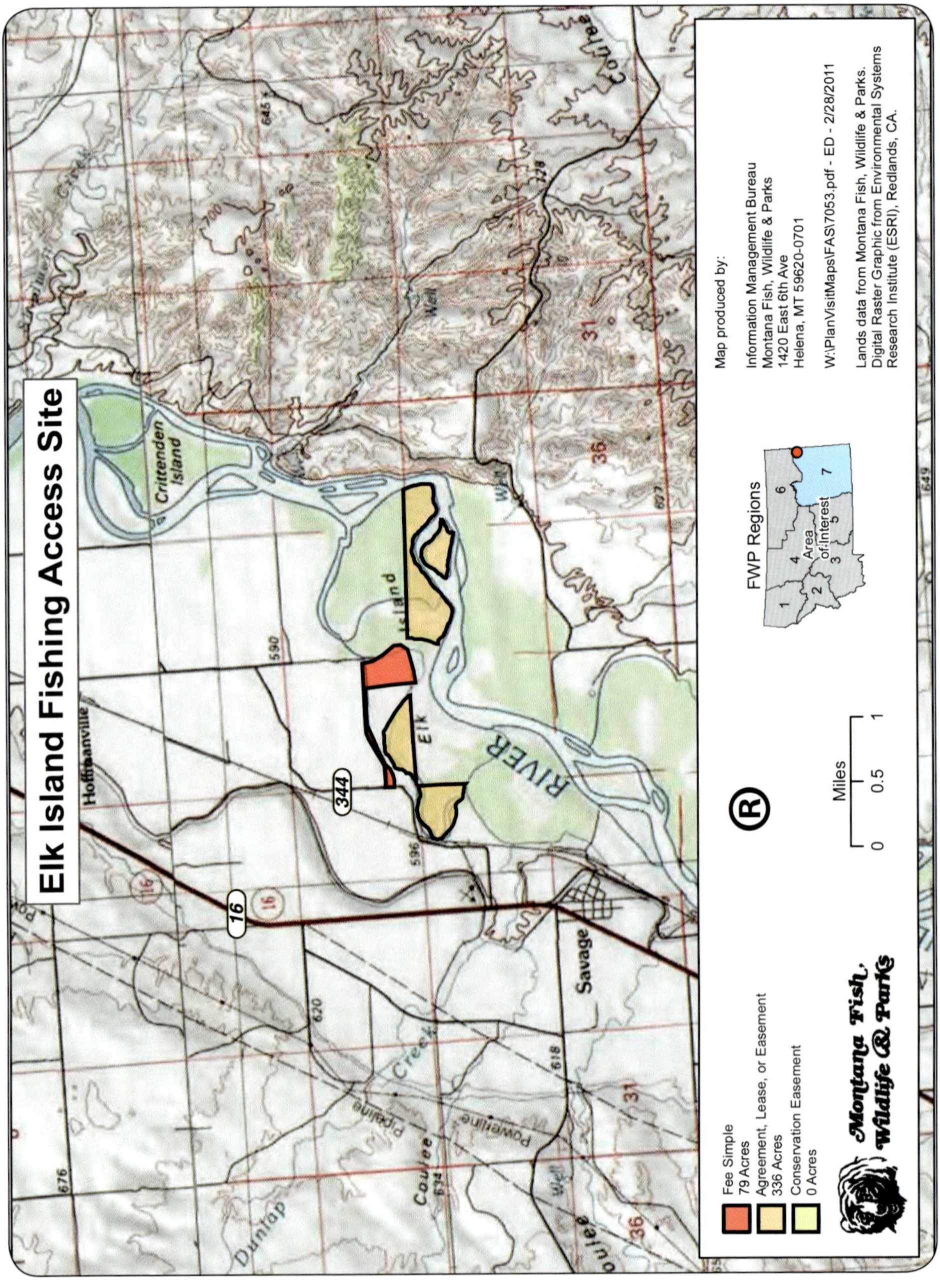

Elk Island Fishing Access Site
Fee Simple
79 Acres
Agreement, Lease, or Easement
336 Acres
Conservation Easement
0 Acres
Montana Fish, Wildlife & Parks
Miles
0
0.5
1
FWP Regions
Area of Interest
Map produced by:
Information Management Bureau
Montana Fish, Wildlife & Parks
1420 East 6th Ave
Helena, MT 59620-0701
W:\PlanVisitMaps\FAS\7053.pdf - ED - 2/28/2011
Lands data from Montana Fish, Wildlife & Parks.
Digital Raster Graphic from Environmental Systems
Research Institute (ESRI), Redlands, CA.
Crittenden Island
Elk Island
RIVER
Savage
Hoffmanville
Dunlap Coulee
Pipeline
Powerline
16
344

Used with permission.

MISSOURI RIVER COUNTRY
#29 Seven Sisters Fishing Access Site

GPS ⊕ **47.576,-104.232**

SOUTH OF SIDNEY ON THE YELLOWSTONE RIVER

KEY BIRDS
Turkey Vulture, Wood Duck, Western Wood-pewee, Eastern Screech Owl, Northern Oriole, American Redstart, Red-winged Blackbird

BEST SEASONS
May through September; June for nesters

AREA DESCRIPTION
River habitat with cottonwood forest, dense shrub understory, grass, sloughs, and cropland

The 560 acres of this FAS and the Yellowstone River attract a variety of songbirds, woodpeckers, waterfowl, wading birds and raptors.

We've hung out here many times, survived merciless skeeter attacks and yet not once can I recall anything like feeling disappointed. Birds of every sort everywhere, and the only thing holding back record check-offs have been our (dare I say it?) too often faulty birding skills.

A search of Montana place names lent no clue as to how "Seven Sisters" got its name; perhaps a local family boasted seven sisters? Or maybe the constellation was at one time particularly prominent and the name stuck...who knows? But I did learn the town of Crane was named after trapper Jimmy Crane who, with partner Frenchy Joe Seymour, built the first cabin near the present town site of Sidney in 1876. Crane was said to be "a dead shot with a rifle, loved whiskey, played a wicked good hand of draw poker, but aside from those had no religious accomplishments worth speaking."

No auto tour; no developed trails; motorized access restricted to established roads. No boat ramp, but small boats can easily be hand launched. Pack-in, pack-out rules apply. Birders should wear blaze orange during the spring (turkey) and fall hunting seasons.

Expect to see whitetails, raccoons, beavers, and mink as well as several species of bats that frequent the area.

Rock hounds might want to stop in at Harmon's Agate and Silver shop in Crane.

DIRECTIONS
Located 9 miles south of Sidney off MT 16. Turn east at Crane (FAS sign), 1 mile to site.

CONTACT
MT FW&P phone: 406-234-0900

Red-winged Blackbird

MISSOURI RIVER COUNTRY

#30 Diamond Willow Fishing Access Site

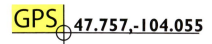 GPS 47.757,-104.055

SIDNEY, ON THE YELLOWSTONE RIVER

KEY BIRDS
Blue Jay, Black-headed Grosbeak, Ovenbird, Red-eyed Vireo, Lark Sparrow, Yellow-breasted Chat, Common Goldeneye

BEST SEASONS
Open year round; spring and fall offers best chance for checking off migrants

AREA DESCRIPTION
Riparian shrub and cottonwood forest

The riparian habitat beside the Yellowstone River attracts a variety of songbirds, waterfowl, wading birds, raptors to this 82-acre FAS. Spring and fall migration is the best time to check off warblers and other migrants.

Once a nice spot to spend a spring or fall day — pack a picnic lunch, take a walk, kick back and watch the birds...alas, now is caught up in the chaos of the Bakken oil boom. Hopefully, some semblance of order will eventually reign...but I for one am not holding my breath.

DIRECTIONS
From MT 16, 1½ miles south of Sidney, turn right (east) on MT 23 for 2½ miles. Turn left (northeast) on CR 122 and go 7 miles; turn left (north) at CR 355 at FAS sign.

Common Goldeneye

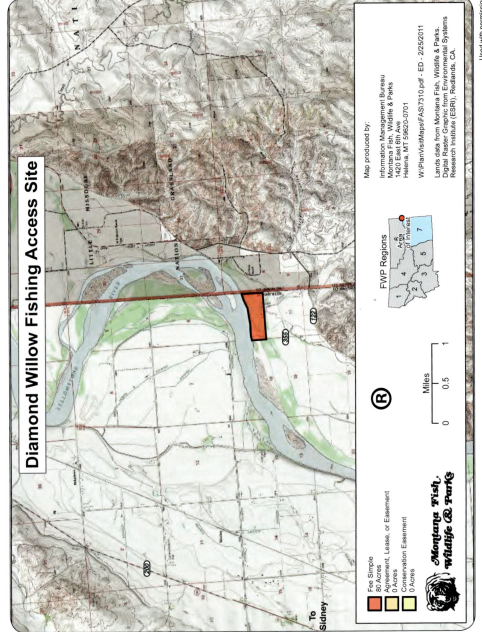

Diamond Willow Fishing Access Site

To Sidney

Montana Fish, Wildlife & Parks

Fee Simple
80 Acres

Agreement, Lease, or Easement
0 Acres

Conservation Easement
0 Acres

Miles
0   0.5   1

FWP Regions

Area of Interest

Map produced by:

Information Management Bureau
Montana Fish, Wildlife & Parks
1420 East 6th Ave
Helena, MT 59620-0701

W:\PlanVisitMaps\FAS\7310.pdf - ED - 2/25/2011

Lands data from Montana Fish, Wildlife & Parks.
Digital Raster Graphic from Environmental Systems
Research Institute (ESRI), Redlands, CA.

Used with permission.

MISSOURI RIVER COUNTRY
#31 | Fort Union Trading Post/Fort Buford National Historic Site

 **GPS** 48.000,-104.045

NORTHEAST OF SIDNEY

KEY BIRDS
Piping Plover, Baird's Sparrow, Least Tern, Sprague's Pipit, Golden Eagle, American White Pelican

BEST SEASONS
Year round; spring and fall migration for largest variety and numbers

AREA DESCRIPTION
At confluence of Missouri and Yellowstone Rivers, a mix of prairie grasslands, cottonwood bottoms, badlands, and sandbars

Technically speaking, this one is not Montana but since it is so nifty and close, I won't tell if you don't. Spring and fall migration attracts waterfowl, raptors, and songbirds, many of which aren't your everyday Montana check-offs. Especially in the fall, due to a peculiar east-to-west curve in the north-south migration pattern, birds show up here on their journey south which are more common farther east. In other words, we should not have been surprised to find a solitary bright male Cape May warbler perched atop the flagpole…Right.

Fort Union Trading Post was operated by the American Fur Company from 1828-1867. Assiniboine, Crow, Cree, Ojibwa, Blackfeet, Hidatsa, and other tribes regularly traded bison hides and other furs for beads, guns, blankets, and more. In 1843, John James Audubon spent the summer here as a base camp, and collected specimens of the Baird's Sparrow and Sprague's Pipit.

Fort Buford is the site where Sitting Bull and his band surrendered in 1881. The nearby recently constructed Confluence Interpretive Center reveals the colorful history surrounding the merging of two great rivers.

There are accessible walkways and interpretive programs at both sites, as well as educational materials. Facilities are open seven days a week, except winter holidays.

Gas, food, and lodging are available nearby in Williston, Fairview, and Culbertson. Note to Birders: As I write this Fall 2012 the area is under siege thanks to the horrendous truck traffic serving the ever expanding Bakken oil boom…e.g. travel with caution.

Piping Plover
(Credit: U.S. Fish and Wildlife Service)

Directions
Located 15 miles southeast of Bainville on MT 327; or 10 miles north of Fairview on ND 58; or 25 miles southwest of Williston on ND 1804.

Contact
Fort Union Trading Post phone: 701-572-9083
Fort Buford Interpretive Center phone: 701-572-9034

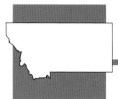

BIRDING TRAILS: MONTANA

Audubon Christmas Bird Count

HISTORY

By the late 1800s, the so-called "Christmas Side Hunt" had grown into a popular holiday tradition. The rules were simple: Choose sides, go afield, shoot anything that moves; side with the "biggest pile of feathered (and furred) critters" wins.

Concerned with the alarming decline of birds on "Christmas Day 1900, ornithologist Frank Chapman, an early officer in the then budding Audubon Society, proposed a new holiday tradition — A "Christmas Bird Census" that would count birds rather than hunt them. Behold, the Christmas Bird Count.

Chapman, along with 27 like-minded cohorts conducted 25 counts that day. Locations ranged from coast to coast, with the large majority in and around the big cities of the northeast; 90 species were tallied.

TODAY

From humble beginnings, the number of counts has grown steadily; 2,248 in 2011/2012. So too the number of participants and sightings; in 2011/2012, 63,277 birders tallied 60,502,185 individuals of 666 species. Montana conducted 31 counts; nearly 600 participants tallied 146 species.

FIND A COUNT NEAR YOU

Anyone can participate and starting this year, there is no fee (used to be $5 to cover the cost of hard-copy summaries which, but are now digital). In Montana, contact your local Audubon Society or Montana Audubon (www.mtaudubon.org). Dates are usually set by mid-November and counts are usually held from mid-December to early January.

BIRDING TRAILS: MONTANA

Great Backyard Bird Count

Anyone can take part in the Great Backyard Bird Count, from novice bird watchers to experts. Participants count birds for as little as 15 minutes (or as long as they wish) on one or more days of the four-day event (February) and report their sightings online. For more information, check out www.birdcount.org.

Spruce Grouse

BIRDING TRAILS: MONTANA

Montana Bird Festivals And Such

INTERNATIONAL MIGRATORY BIRD DAY
Annual event, held the second Saturday in May. Contact www.birdday.org

LOON AND FISH FESTIVAL
Held in Seeley Lake over Memorial Day Weekend (cancelled for 2014). For information, call 406-677-0717

WINGS ACROSS THE BIG SKY
Montana Audubon's Annual Festival is held in June; Bozeman in 2014. Contact information at www.mtaudubon.org

BUZZARD DAY
Annual event held in Makoshika State Park (Glendive) in early June. Contact information at www.Makoshika.org/events.htm

BITTERROOT BIRDING AND NATURE FESTIVAL
Annual event held in June at Lee Metcalf National Wildlife Refuge. For information, call 406-777-5552 or check out the website at www.bitterrootbirdfest.com

BRIDGER RAPTOR FESTIVAL
Annual event held in early October in and around Bozeman. Contact Bridger Bowl at 406-586-1518 or check out the website at www.bridgerraptorfest.org

MONTANA NATURAL HISTORY CENTER
Non-profit organization that holds various nature-oriented programs throughout the year; some relative to birds, some not. Contact MNHC for information and dates at www.montananaturalist.org

MONTANA OUTDOOR BIRDING
An online Yahoo News Group whose members sometimes get together for birding trips. Join in on the fun at www.pets.groups.yahoo.com/group/MOB-Montana/

BIRDING TRAILS: MONTANA

Hire a Guide

GO BIRD MONTANA: WWW.GOBIRDMONTANA.COM

MONTANA: YELLOWSTONE TO GLACIER:
WWW.FIELDGUIDES.COM/BIRD-TOURS/MONTANA

WILD PLANET NATURE AND BIRDING TOURS:
WWW.WILDPLANETNATURETOURS.COM

Anna's Hummingbird

BIRDING TRAILS: MONTANA

Important Bird Areas (IBAs)

The IBA Program is a global initiative implemented in 1995 by the National Audubon Society to identify, monitor, and protect sites deemed critical for the conservation of birds. In January 2002, the Montana IBA Committee voted to identify 26 IBAs from among nearly 60 sites submitted during the first round of nominations. Spread across the state, the sites range in size from 100 acres at Safe Harbor Marsh to more than one million acres at the Charles M. Russell National Wildlife Refuge, collectively encompassing much of the premier bird habitat in the state. Currently, there are 40 IBAs in Montana.

IBAs help focus attention on habitats, but are not legally binding and come with no specific management or conservation plan. That's where dedicated birders, friends, and the various state Audubon Societies step up to the plate through establishing conservation easements, education and, where feasible, putting into motion hands-on plans to conserve and enhance the various sites.

GLOBALLY SIGNIFICANT IBAS

Eleven Montana IBAs are considered globally significant. These include the following sites and trigger species:

- Glaciated Prairie Sage-steppe: Greater Sage Grouse
- Musselshell Sage-steppe: Greater Sage Grouse
- Bridger Sage-steppe: Greater Sage Grouse
- Powder/Carter Sage-steppe: Greater Sage Grouse
- Beaverhead Sage-steppe: Greater Sage Grouse
- Hebgen Lake: Trumpeter Swan
- Little Beaver Creek: Mountain Plover
- North Valley Grasslands: Chestnut-collared Longspur, Sprague's Pipit
- Charles M. Russell National Wildlife Refuge: Greater Sage Grouse, Mountain Plover, Chestnut-collared Longspur, Sprague's Pipit
- Westby Prairie-Wetland Complex: Piping Plover, Sprague's Pipit, Chestnut-collared Longspur
- Glacier National Park: Olive-sided Flycatcher

OVERVIEW OF OTHER STATE IBAs

- Owen Sowerine Natural Area: 65 nesting species
- North Shore Flathead Lake: 229 species observed
- Safe Harbor Marsh: 134 species observed
- Pablo NWR: important shorebird stopover
- Ronan Hawk Roost: largest communal Rough-legged Hawk roost in the world (winter)
- Ninepipe NWR: high number of species use year round
- National Bison Range NWR: 200+ species observed, 6 nesting species of concern
- Clark Fork River/Grass Valley: 230+ species observed, 6 nesting species of concern, high migrant use
- Bitterroot River: 240+ species observed, 9 nesting species of concern, high migrant use
- Blodgett Fire: high density nesting for Lewis's Woodpecker; nesting species of concern are Peregrine Falcon, Williamson's Sapsucker, Black-backed Woodpecker, and Olive-sided Flycatcher
- Kevin Rim: high density nesting of Ferruginous Hawk and other diurnal raptors
- Arod Lakes: one of only 4 nesting colonies of American White Pelican in state
- Freezout Lake: 200+ species, up to 300,000 snow and Ross's Geese stopover in spring, thousands of nesting waterfowl and water birds
- Benton Lake NWR: 240 species, 90 nesting species, thousands of ducks, geese, swans and shorebirds stop by during spring and fall migration; high nesting density of Chestnut-collared Longspur (species of concern); high nesting density of ducks and Franklin's Gull
- Lake Helena: 170 species observed; important breeding and migration stopover for a wide variety of species
- Blackfoot Valley: high nesting density (1,400 pairs) of Brewer's Sparrow (species of concern)
- Canyon Ferry WMA: one of only 4 nesting colonies of American White Pelican in state; Caspian Terns (species of concern) also nest here
- Missouri Headwaters SP: 100+ species observed, 8 nesting species of concern
- Madison Valley: 14 nesting bird species of concern; Ennis Lake is important stopover for Common Loon and other migrating waterfowl and water birds
- Red Rock Lakes NWR: 230 species observed; 15 nesting species of concern including Trumpeter Swan and Brewer's Sparrow
- Lonesome Lake: 100+ species; including at least 11 nesting species of concern
- Bowdoin NWR: 260 species observed; 19 nesting species of concern; one of only 4 nesting colonies of American White Pelican in the state; only nesting site for Arctic terns in state; high density shorebirds in migration
- Halfbreed NWR: 100+ species observed; when water conditions are suitable (not often) important waterfowl and shorebird stopover and Franklin's Gull nesting site

- Bear Canyon: at least 12 nesting species of concern; only known nesting site for the rare Blue-gray Gnatcatcher in state
- Tongue River: 100+ species observed; including 21 species of concern
- Medicine Lake NWR: 270 species observed; including 22 species of global concern and 1 endangered (Whooping Crane); one of only 4 nesting colonies of American White Pelican in the state
- Manning Lake Wetland Complex: one of five nesting colonies of Franklin's Gull in state; four other nesting colonial species; 1,000s of nesting waterfowl; at least 5 nesting shorebird species as well as several songbird species of concern

For more information contact: Amy Cilimburg, Director of Bird Conservation, Montana Audubon
Phone: 406-465-1141
Email: amy@mtaudubon.org
Website: http://www.mtaudubon.org/birds/maps.html

Barred Owl

BIRDING TRAILS: MONTANA

Montana Bird Species of Conservation Concern

LEVEL I PRIORITY
Common Loon, Trumpeter Swan, Harlequin Duck, Greater Sage Grouse, Piping Plover, Mountain Plover, Least Tern, Flammulated Owl, Burrowing Owl, Black-backed Woodpecker, Olive-sided Flycatcher, Brown Creeper, Sprague's Pipit, Baird's Sparrow

LEVEL II PRIORITY
Horned Grebe, White-faced Ibis, Barrow's Goldeneye, Hooded Merganser, Bald Eagle, Northern Goshawk, Ferruginous Hawk, Peregrine Falcon, Ruffed Grouse, Columbian Sharp-tailed Grouse, Long-billed Curlew, Marbled Godwit, Franklin's Gull, Caspian Tern, Common Tern, Forster's Tern, Black Tern, Black-billed Cuckoo, Yellow-billed Cuckoo, Black Swift, Vaux's Swift, Calliope Hummingbird, Lewis's Woodpecker, Red-headed Woodpecker, Red-naped Sapsucker, Williamson's Sapsucker, American Three-toed Woodpecker, Pileated Woodpecker, Willow Flycatcher, Hammond's Flycatcher, Cordilleran Flycatcher, Pacific Wren, Veery, Loggerhead Shrike, Red-eyed Vireo, Lazuli Bunting, Brewer's Sparrow, Lark Bunting, Grasshopper Sparrow, McCown's Longspur, Chestnut-collared Longspur, Black Rosy-finch

THREATENED
Whooping Crane

NEAR THREATENED
Greater Sage Grouse, Long-billed Curlew, Buff-breasted Sandpiper, Red-headed Woodpecker, Olive-sided Flycatcher, Chestnut-collared Longspur, Brewer's Sparrow, Cassin's Finch

VULNERABLE
Piping Plover, Mountain Plover, Pinyon Jay, Sprague's Pipit, Rusty Blackbird

BIRDING TRAILS: MONTANA

Recent Rare (Vagrant) Bird Records

- Pacific Wren: Westby, September, 2010 (first record since the species was split)
- Crested Caracara: Hot Springs, June, 2010
- Carolina Wren: Arlee, March, 2010
- Eastern Meadowlark: Ennis, June, 2009
- Lesser Black-backed Gull: Fort Peck, November, 2008
- Inca Dove: Terry, December, 2006
- Curve-billed Thrasher: Roundup, September, 2006
- Blue-winged Warbler: Bowdoin NWR, May, 2006
- Iceland Gull: Great Falls, December, 2005
- Ross's Gull: Frenchtown, May, 2005
- Eastern Towhee: Red Lodge, December, 2004
- Manx Shearwater: Ninepipe NWR, May, 2004
- Siberian Accentor: Gardiner, November, 2003
- White-tailed Kite: Lee Metcalf NWR, November, 2003
- Sharp-tailed Sandpiper: Somers, November, 2002
- White-eyed Vireo: Beartooth WMA, July, 2002
- Mississippi Kite: Jordan, June, 2002
- Yellow-throated Vireo: Columbus, June, 2002
- Costa's Hummingbird: Corvallis, October, 2001
- Pyrrhuloxia: Billings, December, 2000
- Bewick's Wren: Missoula, October, 2000
- Western Scrub-jay: Great Falls, May, 2000
- Vermilion Flycatcher: Victor, January, 2000
- Cackling Goose and Tufted Duck were also added to the state list during this period, based on earlier records.

BIRDING TRAILS: MONTANA

Chambers of Commerce

Montana State Chamber of Commerce, 406-442-2405 / http://www.visitmt.com/
Anaconda, 406-563-2400 / http://www.anacondamt.org/
Baker, 406-778-2266 / http://www.bakermt.com/
Belgrade, 406-388-1616 / http://www.belgradechamber.org/
Big Sky, 406-995-3000 / http://www.bigskychamber.com/
Big Timber, 406-932-5131 / http://www.bigtimber.com/
Bigfork, 406-837-5888 / http://www.bigfork.org/
Billings, 406-245-4111 / http://www.billingschamber.com
Bitterroot Valley, 406-363-2400 / http://www.bitterrootvalleychamber.com/
Bozeman, 406-586-5421 / http://www.bozemanchamber.com/
Bridger, 406-662-3180 / http://www.valleyprinters.com/bridger.html
Broadus, 406-436-2778
Butte-Silver Bow, 406-723-3177 / http://www.buttechamber.org/
Chinook, 406-357-2339 / http://www.chinookmontana.com
Circle, 406-485-2690 / http://www.circle.visitmt.com/
Colstrip, 406-748-3293 / http://www.semdc.org/
Columbia Falls, 406-892-2072 / http://www.columbiafallschamber.com/
Columbus, 406-322-4505 / http://www.stillwater-chamber.org/
Conner, 406-363-2400 / http://www.bitterrootvalleychamber.com/
Conrad, 406-271-7791 / http://www.conradmt.com/
Corvallis, 406-363-2400 / http://www.bitterrootvalleychamber.com/
Culbertson, 406-787-5821 / http://www.culbertsonmt.com/
Cut Bank, 406-873-4041 / http://www.cutbankchamber.com/
Darby, 406-363-2400 / http://www.bitterrootvalleychamber.com/
Deer Lodge, 406-846-2094 / http://www.powellcountymontana.com/
Dillon, 406-683-5511 / http://bvhd.bmt.net/~chamber/
East Glacier, 406-226-4403 / http://www.glaciermt.com/index.php
Ekalaka, 406-775-6886 / http://www.ekalakachamber.com
Ennis, 406-682-4388 / http://www.ennischamber.com
Eureka, 406-297-7800 / http://www.welcome2eureka.com

Fairfield, 406-467-2531 / http://www.fairfieldmt.com
Florence, 406-363-2400 / http://www.bitterrootvalleychamber.com
Fort Benton, 406-622-3864 / http://www.fortbenton.com/chamber/
Gardiner, 406-848-7971 / http://www.gardinerchamber.com
Glasgow, 406-228-2222 / http://www.glasgowmt.net
Glendive, 406-365-5601 / http://www.glendivechamber.com
Great Falls, 406-761-4434 / http://www.greatfallschamber.org
Hamilton, 406-363-2400 / http://www.bitterrootvalleychamber.com/
Hardin, 406-665-1672 / http://www.hardinmt.com/
Harlowton, 406-632-4694 / http://www.harlowtonchamber.com/
Havre, 406-265-4383 / http://www.havremt.com/
Helena, 406-442-4120 / http://www.helenachamber.com
Hot Springs, 406-741-2662 / http://www.hotsprgs.net/hscofc/
Jordan, 406-557-6158 / http://www.garfieldcounty.com
Kalispell, 406-758-2800 / http://www.kalispellchamber.com
Lakeside, 406-844-3715 / http://www.lakesidesomers.org
Laurel, 406-628-8105 / http://www.laurelmontana.org
Lewistown, 406-535-5436 / http://www.lewistownchamber.com
Libby, 406-293-4167 / http://www.libbychamber.org
Lincoln, 406-362-4949 / http://www.lincolnmontana.com
Livingston, 406-222-0850 / http://www.livingston.avicom.net
Malta, 406-654-1776 / http://maltachamber.com
Manhattan, 406-284-4162 / http://www.manhattanmontana.com
Miles City, 406-234-2890 / http://www.milescitychamber.com
Missoula, 406-543-6623 / http://www.missoulachamber.com
Philipsburg, 406-859-3388 / http://philipsburgmt.com
Plains-Paradise, 406-826-4700 / http://www.plainsmtchamber.com
Plentywood, 406-765-1733 / http://www.plentywood.com
Polson, 406-883-5969 / http://www.polsonchamber.com
Red Lodge, 406-446-1718 / http://www.redlodge.com
Ronan, 406-676-8300 / http://glacier.visitmt.com
Roundup, 406-323-1966 / http://roundupchamber.net
Saco, 406-527-3312 / http://www.sacomontana.net
Scobey, 406-487-2061 / http://www.scobey.org
Seeley Lake, 406-677-2880 / http://www.seeleylakechamber.com
Shelby, 406-434-7184 / http://www.shelbymt.com
Sidney, 406-482-1916 / http://www.sidneymt.com
Superior, 406-822-4891 / http://mineralcounty.info
Terry, 406-635-5782
Thompson Falls, 406-827-4930 / http://www.thompsonfallschamber.com
Three Forks, 406-285-4753 / http://www.threeforksmontana.com
Townsend, 406-266-4101 / http://www.townsendvalley.com
Troy, 406-295-1064 / www.troymtchamber.org

West Yellowstone, 406-646-7701 / http://www.westyellowstonechamber.com
Whitefish, 406-862-3501 / http://www.whitefishchamber.org
Wibaux, 406-796-2412
Wolf Point, 406-653-2012 / http://www.wolfpoint.com

Northern Cardinal

Audubon Societies

Bitterroot Audubon
http://www.bitterrootaudubon.org
Five Valleys Audubon
http://www.fvamissoula.org
Flathead Audubon
http://www.flatheadaudubon.org
Last Chance Audubon
http://www.lastchanceaudubon.org
Mission Mountain Audubon
48901 Hwy 93, Suite A-179, Polson, MT 59860
Pintler Audubon
P.O. Box 432, Twin Bridges, MT 59754
Sacajawea Audubon
http://www.sacajaweaaudubon.org
Upper Missouri Breaks Audubon
P.O. Box 2362, Great Falls, MT 59403

FWP Regional Offices

Region 1, Kalispell, 406-752-5501
Region 2, Missoula, 406-542-5500
Region 3, Bozeman, 406-542-5500
Region 4, Great Falls, 406-454-5840
Region 5, Billings, 406-247-2940
Region 6, Glasgow, 406-228-3700
Region 7, Miles City, 406-234-0900

Montana Bird List

This state bird list is provided courtesy of the Montana Audubon Society. To view updated lists or to purchase a copy of Montana Bird Distribution, log on to www.mtaudubon.org.

† - fewer than 20 records

ANSERIFORMES

ANATIDAE [WATERFOWL]

Anserinae [Geese and Swans]

Greater White-fronted Goose (*Anser albifrons*)
Snow Goose (*Chen caerulescens*)
Ross's Goose (*Chen rossii*)
Brant (*Branta bernicla*) †
Canada Goose (*Branta canadensis*)
Cackling Goose (*Branta hutchinsii*)
Mute Swan (*Cygnus olor*)
Trumpeter Swan (*Cygnus buccinator*)
Tundra Swan (*Cygnus columbianus*)

Anatinae [Ducks]

Duck (*Aix sponsa*)
Gadwall (*Anas strepera*)
Eurasian Wigeon (*Anas penelope*)
American Wigeon (*Anas americana*)
American Black Duck (*Anas rubripes*)
Mallard (*Anas platyrhynchos*)
Baikal Teal (*Anas formosa*)
Blue-winged Teal (*Anas discors*)
Cinnamon Teal (*Anas cyanoptera*)
Northern Shoveler (*Anas clypeata*)
Northern Pintail (*Anas acuta*)
Garganey (*Anas querquedula*) †
Green-winged Teal (*Anas crecca*)
Canvasback (*Aythya valisineria*)
Redhead (*Aythya americana*)
Ring-necked Duck (*Aythya collaris*)
Greater Scaup (*Aythya marila*)

Lesser Scaup (*Aythya affnis*)
Harlequin Duck (*Histrionicus histrionicus*)
Surf Scoter (*Melanitta perspicillata*)
White-winged Scoter (*Melanitta fusca*)
Black Scoter (*Melanitta nigra*) †
Long-tailed Duck (*Clangula hyemalis*)
Bufflehead (*Bucephala albeola*)
Common Goldeneye (*Bucephala clangula*)
Barrow's Goldeneye (*Bucephala islandica*)
Hooded Merganser (*Lophodytes cucullatus*)
Common Merganser (*Mergus merganser*)
Red-breasted Merganser (*Mergus serrator*)
Ruddy Duck (*Oxyura jamaicensis*)

GALLIFORMES

PHASIANIDAE (UPLAND FOWL)

Odontophoridae

California Quail (*Callipepla californica*)

Phasianinae [Old World Fowl]

Chukar (*Alectoris chukar*)
Gray Partridge (*Perdix perdix*)
Ring-necked Pheasant (*Phasianus colchicus*)

Tetraoninae [New World Grouse]

Ruffed Grouse (*Bonasa umbellus*)
Greater Sage-Grouse (*Centrocercus urophasianus*)
Spruce Grouse (*Falcipennis canadensis*)
Willow Ptarmigan (*Lagopus lagopus*) †
White-tailed Ptarmigan (*Lagopus leucura*)
Dusky Grouse (*Dendragapus obscurus*)

Sharp-tailed Grouse *(Tympanuchus phasianellus)*
Greater Prairie-Chicken *(Tympanuchus cupido)* †

Meleagridinae [Turkeys]

Wild Turkey *(Meleagris gallopavo)*

GAVIIFORMES

GAVIIDAE [LOONS]
Red-throated Loon *(Gavia stellata)* †
Pacific Loon *(Gavia pacifica)* †
Common Loon *(Gavia immer)*
Yellow-billed Loon *(Gavia adamsii)* †

PODICIPEDIFORMES

PODICIPEDIDAE [GREBES]
Pied-billed Grebe *(Podilymbus podiceps)*
Horned Grebe *(Podiceps auritus)*
Red-necked Grebe *(Podiceps grisegena)*
Eared Grebe *(Podiceps nigricollis)*
Western Grebe *(Aechmophorus occidentalis)*
Clark's Grebe *(Aechmophorus clarkii)*

PELECANIFORMES

PELECANIDAE [PELICANS]
American White Pelican *(Pelecanus erythrorhynchos)*

PHALACROCORACIDAE [CORMORANTS]
Double-crested Cormorant *(Phalacrocorax auritus)*

CICONIIFORMES

ARDEIDAE [HERONS]
American Bittern *(Botaurus lentiginosus)*
Least Bittern *(Ixobrychus exilis)* †
Great Blue Heron *(Ardea herodias)*

Great Egret *(Ardea alba)*
Snowy Egret *(Egretta thula)*
Little Blue Heron *(Egretta caerulea)* †
Cattle Egret *(Bubulcus ibis)*
Green Heron *(Butorides virescens)* †
Black-crowned Night-Heron *(Nycticorax nycticorax)*
Yellow-crowned Night-Heron *(Nyctanassa violacea)* †

THRESKIORNITHIDAE [IBISES AND SPOONBILLS]

Threskiornithinae [Ibises]

White-faced Ibis *(Plegadis chihi)*

CICONIIDAE [STORKS]
Wood Stork *(Mycteria americana)* †

CATHARTIDAE [NEW WORLD VULTURES]
Turkey Vulture *(Cathartes aura)*

FALCONIFORMES

ACCIPITRIDAE [HAWKS AND ALLIES]

Pandioninae [Ospreys]

Osprey *(Pandion haliaetus)*

Accipitrinae [Hawks and Eagles]

White-tailed Kite *(Elanus leucurus)* †
Mississippi Kite *(Ictinia mississippiensis)* †
Bald Eagle *(Haliaeetus leucocephalus)*
Northern Harrier *(Circus cyaneus)*
Sharp-shinned Hawk *(Accipiter striatus)*
Cooper's Hawk *(Accipiter cooperii)*
Northern Goshawk *(Accipiter gentilis)*
Red-shouldered Hawk *(Buteo lineatus)* †
Broad-winged Hawk *(Buteo platypterus)*
Swainson's Hawk *(Buteo swainsoni)*
Red-tailed Hawk *(Buteo jamaicensis)*
Ferruginous Hawk *(Buteo regalis)*

Rough-legged Hawk *(Buteo lagopus)*
Golden Eagle *(Aquila chrysaetos)*

FALCONIDAE [FALCONS AND ALLIES]

Falconinae [Falcons]

American Kestrel *(Falco sparverius)*
Merlin *(Falco columbarius)*
Gyrfalcon *(Falco rusticolus)*
Peregrine Falcon *(Falco peregrinus)*
Prairie Falcon *(Falco mexicanus)*

GRUIFORMES

RALLIDAE [RAILS AND GALLINULES]

Yellow Rail *(Coturnicops noveboracensis)* †
Virginia Rail *(Rallus limicola)*
Sora *(Porzana carolina)*
Common Moorhen *(Gallinula chloropus)*
American Coot *(Fulica americana)*

GRUIDAE [CRANES]

Gruinae [Typical Cranes]

Sandhill Crane *(Grus canadensis)*
Whooping Crane *(Grus americana)*

CHARADRIIFORMES

CHARADRIIDAE [PLOVERS AND ALLIES]

Charadriinae [Plovers]

Black-bellied Plover *(Pluvialis squatarola)*
American Golden-Plover *(Pluvialis dominica)*
Snowy Plover *(Charadrius alexanderinus)* †
Semipalmated Plover *(Charadrius semipalmatus)*
Piping Plover *(Charadrius melodis)*
Killdeer *(Charadrius vociferus)*
Mountain Plover *(Charadrius montanus)*

RECURVIROSTRIDAE [STILTS AND AVOCETS]

Black-necked Stilt *(Himantopus mexicanus)*
American Avocet *(Recurvirostra americana)*

SCOLOPACIDAE [SANDPIPERS AND ALLIES]

Scolopacinae [Sandpipers]

Greater Yellowlegs *(Tringa melanoleuca)*
Lesser Yellowlegs *(Tringa flavipes)*
Solitary Sandpiper *(Tringa solitaria)*
Willet *(Catoptrophorus semipalmatus)*
Spotted Sandpiper *(Actitis macularius)*
Upland Sandpiper *(Bartramia longicauda)*
Whimbrel *(Numenius phaeopus)*
Long-billed Curlew *(Numenius americanus)*
Hudsonian Godwit *(Limosa haemastica)* †
Marbled Godwit *(Limosa fedoa)*
Ruddy Turnstone *(Arenaria interpres)*
Black Turnstone *(Arenaria melanocephala)* †
Red Knot *(Calidris canutus)*
Sanderling *(Calidris alba)*
Semipalmated Sandpiper *(Calidris pusilla)*
Western Sandpiper *(Calidris mauri)*
Least Sandpiper *(Calidris minutilla)*
White-rumped Sandpiper *(Calidris fuscicollis)*
Baird's Sandpiper *(Calidris bairdii)*
Pectoral Sandpiper *(Calidris melanotos)*
Sharp-tailed Sandpiper *(Calidris acuminata)* †
Dunlin *(Calidris alpina)*
Curlew Sandpiper *(Calidris ferruginea)* †
Stilt Sandpiper *(Calidris himantopus)*
Buff-breasted Sandpiper *(Tryngites subruficollis)* †
Short-billed Dowitcher *(Limnodromus griseus)*
Long-billed Dowitcher *(Limnodromus scolopaceus)*
Wilson's Snipe *(Gallinago delicata)*
American Woodcock *(Scolopax minor)* †

Phalaropodinae [Phalaropes]

Wilson's Phalarope *(Phalaropus tricolor)*
Red-necked Phalarope *(Phalaropus lobatus)*
Red Phalarope *(Phalaropus fulicarius)* †

LARIDAE [Larids]

Stercorariinae [Skuas]

Pomarine Jaeger *(Stercorarius pomarinus)* †
Parasitic Jaeger *(Stercorarius parasiticus)* †
Long-tailed Jaeger *(Stercorarius longicaudus)* †

Larinae [Gulls]

Laughing Gull *(Larus atricilla)* †
Franklin's Gull *(Larus pipixcan)*
Little Gull *(Larus minutus)* †
Bonaparte's Gull *(Larus philadelphia)*
Mew Gull *(Larus canus)* †
Ring-billed Gull *(Larus delawarensis)*
California Gull *(Larus californicus)*
Herring Gull *(Larus argentatis)*
Thayer's Gull *(Larus thayeri)* †
Glaucous-winged Gull *(Larus glaucescens)* †
Glaucous Gull *(Larus hyperborus)* †
Great Black-backed Gull *(Larus marinus)* †
Sabine's Gull *(Xema sabini)* †
Black-legged Kittiwake *(Rissa tridactyla)* †
Ivory Gull *(Pagophila eburnea)* †

Sterninae [Terns]

Caspian Tern *(Sterna caspia)*
Common Tern *(Sterna hirundo)*
Arctic Tern *(Sterna paradisaea)* †
Forster's Tern *(Sterna forsteri)*
Least Tern *(Sterna antillarum)*
Black Tern *(Chlidonias niger)*

ALCIDAE [Alcids]

Long-billed Murrelet *(Brachyramphus perdix)* †
Ancient Murrelet *(Synthliboramphus antiquus)* †

COLUMBIFORMES

COLUMBIDAE [Pigeons and Doves]

Rock Pigeon *(Columba livia)*
Band-tailed Pigeon *(Patagioenas fasciata)* †
Eurasian Collared-Dove *(Streptopelia decaocto)* †
White-winged Dove *(Zenaida asiatica)* †
Mourning Dove *(Zenaida macroura)*

CUCULIFORMES

CUCULIDAE [Cuckoos and Allies]

Coccyzinae [New World Cuckoos]

Black-billed Cuckoo *(Coccyzus erythropthalmus)*
Yellow-billed Cuckoo *(Coccyzus americanus)* †

STRIGIFORMES

TYTONIDAE [Barn and Grass Owls]

Barn Owl *(Tyto alba)*

STRIGIDAE [Typical Owls]

Flammulated Owl *(Otus flammeolus)*
Western Screech-Owl *(Megascops kennicottii)*
Eastern Screech-Owl *(Megascops asio)*
Great Horned Owl *(Bubo virginianus)*
Snowy Owl *(Bubo scandiacus)*
Northern Hawk Owl *(Surnia ulula)*
Northern Pygmy-Owl *(Glaucidium gnoma)*
Burrowing Owl *(Athene cunicularia)*
Barred Owl *(Strix varia)*
Great Grey Owl *(Strix nebulosa)*
Long-eared Owl *(Asio otus)*
Short-eared Owl *(Asio flammeus)*

Boreal Owl (Aegolius funereus)
Northern Saw-whet Owl (Aegolius acadicus)

CAPRIMULGIFORMES

CAPRIMULGIDAE [GOATSUCKERS]

Chordeilinae [Nighthawks]

Common Nighthawk (Chordeiles minor)

Caprimulginae [Nightjars]

Common Poorwill (Phalaenoptilus nuttallii)
Whip-poor-will (Caprimulgus vociferus) †

APODIFORMES

APODIDAE [SWIFTS]

Cypseloidinae [Tropical Swifts]

Black Swift (Cypseloides niger)

Chaeturinae [Spine-tailed Swifts]

Chimney Swift (Chaetura pelagica)
Vaux's Swift (Chaetura vauxi)

Apodinae [Typical Swifts]

White-throated Swift (Aeronautes saxatalis)

TROCHILIDAE [HUMMINGBIRDS]

Trochilinae [Typical Hummingbirds]

Ruby-throated Hummingbird (Archilochus colubris) †
Black-chinned Hummingbird (Archilochus alexandri)
Anna's Hummingbird (Calypte anna) †
Costa's Hummingbird (Calypte costae) †
Calliope Hummingbird (Stellula calliope)
Broad-tailed Hummingbird (Selasphorus platycercus) †
Rufous Hummingbird (Selasphorus rufus)

CORACIIFORMES

ALCEDINIDAE [KINGFISHERS]

Cerylinae [New World Kingfishers]

Belted Kingfisher (Ceryle alcyon)

PICIFORMES

PICIDAE [WRYNECKS AND WOODPECKERS]

Picinae [Woodpeckers]

Lewis's Woodpecker (Melanerpes lewis)
Red-headed Woodpecker (Melanerpes erythrocephalus)
Red-bellied Woodpecker (Melanerpes carolinus) †
Williamson's Sapsucker (Sphyrapicus thyroideus)
Yellow-bellied Sapsucker (Sphyrapicus varius) †
Red-naped Sapsucker (Sphyrapicus nuchalis)
Downy Woodpecker (Picoides pubescens)
Hairy Woodpecker (Picoides villosus)
White-headed Woodpecker (Picoides albolarvatus) †
American Three-toed Woodpecker (Picoides dorsalis)
Black-backed Woodpecker (Picoides arcticus)
Northern Flicker (Colaptes auratus)
Pileated Woodpecker (Dryocopus pileatus)

PASSERIFORMES

TYRANNIDAE [TYRANT FLYCATCHERS]

Fluvicolinae [Typical Flycatchers]

Olive-sided Flycatcher (Contopus cooperi)
Western Wood-Pewee (Contopus sordidulus)

Eastern Wood-Pewee *(Contopus virens)* †
Alder Flycatcher *(Empidonax alnorum)*
Willow Flycatcher *(Empidonax trailii)*
Least Flycatcher *(Empidonax minimus)*
Hammond's Flycatcher *(Empidonax hammondii)*
Grey Flycatcher *(Empidonax wrightii)* †
Dusky Flycatcher *(Empidonax oberholseri)*
Cordilleran Flycatcher *(Empidonax occidentalis)*
Eastern Phoebe *(Sayornis phoebe)* †
Say's Phoebe *(Sayornis saya)*
Vermilion Flycatcher *(Pyrocephalus rubinus)* †

Tyranninae [Kingbirds]

Ash-throated Flycatcher *(Myiarchus cinerascens)* †
Great Crested Flycatcher *(Myiarchus crinitus)* †
Cassin's Kingbird *(Tyrannus vociferans)*
Western Kingbird *(Tyrannus verticalis)*
Eastern Kingbird *(Tyrannus tyrannus)*
Scissor-tailed Flycatcher *(Tyrannus forficatus)* †

LANIIDAE [Shrikes]
Loggerhead Shrike *(Lanius ludovicianus)*
Northern Shrike *(Lanius excubitor)*

VIREONIDAE [Vireos]
White-eyed Vireo *(Vireo griseus)* †
Yellow-throated Vireo *(Vireo flavifrons)* †
Plumbeous Vireo *(Vireo plumbeus)* †
Cassin's Vireo *(Vireo cassinii)*
Blue-headed Vireo *(Vireo solitarius)* †
Warbling Vireo *(Vireo gilvus)*
Philadelphia Vireo *(Vireo philadelphicus)* †
Red-eyed Vireo *(Vireo olivaceus)*

CORVIDAE [Corvids]
Gray Jay *(Perisoreus canadensis)*
Steller's Jay *(Cyanocitta stelleri)*
Blue Jay *(Cyanocitta cristata)*
Western Scrub-Jay *(Aphelocoma californica)* †
Pinyon Jay *(Gymnorhinus cyanocephalus)*
Clark's Nutcracker *(Nucifraga columbiana)*
Black-billed Magpie *(Pica hudsonia)*
American Crow *(Corvus brachyrhynchos)*
Common Raven *(Corvus corax)*

ALAUDIDAE [Larks]
Horned Lark *(Eremophila alpestris)*

HIRUNDINIDAE [Swallows]
Hirundininae

Purple Martin *(Progne subis)*
Tree Swallow *(Tachycineta bicolor)*
Violet-green Swallow *(Tachycineta thalassina)*
Northern Rough-winged Swallow *(Stelgidopteryx serripennis)*
Bank Swallow *(Riparia riparia)*
Cliff Swallow *(Petrochelidon pyrrhonota)*
Barn Swallow *(Hirundo rustica)*

PARIDAE [Tits]
Black-capped Chickadee *(Poecile atricapillus)*
Mountain Chickadee *(Poecile gambeli)*
Chestnut-backed Chickadee *(Poecile rufescens)*
Boreal Chickadee *(Poecile hudsonica)*

SITTIDAE [Nuthatches]
Sittinae [True Nuthatches]

Red-breasted Nuthatch *(Sitta canadensis)*
White-breasted Nuthatch *(Sitta carolinensis)*
Pygmy Nuthatch *(Sitta pygmaea)*

CERTHIIDAE [Treecreepers]
Certhiinae [Typical Creepers]

Brown Creeper *(Certhia americana)*

TROGLODYTIDAE [WRENS]
Rock Wren *(Salpinctes obsoletus)*
Canyon Wren *(Catherpes mexicanus)*
Bewick's Wren *(Thryomanes bewickii)* †
House Wren *(Troglodytes aedon)*
Pacific Wren *(Troglodytes troglodytes)*
Sedge Wren *(Cistothorus platensis)* †
Marsh Wren *(Cistothorus palustris)*

CINCLIDAE [DIPPERS]
American Dipper *(Cinclus mexicanus)*

REGULIDAE [KINGLETS]
Golden-crowned Kinglet *(Regulus satrapa)*
Ruby-crowned Kinglet *(Regulus calendula)*

SYLVIIDAE [OLD WORLD WARBLERS]

Polioptilinae [Gnatcatchers]

Blue-gray Gnatcatcher *(Polioptila caerulea)* †

TURDIDAE [THRUSHES]
Eastern Bluebird *(Siala sialis)*
Western Bluebird *(Sialia mexicana)*
Mountain Bluebird *(Siala currucoides)*
Townsend's Solitare *(Myadestes townsendi)*
Veery *(Catharus fuscescens)*
Gray-cheeked Thrush *(Catharus minimus)* †
Swainson's Thrush *(Catharus ustulatus)*
Hermit Thrush *(Catharus guttatus)*
Wood Thrush *(Hylocichla mustelina)* †
American Robin *(Turdus migratorius)*
Varied Thrush *(Ixoreus naevius)*

MIMIDAE [MIMIDS]
Gray Catbird *(Dumetella carolinensis)*
Northern Mockingbird *(Mimus polyglottos)*
Sage Thrasher *(Oreoscoptes montanus)*
Brown Thrasher *(Toxostoma rufum)*

STURNIDAE [STARLINGS]
European Starling *(Sturnus vulgaris)*

PRUNELLIDAE [ACCENTORS]
Siberian Accentor *(Prunella montanella)* †

MOTACILLIDAE [WAGTAILS AND PIPITS]
American Pipit *(Anthus rubescens)*
Sprague's Pipit *(Anthus spragueii)*

BOMBYCILLIDAE [WAXWINGS]
Bohemian Waxwing *(Bombycilla garrulus)*
Cedar Waxwing *(Bombycilla cedrorum)*

PARULIDAE [WOOD-WARBLERS]
Golden-winged Warbler *(Vermivora chrysoptera)* †
Tennessee Warbler *(Vermivora peregrina)*
Orange-crowned Warbler *(Vermivora celata)*
Nashville Warbler *(Vermivora ruficapilla)*
Northern Parula *(Parula americana)* †
Yellow Warbler *(Dendroica petechia)*
Chestnut-sided Warbler *(Dendroica pensylvanica)*
Magnolia Warbler *(Dendroica magnolia)*
Cape May Warbler *(Dendroica tigrina)* †
Black-throated Blue Warbler *(Dendroica caerulescens)* †
Yellow-rumped Warbler *(Dendroica coronata)*
Black-throated Gray Warbler *(Dendroica nigrescens)* †
Black-throated Green Warbler *(Dendroica virens)* †
Townsend's Warbler *(Dendroica townsendi)*
Blackburnian Warbler *(Dendroica fusca)* †
Yellow-throated Warbler *(Dendroica dominica)* †
Pine Warbler *(Dendroica pinus)* †
Prairie Warbler *(Dendroica discolor)* †
Palm Warbler *(Dendroica palmarum)*

Bay-breasted Warbler *(Dendroica castanea)* †

Blackpoll Warbler *(Dendroica striata)*

Black-and-white Warbler *(Mniotilla varia)*

American Redstart *(Setophaga ruticilla)*

Prothonotary Warbler *(Protonotaria citrea)* †

Ovenbird *(Seiurus aurocapilla)*

Northern Waterthrush *(Seiurus noveboracensis)*

Kentucky Warbler *(Oporornis formosus)* †

Connecticut Warbler *(Oporornis agilis)* †

Mourning Warbler *(Oporornis philadelphia)*

MacGillivray's Warbler *(Oporornis tolmiei)*

Common Yellowthroat *(Geothlypis trichas)*

Hooded Warbler *(Wilsonia citrina)* †

Wilson's Warbler *(Wilsonia pusilla)*

Canada Warbler *(Wilsonia canadensis)* †

Painted Redstart *(Myioborus pictus)* †

Yellow-breasted Chat *(Icteria virens)*

THRAUPIDAE [TANAGERS]
Summer Tanager *(Piranga rubra)* †

Scarlet Tanager *(Piranga olivacea)* †

Western Tanager *(Piranga ludoviciana)*

EMBERIZIDAE [EMBERIZID SPARROWS AND ALLIES]
Green-tailed Towhee *(Pipilo chlorurus)*

Spotted Towhee *(Pipilo maculatus)*

American Tree Sparrow *(Spizella arborea)*

Chipping Sparrow *(Spizella passerina)*

Clay-colored Sparrow *(Spizella pallida)*

Brewer's Sparrow *(Spizella breweri)*

Field Sparrow *(Spizella pusilla)*

Vesper Sparrow *(Pooecetes gramineus)*

Lark Sparrow *(Chondestes grammacus)*

Black-throated Sparrow *(Amphispiza bilineata)* †

Sage Sparrow *(Amphispiza belli)* †

Lark Bunting *(Calamospiza melanocorys)*

Savannah Sparrow *(Passerculus sandwichensis)*

Grasshopper Sparrow *(Ammodramus savannarum)*

Baird's Sparrow *(Ammodramus bairdii)*

Le Conte's Sparrow *(Ammodramus leconteii)* †

Nelson's Sharp-tailed Sparrow *(Ammodramus nelsoni)* †

Fox Sparrow *(Passerella iliaca)*

Song Sparrow *(Melospiza melodia)*

Lincoln's Sparrow *(Melospiza lincolnii)*

Swamp Sparrow *(Melospiza georgiana)* †

White-throated Sparrow *(Zonotrichia albicollis)*

Harris's Sparrow *(Zonotrichia querula)*

White-crowned Sparrow *(Zonotrichia leucophrys)*

Golden-crowned Sparrow *(Zonotrichia atricapilla)* †

Dark-eyed Junco *(Junco hyemalis)*

McCown's Longspur *(Calcarius mccownii)*

Lapland Longspur *(Calcarius lapponicus)*

Smith's Longspur *(Calcarius pictus)* †

Chestnut-collared Longspur *(Calcarius ornatus)*

Snow Bunting *(Plectrophenax nivalis)*

CARDINALIDAE [GROSBEAKS AND ALLIES]
Northern Cardinal *(Cardinalis cardinalis)* †

Pyrrhuloxia *(Cardinalis sinuatus)* †

Rose-breasted Grosbeak *(Pheucticus ludovicianus)*

Black-headed Grosbeak *(Pheucticus melanocephalus)*

Blue Grosbeak *(Passerina caerulea)* †

Lazuli Bunting *(Passerina amoena)*

Indigo Bunting *(Passerina cyanea)*

Painted Bunting *(Passerina ciris)* †

Dickcissel *(Spiza americana)* †

ICTERIDAE [NEW WORLD BLACKBIRDS AND ALLIES]
Bobolink *(Dolichonyx oryzivorus)*

Red-winged Blackbird *(Agelaius phoeniceus)*
Western Meadowlark *(Sturnella neglecta)*
Yellow-headed Blackbird *(Xanthocephalus xanthocephalus)*
Rusty Blackbird *(Euphagus carolinus)*
Brewer's Blackbird *(Euphagus cyanocephalus)*
Common Grackle *(Quiscalus quiscula)*
Great-tailed Grackle *(Quiscalus mexicanus)* †
Brown-headed Cowbird *(Molothrus ater)*
Orchard Oriole *(Icterus spurius)*
Hooded Oriole *(Icterus cucullatus)* †
Bullock's Oriole *(Icterus bullockii)*
Baltimore Oriole *(Icterus galbula)*

FRINGILLIDAE [TYPICAL FINCHES]

Fringillinae [Fringillid Finches]

Brambling *(Fringilla montifringilla)* †

Carduelinae [Carduelid Finches]

Gray-crowned Rosy-Finch *(Leucosticte tephrocotis)*
Black Rosy-Finch *(Leucosticte atratus)*
Pine Grosbeak *(Pinicola enucleator)*
Purple Finch *(Carpodacus purpureus)*
Cassin's Finch *(Carpodacus cassinii)*
House Finch *(Carpodacus mexicanus)*
Red Crossbill *(Loxia curvirostra)*
White-winged Crossbill *(Loxia leucoptera)*
Common Redpoll *(Carduelis flammea)*
Hoary Redpoll *(Carduelis hornemanni)*
Pine Siskin *(Carduelis pinus)*
Lesser Goldfinch *(Carduelis psaltria)* †
American Goldfinch *(Carduelis tristis)*
Evening Grosbeak *(Coccothraustes vespertinus)*

PASSERIDAE [OLD WORLD WEAVERS]

House Sparrow *(Passer domesticus)*

Index

A

Absaroka-Beartooth Wilderness 319, 335
Absarokee 335
Ackley Lake State Park 170
Afterbay Dam 368–369
Afterbay Lake 370
Albright 187
Alder 266, 267, 270
Alder Flycatcher 123, 126, 438
Alva Lake 100
American Avocet 122, 140, 218, 230, 234, 260, 271, 280, 329, 338, 416, 417, 451
American Bittern 23, 31, 98, 101, 149, 296, 331
American Coot 205, 209, 234, 245, 260, 264, 265, 277, 279, 282, 370, 439
American Crow 16, 173, 175, 202, 219, 227, 230, 234, 244, 258, 346, 356
American Dipper 16, 19, 54, 56, 61, 64, 69, 71, 76, 78, 80, 88, 91, 102, 114, 126, 171, 182, 185, 206, 231, 232, 236, 238, 244, 250, 260, 274, 277, 294, 305, 313, 319, 335, 368
American Golden Plover 110, 233, 234
American Goldfinch 78, 149, 175, 180, 204, 227, 251, 264, 348, 356, 430
American Kestrel 43, 54, 89, 136, 138, 149, 173, 175, 179, 194, 202, 209, 210, 218, 219, 221, 226, 241, 248, 251, 254, 258, 260, 265, 273, 286, 288, 346, 366, 370, 387, 432
American Pipit 57, 140
American Prairie Reserve 403, 410
American Redpoll 310
American Redstart 35, 37, 51, 54, 62, 66, 88, 111, 135, 153, 212, 230, 238, 279, 461, 463
American Robin 170, 219, 227
American Three-toed Woodpecker 236, 476
American Tree Sparrow 232, 260, 279, 288, 356, 357
American White Pelican 133, 153, 163, 197, 214, 218, 230, 276, 279, 282, 288, 294, 316, 325, 329, 331, 338, 370, 421, 426, 427, 448, 467, 474, 475
American Wigeon 16, 23, 31, 83, 108, 130, 197, 205, 218, 230, 234, 245, 260, 264, 265, 277, 279, 282, 291, 333, 370, 415, 418, 451
Anaconda 199, 236, 240, 478
Anaconda Copper 233
Anaconda Copper Mule Ranch 238
Anaconda Settling Ponds 233–235
Anna's Hummingbird 472
antelope 138, 161, 164, 173, 257, 380, 416, 418, 428, 435, 442, 458
Arctic Tern 474
Argenta 250
Arlee 477
Arod Lakes 474
Arod Lakes IBA 119, 474
Arod Lakes Waterfowl Production Area 133–134
Arrow Stone Park 231–232
Ashland 343, 376, 378
Ashley Creek 23
Audubon Center 348–349
Audubon Christmas Bird Count 469
Audubon Society 3
Audubon Warbler 323
Augusta 199, 202, 204, 205
Aunt Molly Waterfowl Production Area 207
Avocet 23, 158, 333
Azure Cave 413

B

Babb 115
badger 20, 192, 257, 264, 266, 286, 376, 378, 382, 389, 398, 415, 447, 450
Bainville 468
Baird's Sandpiper 28, 234, 455
Baird's Sparrow 15, 135, 146, 152, 161, 210, 329, 400, 403, 410, 415, 419, 421, 434, 448, 455, 467, 476
Baker 383, 478
Baker's Hole Campground 292, 296–297
Bald Eagle 16, 19, 24, 26, 28, 30, 31, 32, 37, 39, 42, 43, 45, 58, 64, 66, 76, 77, 78, 81, 83, 84, 87, 108, 111, 135, 141, 142, 156, 161, 168, 170, 177, 179, 189, 197, 204, 206, 209, 210, 213, 214, 216, 218, 231, 241, 244, 247, 251, 254, 258, 260, 273, 274, 276, 277, 279, 282, 288, 294, 296, 298, 299, 314, 317, 319, 327, 335, 351, 356, 362, 366, 370, 374, 378, 391, 406, 421, 426, 428, 476
Baltimore Oriole 135, 141, 153, 159, 166, 335, 363, 416, 430, 432, 443, 445
Band-tailed Pigeon 114

Bank Swallow 37, 41, 135, 141, 230, 241, 247, 430, 438
Bannack State Park 256–257, 264
Barker Mines 188
Barn Owl 68, 363
Barn Swallow 32, 91, 141, 202, 204, 227, 230, 245, 251, 302, 316, 366
Barred Owl 111, 475
Barrow's Goldeneye 19, 189, 209, 231, 234, 260, 277, 291, 317, 476
Barry's Landing 370
Bass Creek Fishing Access Site 54–56
Bass Lake 54
bats 461, 463
Battle Ridge Campground 315
Bay-breasted Warbler 445
Bear Canyon Important Bird Area (IBA) 283, 340–342, 475
Bear Creek Trail 61
Bear Gulch Trail 80
Bear Paw Nature Trail 154
Bears Paw Battlefield 152
Bears Paw Mountains 155
Beartooth Mountains 283
Beartooth Wildlife Management Area 210–211, 477
Bear Trap Canyon 277, 279
beaver 254
Beaver Creek 213, 421, 425
Beaver Creek Park 119, 153–154, 155, 180
Beaver Creek Viewing Site 295
Beaver Creek Waterfowl Production Area 425
Beaverhead-Deerlodge National Forest 236, 238, 250, 261, 266, 283
Beaverhead Mountains 241, 261
Beaverhead National Forest 244, 257
Beaverhead River 199, 244, 248, 251, 254–255, 258
Beaverhead Rock 248, 254
Beaverhead Sage-steppe IBA 199, 256, 262–264, 473
beavers 16, 35, 71, 78, 81, 98, 109, 115, 154, 240, 246, 257, 264, 276, 293, 294, 295, 362, 376, 378, 382, 461, 463
Beckman Wildlife Management Area 159–160
Belgrade 291, 301, 478
Belt 185, 186, 187
Belted Kingfisher 16, 19, 32, 37, 71, 76, 80, 83, 97, 98, 100, 106, 189, 206, 230, 232, 238, 244, 256, 260, 274, 277, 296, 317, 335, 370, 373, 390, 391, 395, 429, 438
Bench Road 287

Benton Lake 138, 140, 151, 196
Benton Lake National Wildlife Refuge 119, 191–193, 474
Bewick's Wren 477
Big Belt Mountains 196
Bigfork 103, 104, 478
Big Hole Battlefield 74, 245–246
Big Hole River 199, 241–244
Bighorn Canyon 368
Bighorn Canyon National Recreation Area 368, 370–371
Bighorn River 283, 368, 370
bighorn sheep 16, 34, 76, 128, 161, 204, 236, 274, 276, 342, 407, 413
Big Lake 333
Big Lake Wildlife Management Area 333, 334
Big McNeil Slough 428
Big Mountain Ski Resort 113
Big Muddy Creek 447
Big Sky 478
Big Sky Island 350
Big Snowy Mountains 168
Big Timber 319, 323, 324, 325, 328, 478
Big Timber City Parks 323
Billings 283, 333, 340, 343, 346, 348, 350, 351, 353, 354, 355, 356, 357, 358, 360, 361, 362, 365, 372, 395, 403, 414, 477, 478, 481
Birch Creek 249–250
Birding Guides 472
birding manners 7
Birney 373, 376
bison 34, 297, 411, 419
Bitter Creek Wilderness Study Area 403, 419, 434–435
bitterns 20, 98, 333
Bitterroot Audubon 481
Bitterroot Birding and Nature Festival 471
Bitterroot Birding Trail 51
Bitterroot Range 63, 64
Bitterroot River 11, 47, 64, 66, 81, 84, 474
Bitterroot River Important Bird Area 58–60, 474
Bitterroot Valley 86, 246, 478
Bjornberg Bridge Fishing Access Site 430–431
Black-backed Woodpecker 47, 48, 236, 315, 474, 476
black bear 16, 20, 34, 61, 63, 69, 73, 91, 95, 102, 105, 111, 113, 115, 123, 126, 128, 182, 183, 185, 188, 204, 246, 270, 273, 293, 294, 297, 305, 342, 378
Black Bear Campground 80
Black-bellied Plover 110, 114, 234
Black-billed Cuckoo 476

Black-billed Magpie 149, 159, 175, 189, 202, 205, 210, 227, 230, 232, 234, 241, 249, 251, 258, 260, 264, 265

Black-capped Chickadee 16, 19, 32, 61, 69, 74, 75, 173, 204, 206, 219, 221, 224, 231, 232, 244, 260, 279, 293, 296, 317

Black-chinned Hummingbird 35, 39, 73, 109, 335

Black-crowned Night-heron 133, 216, 222, 241, 370, 426, 429, 451

Black Duck 448

Blackfeet Nation 122

Blackfoot-Clearwater Wildlife Management Area 95–96

black-footed ferret 407, 409, 411, 419

Blackfoot River 207

Blackfoot Valley 474

Blackfoot Valley Important Bird Area 199, 207–209, 279, 474

Black-headed Grosbeak 42, 49, 78, 94, 106, 111, 141, 212, 232, 244, 293, 307, 313, 465

Blackleaf Canyon 125

Blackleaf Wildlife Management Area 123–125, 126, 128

Black-necked Stilt 126, 127, 191, 333, 370, 421, 425, 451

Blackpoll 445

Black Rosy-finch 476

Black's Pond 376–377

black-spotted cutthroat trout 6

Black Swift 114, 476

Blacktail Deer Creek 265, 270

black-tailed prairie dogs 327, 329, 331, 333, 407, 435

black-tail jackrabbit 264

Blacktail Range 265

Blacktail Road 265–266

Blacktail Wildlife Management Area 267

Black Tern 20, 103, 104, 161, 207, 209, 416, 447, 476

Black Turnstone 114

Blanchard Lake 100

Blasdel Waterfowl Production Area 108

Blodgett Canyon 62

Blodgett Fire 474

Bluebill 20, 234

bluebirds 48, 166, 171, 244

Blue-gray Gnatcatcher 340

Blue-headed Vireo 453

Blue Jay 279, 360, 363, 387, 395, 465

Blue Mountain Nature Trail 47–48

Blue-winged Teal 16, 28, 83, 123, 140, 196, 230, 234, 245, 251, 256, 264, 265, 270, 291, 302, 370, 415, 426, 439

Blue-winged Warbler 477

bobcat 16, 20, 52, 113, 115, 266, 305, 376, 378, 382, 398, 407

Bob Marshall Wilderness 105, 125, 205

Bob Niebuhr Trail 171

Bobolink 15, 54, 87, 126, 158, 205, 207, 209, 212, 214, 219, 228, 230, 232, 461

Bohemian Waxwing 19, 41, 231, 232, 249, 250, 254, 264, 279, 305

Bonaparte's Gull 209, 234

Boreal Chickadee 16, 19

Boreal Owl 52, 74

Boulder Creek Trail 69

Boulder Forks FAS 319

Boulder River 319–322, 323

Bowdoin National Wildlife Refuge 147, 403, 415, 418, 425, 428, 429, 474, 477

Bowdoin National Wildlife Refuge (IBA) 421–423

Box Elder 155

Boyd 338

Boyes 380

Boy Scout Road 97

Bozeman 199, 283, 301, 302, 304, 305, 306, 307, 308, 309, 311, 312, 313, 314, 315, 471, 478, 481

Bozeman Creek 307

Bozeman Trail System 310

Brant 146

Brewer's Blackbird 26, 177, 204, 219, 234, 265, 282, 323, 370, 395, 426

Brewer's Sparrow 114, 135, 138, 146, 179, 199, 202, 207, 209, 212, 218, 256, 265, 273, 274, 290, 340, 434, 440, 448, 474, 476

Brewer's Sparrow (subspecies: Timberline) 114

Brewer's Vesper 240

Brewery Flats Fishing Access Site 166–167

Bridger 342, 478

Bridger Bowl Ski Area 314, 471

Bridger Creek 313

Bridger Mountains 315, 316

Bridger Raptor Festival 314, 471

Bridger Sage-steppe Important Bird Area 283, 473

Broad Ax Lodge 76–77

Broad-tailed Hummingbird 274, 275, 335

Broadus 380, 478

Broad-winged Hawk 314

brook trout 61

Brown-breasted Nuthatch 19, 64

Brown Creeper 19, 62, 64, 69, 86, 236, 296, 306, 353, 476

Brown-headed Cowbird 204, 265

Brown's Lake 207, 209

Brown Thrasher 149, 163, 189, 313, 340, 360, 363
brown trout 61
Brush Lake State Park 451
Buff-breasted Sandpiper 476
Bufflehead 64, 65, 230, 234, 260
Bull Lake 19
Bullock's Oriole 16, 39, 43, 66, 78, 81, 89, 91, 106,
    135, 141, 159, 163, 166, 189, 209, 219, 222,
    228, 230, 232, 244, 251, 264, 288, 290, 310,
    335, 346, 360, 393, 395, 396, 443, 445
bull snake 407
bull trout 37
buntings 248
Burma Road (Glen) 247–248
Burrowing Owl 135, 136, 146, 158, 195, 247, 325,
    327, 329, 380, 381, 382, 387, 397, 400, 403,
    406, 410, 419, 434, 440, 448, 458, 476
Busby 374
bushy-tailed woodrat 342
Butte 199, 233, 478
Butte Mining District 233
Buzzard Day 471
Bynum 123
Bynum Reservoir 123

C

Cackling Goose 477
California Gull 133, 145, 153, 197, 218, 443, 445,
    448
Calliope Hummingbird 19, 24, 26, 35, 39, 69, 73,
    80, 89, 91, 106, 111, 123, 126, 183, 187,
    202, 204, 224, 226, 307, 335, 340, 476
Camas Creek 63
Campanula Creek 292
Camp Baker 177
Camp Creek Campground 413–414
Camp Fortunate 260
Canada Goose 16, 28, 31, 39, 81, 83, 122, 130, 133,
    135, 146, 147, 194, 205, 218, 222, 230, 231,
    234, 251, 258, 260, 264, 276, 282, 291, 356,
    366, 370
Canada Jay 305
Canada Warbler 445
Canvasback 111, 112, 234, 271, 329, 333
Canyon Ferry Reservoir 227
Canyon Ferry Wildlife Management Area 474
Canyon Ferry Wildlife Management Area Import-
    ant Bird Area 199, 228–230
Canyon Wren 288, 340, 351, 370
Cape May Warbler 467

Cardinal 480
Carolina Wren 477
Cascade 196, 197
Caspian Tern 126, 218, 228, 230, 290, 443, 474, 476
Cassin's Finch 26, 53, 183, 271, 340, 476
Cassin's Vireo 24, 71, 87, 93, 111
catbirds 98, 166
Cattail Marsh Nature Trail 258
Cattail Marsh Self-Guided Interpretive Trail 254
Causeway (Lake Helena to Hauser Lake) 213
Cedar Waxwing 5, 19, 35, 41, 87, 106, 159, 219,
    222, 227, 230, 232, 251, 264, 302, 354, 355,
    357, 390
Centennial Grove Nature Trail 80
Centennial Mountains 273
Centennial Range 273
Centennial Valley 199, 265
Central Park Pond 291
Chain of Lakes 100
Chambers of Commerce 478–480
Charles M. Russell National Wildlife Refuge 165,
    397, 403, 411, 473
Charles M. Russell National Wildlife Refuge (IBA)
    406–409
Cherry River Fishing Access Site 302–303
Chester 140, 141
Chestnut-collared Longspur 145, 191, 338, 415,
    440, 447, 455, 473, 474, 476
Chestnut Mountain Trail 312
chickadees 323
Chief Cameahwait 260
Chief Joseph 244
Chief Joseph Pass Ski Trails 74–75
Chief Plenty Coups State Park 346–347
Chinook 119, 147, 152, 478
Chipping Sparrow 16, 87, 89, 135, 151, 194, 224,
    227, 302, 340, 355
Choteau 119, 122, 123, 125, 126, 127, 128, 130, 134
Choteau Loop 119, 126–127
Chris Boyd Trail 310
Church Slough 108
Cinnamon Teal 20, 83, 84, 100, 110, 140, 230, 245,
    251, 256, 264, 265, 270, 287, 296, 302, 425,
    426, 429
Circle 478
Clark Canyon Dam 254, 261
Clark Canyon Reservoir 258–260, 264
Clark Fork River 37–38, 41, 45–46, 47, 87, 199,
    232, 234, 474
Clark Fork River/Grass Valley Important Bird Area
    474

Clark's Grebe 153, 233
Clark's Nutcracker 32, 74, 114, 116, 173, 183, 185, 224, 232, 236, 240, 249, 250, 261, 292, 293, 295, 315, 340, 413
Clay-colored Sparrow 108, 126, 138, 146, 152, 158, 209, 210, 214, 222, 286, 288, 290, 308
Clearwater Crossing 209
Clearwater Junction 95
Clearwater Lake 100
Clearwater River 97, 98, 100
Clearwater River Canoe Trail 98
Cliff Swallow 32, 76, 89, 91, 128, 135, 141, 149, 195, 230, 234, 245, 248, 274, 351, 366, 370
Clover Divide 265
Clown Duck 114
Clyde Park 317
Cole Ponds 429
Colstrip 478
Columbia Falls 478
Columbian ground squirrel 20
Columbian Sharp-tailed Grouse 15, 476
Columbus 335, 338, 477, 478
Common Goldeneye 16, 19, 98, 189, 213, 230, 231, 234, 258, 260, 277, 282, 291, 295, 465
Common Grackle 323, 393, 394
Common Loon 19, 24, 28, 64, 97, 98, 100, 103, 104, 122, 189, 209, 213, 222, 276, 277, 279, 338, 358, 476
Common Merganser 37, 66, 78, 87, 230, 244, 245, 256, 258, 260, 276, 282, 335, 443
Common Nighthawk 140, 149, 163, 173, 175, 179, 204, 234, 264, 374
Common Poorwill 156, 210, 340
Common Raven 16, 128, 173, 175, 219, 227, 230, 232, 241, 249, 251, 258, 260, 264, 265, 311
Common Redpoll 305
Common Snipe 20, 49, 140
Common Tern 476
Common Yellowthroat 26, 35, 78, 83, 135, 152, 166, 204, 212, 232, 256, 264, 370
Common Yellowthroat Warbler 230, 240
Condon 102
Confederated Salish Tribe 28
Connecticut Warbler 451
Conner 478
Conrad 478
Cooney Reservoir State Park 338–339
Cooper's Hawk 89, 106, 109, 155, 221, 230, 306, 340, 387, 390, 428
coot 28, 205, 241
Cordilleran Flycatcher 45, 126, 210, 312, 315, 476

Corps of Discovery 162
Corvallis 78, 81, 477, 478
Costa's Hummingbird 78, 79, 477
cottontail rabbit 257, 264
Cottonwood Creek 95, 270
Cottonwood Reservoir 316
Council Grove State Park 43–44, 45
Cow Creek Burn Important Bird Area 62
Coyote Coulee Trail 63
coyotes 34, 81, 113, 154, 161, 192, 240, 246, 254, 257, 260, 264, 266, 270, 286, 297, 301, 305, 329, 331, 333, 342, 372, 374, 376, 378, 380, 382, 389, 398, 407, 411, 415, 416, 418, 419, 426, 432, 436, 439, 442, 447, 450, 458
Craig 210
Crazy Canyon 86
Crazy Creek Campground 71
Crazy Mountains 316, 328
creepers 48
Crested Caracara 477
Crow Agency 372, 373, 374
Crow Indian Reservation 368, 370
Crow Indians 329
Crow Indian Tribal Land 346
Crystal Lake 168–169
Culbertson 447, 448, 450, 453, 467, 478
Curve-billed Thrasher 477
Custer National Forest 283, 335, 342, 376, 382
Cut Bank 478
cutthroat trout 6

D

Dagmar 451
Dahl Lake 20
Dancing Prairie Preserve 15
Danny On Trail 113
Darby 63, 64, 66, 76, 478
Dark-eyed Junco 69, 72, 95, 173, 226, 232, 260
deer 34, 61, 63, 69, 71, 73, 173, 329, 331, 333, 342, 428
Deer Lodge 232, 233, 478
Dell 260, 262, 264
Denny Creek Road 299–300
Denton 119, 159
desert cottontail 342, 389, 398
Diamond Willow Fishing Access Site 465–466
Dillon 199, 246, 247, 249, 250, 251, 253, 254, 255, 256, 257, 258, 260, 261, 262, 264, 265, 266, 267, 270, 363, 478
dippers 25, 83, 166, 171, 249, 319
Divide 246

Dodson 415
Dodson Creek Unit 416
Dodson Dam Unit 416
Dornix Park 323
Double-crested Cormorant 64, 83, 133, 145, 197, 218, 228, 230, 276, 288, 448
Dowitcher 20
Downstream Recreation Area 445–446
Downy Woodpecker 19, 32, 135, 170, 183, 185, 210, 219, 221, 226, 230, 232, 249, 250, 251, 256, 279, 296, 305, 311, 340, 393, 436
Dry Creek Road 301
Dry Fork Creek 435
Dry Fork Road 186
Dry Wolf Creek 171
Duck Creek 292
Ducks Unlimited 376, 425
Dupuyer 122
Dupuyer Creek 122
Dusky Flycatcher 16, 123, 186, 210
Dusky Grouse 32, 87, 91, 93, 100, 111, 128, 173, 175, 187, 236, 240, 246, 250, 267, 293, 299, 413
Dyrdahl Waterfowl Production Area 418

E

eagles 30, 245
Eared Grebe 24, 103, 104, 130, 191, 209, 218, 230, 331, 338, 358, 370, 426, 447
Earl Guss Park 355
Ear Mountain Wildlife Management Area 126, 128–129
Earthquake Lake Boat Launch 276
Eastern Bluebird 461
Eastern Kingbird 76, 89, 149, 152, 166, 202, 219, 222, 226, 232, 238, 256, 264, 265, 288, 302, 338, 346, 374, 391, 432, 438
Eastern Kingfisher 135
Eastern Meadowlark 477
Eastern Screech Owl 378, 391, 410, 461, 463
Eastern Towhee 477
East Fork Bitterroot River 76
East Fork Lolo Creek 51
East Gallatin Recreation Area 304
East Gallatin River 302
East Glacier 114, 478
East Rosebud Creek 335
Ekalaka 382, 383, 478

elk 16, 20, 34, 52, 61, 63, 69, 71, 73, 84, 95, 115, 123, 126, 128, 140, 161, 173, 175, 182, 183, 185, 188, 204, 240, 246, 250, 257, 260, 264, 266, 270, 273, 274, 276, 292, 293, 294, 295, 297, 378, 398, 407, 411, 413, 442
Elk Island Fishing Access Site 461–462
Elk Lake 273
Ennis 277, 279, 477, 478
Ennis Lake 199, 277
Erskine Fishing Access Site 35–36, 45
Eurasian Collared-dove 212, 232, 248, 251, 264, 265, 317
Eureka 15, 478
Eureka Reservoir 126
European Starling 227, 232, 260
Evening Grosbeak 236

F

Fairfield 119, 130, 479
Fairview 467, 468
Faraasen Park Recreation Site 438
Ferruginous Hawk 15, 30, 126, 135, 136, 138, 142, 143, 146, 153, 156, 158, 159, 173, 177, 195, 202, 230, 241, 247, 262, 267, 279, 301, 316, 360, 395, 406, 419, 434, 458, 474, 476
finches 244, 312
Fir Ridge Cemetery 292
First Peoples Buffalo Jump State Park 195
fisher 16, 20, 52, 115
Fish Hatchery (Bozeman) 313
Fishtail Creek 335
Fish, Wildlife and Parks Regional Offices 481
Five Valleys Audubon 89, 481
Flammulated Owl 86, 476
Flathead Audubon 481
Flathead Audubon Society 112
Flathead Lake 11, 24, 26, 108
Flathead National Forest 11, 24, 112
Flathead River 106, 108
Flathead Tribal Lands 31
Flathead Tribal Wildlife Program 28
flicker 173
Flint Creek Range 236
Florence 54, 479
flycatchers 48, 51, 78, 221, 244, 245, 335, 362
Forster's Tern 145, 214, 218, 360, 370, 447, 476
Fort Benton 119, 156, 162, 479
Fort Buford National Historic Site 467–468
Fort Fizzle 51
Fort Peck 477
Fort Peck Assiniboine Reservation 447

Fort Peck Campground 445–446
Fort Peck Dam 443, 445
Fort Peck Dredge Cut Ponds 443–444
Fort Peck Indian Reservation 447
Fort Peck Lake 402
Fort Peck Reservoir 406, 407
Fort Smith 368, 370
Fort Union Trading Post 467–468
Four Corners 108
Four Dances Natural Area 353–354
fox 154, 279, 376
Fox Lake Wildlife Management Area 458–460
Fox Sparrow 52, 113, 308
fox squirrel 109, 362, 391
FR 989 294
Franklin's Grouse 249
Franklin's Gull 130, 191, 197, 214, 331, 360, 443, 445, 447, 448, 450, 474, 475, 476
Fred Robinson Bridge 163
Freezout Lake 3, 119, 474
Freezout Lake Wildlife Management Area 130–132
French Creek 249–250
Frenchman Creek 435
Frenchman River 419
Frenchtown 477
Fresno Reservoir Wildlife Management Area 143–145
Froid 403
Furnell Waterfowl Production Area 140

G

Gadwall 20, 23, 28, 197, 205, 218, 230, 234, 260, 282, 291, 370, 376, 415, 426
Gallagator Trail 310
Gallatin County Pheasants Forever Chapter 425
Gallatin National Forest 283, 293, 299, 305, 315, 328
Gallatin River 288
Gallatin Valley Land Trust 310
Gardiner 477, 479
geese 426
Geraldine 158
Ghost Village Road 294
Giant Springs State Park 189–190
Gibson Reservoir Dam 206
Girard Grove 97
Glaciated Prairie Sage-steppe 473
Glacier National Park 11, 114–117, 473
Glacier National Park (IBA) 114

Glasgow 403, 410, 434, 435, 438, 439, 440, 442, 443, 446, 479, 481
Glaucous Gull 443, 445
Glendive 343, 385, 386, 471, 479
Glen Lake 304
Golden-crowned Kinglet 16, 236, 271
Golden Eagle 57, 76, 114, 122, 123, 126, 136, 140, 142, 146, 154, 155, 158, 161, 164, 173, 175, 179, 183, 184, 194, 195, 202, 204, 205, 206, 221, 231, 236, 244, 247, 250, 254, 256, 258, 260, 261, 262, 264, 265, 267, 271, 273, 274, 276, 277, 287, 301, 314, 316, 317, 324, 328, 329, 346, 351, 370, 383, 385, 387, 397, 406, 410, 418, 419, 428, 467
goldeneye 205, 264
grackles 248
Granite Peak 4, 6
Grant (Beaverhead County) 261
Grant Kohrs Ranch 231–232
Grant Marsh Wildlife Management Area 366–367
Grasshopper Creek 256, 257
grasshopper sparrow 15, 32, 135, 145, 146, 158, 164, 195, 222, 400, 419, 434, 447, 476
Grasslands National Park (Canada) 419–420
Grass Range 164
Grass Valley 45
Grass Valley IBA 45–46
Gravelly Mountains 273
Gravelly Range 265, 274
Gray Catbird 35, 41, 43, 66, 97, 100, 106, 171, 189, 212, 222, 227, 230, 232, 256, 279, 288, 302, 304, 313, 355, 430, 432
Gray-cheeked Thrush 453
Gray-crowned Rosy Finch 57, 114, 333, 413
Gray Flycatcher 256
Gray Jay 32, 74, 182, 183, 185, 210, 224, 232, 240, 249, 250, 296, 315
Gray Partridge 133, 134, 138, 140, 141, 147, 149, 151, 154, 158, 159, 164, 170, 195, 196, 205, 231, 249, 258, 260, 267, 277, 333, 419, 420, 426
gray wolf 115, 246, 273, 293
Great Backyard Bird Count 470
Great Blue Heron 16, 22, 37, 39, 42, 66, 81, 83, 87, 97, 98, 100, 106, 109, 145, 166, 216, 222, 232, 241, 244, 251, 258, 264, 267, 282, 291, 298, 299, 370, 428, 439, 448
Great Egret 421, 423
Greater Sage Grouse 165, 256, 262, 340, 343, 403, 407, 410, 440, 473, 476
Greater Scaup 108

Greater White-fronted Goose 356
Greater Yellowlegs 192, 205, 234, 280, 333, 390, 416, 458
Great Falls 119, 156, 188, 189, 191, 195, 210, 403, 409, 477, 479, 481
Great Gray Owl 19, 35, 74, 80, 97, 103, 104, 111, 236, 238, 249, 250, 264, 306
Great Horned Owl 16, 19, 32, 41, 71, 76, 78, 100, 106, 111, 135, 136, 141, 146, 163, 191, 210, 219, 226, 230, 240, 250, 265, 279, 309, 324, 370, 387, 393, 395
Great-tailed Grackle 265
grebes 101, 122, 213, 316, 329, 333
Greenhorn Creek 221
Greenough Park 88
Green-tailed Towhee 78, 156, 163, 219, 222, 224, 226, 241, 244, 310, 313, 340, 406
Green-winged Teal 20, 24, 28, 83, 140, 196, 230, 231, 234, 245, 251, 256, 260, 264, 265, 270, 295, 302, 304, 426
Greycliff Prairie Dog Town State Park 325
Greycliff State Park 325
grizzly bears 6, 20, 95, 102, 105, 115, 123, 126, 128, 204, 273, 292, 294, 297, 298
Grizzly Gulch 226
ground squirrel 34, 246
gulls 122, 329
Gyrfalcon 301

H

Hailstone Basin 329
Hailstone National Wildlife Refuge 329–330, 331, 333, 334
Hairy Woodpecker 19, 32, 63, 69, 80, 135, 161, 163, 171, 183, 185, 210, 219, 221, 226, 232, 250, 251, 256, 305, 311, 360, 361, 393
Halfbreed National Wildlife Refuge 329, 333, 334, 474
Halfbreed National Wildlife Refuge (IBA) 331–332
Hamilton 58, 62, 63, 78, 80, 479
Hammond's Flycatcher 26, 41, 45, 69, 71, 80, 210, 312, 315, 476
Hannan Gulch 206
Hannon Memorial Fishing Access Site 66
Hardin 366, 368, 370, 479
Hardy 197
Harlan's Hawk 428
Harlequin Duck 16, 19, 114, 115, 476
Harlowton 168, 175, 479
Harper's Lake 100
Harrison Reservoir Important Bird Area 199, 280–282

Harris's Sparrow 260
Hartelius Waterfowl Production Area 194
Hauser Lake 213
Havre 119, 146, 149, 151, 153, 155, 479
hawks 30, 31, 245, 267, 428
Haymaker Wildlife Management Area 175–176
Hebgen Lake 276, 292, 293, 294, 295, 297, 298, 299, 473
Hebgen Lake Road 299–300
Helena 199, 210, 212, 213, 214, 216, 218, 219, 221, 222, 224, 226, 227, 479
  Floweree Drive 219
  McHugh Drive 219
  Sierra Road 219
Helena Valley 214
Helena Valley Regulating Reservoir 218
Hell Creek 406
Hellgate Canyon 87
Henry's Lake, Idaho 266, 271, 273
Hermit Thrush 86, 113, 182, 224, 236, 238, 293
Hewitt Lake 428, 429
Hewitt Lake NWR 428
Hieronymous Park (Hamilton) 78–79
Highland Ridge Trail 310
Highwood Mountains 158
Hi-Line 119
Hinsdale 403, 432, 434, 436
Hinsdale Wildlife Management Area 432–433
hoary marmot 61, 62, 69
Hobson 170, 173
Holland Lake 100
Holm Waterfowl Production Area 147–148
Holter Lake 210
Home Gulch 206
Homestead Lake 448
Hooded Merganser 37, 45, 83, 109, 228, 230, 260, 299, 300, 368, 476
Horned Grebe 103, 104, 230, 358, 368, 476
Horned Lark 15, 87, 140, 164, 222, 231, 232, 260, 264, 301, 313, 338, 372, 374
Horse Prairie Creek 258
Hot Springs 477, 479
House Finch 232, 251, 348, 349, 356
House Sparrow 260, 445
House Wren 219, 230, 351, 358, 370
Howrey Island 343
Howrey Island Recreation Area 362
huckleberries 25
Hughesville Road 186
hummingbirds 312
Huson 45
Hyalite Canyon 305
Hysham 343, 362, 363

I

Iceland Gull 477
Idaho Falls 199
Important Bird Areas (IBAs) 340, 473–475
Inca Dove 477
Indian pictographs 288
Indian Trees Campground 73, 74
Indigo Bunting 391
Inez Lake 100
International Migratory Bird Day 471
Isaac Homestead Wildlife Management Area
    363–365
Isaac Homestead WMA 343
Itch-Kep-Pe Park 335

J

jackrabbits 257
Jackson 241, 244
James P. Sunderland Park 227
Jarina Waterfowl Production Area 122
jays 48
Jefferson River 199, 282, 288, 290
Jones Creek 400
Jordan 477, 479
Judith River Wildlife Management Area 173–174
Jumping Creek 182
juncos 64

K

Kalispell 11, 106, 108, 109, 110, 479, 481
kangaroo rat 342
Kelly Island 37, 45
Kelly Island Fishing Access Site 39–40
Kevin Rim 474
Kevin Rim Important Bird Area 119, 136–137
Killdeer 2, 20, 23, 66, 89, 146, 149, 170, 173, 196,
    234, 270, 271, 325, 370, 439
Kim Williams Trail 87
kingbirds 209, 241
kingfishers 83, 166
kinglets 54, 244
Kingsbury Lake Waterfowl Production Area 158
Kings Hill Pass 183–184
Kipp Recreation Area 163
Kirk Hill 306
kit fox 411
Kleinschmidt Lake 207
Knowlton Reservoir 123
Kootenai Falls WMA 16–18

Kootenai National Forest 11
Kootenai River 4, 6, 11, 16
Kootenai Tribe 28
Korsbeck Waterfowl Production Area 415

L

Lake Como National Recreation Trail 64–65
Lake Elmo State Park 358–359
Lake Elwell 141
Lake Helena 213, 214, 474
Lake Helena Drive 216–217
Lake Helena Important Bird Area 474
Lake Helena Wildlife Management Area 214–215
Lake MacDonald 114
Lake Mary Ronan State Park 24–25
Lake Mason National Wildlife Refuge 400–401
Lakeside 479
Lambert 458
Lame Deer 373
Lapland Longspur 110, 232, 301
Larb Hills 442
largemouth bass 28
Lark Bunting 15, 138, 146, 333, 351, 370, 434, 447,
    476
Lark Sparrow 138, 146, 149, 158, 210, 222, 323,
    338, 340, 372, 465
Last Chance Audubon 481
Last Chance Audubon Society 213, 216, 217, 218,
    219, 221, 222, 223
Laurel 479
Lavold Reservoir 324
Lawrence Park 109
Lazuli Bunting 15, 32, 45, 49, 87, 88, 89, 106, 109,
    126, 153, 171, 172, 202, 204, 205, 210, 212,
    224, 228, 230, 240, 279, 292, 313, 340, 351,
    360, 370, 378, 390, 395, 406, 476
least chipmunk 342
Least Flycatcher 35, 135, 149, 197, 209, 221, 230,
    232, 256, 279, 288, 319, 429, 436, 438
Least Sandpiper 28, 234
Least Tern 467, 476
Le Conte's Sparrow 161, 447, 448, 455
Ledford Creek 270
Lee Metcalf National Wildlife Refuge 83–85, 471,
    477
Lemhi Pass 261
Lesser Black-backed Gull 477
Lesser Scaup 20, 218, 230, 234, 271, 331, 368, 370
Lesser Yellowlegs 192, 205, 233, 234, 333, 390
Lewis and Clark 156, 189, 260, 360, 365, 407, 410

Lewis and Clark National Forest 180, 182, 183, 185, 186, 283
Lewis's Woodpecker 32, 35, 39, 45, 54, 58, 60, 62, 64, 69, 71, 84, 86, 88, 102, 117, 185, 206, 210, 244, 311, 474, 476
Lewistown 119, 161, 162, 163, 164, 166, 168, 406, 409, 410, 412, 414, 479
Libby 16, 479
Lima 264, 266, 273
Lima Reservoir 264, 266
Limestone Creek 308
Lincoln 479
Lincoln's Sparrow 95, 236, 298, 315
Lindbergh Lake 100
Lindley Park 309
Little Beaver Creek 473
Little Beaver Creek Important Bird Area 403, 440–442
Little Bighorn National Monument 372
Little Bitterroot Lake 22
Little Prickly Pear Creek 212
Little Rock Creek 64
Little Rockies 413–414
Livingston 316, 317, 479
Livingston County Parks 317–318
Logan 290
Logan Creek 111
Logan Pass 114
Loggerhead Shrike 113, 135, 145, 146, 256, 340, 358, 360, 363, 406, 418, 434, 458, 476
Lolo 49, 58
Lolo Creek 49
Lolo Creek Campground 51
Lolo National Forest 11, 97, 99, 101
Lolo Pass 52–53
Loma 156
Lonesome Lake 474
Long-billed Curlew 15, 16, 18, 110, 123, 126, 130, 140, 146, 147, 153, 158, 161, 168, 192, 194, 195, 202, 207, 209, 212, 214, 218, 232, 234, 245, 249, 251, 265, 267, 271, 280, 288, 291, 292, 331, 382, 400, 401, 410, 419, 421, 434, 440, 447, 448, 476
Long-billed Dowitcher 110, 192, 233, 234
Long-eared Owl 32, 34, 163, 241, 306, 387
Long-tailed Duck 114, 233, 279, 368
Loon and Fish Festival 471
loons 101, 103, 111, 199
Loring 418
Lost Creek State Park 236–237
Lost Trail National Wildlife Refuge 20
Lost Trail Pass 246

Lovell, Wyoming 370
Lower Glaston Lake 324
Lower Skelly Gulch 221
Lower Valley Road 108
lynx 20, 115

M

MacDonald Creek 114
MacGillivray's Warbler 19, 35, 58, 73, 91, 111, 113, 183, 185, 186, 210, 307, 313, 315, 340, 355, 395
Maclay Flat Nature Trail 42
Madison River 274, 277, 279, 288, 294, 296
Madison Valley 474
Madison Valley Important Bird Area 199, 277–279, 474
Makoshika State Park 343, 385–386, 471
Mallard 16, 23, 28, 29, 35, 66, 140, 146, 149, 152, 173, 194, 196, 204, 205, 216, 218, 222, 230, 231, 234, 244, 245, 251, 256, 258, 260, 264, 265, 270, 277, 282, 291, 302, 366, 370, 376, 415, 418, 426, 439, 451
Malta 403, 409, 410, 412, 414, 415, 416, 417, 418, 419, 420, 421, 422, 425, 426, 428, 429, 432, 479
Manhattan 479
Manning Lake 447, 475
Manning Lake Wetland Complex 475
Manning Lake Wetland Complex Important Bird Area 403, 447
Manx Shearwater 477
Many Glacier 114
Marbled Godwit 126, 130, 143, 146, 158, 192, 196, 260, 271, 419, 447, 458, 476
Marias River 141, 156
Marias River State Park 135
Marias River Wildlife Management Area 135
Marion 20
Marsh Wren 49, 81, 83, 101, 108, 216, 222, 227, 230, 234, 251, 256, 258, 260, 271, 302, 376
marten 240
Martinsdale 175
Matador Ranch 266
Matthews Recreation Area 390
May Creek Campground 74
McCown's Longspur 15, 138, 143, 146, 194, 210, 256, 415, 434, 440, 476
McLeod 319
McNab Pond 382
McNeil Slough Waterfowl Production Area 428
meadowlarks 89, 149, 195

Medicine Lake 451
Medicine Lake National Wildlife Refuge 403, 455, 457, 475
Medicine Lake National Wildlife Refuge Important Bird Area 448–450
Medicine Rocks State Park 383–384
Melrose 244
Melville 328
Memorial Creek 185
Memorial Falls 185
merganser 248
Merlin 89, 126, 128, 142, 218
Merritt Lane 216–217
Mexico 453
Middle Lake 133
Miles City 343, 362, 383, 390, 391, 393, 394, 479, 481
Miles City Parks 393–394
Milk River 119, 143, 421, 428, 429, 430, 436, 438
Milk River Wildlife Management Area 416–417, 429
Mill Canyon 62
Mill Creek 234
mink 16, 78, 109, 154, 192, 240, 246, 254, 378, 391, 447, 450, 463
Mission Creek 317
Mission Mountain Audubon 481
Mission Mountain Range 104
Mission Mountains 100
Mission Mountains Wilderness 105
Mission Valley 28, 30, 31
Mississippi Kite 477
Missoula 11, 37, 39, 41, 42, 43, 45, 47, 75, 81, 86, 87, 88, 89, 91, 93, 477, 479, 481
Missouri Headwaters State Park 474
Missouri Headwaters State Park Important Bird Area 288–290
Missouri River 156, 161, 162, 163, 189, 197, 199, 213, 228, 288, 397, 398, 406, 407, 409, 412, 443, 445, 467
Missouri River Breaks 163
Molt/Big Lake Complex 333–334
Monida 199, 266, 271, 273
Montana Audubon 1, 136, 197, 279, 348, 469, 471, 475
Montana Audubon Annual Bird Festival 440
Montana Audubon Society 107, 214, 264, 279
Montana Bird Festivals 471
Montana Bird List 482–499
Montana Bird Species of Conservation Concern 476
Montana Central Railroad 188
Montana City 227

Montana Natural History Center 471
Montana Outdoor Birding 471
Monture Creek 95
moose 16, 20, 52, 69, 71, 78, 81, 84, 115, 140, 240, 246, 257, 260, 264, 266, 270, 273, 276, 292, 293, 294, 295, 297, 298, 305
Mountain Bluebird 15, 19, 32, 39, 42, 43, 47, 54, 62, 64, 71, 76, 89, 91, 126, 128, 134, 135, 140, 141, 147, 149, 153, 159, 161, 163, 164, 168, 171, 173, 177, 179, 202, 204, 205, 206, 210, 216, 221, 224, 226, 227, 230, 238, 249, 251, 256, 258, 264, 265, 267, 274, 286, 287, 292, 301, 306, 308, 310, 311, 313, 324, 328, 351, 370, 387, 395
Mountain Chickadee 30, 32, 61, 74, 95, 171, 177, 186, 187, 224, 231, 232, 260, 279, 293, 296, 305, 313, 315, 317, 413
mountain cottontail 378
mountain goats 34, 91, 115, 236, 274, 276, 293, 295
mountain lion 16, 91, 113, 266, 407, 413
Mountain Plover 15, 161, 164, 204, 400, 403, 406, 410, 419, 434, 440, 473, 476
Mount Ellis 308, 311
Mount Haggin Wildlife Management Area 238–240
Mount Helena City Park 224–225
Mount Jumbo 93–94
Mount Sentinel 87
Mourning Dove 32, 134, 135, 149, 173, 230, 234, 248, 251, 264, 265, 317, 325, 366, 372, 374, 391, 436
Mourning Warbler 445
"M" Trail (Bozeman) 313
mule 415
mule deer 16, 20, 52, 95, 115, 123, 126, 128, 134, 138, 140, 154, 161, 164, 175, 182, 183, 185, 188, 192, 204, 240, 246, 250, 257, 260, 264, 266, 270, 273, 274, 276, 286, 293, 294, 295, 301, 305, 342, 374, 376, 378, 380, 382, 389, 391, 398, 407, 411, 413, 418, 419, 435, 439, 442, 458
muskrat 254
muskrats 16, 20, 23, 37, 78, 81, 84, 192, 246, 257, 391, 447, 450
Musselshell River 283, 395, 397, 398
Musselshell Sage-steppe Important Bird Area 343, 397–399, 473
Mystic Island Park 350

N

Nashville Warbler 87
National Audubon Society 473

National Bison Range Important Bird Area 32–34
National Bison Range National Wildlife Refuge 474
Nature Conservancy 1, 15, 26, 103
Neihart 185
Nelson Reservoir 416, 426–427, 428, 429
Nelson's Sharp-tailed Sparrow 448
Nelson's Sparrow 447, 455
Newlan Creek Reservoir Fishing Access Site 179–181
Nez Perce Historic Trail 162
Nez Perce National Historic Park 152
Nilan Lake 205
Ninepipe National Wildlife Refuge 474, 477
Ninepipe National Wildlife Refuge Important Bird Area 31
Ninepipe Reservoir 31
Norm Shoenthal Island 356
Norris 279
North Chinook Reservoir 147
Northern Cheyenne Indian Reservation 373, 378
Northern Flicker 61, 163, 204, 230, 232, 234, 250, 251, 258, 260, 261, 286, 348, 357, 391
Northern Goshawk 54, 61, 74, 86, 101, 103, 104, 161, 179, 232, 236, 249, 250, 265, 292, 299, 306, 360, 395, 476
Northern Harrier 54, 58, 84, 100, 135, 136, 138, 140, 142, 143, 149, 151, 152, 164, 168, 173, 175, 194, 195, 196, 202, 204, 205, 209, 210, 212, 214, 216, 218, 219, 221, 230, 231, 234, 240, 241, 249, 251, 258, 260, 265, 267, 273, 277, 286, 287, 288, 292, 293, 299, 301, 308, 311, 313, 324, 325, 329, 451, 458
Northern Oriole 32, 153, 370, 461, 463
Northern Pintail 23, 28, 83, 108, 130, 197, 230, 234, 271, 277, 333, 368, 415, 418
Northern Pygmy Owl 42, 186, 210, 226, 236, 238, 240, 279
Northern Rough-winged Swallow 32, 106, 135, 141, 234, 302, 432, 438
Northern Saw-whet Owl 24, 32, 111
Northern Shoveler 31, 130, 143, 197, 216, 217, 218, 234, 370, 415, 418, 439
Northern Shrike 44, 232, 260, 368
Northern Waterthrush 35, 39, 111, 227, 232, 238, 298, 304, 313, 443
North Fork Blackfoot River 209
North Shore Flathead Lake Important Bird Area 474
North Valley Grasslands 473
Norwegian Gulch 206
nuthatches 48, 159, 306, 309

O

Odell Creek 271
Oldsquaw 368
Old Town Road 286
Olive-sided Flycatcher 62, 64, 210, 238, 271, 293, 473, 474, 476
Opheim 419, 420, 435
Orange-crowned Warbler 41, 42, 58, 66, 81, 111, 113, 135, 221, 226, 307, 313, 395
Orchard Oriole 393, 445
orioles 48
Orofino Gulch 226
Osprey 19, 24, 26, 31, 37, 39, 41, 42, 43, 64, 66, 76, 78, 81, 83, 87, 106, 109, 111, 135, 149, 156, 168, 169, 170, 197, 206, 209, 210, 218, 230, 232, 234, 241, 244, 251, 254, 258, 273, 274, 276, 277, 288, 294, 296, 298, 299, 314, 318, 319, 323, 327, 335, 356, 390, 426
otter 16, 78, 81, 109, 115, 240, 246, 294, 378
Otter Creek Road 324
Our Lake 126
Ovando 199, 207, 209
Ovenbird 106, 355, 378, 443, 445, 461, 465
Owen Sowerine Natural Area 474
Owen Sowerwine Natural Area Important Bird Area 106–107
owls 25, 31, 245, 305, 428

P

Pablo National Wildlife Refuge 474
Pablo National Wildlife Refuge Important Bird Area 28–29
Pablo Reservoir 28
Pacific Wren 16, 26, 45, 49, 54, 61, 69, 71, 86, 166, 204, 476, 477
Packer Meadows 52
Pah-Nah-To Recreation Park 155
Painted Hills Trail 310
painted turtle 35, 37, 83, 98, 461
Paradise 479
Paradise Valley 283
Pattee Canyon National Recreation Area 86
Paulo Reservoir 439
Pearce Waterfowl Production Area 422
Pectoral Sandpiper 110, 234, 331
Pelican Fishing Access Site 325–327, 328
Pelican Point Fishing Access Site 197
pelicans 327
Peregrine Falcon 45, 57, 61, 62, 136, 161, 199, 265, 270, 271, 273, 288, 294, 329, 351, 353, 360, 370, 421, 428, 474, 476

phalaropes 23, 329
Pheasants Forever 425
Philadelphia Vireo 451, 453
Philipsburg 479
Pictograph Cave State Park 351–352
Pied-billed Grebe 24, 103, 104, 233, 331, 370, 416, 426
pika 57, 61, 62, 69
Pileated Woodpecker 16, 19, 24, 25, 26, 39, 42, 45, 47, 51, 54, 58, 64, 69, 71, 73, 80, 83, 84, 86, 88, 106, 109, 210, 226, 236, 476
Pine Butte Swamp Preserve 126
Pine Grosbeak 61, 63, 155, 183, 236, 296
pine marten 20, 52, 115, 246
Pine Siskin 236, 261, 323, 333, 348
Pintler Audubon 481
Pinyon Jay 219, 222, 333, 340, 353, 397, 413, 476
Piping Plover 403, 425, 448, 455, 467, 468, 473, 476
Pirogue Island State Park 391–392
Pishkun Reservoir 128
Placid Lake 100
Plains 479
Plentywood 453, 455, 479
Plum Creek Timberlands 20
Poindexter Slough Fishing Access Site 251–253
Polaris 257
Polebridge 114
Polson 26, 28, 34, 479, 481
Pompey's Pillar National Monument 360–361
Pond Trail 310
poorwill 397
porcupine 81, 192, 266, 389, 398, 426, 432, 436, 447, 450
Porphyry Peak Lookout 183–184
Powder Carter Sage-steppe Important Bird Area 343, 380–381, 473
prairie dogs 161, 164, 327, 372, 376, 382, 398, 411, 419
Prairie Falcon 26, 76, 87, 93, 126, 128, 136, 138, 141, 143, 146, 158, 161, 209, 232, 247, 248, 256, 265, 271, 274, 288, 301, 324, 351, 370, 385, 387
prairie rattlesnake 34, 161, 264, 286, 407, 442
Prickly Pear Creek 210, 219, 227
pronghorn 34, 140, 164, 192, 246, 260, 266, 270, 273, 286, 301, 329, 331, 333, 372, 376, 382, 389, 398, 407, 411, 415, 426, 432, 436, 439
Pryor 346
Pryor Mountains 340, 354
ptarmigan 114
Pygmy Nuthatch 32, 42, 43, 61, 81

Pygmy Owl 19
pygmy rabbit 257, 264
Pyrrhuloxia 477

Q

Quake Lake 274, 276, 294

R

raccoons 254, 363, 391, 458, 461, 463
rainbow trout 61
Rainy Lake 100
Rapelje 329, 331
Rare (Vagrant) Bird Records 477
rattlesnake 410
Rattlesnake Creek 92, 250
Rattlesnake National Recreation Area 91–92
rattlesnakes 91, 164, 195, 248, 257, 327, 329, 331, 354, 372, 411, 435
Raynold's Pass Bridge 274–275
Red-breasted Merganser 122, 279
Red-breasted Nuthatch 26, 32, 61, 74, 81, 141, 173, 177, 224, 231, 232, 240, 296, 306, 357
Red Crossbill 54, 61, 62, 74, 155, 236, 271
Red-eyed Vireo 19, 45, 58, 62, 84, 106, 163, 210, 378, 465, 476
red fox 23, 81, 254, 266, 342, 362, 374, 378, 382, 416, 447, 450, 458
Redhead 20, 28, 31, 107, 108, 145, 216, 218, 230, 234, 271, 277, 279, 329, 331, 333, 368, 426
Red-headed Woodpecker 358, 362, 378, 393, 476
Red Lodge 335, 477, 479
Red-naped Sapsucker 16, 19, 20, 32, 45, 47, 58, 63, 64, 71, 81, 84, 86, 91, 102, 106, 109, 128, 183, 185, 186, 187, 204, 206, 209, 210, 230, 232, 244, 265, 277, 279, 288, 293, 299, 305, 308, 476
Red-necked Grebe 24, 28, 31, 97, 103, 104, 126, 209, 218, 330, 429
Red-necked Phalarope 233, 234, 241
Red Phalarope 279
Redpoll 374
Red Rock Lake 273
Red Rock Lakes National Wildlife Refuge 198, 199, 264, 266, 267, 271–273, 474
Red Rock River 199, 258, 265
Red-shafted Flicker 41, 66, 69, 88
red squirrel 342
Redstart 378

Red-tailed Hawk 30, 32, 41, 43, 89, 93, 100, 106, 123, 136, 157, 164, 173, 175, 177, 179, 204, 209, 210, 219, 230, 236, 241, 244, 260, 265, 273, 288, 293, 299, 372, 378, 387, 434

Red-throated Loon 64, 114

Red-winged Blackbird 16, 26, 42, 83, 87, 140, 152, 204, 216, 222, 227, 230, 232, 234, 241, 251, 264, 265, 282, 302, 328, 370, 395, 426, 463, 464

Richardson's ground squirrel 266

Ring-billed Gull 110, 133, 218, 228, 230, 234, 443, 448

Ring-necked Duck 37, 218, 234, 260, 276, 295, 368

Ring-necked Pheasant 31, 83, 133, 141, 147, 149, 151, 152, 156, 159, 163, 164, 170, 171, 247, 248, 277, 301, 325, 363, 366, 368, 416, 421, 425, 426, 428, 429, 432, 440, 458, 461

river otter 78, 84, 109, 115, 246, 254

River Park (Hamilton) 78–79

Robb-Ledford Wildlife Management Area 267

Robin 149

Rock Creek 64

Rock Dove 152

Rock Pigeon 232, 251, 260, 353

Rockvale 342

Rock Wren 57, 87, 93, 155, 158, 195, 226, 288, 340, 351, 353, 383, 385

Rocky Boy Indian Reservation 155

Roe River 189

Ronan 30, 31, 34, 479

Ronan Creek 25

Ronan Hawk Roost 474

Ronan Hawk Roost Important Bird Area 30

Rookery Wildlife Management Area 149–150

Rosebud Battlefield State Park 373, 374

Rosebud Creek 335

Ross Cedar Grove 19

Ross Creek Falls 19

Ross's Goose 110, 130, 133, 192, 209, 474

Ross's Gull 477

Rosy Finch 114

Rough-legged Hawk 28, 30, 32, 123, 202, 231, 247, 260, 279, 288, 301, 314, 317, 368, 370, 434, 474

Rough-winged Swallow 37, 370

Round Lake 133, 455

Roundup 343, 395, 397, 400, 477, 479

Roundup River-Walk Heritage Trail 395–396

Ruby-crowned Kinglet 19, 24, 54, 61, 63, 64, 87, 226, 236, 271, 296, 312, 324, 353

Ruby River 199, 270

Ruddy Duck 28, 31, 122, 130, 145, 207, 234, 271, 280, 368, 426

Ruffed Grouse 19, 20, 26, 73, 76, 92, 98, 100, 101, 102, 103, 104, 106, 177, 183, 186, 238, 240, 293, 476

Rufous Hummingbird 19, 26, 35, 39, 69, 73, 80, 91, 111, 123, 126, 183, 224, 226, 251, 253, 292, 307, 335

Rusty Blackbird 476

S

Sacagawea 260

Sacagawea Park 317

Sacajawea Audubon 481

Saco 430, 479

Safe Harbor Marsh 473, 474

Safe Harbor Marsh Important Bird Area 26–27

Sage Creek 146

Sage Grouse 143, 161, 164, 256, 264, 265, 267, 271, 273, 324, 343, 380, 382, 383, 387, 397, 398, 400, 406, 413, 415, 416, 434

Sage Sparrow 265, 270

Sage Thrasher 212, 256, 267, 273, 286, 287, 290, 340, 397

Sally Tollefson Memorial Trail 103

Salmon-Challis National Forest 261

Salmon Lake 100

Sam Billings Memorial Campnground 69

Sanderling 455

Sandhill Crane i, 20, 23, 43, 98, 110, 123, 126, 143, 151, 159, 168, 173, 179, 182, 194, 196, 209, 210, 216, 218, 230, 232, 234, 240, 244, 245, 251, 264, 265, 267, 271, 279, 282, 287, 288, 290, 291, 292, 295, 323, 325, 331, 370, 410, 412, 428, 448, 458

sandpipers 20, 39, 260

Sands Lake 151

Sands Waterfowl Production Area 151

Sanford Bluebird Trail 119

sapsuckers 48

Savannah Sparrow 15, 43, 81, 87, 108, 140, 143, 152, 173, 175, 194, 218, 219, 232, 234, 240, 251, 265, 288, 292, 301, 302, 308, 311, 324, 328

Say's Phoebe 141, 195, 324, 373

Scarlet Tanager 391, 451, 453, 454

Schrammeck Lake Waterfowl Production Area 196

Scobey 479

Scratchgravel Hills 222–223

Sedge Wren 455

Seeley Lake 97, 98, 100, 471, 479

Seeley-Swan 11

Selway-Bitterroot Wilderness 54

Semipalmated Plover 28, 83, 234
Semipalmated Sandpiper 28, 332, 455
Seth Diamond Nature Trail 97
Seven Sisters Fishing Access Site 463–464
Shambo Pond 271
Sharp-shinned Hawk 230, 231, 312, 324
Sharp-tailed Grouse 123, 126, 135, 138, 140, 141, 143, 145, 147, 148, 151, 154, 155, 156, 158, 159, 161, 164, 171, 191, 192, 195, 329, 333, 363, 366, 373, 380, 382, 383, 387, 406, 410, 416, 421, 425, 426, 428, 451, 458
Sharp-tailed Sandpiper 477
Sharp-tailed Sparrow 447, 455
Sheep Creek 122
Sheep Mountain 274
Shelby 119, 135, 136, 479
Sheridan 270
Short-eared Owl 30, 58, 84, 108, 135, 140, 146, 151, 158, 194, 195, 273, 287, 329, 333, 448
Showdown Ski Area 183
shrikes 360
Siberian Accentor 477
Sidney 458, 461, 463, 464, 465, 479
Silver City 212
Sioux Indian Reservation 447
Sitting Bull 467
Skalkaho Pass 80
Skelly Gulch 221
skunks 23, 81, 84, 447, 450
Sleeping Buffalo 416, 426, 428
Sleeping Buffalo Unit 416
Sluice Boxes State Park 187–188
Smith Lake Waterfowl Production Area 23
Smith River Wildlife Management Area 177–178
Snipe 98, 123, 170, 241
Snow Bunting 108, 110, 140, 232, 240, 245, 301
Snowcrest Mountain 267
Snow Goose 110, 130, 131, 133, 191, 209, 356
snowshoe hare 63, 98
Snowy Owl 28, 30, 31, 110, 141, 262, 264, 395, 428
Solitary Sandpiper 234, 288
Solitary Vireo 95
Somers 477
Song Sparrow 16, 26, 31, 43, 78, 83, 101, 123, 135, 151, 152, 170, 219, 222, 232, 240, 251, 260, 279, 288, 302, 304, 308, 325, 368, 369, 370
Sora 31, 42, 81, 123, 125, 134, 153, 209, 216, 222, 232, 241, 244, 245, 264, 271, 295, 296, 299, 426, 458
Sora Rail 101
Sourdough Nature Trail 307
South Fork Madison River 298
Spalding's Catchfly 15

Sparrow Pond 271
sparrows 78, 168, 230, 244, 248, 250, 265, 312
Spotted Sandpiper 37, 66, 78, 135, 145, 149, 170, 179, 196, 218, 232, 234, 271, 274, 280, 288, 370
Spotted Towhee 43, 87, 89, 93, 141, 156, 224, 226, 313, 362, 376, 406, 432
Sprague's Pipit 15, 135, 140, 146, 152, 158, 194, 202, 204, 210, 277, 403, 410, 416, 419, 421, 434, 447, 455, 467, 473, 476
Springhill-Dry Creek Loop 301
Springhill Road 301
Spring Meadow State Park 222–223
Spruce Grouse 20, 70, 91, 238, 240, 249, 250, 470
Stanford 171
Stanford Bluebird Trail 171–172
starlings 149, 264
Steller's Jay 16, 19, 32, 52, 57, 74, 91, 101, 113, 182, 183, 185, 224, 236, 240, 249, 250, 296, 306, 315, 387
Stevensville 54, 57, 83
Stevensville River Trail 84
Stillwater River 106, 335–337
Stilt Sandpiper 28, 110, 234, 455
St. Mary 114
St. Mary's Peak 57
Story Mill Spur Trail 310
St. Paul, Minnesota 323
striped skunk 78, 363, 416
Sula 71, 73, 74, 76
Summit Lake 100
Sunburst 138
Sun River Backcountry Loop 205–206
Sun River Wildlife Management Area 202–204, 206
Superior 479
Surf Scoter 279
Swainson's Hawk 15, 45, 54, 100, 136, 138, 140, 142, 146, 153, 156, 158, 159, 182, 195, 197, 219, 221, 230, 241, 247, 262, 265, 267, 273, 292, 301, 314, 324, 439
Swainson's Thrush 111, 123, 155, 189, 238, 317, 376
swallows 106, 212, 244, 248, 258
Swan Lake 104
Swan Mountain Range 104
Swan River 103
Swan River National Wildlife Refuge 104–105
Swan River Oxbow Preserve 103
Swan River State Forest 102
swans 426
Sweet Grass Creek 328
Sweet Grass Creek Loop 328

Sweet Grass Hills 118, 119, 138, 140, 142, 265
Swift Dam 122
swift fox 378, 398, 415, 435
Swift Reservoir 122

T

Tally Lake 111–112
Tally Lake Warbler Weekend 111
teal 149, 159, 194, 205, 216, 251, 254, 258, 271, 282, 292
Teller Wildlife Refuge 81–82
Tennessee Warbler 111, 445
Terry 343, 389, 477, 479
Terry Badlands 343
Terry Badlands Wilderness Study Area 387–388
Teton River 126
Thayer's Gull 443, 445
Thief Creek 249–250
thirteen-lined ground squirrel 458
Thompson Falls 19, 479
Three Forks 279, 280, 282, 286, 287, 288, 479
Three Forks Area 288–290
Three Forks Ponds 290
Three-toed Woodpecker 47, 62, 114, 126, 161
thrushes 52, 113, 126, 312
Tiber Dam 141
Tobacco Plains 15
Tongue River 475
Tongue River Birding Route 373
Tongue River Important Bird Area 343, 378–379, 475
Tongue River Reservoir State Park 374–375
Tongue River Road 373
Toole County Waterfowl Production Areas 138–139
Tower Street Park 41
Townsend 199, 216, 227, 230, 479
Townsend's Solitaire 62, 113, 210, 222, 231, 232, 238, 250, 260, 313, 317, 348, 357
Townsend's Warbler 19, 51, 52, 63, 71, 81, 91, 106, 111, 113, 238, 261
Trail Creek Road 312
Trapper Peak 69
Traveler's Rest State Park 49–50
Tredson Reservoir 122
Tree Sparrow 348, 370
Tree Swallow 32, 39, 42, 87, 89, 91, 135, 141, 149, 173, 197, 204, 227, 230, 234, 241, 248, 251, 254, 288, 302, 325, 429
Tribal Trust Lands 28
Triple Tree Trail 308

trout 98
Troy 19, 479
Trumpeter Swan 28, 83, 199, 271, 273, 277, 279, 291, 299, 316, 473, 474, 476
Tufted Duck 477
Tundra Swan 23, 108, 130, 196, 234, 265, 276, 277, 282, 291, 325
turkey 23, 26
Turkey Vulture 15, 39, 204, 210, 227, 247, 248, 323, 370, 372, 373, 385, 387, 463
Twin Bridges 241, 244, 254, 266, 481
Twin Lakes 122
Two Dot 175
Two Medicine 114
Two Moon Park 357

U

UL Bend National Wildlife Refuge 409, 411
Ulm 195
Ulm Pishkun State Park 195
Upland Sandpiper 146, 158, 175, 205, 400, 447
Upper Missouri Breaks Audubon 481
U.S. Fish and Wildlife Service 1
U.S. Forest Service 376
Utica 173

V

Val Marie (Canada) 420
Vandalia Wildlife Management Area 436–437
Varney Bridge 277
Vaughn 194
Vaux's Swift 42, 91, 106, 109, 114, 476
Veery 16, 43, 48, 62, 63, 106, 126, 159, 210, 212, 221, 226, 227, 230, 279, 288, 306, 476
Vermilion Flycatcher 477
Vesper Sparrow 32, 87, 89, 93, 135, 138, 140, 143, 146, 152, 158, 164, 173, 175, 177, 179, 194, 195, 212, 218, 224, 232, 234, 273, 288, 301, 308, 313, 324, 328, 338, 370, 436
Victor 61, 81, 477
Violet-green Swallow 91, 149, 230, 241, 244, 288, 302, 304, 325
vireos 48, 306
Virginia Rail 101, 232, 287, 426, 458

W

warblers 51, 78, 98, 221, 224, 244, 245, 248, 250, 306, 309, 335, 362, 453

Warbling Vireo 20, 28, 49, 54, 58, 61, 62, 63, 73, 106, 113, 159, 209, 212, 221, 226, 236, 271, 279, 288, 292, 306, 307, 312, 340, 376, 378
War Horse Lake 164
War Horse National Wildlife Refuge 164
Warm Springs Creek 234
Warm Springs Wildlife Management Area 199, 233–235
Waterworks Hill 89–90
waxwings 249
Webb Waterfowl Production Area 418
Westby 403, 453, 454, 455, 477
Westby City Park 453–454
Westby Prairie-Wetland Complex 473
Westby Prairie-Wetland Complex Important Bird Area 403, 455–457
Western Bluebird 15, 19, 42, 43, 89, 91, 202, 210, 304, 313, 351
Western Grebe 24, 28, 31, 97, 103, 104, 130, 153, 179, 209, 218, 230, 331, 338, 358, 368, 370
Western Kingbird 76, 89, 149, 163, 202, 226, 227, 230, 232, 256, 258, 264, 265, 288, 302, 338, 346, 373, 391, 438
Western Kingfisher 135
Western Meadowlark 6, 32, 54, 81, 87, 134, 140, 141, 147, 151, 152, 159, 164, 168, 177, 194, 205, 210, 212, 216, 218, 219, 224, 230, 244, 265, 267, 271, 274, 282, 286, 301, 304, 324, 325, 328, 366, 370, 374, 376, 377, 410
Western Screech Owl 26, 69, 76, 80, 88, 141, 210, 306, 416
Western Scrub-jay 477
Western Tanager 16, 20, 35, 37, 39, 42, 43, 47, 49, 61, 62, 63, 64, 76, 83, 86, 89, 90, 91, 111, 171, 206, 210, 219, 220, 221, 224, 228, 236, 238, 247, 248, 251, 256, 264, 265, 271, 279, 305, 306, 310, 312, 319, 382
Western Wood-pewee 26, 43, 54, 73, 83, 135, 222, 230, 232, 271, 288, 290, 307, 346, 436, 463
West Fork of the Bitterroot River 69
West Glacier 114
West Rosebud Creek 335
West Valley Ponds 110
West Yellowstone 274, 276, 292, 293, 294, 295, 296, 297, 298, 299, 480
White-breasted Nuthatch 19, 43, 54, 61, 62, 63, 69, 81, 204, 219, 221, 224, 226, 236, 261, 311, 357
White-crowned Sparrow 52, 113, 123, 170, 210, 236, 271, 311, 338, 357
White-eyed Vireo 477

White-faced Ibis 143, 191, 264, 265, 447, 476
Whitefish 111, 113, 480
white-footed mice 342
White-fronted Goose 233, 279
White-headed Woodpecker 114
White-rumped Sandpiper 455
White Sulphur Springs 177, 179, 180, 182
white-tailed deer 16, 20, 23, 35, 37, 78, 81, 84, 95, 98, 102, 105, 109, 111, 115, 123, 128, 134, 154, 182, 183, 185, 188, 192, 204, 248, 254, 260, 264, 266, 270, 273, 301, 305, 374, 376, 378, 380, 382, 389, 391, 407, 415, 416, 419, 426, 432, 436, 450, 458, 461, 463
white-tailed jackrabbit 342, 378, 389, 398, 415
White-tailed Kite 477
White-tailed Ptarmigan 114
white-tail jackrabbit 257, 264
whitetails 362, 363
White-throated Sparrow 279
White-throated Swift 62, 76, 91, 123, 187, 241, 244, 264, 288, 340, 351, 370, 413
Whitewater Creek 429
Whit's Lake Road (FR 971) 293
Whooping Crane 448, 476
Wibaux 480
Wild Horse Lake 146, 165
wild horses 342
Wild Turkey 20, 23, 26, 102, 103, 104, 106, 135, 159, 247, 248, 301, 319, 324, 328, 333, 362, 363, 365, 368, 372, 373, 374, 376, 380, 382, 413, 432, 436, 461
Willet 145, 146, 158, 260, 271, 280, 447, 458, 460
Williamson's Sapsucker 62, 71, 209, 210, 236, 315, 474, 476
Williston, North Dakota 467, 468
Willow Creek 234, 287, 290, 317
Willow Creek Reservoir 280–282
Willow Creek Reservoir (Augusta) 206
Willow Flycatcher 20, 26, 32, 35, 37, 45, 51, 58, 66, 83, 84, 103, 104, 106, 111, 128, 135, 152, 166, 186, 189, 197, 206, 209, 212, 214, 227, 232, 238, 250, 279, 302, 476
Wilsall 316
Wilson's Phalarope 58, 84, 130, 139, 140, 147, 158, 214, 218, 234, 260, 264, 271, 370, 418, 447, 455
Wilson's Snipe 42, 97, 98, 100, 134, 153, 158, 212, 216, 222, 230, 232, 234, 256, 260, 264, 291, 296
Wilson's Warbler 52, 88, 93, 153, 189, 240, 256, 298

Wings Across the Big Sky 471
Winifred 162
Winnett 165
Wisdom 74, 240, 244, 245, 246
Wise River 240
wolf 113
Wolf Creek 210
Wolf Point 480
wolverine 20, 115
wolves 52
Wood Bottom Recreation Area 156–157
Wood Duck 16, 19, 20, 26, 35, 42, 78, 83, 88, 98, 106, 109, 222, 230, 232, 317, 323, 363, 393, 425, 429, 463
Woodhawk Recreation Site 161–162
Wood Lake 205
Wood Mountain Regional Park 419
woodpeckers 48, 51, 54, 61, 159, 179, 186, 248, 306, 309, 335, 376, 428, 436, 463
wood-pewee 149
Wood Warbler 222

Y

Yellow-bellied Flycatcher 451, 453
yellow-bellied marmot 288
Yellow-billed Cuckoo 476
Yellow-billed Loon 114, 358
Yellow-breasted Chat 141, 153, 156, 378, 391, 395, 461, 465
Yellow-crowned Kinglet 19, 64, 240
Yellow-headed Blackbird 26, 31, 42, 83, 98, 101, 134, 140, 213, 214, 216, 222, 230, 232, 234, 241, 245, 251, 254, 264, 271, 302, 324, 328, 395, 426, 455, 457
yellowlegs 23
yellow perch 28
yellow pine chipmunk 342
Yellow Rail 455
Yellow-rumped Warbler 28, 39, 42, 49, 61, 63, 64, 71, 73, 135, 166, 170, 189, 221, 226, 227, 230, 236, 238, 240, 251, 256, 264, 302, 307, 312, 393, 395
Yellowstone National Park 283
Yellowstone Park 296
Yellowstone River 317, 323, 327, 328, 335, 348, 357, 461, 463, 465, 467
Yellowstone Valley Audubon 348
Yellowtail Dam 368
Yellow-throated Vireo 477

Yellow Warbler 16, 20, 28, 37, 39, 42, 49, 78, 83, 88, 135, 152, 166, 170, 175, 226, 227, 230, 232, 234, 236, 238, 241, 251, 279, 288, 292, 302, 307, 312, 319, 322, 338, 370, 395
Yellow Water Reservoir 165
Yucatan Peninsula 453
Yukon 453

Z

Zortman 410, 412, 413, 414